REFERENCE
ONLY

How They Lived

How They Lived

An Annotated Tour of Daily Life through History in Primary Sources

Volume 1
Ancient and Medieval World

James Ciment

Foreword by Robert André LaFleur

 GREENWOOD™

An Imprint of ABC-CLIO, LLC
Santa Barbara, California • Denver, Colorado

Copyright © 2016 by ABC-CLIO, LLC

Library of Congress Cataloging-in-Publication Data

Names: Ciment, James.
Title: How they lived : an annotated tour of daily life through history in primary sources / James Ciment; foreword by Robert André LaFleur.
Description: Santa Barbara, California : Greenwood, an Imprint of ABC-CLIO, LLC, 2016-
Identifiers: LCCN 2015017582| ISBN 9781610698955 (hardback : v. 1) | ISBN 9781610698962 (ebook)
Subjects: LCSH: Civilization—History—Sources. | Civilization—History—Juvenile literature. | World history—Sources. | World history—Juvenile literature. | BISAC: HISTORY / World. | HISTORY / Study & Teaching.
Classification: LCC CB69.2 .C56 2016 | DDC 930.1—dc23 LC record available at http://lccn.loc .gov/2015017582

ISBN: 978-1-61069-895-5
EISBN: 978-1-61069-896-2

20 19 18 17 16   1 2 3 4 5

This book is also available on the World Wide Web as an eBook.
Visit www.abc-clio.com for details.

Greenwood
An Imprint of ABC-CLIO, LLC

ABC-CLIO, LLC
130 Cremona Drive, P.O. Box 1911
Santa Barbara, California 93116-1911

This book is printed on acid-free paper ∞

Manufactured in the United States of America

Contents

Contents

Contents

Volume 2

Part 12: The Emergence of Modern Europe: 1500–1700 CE

Part 13: The World beyond Europe: Sixteenth–Eighteenth Centuries CE

Part 15: The Rise of Nationalism: Late Eighteenth–Early Twentieth Centuries

Foreword

Robert André LaFleur

Sources Behind the Footnotes

A decade ago, the eminent early-modern historian Anthony Grafton published a brilliant little book called *The Footnote*. An editor sent it to me when it was published, and asked if I was interested in writing a review. "Footnotes—they're the kind of thing you would be interested in," she wrote with just the trace of condescension. She was right about me, but wrong about the fascination that footnotes hold. The book is a marvel, and Grafton takes the reader on what becomes almost a detective tale that leads to the origin of the footnote in Western historical writing. It is a breathtaking story about an aspect of historical study that dominates everything that we do, from junior high school classes to the highest reaches of the professional history.

But it is not the footnote itself that is the real draw; it is what lies behind those little jottings. Those are the sources—of precisely the kind that you will encounter in this book. Sources are the most important things of all in historical studies. Everything that we know about the past—absolutely everything—comes from them. We are indebted to them and more than occasionally frustrated by how little they seem to tell us about how people lived their daily lives in earlier eras, distant lands, or both. And yet they are all we have. Better to learn, as this book will teach you, how to tease answers from those precious remnants of past life.

Unlike the historian's colleague down the hall, the anthropologist, she cannot "go to" the past the way her colleague can take a flight that eventually lands her in Greece, China, Tanzania, or Borneo. The only thing the historian has is a set of materials—carry-overs from lives that were lived decades, centuries, or even millennia before. Many of these sources are written and exist on papyrus, bamboo, in handwriting, and in print. There are edicts, diaries, letters, newspapers, pamphlets, and learned studies. And that is only the beginning. As this book will teach you, the written sources are only a fragment of what we need to consider if we are to gain a better understanding of how people occupied their days from sunup to sundown, and beyond. For that, we need to widen the scope of what we consider a source—far beyond what historians of earlier eras would have ever noticed. There are, of course, artworks, statuary, coins, and war machinery. These have always been part of the source record of even very traditional historians.

But what of the rest of everyday life? As you know, just by thinking about the things you have encountered in your day before reading this, there is much more to say about daily life that cannot be known through written records or even artworks and coinage. What about the rest of life as we live it? For that, we need to broaden our inquiry to a wide array of materials ranging from household products to farm implements, and from school supplies to groceries. These (and many more) are the sources of daily life.

Always Perishing, Always Growing

In one way of thinking, everything is a source—everything. From the Declaration of Independence to the spoons in a colonial American kitchen, any bit of life can teach us at least a bit about the ways people made choices, instructed others, and figured out how to function in a complicated world. To be sure, historians make several distinctions about sources, categorizing them as *primary*, *secondary*, and sometimes even *tertiary*. These distinctions will become more familiar to you as you make your way through this book, but it is important to note that even these categories shade from one into the other in various ways. A book written about the French Revolution a hundred years later would usually be considered a secondary source—the book relies on other primary documents to tell a story of a bygone era. On the other hand, let us imagine that we are writing our own papers about the author of that book about the French Revolution. Well, now, suddenly, his account of an earlier era is a primary source for his thought.

Gaining that kind of perspective is precisely what this book will teach you.

* * *

The source materials in this book are widely varied and reflect the range of possibilities for historians to consider as they assess daily life in the past. The inevitable nature of daily life also leads to something that few of us consider in the course of our busy days. Almost everything that happens, large and small, in any day during human history is lost almost immediately. The details of the meals we eat, the people with whom we talked, and what we thought about the thousands of little movements we make each day—all but a fraction are lost the moment they occur.

Most daily life is made up of repeated, lived experiences that almost no one would think to remember. Brushing your teeth, making the bed—even sitting down for breakfast—blurs together from one day to another. Once enough time goes by, it is so routine, so common, that only extraordinary changes (such as breakfast with a royal family) gets recorded. Those "big" events go into the letters, diaries, and other accounts that we study, but they are only a tiny fraction of what we do in any day.

Are they the "most important" Not always, and maybe not even usually.

One thing is certain, though. It does not take long before such routine knowledge blends right into the past. Ironically enough, that also means that the most common (taken-for-granted) features of daily life in the past are often the strangest once enough time has gone by. One of the greatest of French historians, Georges Duby, said that he spent an inordinate amount of time in his career wondering exactly how thirteenth-century knights got onto their horses. Hopping onto a horse is both a physical and a cultural act, and the particular details are lost to the past. So, too, are precisely the ways that colonial spoons might have been used decades later in an Ohio cabin made by pioneers from the eastern seaboard.

It is not just material things that are lost, either; the vast bulk of written sources are quickly discarded. Families overwhelmed by the loss of an elderly loved one quite often discard large volumes of material (I have heard countless stories of this). On one level or another, it happens all the time and in every corner of life in the world. In a profound manner, then, the record of the past is always shrinking. There will never be the range of source materials again after the lived experiences of any day's life passes into history.

And yet . . . it is also always growing, too. How can this be? In an absolute sense, it becomes radically smaller with each passing day, before settling into a slow loss of material after several decades, and then centuries. But that record does eventually "grow," and in meaningful ways. For example, many governments have "50-year" rules, after which most classified documents are made public. This means that historians are always discovering things about the world of 50 years ago that had not been known by all but a few in the intervening years.

And there is more. As historians change the way they think about the past, things that were never considered "sources" become so. A history profession focused only on kings, queens, presidents, and prime ministers had no use for most everyday objects (and too, many were thrown away). Yet the history profession today emphasizes the enormous importance of daily life in understanding the past. Suddenly, a tractor wheel from the 1930s becomes relevant, as does a mortar and pestle from ancient China.

As our questions change, "new" sources appear.

We are always losing the record of the past, and yet always gaining it as well.

Points of Knowledge

As you work your way through the sections in this book, you may feel a bit bewildered—the way that every historian feels at some points in her or his work. There is an enormous array of objects, written and material, and sometimes it will seem that they are just arbitrary fragments of society and culture—tidbits of life in a past world. At times, it can seem that there are too few pieces to a complex puzzle and this is because the sources are, indeed, fragments of lived experience. They are a small number of the items that were *not* lost (or were rediscovered) by historians. And yet those sources do not, in themselves, tell a story. The sources, in short, can never "speak for themselves."

Making them speak is our job—the work of historians.

One way to think about the primary source materials you will encounter in this book is that they are isolated points "out there." Take a blank sheet of paper, make 20 dots on it, and then think about ways that you might connect them (note, too, that there is much more blank page than dots). Even such a simple project can be done in numerous, and sometimes highly creative, ways. "Doing" the history of daily life works in a similar manner. The "dots" are much more complex than pen marks on paper, of course, but the ways that we connect them are shaped by our cultural heritages (many Westerners like straight lines), the characteristics of the dots themselves (even those little things are not all the same), and the combined discipline and creativity that we bring to the task. Twenty of us can connect the dots, and we will have 20 very different approaches.

The sources are the dots, the points (except infinitely more complex). The weave, the story, the analysis—those are up to us.

This book will introduce you to the sources of daily life all over the world and to the ambitious work you will share with all serious historians.

Note: Robert André LaFleur is professor of history and anthropology at Beloit College.

Introduction

How They Lived: An Annotated Tour of Daily Life through History in Primary Sources offers readers nearly 400 historical primary sources—text and visual—ranging from the Paleolithic era to the present day and from cave paintings to "tweets." They range as far afield geographically as they do chronologically. Every major region of human habitation is represented—from the heart of Europe to the far-flung islands of the South Pacific, from Patagonia to Siberia.

Still, as diverse as the eras and cultures represented are, the primary sources in the book do have one thing in common; they all focus on the everyday life of ordinary and not-so-ordinary people, on the quotidian doings of human beings as they make history and make their way through history. But what exactly is meant by daily life? Broadly speaking, it is defined here as the routine, the repeated, the ritualized—daily occurrences, not epochal events. A statesman's grand declaration of war is not everyday life; the simple soldier's account of what it was like to fight in that war most definitely is.

For all that, daily life is interpreted as broadly as possible. The primary sources explore the realm not just of the physical world but that of the mind as well. Thus, the selections include some obvious choices—the contents of a typical Roman's supper; the medicine practiced by a medieval Arab doctor; the factory routine of a Japanese autoworker—but some not so obvious ones, too. When a precolonial era Yoruba man of West Africa paused in his day to contemplate his existence, what was he thinking? How did the ancient Greeks understand the significance of democracy to their everyday lives?

Just as extraordinary events, such as, say, the assassination of Julius Caesar or the discovery of penicillin, cannot be understood outside of their historical context, so too, ordinary daily life can only be made sense of within the context of larger historical forces. And so while this book is about the things, thoughts, and doings of everyday life, the primary sources it contains may have a political or geopolitical significance or say something about a civilization's economy, art, culture, and society.

How to Use this Book

This book is divided into two chronological volumes: Volume 1 covers human history from the Paleolithic era to around the year 1500 of the common era (CE, sometimes referred to as AD).

Volume 2 examines history from around the midpoint of the second millennium to the present day. The break is one many students of world history will be familiar with, for it was in the fifteenth and sixteenth centuries that the world underwent a dramatic transformation with the establishment of contact between the Western and Eastern Hemispheres and the beginning of the rise of the West as the world's global hegemon.

Each volume is then divided into parts: 11 in the first, 8 in the second. These parts are organized both by place and time. So, for example, Volume 1 contains several different parts on the period between roughly 3000 BCE (before the common era, also referred to as BC) and 500 BCE to 500 CE. These parts correspond to various parts of the globe which, at the time, were often quite isolated from one another: Egypt and the Middle East; South Asia; East and Southeast Asia; the ancient Mediterranean civilizations of ancient Greece and Rome; and sub-Saharan Africa. As distant civilizations come into increasing contact with one another after 1500 and a common global history begins to emerge, the parts in Volume 2 follow a more straightforward chronological organization, from the emergence of Europe as a global power from 1500 to 1700 to the Industrial Revolution of the late eighteenth to early twentieth centuries to the era of economic and cultural globalization at the end of the twentieth and beginning of the twenty-first centuries.

The nineteen parts contain varying numbers of primary sources. How many went into each part was the result of various considerations—which sometimes were at cross-purposes with each other—including the length of the era and the number of civilizations and peoples covered, admittedly subjective decisions about the era's importance to the overall thrust of human history, as well as the sheer availability of primary sources from that era, the latter a particularly important consideration in the first volume.

The format of the book has been designed for the ease of the reader, with the primary source on one side of a two-page spread and the descriptive material about it on the other. Each of these page spreads is headed by a descriptive title for the primary source; the region, culture, or civilization it came from; and the date of its writing, publication, or production. In the case of older primary sources, the dates are, by necessity, listed as a time span, corresponding to when scholars believe the primary source was created or, in cases of historical writings, the period those writings are examining.

Each primary source is also accompanied by two annotations, titled "What You Need to Know" and "A Closer Look," as well as a citation as to the source of the object or document. The first section gives a brief description of the primary source and its historical context. The second focuses on what it tells us about daily life, as well as providing an analysis of the source and its significance. Together, the two annotations provide not just a description of daily life in the past but what that daily life reveals about the nature of the people, era, or civilization in question.

About Primary Sources

As noted, the primary sources are of two types: text and visual. Textual primary sources, or documents, include selections from both private life—such as journals, diaries, and letters—and those from public sources, including the following: legal codes, government documents, religious scripture, essays, travelogues, philosophical writings, discourses on etiquette and manners, histories (not recent ones but those written around or near the era in question), newspaper and magazine content, advertisements, and literature, including everything from epics and sagas to lyrical poetry. In many cases, longer documents have been excerpted, sometimes significantly but always with an emphasis on the most revealing elements of the document, so that they can fit into the format of the book.

In most cases, the documents come from sources within the culture being examined, such as an essay by a Confucian scholar from third century BCE on filial piety or a speech by activist Desmond Tutu on the daily struggle against the apartheid regime in late twentieth-century South Africa. In other cases, however, the documents were written by outside observers. The decision to include such documents was made by necessity, in the case of nonliterate cultures, such as those of hunting and gathering societies, or from civilizations whose written tradition has largely been lost, such as those of the pre-Columbian peoples of Mesoamerica. These documents present both advantages— an ability to see things with fresh eyes—and disadvantages, the obvious prejudices held by literate peoples against nonliterate ones. This is particularly the case in the modern era, as Europeans confronted and conquered peoples and nations across the globe.

The visual material in the book consists of two basic types. The first are images of the primary sources of daily life themselves. These primary sources range widely from weapons to household goods, from the paraphernalia of commerce to items of personal adornment, such as clothing and jewelry, from religious objects to those related to sports and games. The second type consists of images of the activities of daily life. For early eras, this might include drawings, paintings, mosaics, and sculpture. From the nineteenth century onward, the visual material is largely photographic.

Evaluating Primary Sources

For historians, a primary source is a visual, textual, or—since the invention of mechanical and chemical sound and visual recording in the late nineteenth century—audible and video primary sources from the past, usually from the period and place a historian is studying and writing about. Virtually all of the primary sources in this book are primary sources. The exceptions are histories, such as those written by ancient Roman scholars about earlier Mediterranean civilizations.

As noted earlier in regard to the selections in this book, there are many, many types of primary sources, although most fall into one of two categories. There are primary sources of a private nature originally meant for the eyes, touch, or minds of the individual creator or user, or her family or his close circle of acquaintances: a diary, a letter, or an object of personal use, such as a hair brush or a snuff box. Public sources are those with a wider original audience—newspaper accounts, laws, architecture, and the like.

Aside from recent history, where a researcher can talk to participants of the events in question, primary sources represent the only building materials from which historians can reconstruct the past, or, at least, their interpretation of it. That is to say, a primary source may say different things to different historians. Take the final part of Volume 2 on the present era, "A New Millennium," where there is a photo of an Egyptian man holding up a protest sign. From that primary source alone, would some future historian assume Egyptians enjoyed a free society, where they could say what they please, or a restrictive one, where people were forced to take to the streets to make their voices heard? The historian has to decide. Just as no two artists would carve the same sculpture from the same hunk of marble, so no two historians will write the same history from the same set of primary sources.

Still, historians seek the truth, as they understand it. To achieve this, to make their histories as true to the past as possible, historians amass, interpret, and synthesize as many primary sources as they can. For ancient eras, where extant sources are limited, this might include quite literally everything the scholar can lay his or her hands on. For more recent periods, the historian must be more selective, deciding what source is more important, what source is more representative or revealing of the person, event, idea, or place he or she is researching and writing about.

More frequently than not, various primary sources may say very different things about the same historical event or person. What, then, to do? This is where the historian must weigh the credibility and accuracy of sources, particularly of textual or representational ones, as opposed to historical objects themselves. In doing so, he builds his argument for a particular version of the past in a fashion not too dissimilar from a lawyer making a case in court. Is the primary voice hearsay, or did the creator of it actually witness the historical event or know the historical person? Do the creators of other primary sources—that is, other witnesses—contradict the witness in question? Does the witness to history have a motive for lying or exaggerating the truth, or simply a cultural bias to the same end? Medieval European chroniclers, for example, were notorious for exaggerating numbers. They may tell us that a particular ruler put hundreds of thousands of soldiers into battle when historians know that the technology and resources of the era could not have supported more than a few thousand.

For representational images, similar problems apply. Even photographs, seemingly mechanically exact representations of the past, can be questioned: Are they selectively shot? Do they provide the whole picture? Were the scenes set up before being photographed? Was the image manipulated afterward, a particular problem in the age of digital photography and video for future historians?

With the actual objects of history, the problem is not bias—they are what they are—but making sense of them. Objects are mute and sometimes seemingly inscrutable, especially when they come from nonliterate societies or societies whose text we cannot decipher. What do we make of the patterns on the sixteenth century BCE *pithoi* of Knossos, Crete (Volume 1, Part 4) or the subject matter in the more recent Dogon rock paintings of West Africa? With such objects, historians are forced to make guesses, although informed ones made by piecing together meaning from the rest of the archaeological record of the society in question or based on comparisons with objects from societies we know more about.

Studying the primary sources of the everyday life of civilizations of the past presents unique challenges of its own. Oftentimes the quotidian did not warrant the attention of chroniclers, so there is a dearth of primary textual documents on, say, what ancient Persians ate or the kinds of beds the Aztecs slept on. It is often difficult to make sense of everyday objects. What do we make, for instance, of the glass perfume bottles from ancient Rome (Volume 1, Part 5)? We know what perfume is, of course, and how it was generally used, but how can we discern how it was used in ancient Rome, or by whom, or what it meant to ancient Romans? The answer comes from piecing together other primary sources a combination of things, by comparisons to other civilizations, and from the plain common sense of the historian, as informed by his or her extensive understanding of the civilization in question.

As the author of these volumes, I have given my own, best interpretation to the meaning and significance of the 400 primary sources collected here, based on what historians and archaeologists have written about the peoples, societies, and civilizations that produced them. But, of course, I had to weigh the evidence and come to conclusions of my own. Perhaps, you will choose to interpret these primary sources on the everyday life of the past 20,000 years of prehistory and history in your own, informed way. As a professional historian, I would expect nothing less from my readers.

Part 1:
Ancient Australia

40,000 BCE–Fourth Millennium BCE

1.1.1 Australian Aboriginal Cave Paintings

Queensland, Australia
After 40,000 BCE

Credit: DeAgostini/Getty Images

What You Need to Know

An example of aboriginal artwork from Queensland, in northeastern Australia, is shown here. The exact date is unknown, but archaeologists believe it was created after 40,000 BCE.

The Aborigines, or native inhabitants of Australia, are believed to have migrated to that continent from Southeast Asia around 50,000 years ago, a migration made possible by the lower sea levels of that period, which created a near continuous land bridge between the two continents. Although the sea journeys would have been shorter then, the Aborigines' migration nevertheless represents the first-ever human crossing of a large body of water. They quickly spread across the far reaches of the island continent. When the oceans rose again, Australia was cut off from Asia once more, allowing the Aborigines to develop almost completely undisturbed by outsiders until the modern age of European exploration. Thus, the Aborigines are the only known people to have maintained a hunting and gathering economy across a continental expanse into the modern era. Although their material culture was relatively scant, there is evidence that trade existed across the continent, as shell beads from specific regions are found far and wide in archaeological digs.

A Closer Look

Among the most moving and interesting of early Aboriginal creativity are the cave and rock paintings they made in various parts of the continent. As some of them depict megafauna that disappeared from Australia some 40,000 years ago, probably as a result of their own hunting practices, archaeologists conjecture that the work represents the earliest known human artwork.

The artist or artists of this work made it by placing their hands against the rock and then blowing ocher, a reddish pigment made from impure iron ore dust, mixed with water, through a reed, thereby outlining the hand. Because ocher is a nonorganic substance, it cannot be carbon dated, and thus the exact age of this painting is unknown.

Still, such hand paintings are found in sites featuring prehistoric art in various parts of the world by various peoples who could not have taught the practice to each other. Their ubiquity has led archaeologists to suggest deeper, psychological reasons behind them. Some scholars believe that they represent the emergence of self-identity in early cultures. Because they accompany other kinds of imagery, it is hypothesized that they represent a kind of artist's "signature." Many also feature patterns within or around the hands, suggesting that they may have something to do with healing or were part of a ritualistic ceremonies, such as the passage from adolescence to adulthood and membership in the group, although this example does not have those patterns.

1 100 200 300 400 500 600 700 800 900 1000 1100 1200 1300 1400 1500 1600 1700 1800 1900 2000 CE

1.1.2 Late Paleolithic Mortar and Pestle

Southern Europe
ca. 25,000–10,000 BCE

Credit: DeAgostini/Getty Images

TIMELINE 40,000 35,000 30,000 25,000 20,000 15,000 10,000 5000 1 BCE

What You Need to Know

The artifact shown here is a stone mortar and pestle—the former is the flat surface at the bottom, and the latter is the club-shaped object on top—that was unearthed near the village of Picinisco in central Italy.

Archaeologists have found evidence of the presence of humans in the region as far back as 45,000 years ago, with some scholars theorizing it may go back a lot longer than that. The tool's exact date has not been determined, but it probably dates back to the late Paleolithic period from around 25,000 to 10,000 BCE. A mortar and pestle is a tool for the crushing, grinding, and mixing of substances. This particular one could have been used for any number of purposes, including the grinding of grass seeds into flour or meal, the processing of medicinal plants, and the production of mineral pigments for rock painting or the adornment of bodies and implements of daily use, such as baskets or clothes. The hunting and gathering society that fashioned this mortar and pestle may have also used it for the grinding of grains they themselves planted, as they may have been one of many cultures making the transition from the gathering of food plants to the growing of them at that time. While humans in Italy and elsewhere did not practice agriculture until the Neolithic age after 10,000 BCE, they often sowed the seeds of edible plants that they gathered later.

A Closer Look

Humans, of course, are the masters of tool making—that is, of manipulating a natural object to make it more useful for some purpose. Other animals make tools, but none are remotely as adept at this skill as human beings. Archaeologists have unearthed primitive cutting and hammering tools made of stone that date back 2.6 million years, long before modern *Homo sapiens* evolved. The evolution of both the human brain and body contributed to our increasingly sophisticated capacity to make and use tools. A larger brain allowed for conceptualization of how to manipulate nature. Our vocal chords permitted sophisticated language to more readily pass on the techniques of tool making and use to others. Finally, our upright stance freed the arms, while our opposable thumbs gave us unparalleled dexterity in manipulating objects. At the same time, the very use of tools contributed to this evolution, as those whose brains and bodies could better fashion and utilize them passed on their genes to offspring who also enjoyed these advantages. At first, the tools were small and portable, reflecting the nomadic and seminomadic lifestyles of prehistoric human communities. The development of agriculture called forth the need for planting and reaping tools, such as simple ploughs and scythes. Agriculture also permitted humans to settle in fixed communities. Not needing to move about, they could accumulate larger and heavier tools, particularly those that required animal power to operate, such as oxen-pulled ploughs and pottery wheels.

1 100 200 300 400 500 600 700 800 900 1000 1100 1200 1300 1400 1500 1600 1700 1800 1900 2000 CE

1.1.3 Neolithic Arrowhead

Western Africa
ca. 10,000–3000 BCE

Credit: DeAgostini/Getty Images

What You Need to Know

This artifact is a stone arrowhead, found in the country of Niger in the Sahel region of western Africa. It dates from the Neolithic era, also referred to as the New Stone Age, which lasted from about 10,000 to 3000 BCE. The arrowhead could have been used for hunting, particularly of the various kinds of cervine, or deer-like animals, such as impalas, or in conflicts over resources between different clans of prehistoric humans.

Before the development of agriculture in the Neolithic period, human societies survived by hunting and gathering, usually roaming from place to place in search of good foraging and game animals. Typically, men would engage in the hunt for large game, while women would maintain the home camps, including the all-important fires, and roam the vicinity for edible plants, insects, and small game and fish. By the Neolithic period, some foraging societies engaged in rudimentary agriculture, scattering edible grass seeds in particularly fertile and well-watered spots and then returning later to harvest them.

Such an existence was precarious, with humans dependent on the whims of nature. It also did not allow for the development of stable communities, the growth of large-scale populations, or craft specialization. Such groups, which usually numbered no more than 50 to 100 persons, required extensive amounts of land to survive, up to 500 square miles depending on the terrain and the climate. Although most of their food was provided by foraging, hunting represented a key source of protein.

A Closer Look

Early arrows were throwing weapons, not ones shot from bows. The makers of such weapons would carve sticks into narrow shafts, then attach the carefully sculpted arrowhead onto one end of the shaft, with twine, vines, or even animal sinew. In some places, where pitch or tar, was available, that might be used to attach the arrowhead to the shaft. Because only the arrowheads were made of nonorganic material, they alone survived to be dug up by archaeologists.

Arrows were an improvement on simple throwing spears in that they had fletching, or stabilizers, at the back end of the shaft that supported the arrowhead. Arrows are among the earliest of human weapons. Primitive ones have been found in what is now South Africa dating as far back as 60,000 BCE.

Bows, or instruments with a flexible arc connected by a string and used to increase the distance and accuracy of an arrow, came much later. The earliest evidence for those goes back only 20,000 years. Moreover, many hunting and gathering societies never developed this tool. The bow and arrow offered great advantages over thrown weapons in three ways. First, by allowing the hunter to keep his distance from his prey, it lowered the threat of injury that big game could inflict. Second, it also allowed hunters the ability to take down game too fast to be pursued on foot. Finally, by keeping their distance, hunters had a better chance of ambushing prey.

1 100 200 300 400 500 600 700 800 900 1000 1100 1200 1300 1400 1500 1600 1700 1800 1900 2000 CE

1.1.4 Mesolithic Ornamental Club

Denmark
ca. 9000–6000 BCE

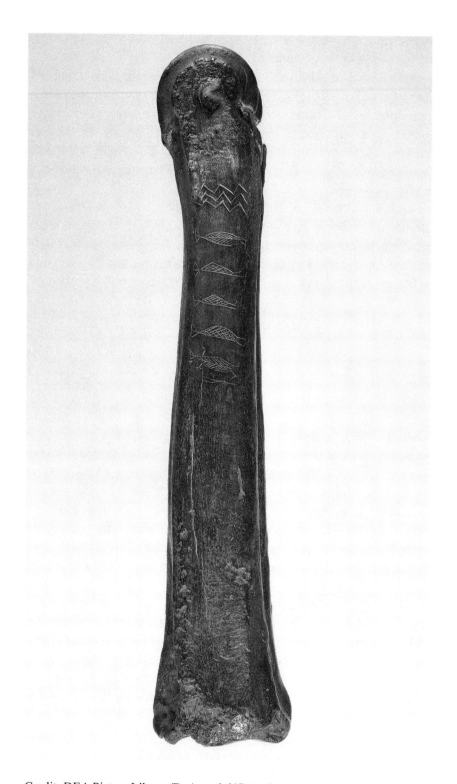

Credit: DEA Picture Library/DeAgostini/Getty Images

What You Need to Know

This ornamental club was unearthed near the town of Soro, Denmark, and dates back to the Mesolithic period, or the Middle Stone Age. As its name implies, the Mesolithic period falls between the long Paleolithic, or Old Stone Age, and the Neolithic, or New Stone Age, which saw the birth of systematic agriculture and the beginnings of civilization. Its precise years vary from one part of the world to another; in Europe, it stretches roughly from about 10,000 to 5000 BCE.

The club is made from the femur bone of a large quadruped, such as an auroch, a precursor of domestic cattle. What the club was used for is unknown. It could have been used in hunting to dispatch an animal already weakened by other weapons. By the Mesolithic period, humans in various parts of the world had already developed the bow and arrow and the slingshot. Or it could have been used in intrahuman conflict. Presuming the latter, the population of Paleolithic peoples was thin enough on the land that a potential conflict over resources was more easily achieved by migration than through deadly conflict. Small hunting and gathering bands lived on edge of existence, thus any loss of life was costly. But as the population expanded during the Mesolithic period, that ability to move away diminished. Also notable is the fact that the club features ornamentation, a sign, along with the lack of obvious wear and tear, that it may have been used in ritual as well as hunting or warfare.

A Closer Look

One of the most contentious questions in anthropology concerns warfare. Specifically, are human beings biologically predisposed toward fighting with one another? The various methods used to answer that question—the archaeological record, the study of nonhuman apes, and observations of modern hunting and gathering society—provide mixed evidence.

Still, prehistoric hunting and gathering societies were, by necessity, thin on the land, as there were simply not enough resources to support large populations. Thus, communities of such people could move on, if there was too much competition with other groups for scarce resources or if they were the targets of more aggressive groups, looking to poach their women and children to bolster their ranks. There might also be internal strife among members seeking dominance within the group. In the latter case, communities would often split apart, with one group leaving the area.

With the advent of agriculture, people began settling in villages—that is, in larger numbers and in closer proximity to one another. Moreover, they could not simply pack up and leave. Such communities depended on cooperation and the nonviolent resolution of conflict to survive. Thus, instead of resolving disputes through violence, people developed laws and gave the power to enforce such laws to governments, which were granted a monopoly on legitimate force.

1   100 200 300   400   500   600   700   800   900   1000 1100 1200 1300   1400   1500   1600   1700 1800 1900 2000 CE

1.1.5 Beaker Culture Drinking Vessel

Western Europe
ca. 4000 BCE

Credit: Universal History Archive/Getty Images

What You Need to Know

The Beaker folk lived in Europe's temperate zones from about 4500 BCE to 2000 BCE. Their name comes from the prevalence of a specific kind of pottery they made—bell-shaped ceramic beaker jars—found in the remains of their settlements and gravesites. An example is shown here.

The shift from hunting and gathering to agriculture as a source of sustenance dramatically altered the content of prehistoric people's diets. The former had its drawbacks. Finding food was a hit-and-miss prospect, so people often went hungry or even starved. Moreover, most of the food gathered—meat, grass seed, fruit, and leafy plants, was not easily stored against lean times. At the same time, however, such a mix of foods provided a well-balanced diet, as long as there was enough of it. The advent of agriculture created a shift toward a more homogenous diet of carbohydrates, the primary source of food energy in grains. But growing grains offered three major advantages: abundance, predictability, and the ability to be stored. Thus, there arose a need for containers, such as ceramics, to store it. And because most grains require processing to eat, often in the form of mush or porridges, there arose the need for water- and heat-resistant implements, for which ceramic is the ideal material.

A Closer Look

The Beaker culture's jars were decorated with abstract patterns made from intricate toothed stamps. What the beakers were used to hold is highly conjectural, although many scholars say it may have held alcoholic beverages, such as beer and mead, the latter a drink concocted from honey, fruit, and other ingredients.

The Beaker people were practicing one of the oldest known industries of humankind. Ceramics are heat- and corrosion-resistant materials, derived from minerals, typically different kinds of clay, that are then shaped and fired to a greater hardness and impermeability at high temperatures. Evidence of ceramics dates back at least 20,000 years. Archaeologists believe that the technique for making ceramics was probably discovered by accident and then improved on by experimentation.

Pottery developed around the same time as agriculture, which was no coincidence, given that farming produced large surpluses that had to be stored safely for future consumption. Pottery was not just used to store dry and liquid goods, the latter including oil and alcoholic beverages, but for cooking and eating off as well. Pottery is heavy and fragile, and so not to be moved about easily. But with agriculture, people settled into fixed communities, so portability of containment vessels was no longer as essential.

1 100 200 300   400   500   600   700   800   900   1000 1100 1200 1300   1400   1500   1600   1700 1800 1900 2000 CE

Part 2:
Egypt and the Near East

Fourth Millennium BCE–First Century CE

1.2.1 Egyptian Bronze Age Sickle

Egypt
ca. 3300–1200 BCE

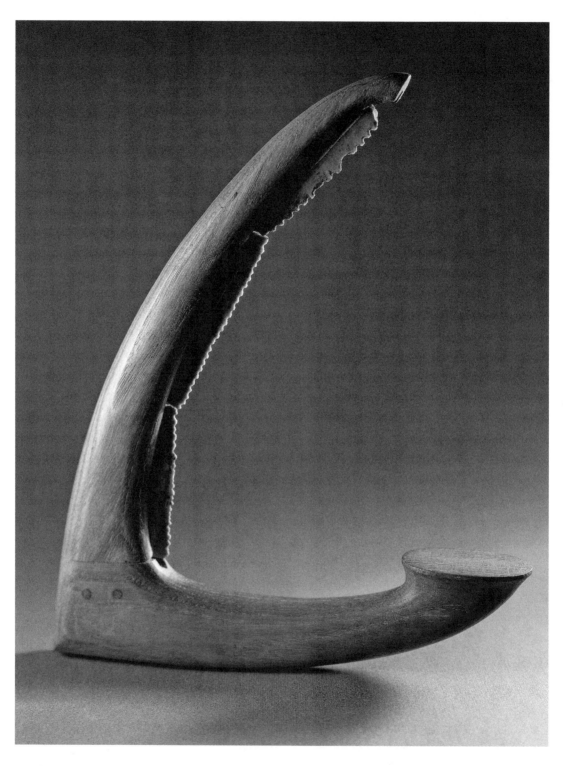

Credit: DEA/G. Dagli Orti/DeAgostini/Getty Images

What You Need to Know

The sickle shown here was used for harvesting grain in Egypt sometime between the late fourth century BCE and the late second century BCE.

During the early Neolithic era, just after the last Ice Age ended, around 8000 to 7000 BCE, humans began to shift from nomadic and seminomadic hunting and gathering societies to more settled communities based on agriculture. Remarkably, this occurred almost simultaneously in several places around the globe, including the Nile valley of Egypt. At first, the people there simply planted wild edible grass seeds in the mud left behind by the great river's annual flood. They did little to tend the crops, allowing the naturally fertile and moisture-laden soil to do the job. They would then return months later to reap the crop by hand. Millennia later, the Greek historian Herodotus would describe how easy growing crops in the Nile valley was when he noted that the Egyptians "obtain crops from the land more easily than all other men." Such fecundity eased the transition from hunting and gathering to early forms of agriculture, as merely planting seeds in the mud led to harvests without people having to tend the crops.

A Closer Look

By around the fourth century CE, Egyptians began to practice more intense agriculture, which required them to settle into stable communities. This produced a greater output, which allowed for surpluses to support people who specialized in the making of tools for agriculture and other activities. One of those tools is pictured here: a stone sickle blade for harvesting cereal grains. The two most important of these in ancient Egypt were barley and emmer, an early variety of wheat.

Grains needed to be harvested quickly once they were ripe. This required coordinated effort by large gangs of reapers who would use sickles like this to cut down the plants, gather them, and take them to a central place to be processed into flour. Women and children would typically follow the men to pick up any stalks they missed or dropped. Children would also be employed to chase away or trap birds that descended on the fields as the grain ripened.

Egyptian craftsmen used nature itself to shape the sickles, using cattle jawbones as a model. Indeed, sickles were made from actual bones, with the teeth as the cutting edge. Where wood was used, flint would be implanted to provide serration.

1 100 200 300 400 500 600 700 800 900 1000 1100 1200 1300 1400 1500 1600 1700 1800 1900 2000 CE

1.2.2 Old Kingdom Sculpture of Man Making Beer

Egypt
ca. 2650–2130 BCE

Credit: Ann Ronan Pictures/Print Collector/Getty Images

What You Need to Know

The accompanying artifact is a figurine of a man making beer and dates back to Old Kingdom Egypt.

Alcohol is a colorless and volatile organic compound that is made through fermentation, an aerobic process in which yeast breaks down the sugars and starches in food. Alcohol can be used, in its denatured form, as a nonconsumable solvent or, in its natural form, as a consumable intoxicant. Nobody knows exactly when humans encountered alcohol—that event first occurred in prehistoric times—but it was probably a discovery rather than an invention. That is, given time and heat, any food substance with a high sugar content will ferment and produce alcohol without any human intervention.

Archaeologists, however, have discovered stone containers from the late Neolithic period around 10,000 BCE that were used to hold beer, indicating that humans actively produced the stuff that far back in time. Indeed, the evidence points to the fact that humans brewed beer even before they began making flour and baking it into bread. All of the great ancient civilizations of the world inherited this prehistoric legacy, including the Egyptians.

A Closer Look

Reliefs on tombs, dating from as early as 2400 BCE, describe the ancient Egyptian process for making beer. They show barley being crushed, mixed with water, and then molded into cakes. Once the latter had dried, they were crushed again and remixed with water and then left in fermenting bowls or vats. Yeast and other microorganisms would settle on the surface and feast on the sugar in the barley-infused liquid, creating alcohol. What part of the process is shown in this figurine of an Egyptian laborer making beer is not clear.

Along with wine, which was also produced in abundance, beer was a central element in the ancient Egyptian diet. Easy to make and requiring no special tools, it was fermented in virtually every Egyptian home, rich or poor. And it was not just enjoyed for its intoxicating affect; it was also a nutriment, a medicine, and a form of money. Beer also played an important role in Egyptian rituals and religion. Indeed, one of the central gods of the Egyptian pantheon, Osiris, was believed to have created beer and given it to humans. And Egyptians routinely offered beer as a sacrifice to the gods.

Finally, the historical record also reveals that Egyptians were aware of the social problems alcohol could cause. Inscriptions on the tombs of pharaohs talk of how taverns, which were also houses of prostitution, corrupted people. They also praised the virtue of moderation in drinking.

1 100 200 300 400 500 600 700 800 900 1000 1100 1200 1300 1400 1500 1600 1700 1800 1900 2000 CE

1.2.3 Vizier Ptah-Hotep's Advice on Family Life

Egypt
Twenty-Fourth Century BCE

If thou art a wise man, bring up a son who shall be pleasing to [Ptah]. If he conforms his conduct to thy way and occupies himself with thy affairs as is right, do to him all the good thou canst; he is thy son, a person attached to thee whom thine own self hath begotten. Separate not thy heart from him. . . . But if he conducts himself ill and transgresses thy wish, if he rejects all counsel, if his mouth goes according to the evil word, strike him on the mouth in return. Give orders without hesitation to those who do wrong, to him whose temper is turbulent; and he will not deviate from the straight path, and there will be no obstacle to interrupt the way. . . .

If thou desirest to excite respect within the house thou enterest . . . keep thyself from making advances to a woman, for there is nothing good in so doing. . . .

If thou are wise, look after thy house; love thy wife. Fill her stomach, clothe her back; these are the cares to be bestowed upon her person. Caress her, fulfill her desires during the time of her existence; it is a kindness which does honor to its possessor. Be not brutal; tact will influence her better than violence. . . . Behold to what she aspires, at what she aims, what she regards. It is that which fixes her in thy house; if thou repellest her, it is an abyss. Open thy arms for her, respondent to her arms; call her, display to her thy love. . . .

Source: Ptah-hotep. Excerpts from *The Instruction of Ptah-Hotep*. In *The Sacred Books and Early Literature of the East*. Vol. 2. Edited by Charles F. Horne. New York: Parke, Austin and Lipscombe, Inc., 1917, pp. 66–67.

TIMELINE   40,000   35,000   30,000   25,000   20,000   15,000   10,000   5000   1 BCE

What You Need to Know

This excerpt is from *The Instruction of Ptah-Hotep* on family life in ancient Egypt. Ptah-Hotep was a vizier, or high official, in the Egyptian government, who lived in the 24th century BCE.

At the heart of ancient Egyptian society was the nuclear family. Egyptians were monogamous in marriage, and most households consisted of two parents and their children, although wealthier households would also contain numerous servants, and elderly parents lived with the families of their grown-up children. Indeed, so important was the nuclear family that Egyptians arranged their pantheon of gods into groupings that resembled it. In addition, the ancient Egyptian language contained no specific words for extended family members; the word for *mother* was applied to a grandmother, for instance, and the word for *brother* applied to an uncle. Families were also a source of great pride, and lineages were traced both through the mother's and the father's side of the family. The laws of Egypt even stated that slave families could not be broken up by their masters.

A Closer Look

Binding the Egyptian nuclear family together were a set of mutual obligations—the father was to provide for the household and the mother the care of the children. In return, the children owed their parents respect. Indeed, it was one of highest obligations of the eldest son or, where there were no sons, the eldest daughter to care for parents in their dotage. In *The Instruction of Ptah-Hotep*, vizier makes clear the importance of respecting parents, saying that it is right for a father to strike a son who sasses him.

At the same time, Ptah-Hotep also dwells on the relationships between men and women. He offers his own equivalent of the biblical injunction not to covet thy neighbor's wife. But there is also a gentler side to Ptah-Hotep's advice to husband, that seems almost modern in its attention to what makes for a loving relationship. Not only must a good husband provide for the physical wants of his wife but he should fulfill her emotional needs as well. "Caress her," he writes, "fulfill her desires during the time of her existence; it is a kindness which does honor to its possessor." He also touches on the topic of problems within the relationship, when he says, "if thou repellest her, it is an abyss." Although Egyptians held the marriage bonds to be the foundation of a family, and hence of society, they also allowed for divorce for any number of reasons—adultery, abuse, infertility—and for no reason beyond simple incompatibility.

1　100　200　300　400　500　600　700　800　900　1000　1100　1200　1300　1400　1500　1600　1700　1800　1900　2000 CE

1.2.4 Sumerian Administrative Tablet with Cuneiform Script

Ngirsu, Sumeria
ca. 2360 BCE

Credit: DEA/G. Dagli Orti/DeAgostini/Getty Images

What You Need to Know

This cuneiform tablet dates from the Sumerian civilization of the third millennium BCE. The tablet, which includes an accounting of rams and goats, dates from around 2360 BCE.

Cuneiform was not what the Sumerians called their script. Rather, it is a term applied by scholars and is derived from the Latin term for "wedge-shaped." A quick glance at the image reveals why scholars use this term. In this tablet, the cuneiform imprints are divided into boxes, each of which refers to a separate account. Scribes employing cuneiform script would use special instruments to impress wedge-shaped forms into wet clay. The clay would then dry quickly in the hot Mesopotamian sun, leaving behind a permanent written record.

The contents of the tablet also reveal much about this oldest of writing systems. Scholars theorize that writing emerged out of accounting, that is, the keeping track of property and trade deals, themselves the result of the surpluses made possible by early civilizations based on irrigated agriculture.

A Closer Look

As early as the ninth millennium BCE, the peoples of Mesopotamia were using tokens as a form of record keeping. This form of accounting lasted some five thousand years, until it was replaced by its logical successor, the etching of pictures onto clay tablets. This allowed various things to be counted on the same tablet—that is, an image of a house could be combined with that of three goats.

Gradually, the images became more abstract, but they had the limitation that they could not express abstract concepts. Eventually, scribes figured out how to combine the shapes in ways that would allow for such expression. Because slaves were usually obtained from the mountain areas around Mesopotamia, the image of a mountain was combined with that of a man to form the concept *slave*. The most important breakthrough, however, came during the early third millennium, when scribes began using shapes to signify sounds, thus developing the first phonetic alphabet.

These developments were aided by the spread of special schools for scribes, the students of usually consisting of the sons of wealthy families. Schools included a principal, teachers, and teaching assistants who also disciplined the students. Caning was a common form of punishment for poor work.

1 100 200 300 400 500 600 700 800 900 1000 1100 1200 1300 1400 1500 1600 1700 1800 1900 2000 CE

1.2.5 Egyptian Hymn to the Nile

Egypt
2100 BCE

Hail to thee, O Nile ! Who manifesteth thyself over this land and comest to give life to Egypt! Mysterious is thy issuing forth from the darkness, on this day whereon it is celebrated! Watering the orchards created by Ra to cause all the cattle to live, thou givest the earth to drink, inexhaustible one! Path that descendest from the sky, loving the bread of Seb and the first-fruits of Nepera, thou causest the workshops of Ptah to prosper! . . .

Lord of the fish, during the inundation, no bird alights on the crops. Thou Greatest the corn, thou bringest forth the barley, assuring perpetuity to the temples. If thou ceasest thy toil and thy work, then all that exists is in anguish. If the gods suffer in heaven then the faces of men waste away.

Then he torments the flocks of Egypt, and great and small are in agony. But all is changed for mankind when he comes; he is endowed with the qualities of Num.

If he shines, the earth is joyous, every stomach is full of rejoicing, every spine is happy, every jaw-bone crushes (its food).

He brings the offerings, as chief of provisioning; he is the creator of all good things, as master of energy, full of sweetness in his choice. If offerings are made it is thanks to him.

He brings forth the herbage for the flocks, and sees that each god receives his sacrifices.

All that depends on him is a precious incense. He spreads himself over Egypt, filling the granaries, renewing the marts, watching over the goods of the unhappy.

He is prosperous to the height of all desires, without fatiguing himself therefore. He brings again his lordly bark; he is not sculptured in stone, in the statutes crowned with the uraeus serpent, he cannot be contemplated. No servitors has he, no bearers of offerings!

He is not enticed by incantations! None knows the place where he dwells, none discovers his retreat by the power of a written spell.

No dwelling (is there) which may contain thee! None penetrates within thy heart! Thy young men, thy children applaud thee and render unto thee royal homage. Stable are thy decrees for Egypt before thy servants of the North! He stanches the water from all eyes and watches over the increase of his good things.

Source: *Hymn to the Nile*. In *The Library of Original Sources*. Vol. I, *The Ancient World*. Edited by Oliver J. Thatcher. Milwaukee: University Research Extension Co., 1907, pp. 79–83.

TIMELINE   40,000   35,000   30,000   25,000   20,000   15,000   10,000   5000   1 BCE

What You Need to Know

This passage is from the *Hymn to the Nile*, written down by an unknown scribe around 2100 BCE.

Perhaps no civilization of the ancient Western world was so dominated by a single geographic feature as Egypt was by the Nile. The river provided not only water to an arid land, but its annual floods renewed the earth with fresh nutriments. Navigable far along its length—until the first cataracts at Aswan, in what is now southern Egypt—it helped to unify the people of Egypt. It is for good reason that the Greek historian Herodotus called Egypt, "the gift of the Nile."

The Nile is the longest river in the world, 4,238 miles from its origins in Lake Victoria, the greatest of East Africa's Great Lakes, to its mouth in the eastern Mediterranean. It is actually formed from two rivers, the Blue and the White Nile, which come together at the modern-day city of Khartoum, in Sudan. Heavy summer rains in the Ethiopian Highlands and Great Lakes region produce surfeits in the two feeder rivers, which gradually made their way down to Egypt by the beginning of September and continued into October. Today, however, the Aswan High Dam prevents the flood from reaching Lower Egypt, where farmers now depend on modern fertilizers to make their crops grow.

A Closer Look

As the writer of the poem relates, virtually every aspect of Egyptian life and culture was determined by the Nile. The ancient Egyptian calendar was divided into three seasons, based on the cycles of the river: *Akhet* (Inundation), *Peret* (Growth), and *Shemu* (Harvest). The Egyptians conceptualized the land of Egypt as being of two parts—the western side of the river was the land of the setting sun and was home to the kingdom's necropolis, or cities of the dead. The Nile's annual flood was considered a god, as the ancient Egyptians well understood that it was the source of their sustenance and hence their lives. Interestingly, says the scribe, this god cannot be "sculptured in stone . . . cannot be contemplated . . . [n]o dwelling (is there) which may contain thee!" And, indeed, archaeologists have yet to discover any Egyptian temple dedicated to the Nile. Perhaps, say historians, this is because the river was so intimately connected to people in their everyday lives, unlike the other gods of their pantheon, such as those of the underworld or the creator, Ra. Still, Egyptians knew very little about the river's origins or the source of those life-giving floods. "Mysterious," the scribe writes, "is thy issuing forth from the darkness."

1 100 200 300 400 500 600 700 800 900 1000 1100 1200 1300 1400 1500 1600 1700 1800 1900 2000 CE

1.2.6 The Sumerian Flood Myth from the *Epic of Gilgamesh*

Sumer
2100 BCE

Per-napishtim then said unto Gilgamesh: "I will reveal unto thee, O Gilgamesh, the mysterious story, and the mystery of the gods I will tell thee. The city of Shurippak, a city which, as thou knowest, is situated on the bank of the river Euphrates. That city was corrupt, so that the gods within it decided to bring about a deluge, even the great gods, as many as there were: their father, Anu, their counsellor, the warrior Bel; their leader Ninib; their champion, the god En-ui-gi. But Ea, the lord of unfathomable wisdom, argued with them. Their plan he told to a reed-hut, [saying]: 'Reed-hut, reed-hut, clay-structure, clay-structure! Reed-hut, hear; clay-structure, pay attention! Thou man of Shurippak, son of Ubara-Tutu, build a house, construct a ship; forsake thy possessions, take heed for thy life! Abandon thy goods, save [thy] life, and bring living seed of every kind into the ship. As for the ship, which thou shalt build, let its proportions be well measured: Its breadth and its length shall bear proportion each to each, and into the sea then launch it.'

"Six days and nights the wind blew, and storm and tempest overwhelmed the country.

"When the seventh day drew nigh the tempest, the storm, the battle which they had waged like a great host began to moderate. 'The sea quieted down; hurricane and storm ceased.'

"I looked out upon the sea and raised loud my voice, but all mankind had turned back into clay. Like the surrounding field had become the bed of the rivers. I opened the air-hole and light fell upon my cheek. Dumbfounded I sank backward, and sat weeping, while over my cheek flowed the tears. I looked in every direction, and behold, all was sea. Now, after twelve [days?] there rose [out of the water] a strip of land. To Mount Nisir the ship drifted. On Mount Nisir the boat stuck fast and it did not slip away.

"The first day, the second day, Mount Nisir held the ship fast, and did not let it slip away.

"The third day, the fourth day, Mount Nisir held the ship fast, and did not let it slip away.

"The fifth day, the sixth day, Mount Nisir held the ship fast, and did not let it slip away.

"When the seventh day drew nigh I sent out a dove, and let her go. The dove flew hither and thither, but as there was no resting-place for her, she returned. Then I sent out a swallow, and let her go. The swallow flew hither and thither, but as there was no resting-place for her she also returned. Then I sent out a raven, and let her go. The raven flew away and saw the abatement of the waters. She settled down to feed, went away, and returned no more. Then I let everything go out unto the four winds, and I offered a sacrifice. I poured out a libation upon the peak of the mountain. I placed the censers seven and seven, and poured into them calamus, cedar-wood, and sweet-incense.

"The gods smelt the savour; yea, the gods smelt the sweet savour; and gods gathered like flies around the sacrificer."

Source: Excerpts from *The Epic of Gilgamesh*. In "The Gilgamesh Narrative, Usually Called the Babylonian Nimrod Epic." Translated by William Muss-Arnolt. In *Assyrian and Babylonian Literature: Select Translations. The World's Great Books.* Edited by Rossiter Johnson. New York: D. Appleton, 1901, pp. 351–352, 355–357.

TIMELINE 40,000   35,000   30,000   25,000   20,000   15,000   10,000   5000   1 BCE

What You Need to Know

The document excerpted here comes from the Epic of Gilgamesh, a Sumerian poem from around 2100 BCE.

The first great civilization of Mesopotamia, in what is now Iraq, and arguably, the first civilization in human history was that of the Sumer. Like many of the other early civilizations, it arose in an arid climate and in a land watered by a river or, in the case of Mesopotamia, a river system. To put the river's water to use, however, required an elaborate irrigation system, which had to be built and administered under a central government, although it should be noted that the complex riverine environment of Mesopotamia made it impossible for kings of Sumer to directly rule but a small part of the entire land of the Tigris and Euphrates. Still, from this basic need to harness the rivers arose all the hallmarks of civilization—cities, government palaces, religious temples, a priestly class, and rituals to placate the gods who controlled nature. And it gave rise to writing, a means through which people could keep track of the crop surpluses irrigated agriculture produced and record the deeds of gods and kings.

A Closer Look

Egypt and Mesopotamia provide two contrasting examples of how environments shaped the culture of earliest civilizations. Egypt was located in the Nile Valley, unified by a single navigable river, which flooded on a predictable basis every fall, leaving behind not wreckage but refertilized farmland. It was also largely isolated from outside invaders. Mesopotamia, on the other hand, was at the crossroads of many peoples and was frequently invaded by outsiders. Rather than being a unifying force, its complex river system divided the land into often warring states. Moreover, those rivers were far from placid. Their unpredictable floods could be devastating to life, farmland, and structures. It was out of this environment that Mesopotamian religion—with its vengeful and capricious gods, who always had to be placated with sacrifices—emerged. When they were not, or when humanity disappointed the gods, disaster struck.

One such disaster was the so-called great flood, described here in an excerpt from the *Gilgamesh,* which relates the story of the eponymous hero, king of the Sumerian city of Uruk. As the poet, or poets, of the epic relate, "the city was corrupt so that the gods within it decided to bring about a deluge." But, not wishing to wipe out the world for good, they picked a man to "construct a ship . . . and bring living seed of every kind into the ship."

If the story sounds familiar, there is a good reason for this, as the tale of the "great flood," permeated cultures around the Mediterranean, including that of the ancient Hebrews, who are believed to have originated in Mesopotamia.

1.2.7 Terracotta Relief of a Babylonian Harp Player

Babylonia
ca. 2000 BCE

Credit: DeAgostini/Getty Images

TIMELINE   2000 1900 1800 1700 1600 1500 1400 1300 1200 1100 1000 900 800 700 600 500 400 300 200 100 1 BCE

What You Need to Know

This Babylonian relief made of clay depicts a seated man playing the harp and is from early in the second millennium BCE.

The Babylonians were a Semitic people who had migrated in prehistoric times from the Arabian desert to the well-watered valley formed by the Tigris and Euphrates Rivers. The heart of Babylonian civilization was the eponymous capital, Babylon. Its location near where the two rivers come closest together made it a natural place for trade and for the administration of an empire that encompassed much of Mesopotamia. Traders from Babylon spread ideas, skills, and arts across the Middle East, influencing cultures in Anatolia, Palestine, and into the Mediterranean Basin. The Babylonians, however, were not just spreaders of culture but adopters as well, confident that their civilization was enhanced by new ideas from abroad. Babylon's wealth and power reached their zenith during the long reign of Hammurabi, who ruled the state from 1792 to 1750 BCE.

A Closer Look

Much of what we know about everyday Babylonian life comes from those laws created by Hammurabi. But, of course, they give us a somewhat limited picture of that life. Babylon, which took its name from its eponymous capital city, near modern-day Baghdad, had a rich culture, of which music was an important part.

As in all cultures, there was the music of ordinary daily life and the music of special occasions. The former was played with simple wind and percussion instruments, accompanied by clapping and vocalizations, usually in a nasal tone. But, as with much about the culture of everyday life in ancient times, it has been lost to the past. What we see in surviving art are depictions of the music played at formal occasions, as depicted in this terracotta relief of a Babylonian harp player from early in the second millennium BCE. The harp was made of a hollow wooden sounding box, with a wood pedestal extending from the bottom. The strings, made of the intestines of domesticated animals such as sheep or cattle, wrapped around the pedestal and then stretched vertically to the top of the sound box. As shown, the harp is much smaller than its modern-day equivalent and so was held by the player on his lap. It was featured in the music played at ceremonies, probably in wealthier households, including weddings, funerals, and coming-of-age rites.

1.2.8 Code of Hammurabi on Property Crime

Babylonia
Eighteenth Century BCE

2. If any one bring an accusation against a man, and the accused go to the river and leap into the river, if he sink in the river his accuser shall take possession of his house. But if the river prove that the accused is not guilty, and he escape unhurt, then he who had brought the accusation shall be put to death, while he who leaped into the river shall take possession of the house that had belonged to his accuser. . . .

5. If a judge try a case, reach a decision, and present his judgment in writing; if later error shall appear in his decision, and it be through his own fault, then he shall pay twelve times the fine set by him in the case, and he shall be publicly removed from the judge's bench, and never again shall he sit there to render judgement. . . .

8. If any one steal cattle or sheep, or an ass, or a pig or a goat, if it belong to a god or to the court, the thief shall pay thirtyfold therefor; if they belonged to a freed man of the king he shall pay tenfold; if the thief has nothing with which to pay he shall be put to death. . . .

14. If any one steal the minor son of another, he shall be put to death. . . .

21. If any one break a hole into a house (break in to steal), he shall be put to death before that hole and be buried.

22. If any one is committing a robbery and is caught, then he shall be put to death.

23. If the robber is not caught, then shall he who was robbed claim under oath the amount of his loss; then shall the community, and . . . on whose ground and territory and in whose domain it was compensate him for the goods stolen. . . .

25. If fire break out in a house, and some one who comes to put it out cast his eye upon the property of the owner of the house, and take the property of the master of the house, he shall be thrown into that self-same fire.

Source: King, L. W., trans. *The Code of Hammurabi.* New York: 1915.

What You Need to Know

The accompanying text comes from the Code of Hammurabi. It is a compilation of the laws regarding property.

Hammurabi was born at an unknown date in the late nineteenth century BCE and ruled as the sixth king of Babylon, from 1792 until his death in 1750. The kingdom he ruled over had just been one of many small kingdoms in the fractured landscape of the Tigris and Euphrates valley. But under Hammurabi's leadership, it came to dominate the region militarily and politically. It was centered on its eponymous capital city, the culture of which also dominated the Mesopotamia.

Hammurabi's achievement is remarkable, given how difficult it was to control a landscape divided by numerous rivers and marshes and to keep it safe from outside invaders, who looked upon its riches with envy. Indeed, Babylon survived for more than two centuries, until conquered by the Hittites, who sacked its capital city, in 1531 BCE. Far greater than uniting Mesopotamia for several hundred years was Hammurabi's legacy as a lawgiver.

A Closer Look

The Code of Hammurabi, developed and written down sometime in the early eighteenth century BCE, is not the first legal code in Mesopotamian history, nor is it the earliest extant code we have. But it is the most systematic of its kind for the early ancient world. Four things distinguish it and underline its importance in the history of jurisprudence. One was the way it was promulgated. It was written down not only on tablets stored in the king's palace but also onto public stele, in the common Akkadian language of the day, so that any literate person could read it. Thus, there would be no excuse for perpetrators in pleading ignorance of the law.

The second notable characteristic is that it distinguished among classes of people, as in code number 8. Aristocrats were to be treated differently than commoners. Although this offends modern-day sensibilities, it is nevertheless how laws have operated through much of human history. Third, the laws largely rested on the presumption that the accused was innocent until evidence had been collected to prove his or her guilt, although that evidence could take magical form, as in law code number two. Finally, although its punishments seem quite harsh to us—in laws number 14 and 25, for instance the death penalty is employed for any number of crimes that do not involve the taking of a life—they were designed to fit the severity of the crime, at least according to the customs and beliefs of the time. This idea, along with the presumption of innocence and the providing of evidence to prove guilt, are principles by which modern law is informed.

1.2.9 Medical Strictures from the Code of Hammurabi

Babylonia
Eighteenth Century BCE

215. If a physician make a large incision with an operating knife and cure it, or if he open a tumor (over the eye) with an operating knife, and saves the eye, he shall receive ten shekels in money.

216. If the patient be a freed man, he receives five shekels.

217. If he be the slave of some one, his owner shall give the physician two shekels.

218. If a physician make a large incision with the operating knife, and kill him, or open a tumor with the operating knife, and cut out the eye, his hands shall be cut off.

219. If a physician make a large incision in the slave of a freed man, and kill him, he shall replace the slave with another slave.

220. If he had opened a tumor with the operating knife, and put out his eye, he shall pay half his value.

221. If a physician heal the broken bone or diseased soft part of a man, the patient shall pay the physician five shekels in money.

222. If he were a freed man he shall pay three shekels.

223. If he were a slave his owner shall pay the physician two shekels.

Source: King, L. W., trans. *The Code of Hammurabi*. New York: 1915.

TIMELINE   2000 1900 1800 1700 1600 1500 1400 1300 1200 1100 1000 900 800 700 600 500 400 300 200 100 1 BCE

30

What You Need to Know

This selection from the Code of Hammurabi includes the laws relating to the field of medicine. Early in the eighteenth century BCE, Hammurabi, the king of the Babylonians, developed new laws and systematized existing ones into what became known as the Code of Hammurabi, one of the earliest legal codes we know of. The code covered virtually every aspect of ancient Mesopotamian life. To the modern reader, the punishments in the code seem harsh, but there was a certain justice in them, as Hammurabi attempted to match the punishment to the offense.

A surprisingly large number of medical texts—written in cuneiform, the script first developed by the Sumerians, and etched into clay tablets—survive from the ancient civilizations of Mesopotamia. What they reveal is a remarkable treasure of knowledge about the human body, as well as diverse methods to treat the various ailments that befell it. Although there is a certain amount of sorcery in the medicine these tablets describe, much of the diagnostic methods and treatments reveal a rational approach to healing, even if the measures they prescribed may have done little good and even done harm to patients. But, of course, that was the case for medical treatment as recently as the nineteenth century CE. Still, the ancient peoples of Mesopotamia tended to believe that ailments were caused by spirits who have been displeased by the actions of the sufferer or, in the case of epidemics, by society at large.

A Closer Look

The excerpt of the Code of Hammurabi here covers the medical profession, revealing the severity of the code with various types of malpractice being punished to the extreme. For example, should a physician "cut out the eye" of a patient, the physician's "hands shall be cut off," which, of course, would end his career and livelihood as a healer. The code also reveals that physicians were paid by the procedure, somewhat like doctors in the United States today.

There were, in fact, two kinds of healers in ancient Mesopotamia. One was known as the *ashipu*, who was a kind of sorcerer who used charms and spells to cure an ailing person. It was typically to him that the sufferer first went. Should such measures fail, the *ashipu* might refer the patient to an *asu*, a person we would more typically associate with medicine and to whom the strictures in the code applied. The *asu* was an expert in the use of plant-based cures, which would often be applied to the patient in the form of a plaster laid on the body. Surgery would also be part of his practice though was probably used sparingly as the surgeon risked much should he botch an operation.

1.2.10 Egyptian Wood Lyre

Qurnet Murai, Thebes
ca. 1550–1075 BCE

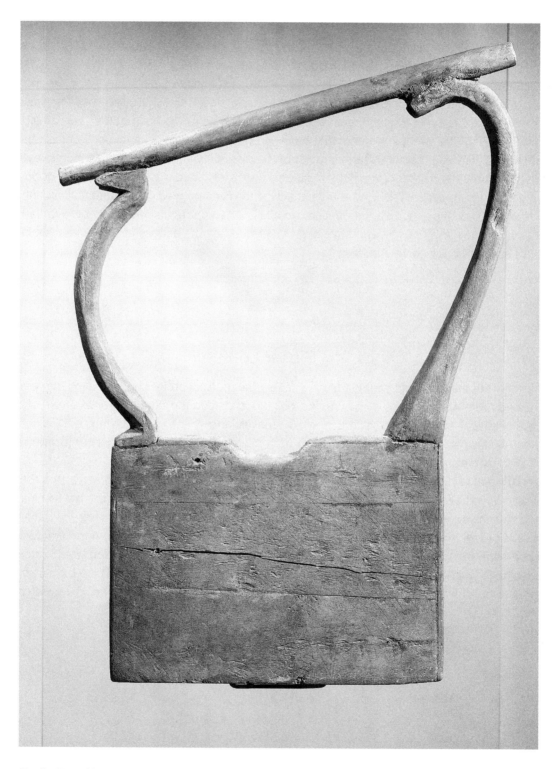

Credit: DEA/G. Dagli Orti/DeAgostini/Getty Images

What You Need to Know

The wood lyre pictured here comes from Qurnet Murai, a necropolis outside of the ancient Egyptian city of Thebes. It dates to the New Kingdom.

Archaeological remains point to the ubiquity of music in ancient Egyptian life. It was played in virtually every setting: religious centers, palaces, workshops, farms, in military camps and on the battlefield, and in funeral ceremonies. Indeed, the Egyptian pantheon included several gods associated with music, including Hathor and Bes, who were also connected to dance and fertility.

There was also a professional class of musicians, ranked according to social status. Those who played in the temples—many of whom were women—were the most respected, as were those who performed for the pharaoh and his court. There were also itinerant musicians who played for hire, typically for celebrations and festivals. From the archaeological evidence, there does not appear to have been amateur musicians in Egypt, nor does it seem that music was an important part of the education of children.

A Closer Look

Although it is possible to use art and artifacts to reconstruct the sounds of Egyptian music, it impossible to know what its melodies and rhythms were because the ancient Egyptians before the fourth century BCE, when they became influenced by Greek civilization, did not notate their music. However, found artifacts, such as this wooden lyre, allow us a glimpse into what was played.

The ancient Egyptian possessed instruments that fell into all the categories we know today, barring pneumatic and hydraulic instruments, such as the organ, although some historians of music believe that the Western world's first organ was the invention of a third-century BCE Greek inventor named Ctesibus, who lived in Egypt. Along with natural sources of musical sound, such as the human voice (both male and female) and hand clapping, the instruments known to the pre-Hellenistic Egyptians included percussion instruments, both beaten, such as hand drums, and shaken, such as castanets and sistrums. The Egyptians also knew both reeded and unreeded wind instruments, while stringed instruments included harps, lutes, and lyres; one of the latter, made of wood and found in the cemetery of Qurnet Murai, near Thebes in central Egypt, is shown in the accompanying image.

The Egyptian lyre was made of wood and consisted of a hollow body, which resonated the sound made by the strings, and a cross bar. Together, the two held the strings, which were made from the intestines of domesticated animals and is known today by the misnomer "catgut." In fact, there is no evidence that the Egyptians, who revered cats, or any other people in history for that matter, have used the intestines of cats to make strings for instruments.

1 100 200 300   400   500   600   700   800   900   1000 1100 1200 1300   1400   1500   1600   1700 1800 1900 2000 CE

1.2.11 Egyptian Alabaster Canopic Jar

Thebes, Egypt
ca. 1550–1075 BCE

Credit: DeAgostini/Getty Images

What You Need to Know

The canopic jar pictured here was used by Egyptians to hold the organs from mummified corpses.

Like all civilizations, ancient Egypt was shaped by its environment. In Egypt's case, this included a steady, dry climate and a river that never ran dry and provided a life-giving inundation of farmland every fall. The former meant that few things decayed quickly; the latter set a rhythm for life. From this, Egyptians concluded that the world was a stable and predictable place. So, too, were their notions of the cycle of life and death.

According to Egyptian religious beliefs, Osiris was the god of both the underworld and fertility; he brought the floods that kept Egypt alive, and he weighed the souls of the dead to see if they deserved everlasting life. Each year he died and then was revived by his wife Isis, aided by the jackal-headed god Anubis, who was also the deity for mummification, the preservation of the body for the afterlife.

A Closer Look

Why the ancient Egyptians came to believe that preserving the body was essential to the soul's progress in the afterlife is unknown as it dates from prehistoric times. But the climate probably had something to do with it. In the dry desert, a buried body would stay remarkably well preserved for a long period of time.

By the historical era of the third millennium BCE, the Egyptians had developed the idea of the *ka*, a kind of second body that survived death and embodied the essence of the *khat*, the body that one had during life. To ensure that the *ka* survived, the *khat* had to be well preserved, and so the Egyptians added their own ingenuity to the desert's capacity for preservation. Thus was developed the art of mummification. After a person died—presuming their family had the means to conduct the process—his or her organs would be removed and the body treated with resin, a natural preservative, and then wrapped in linen.

The Egyptians understood that the internal organs were essential to the body's functioning and so must be carefully preserved as well. As noted, in early Egyptian civilization, the organs would be removed from the body, preserved, and then placed in a canopic jar, one of which, made of alabaster, is pictured here. It is topped with the head of Imseti, a human-headed god associated with the liver. The hieroglyphs on the body of the jar tell the story of the various gods associated with the death process. The canopic jar would then be buried along with the mummified body. Later, when embalming methods improved, the preserved organs were put back into the body for internment.

1 100 200 300   400   500   600   700   800   900   1000 1100 1200 1300   1400   1500   1600   1700 1800 1900 2000 CE

1.2.12 Hymns from the Egyptian Book of the Dead

Egypt
1500–50 BCE

Homage to thee, Osiris, Lord of Eternity, King of the Gods, whose names are manifold, whose forms are holy, thou being of hidden form in the temples, whose Ka is holy. Thou art the governor of Tattu (Busiris), and also the mighty one in Sekhem (Letopolis). Thou art the Lord to whom praises are ascribed in the name of Ati, thou art the Prince of divine food in Anu. Thou art the Lord who is commemorated in Maati, the Hidden Soul, the Lord of Oerrt (Elephantine), the Ruler supreme in White Wall (Memphis). Thou art the Soul of Ra, his own body, and hast thy place of rest in Henensu (Herakleopolis). Thou art the beneficent one, and art praised in Nart. Thou makest thy soul to be raised up. Thou art the Lord of the Great House in Khemenu (Hermopolis). Thou art the mighty one of victories in Shas-hetep, the Lord of eternity, the Governor of Abydos. The path of his throne is in Ta-tcheser (i.e., a part of Abydos).

Thy name is established in the mouths of men. Thou art the substance of the Two Lands (Egypt). Thou art Tem, the feeder of the Kau (Doubles), the Governor of the Companies of the gods. Thou art the beneficent spirit among the spirits. The god of the Celestial Ocean (Nu) draweth from thee his waters. Thou sendest forth the north wind at eventide, and breath from thy nostrils to the satisfaction of thy heart. Thy heart reneweth its youth, thou producest the . . . The stars in the celestial heights are obedient unto thee, and the great doors of the sky open themselves before thee. Thou art he to whom praises are ascribed in the southern heaven, and thanks are given for thee in the northern heaven. . . .

May Ra give glory, and power, and truth-speaking, and the appearance as a living soul so that he may gaze upon Heru-khuti, to the Ka of the Osiris the Scribe Ani, who speaketh truth before Osiris, and who saith: Hail, O all ye gods of the House of the Soul, who weigh heaven and earth in a balance, and who give celestial food [to the dead]. Hail, Tatun, [who art] One, thou creator of mortals [and] of the Companies of the Gods of the South and of the North, of the West and of the East, ascribe ye praise to Ra, the lord of heaven, the King, Life, Strength, and Health [be to him], the maker of the gods. Give ye thanks unto him in his beneficent form which is enthroned in the Atett Boat; beings celestial praise thee, beings terrestrial praise thee. Thoth and the goddess Ma'at mark out thy course for thee day by day and every day. Thine enemy the Serpent hath been given over to the fire. The Serpent-fiend Sebau hath fallen headlong, his forelegs are bound in chains, and his hind legs hath Ra carried away from him. The Sons of Revolt shall never more rise up. The House of the Aged One keepeth festival, and the voices of those who make merry are in the Great Place.

Source: Excerpt from *The Egyptian Book of the Dead*. In *The Papyrus of Ani (The Book of the Dead)*. Vols. I and II. Translated by Ernest Alfred Wallis. New York: G. P. Putnam and Sons, 1913, 59, pp. 340–344.

What You Need to Know

The passage here contains parts of hymns to the gods Osiris and Ra from the Egyptian Book of the Dead.

Perhaps because life was so precarious, peoples of the ancient world expended a good deal of thought on what happened after one died. The Egyptians were no different. Much of the energy spent in paying obeisance and making sacrifices to the gods during one's lifetime was rewarded by their protection after death. Such protection was essential as the Egyptian underworld was a terrifying place, filled with all kinds of obstacles and dangers for the soul of the deceased as it made its way from underworld to the Hall of Judgment. Once there, the heart of the deceased was weighed by the jackal-headed god of the dead, Anubis. On the other side of the scale was a feather, which represented Ma'at, goddess of truth. If the scales balanced, the soul went on to everlasting life. If, on the other hand, the heart was found wanting, the body and soul of the deceased were devoured by the evil gods of the Egyptian pantheon.

A Closer Look

The Egyptian Book of the Dead, a collection of writings in use from about 1500 to 50 BCE, consisted largely of two elements: hymns to the various gods of the Egyptian pantheon and spells that would ward off the many evils confronting the deceased in the underworld. Indeed, the ancient Egyptian name for the texts is best translated as "Spells for Going Forth by Day." By chanting these hymns, which were similar to the ones living priests chanted in temples, the deceased would invoke the protection of these gods as they made their way through the underworld toward immortality, if their lives on Earth justified that fate.

Osiris was, like Anubis, a god who was identified with the underworld and the afterlife. Osiris was also the underworld deity who granted life in the world above and was responsible for the process through which seeds turned into plants and for the annual flooding of the Nile, which brought fertile new soil to Egypt. Ra was the Egyptian god associated with the sun. He was also the god of creation, as Egyptians believed that Ra created the three parts of the universe—the Earth, the heavens, and the underworld. All life was a creation of Ra.

1 100 200 300 400 500 600 700 800 900 1000 1100 1200 1300 1400 1500 1600 1700 1800 1900 2000 CE

1.2.13 Model of an Assyrian Home

Tell Munbaqa, Syria
ca. 1400–1200 BCE

Credit: DeAgostini/Getty Images

TIMELINE   2000 1900 1800 1700 1600 1500 1400 1300 1200 1100 1000 900 800 700 600 500 400 300 200 100 1 BCE

What You Need to Know

This clay model of an Assyrian home is from the fourteenth or thirteenth century BCE.

Around the beginning of the ninth century BCE, there arose in northern Mesopotamia a great new power. These people were known as the Assyrians, and they were among the most warlike people in history. Themselves the subject of constant attack, they developed a strong state and army. Over the next 200 years, they conquered all of Mesopotamia and then moved into the Levant and finally Egypt, which fell to their armies in 717 BCE. Determined on the battlefield, the Assyrians were ruthless as conquerors, demanding large tribute payments from the civilizations they ruled and exacting terrible vengeance on those who refused to pay or who rose up in rebellion. But they were also great empire builders. The Assyrian kings laid roads across their realm and constructed enormous palace complexes at their capital, Nineveh, in what is now northern Iraq. Assyria's fall was as swift as its rise. By the late seventh century BCE, they had been conquered by Babylonians and Persians, and their capital was sacked in 612.

A Closer Look

As with many ancient civilizations, what we know about Assyrian art and architecture mostly comes from the ruins of great public structures—in this case, those palace complexes their kings built. Many of these are covered in stone reliefs of exquisite detail and anatomical precision, most of them devoted to scenes of warfare and hunting. Most Assyrians, however, lived in far more humble surroundings.

The Assyrians, Mesopotamian homeland was essentially a vast river valley—actually the twin river valley of the Tigris and Euphrates—surrounded by forbidding desert. Forests were almost unknown, and timber was scarce. But mud from the riverbanks was plentiful, and so the Assyrians built their dwellings from it, using wood sparingly, for such things as doors. Most houses had a square center room, with other rooms built off of it. But even a modest dwelling of a few mud rooms might have been more than the poorest Assyrians could afford. These latter folk probably lived in simple huts, made from the reeds that grew in abundance in the marshlands that flourished in Mesopotamia, a name derived from the Greek for "land between rivers." Indeed, this model may depict one of those huts, at the top of which is a small round opening to let out smoke from cooking fires.

1 100 200 300   400   500   600   700   800   900   1000 1100 1200 1300   1400   1500   1600   1700 1800 1900 2000 CE

1.2.14 Clean and Unclean Foods according to the Book of Deuteronomy

Israel
ca. Seventh Century BCE

Don't eat any disgusting animals. You may eat the meat of cattle, sheep, and goats; wild sheep and goats and gazelles, antelopes and all kinds of deer. It is all right to eat meat from any animals that have divided hoofs and also chew the cud.

But don't eat camels, rabbits, and rock badgers. These animals chew the cud but do not have divided hoofs. You must treat them as unclean. And don't eat pork, since pigs have divided hoofs, but they do not chew their cud. Don't even touch a dead pig!

You can eat any fish that has fins and scales. But there are other creatures that live in the water, and if they do not have fins and scales, you must not eat them. Treat them as unclean.

You can eat any clean bird. But don't eat the meat of any of the following birds: eagles, vultures, falcons, kites, ravens, ostriches, cormorants, storks, herons, and hoopoes. You must not eat bats. Swarming insects are unclean, so don't eat them. However, you are allowed to eat certain kinds of winged insects.

You belong to the LORD your God, so if you happen to find a dead animal, don't eat its meat. You may give it to foreigners who live in your town or sell it to foreigners who are visiting your town.

Don't boil a young goat in its mother's milk.

Source: Deuteronomy 14.3–21. *The Holy Bible: Contemporary English Version*. New York: American Bible Society, 1995.

TIMELINE   2000 1900 1800 1700 1600 1500 1400 1300 1200 1100 1000 900 800 700 600 500 400 300 200 100 1 BCE

What You Need to Know

The ancient Hebrews had strict dietary laws, such as these from the book of Deuteronomy, which they believed came directly from their god, Yahweh.

For various reasons, including the collapse of the Hittite Empire and an uncharacteristic breakdown of Egyptian society in the thirteenth century BCE, the region known today as the Levant became free of outside control, allowing it to give rise to a number of small independent kingdoms, most notably, the seafaring Phoenicians and, to their south, the monotheistic Hebrews. In ancient Egypt and Mesopotamia, the latter were known as the *habiru* and *hapiru*, respectively, both of which designate homeless but independent nomads. In fact, it is believed that the Hebrews originated in northern Mesopotamia; the Old Testament, a collection of Hebrew legends, proverbs, laws, and songs, among other things, also speaks of their being enslaved in Egypt. According to the Old Testament's book of Exodus, a prophet named Moses led the Hebrews out of Egyptian bondage into the land of Canaan, or modern-day Israel and Palestine where, under Kings Saul and David, they established hegemony for the first time.

A Closer Look

By all accounts, the Hebrews were a minor people, and their kingdom a relative backwater in the Middle East and Mediterranean basin of their time, especially compared to the great civilizations of Mesopotamia, Egypt, and Anatolia. But, arguably, they had a more lasting legacy in the history of Western Civilization than any of these. For the Hebrews, with their unwavering belief in a single, omnipotent god, shaped the religious destiny of billions of people to come—Jews, Christians, and Muslims alike.

Yahweh, the Hebrew God, was unique among ancient deities in that He was a lone god, with no parents, no wife or consort, and no family. This allowed for a more effortless transition from an anthropomorphic god, which Yahweh was originally, to a purely spiritual being, without any of the flaws associated with gods that took human form, such as those of Egypt, Mesopotamia, and eventually the Greco-Roman world. At the heart of the Hebrew religion was the pact, or covenant, between Yahweh and His people. If they would take no gods before Him, He would protect them from their enemies. And to worship Him was to accept His laws, including those dietary laws laid down in this excerpt from Old Testament's book of Deuteronomy. Theologians and historians provide two explanations for these dietary laws and the Hebrew's insistence that Yahweh had laid them down. One was practical; the pig, for example, eats refuse and, if not fully cooked, can cause disease. The other is that by adhering to these laws the Hebrews distinguished themselves from others, including those who ruled over them.

1.2.15 Gold Model Chariot from Ancient Persia

Achaemenid Empire
600–400 BCE

Credit: Jupiterimages

What You Need to Know

A model of a Persian chariot, rendered in gold, is shown here. It dates to the Achaemenid Empire.

The Persians were an Indo-European people who migrated in prehistoric times from central Europe and what is now Russia into the region between Caspian Sea and the Persian Gulf, land that comprises present-day Iran. Initially, they lived in small kingdoms and came under the cultural influence of the neighboring peoples of Mesopotamia. With the exception of its well-watered central plateau, the land the Persians occupied was a harsh one of arid deserts and forbidding mountains. But it was also a land rich in minerals, including iron, copper, and the blue-green gemstone lapis lazuli. This gave Persians the wealth to conduct trade, but it also invited raids and invasions, most notably by the Assyrians in the first half of the first millennium BCE. The Persians also competed for supremacy with the Medes, a culturally akin people who had migrated into the region around the same time. From the eighth and seventh centuries BCE, the Medes ruled over the Persians, until the rise of the greatest of Persian kings, Cyrus II, also known as Cyrus the Great, who threw off Median control and expanded Persia mightily during his reign from 559 to 530 BCE.

A Closer Look

Under Cyrus the Great and his Achaemenid dynasty successors Darius I and Xerxes I, who ruled from Cyrus's death in 530 BCE until 465 BCE, Persia became one of the most expansive and successful empires in ancient history, stretching from the Indus Valley of present-day Pakistan to Macedonia in the Balkans of Europe.

Cyrus was a great military leader who used one of the Persians' most important assets, their ability to train and raise war-horses, to singular effect. The model of a Persian chariot shown here is pulled by a team of four horses and contains a driver and warrior, who wielded bows and arrows for distance fighting and spears for closeup combat, although the weapons are not included in the model.

Persia's armies were effective not just because of their great size but also because they employed superior tactics, of which the chariot-mounted archers were critical. Typically, however, attacks began with the infantry. After establishing a phalanx in front of the enemy, they would kneel on the ground, using their shields for protection against enemy archers. They would then let loose a stream of arrows of their own and quickly attack using the falling arrows as a diversion. At the same time, the cavalry would advance to prevent similar moves by the enemy's horsemen and to keep the enemy's infantry in a confined space where the Persian infantry could then finish them off.

1 100 200 300 400 500 600 700 800 900 1000 1100 1200 1300 1400 1500 1600 1700 1800 1900 2000 CE

1.2.16 Terracotta Figurine of an Egyptian Scribe

Thebes, Egypt
ca. 520–480 BCE

Credit: DEA/G. Dagli Orti/DeAgostini/Getty Images

TIMELINE   2000 1900 1800 1700 1600 1500 1400 1300 1200 1100 1000 900 800 700 600 500 400 300 200 100 1 BCE

What You Need to Know

The terracotta sculpture in the accompanying image is of an Egyptian scribe from the late sixth or early fifth century BCE.

The very definition of history is bound up with writing, for it is only when people put down their thoughts in permanent form that we have a record of who they were, what they did, and what they believed. Conversely, the rise of agriculture—and with it, stable communities and surpluses—generated a need for keeping track of things. Thus, early writing was a form of tallying. That was the origin of the cuneiform system of writing among the ancient Mesopotamians, who are believed to be the first humans to discover writing, perhaps as early as the ninth millennium BCE, although proper cuneiform—that is, the use of abstracted symbols—came much later.

Ancient Egypt did not come to writing until around the fourth millennium BCE, although most archaeologists believed they did so independent of developments in Mesopotamia, which was separated from the Nile Valley by hundreds of miles of forbidding desert. Our earliest examples of Egyptian hieroglyphic writing come from tombs, and although these early hieroglyphs remain unintelligible to us, it is clear they recorded the identity of the dead.

A Closer Look

Hieroglyphs such scribes drew are abstracted images used to convey basic elements of meaning and sound. Thus, they are both logographic and alphabetic. Indeed, although we cannot read exactly what the earliest of hieroglyphs say, we do know that the images do not exactly correspond to what they are referring to. Instead, they represent other words phonetically related to the object they are describing. Thus, we know that from almost the beginning, Egyptian writing was phonetically based. We can also discern that the earliest hieroglyphs are related to and are part of the same system that produced later hieroglyphic writing, which we can decipher.

As in many ancient civilizations, writing was the preserve of a select elite of scribes, like this one from Thebes. Most of these scribes worked either for the court of the pharaoh, where they would have kept essential administrative records, or were part of the priestly class, who would have used writing to tell the story of the gods and the pharaohs, who Egyptians believed were the mortal incarnation of the falcon-god Horus. The only other people who had writing skills were specialized craftsmen, who created the various inscriptions on funerary items and monuments.

1   100   200   300   400   500   600   700   800   900   1000   1100   1200   1300   1400   1500   1600   1700   1800   1900   2000 CE

1.2.17 Herodotus Describes the Domestic Animals in Egypt

Egypt
Fifth Century BCE

66. The number of domestic animals in Egypt is very great, and would be still greater were it not for what befalls the cats. As the females, when they have kittened, no longer seek the company of the males, these last, to obtain once more their companionship, practise a curious artifice. They seize the kittens, carry them off, and kill them, but do not eat them afterwards. Upon this the females, being deprived of their young, and longing to supply their place, seek the males once more, since they are particularly fond of their offspring. On every occasion of a fire in Egypt the strangest prodigy occurs with the cats. The inhabitants allow the fire to rage as it pleases, while they stand about at intervals and watch these animals, which, slipping by the men or else leaping over them, rush headlong into the flames. When this happens, the Egyptians are in deep affliction. If a cat dies in a private house by a natural death, all the inmates of the house shave their eyebrows. . . .

67. The cats on their decease are taken to the city of Bubastis, where they are embalmed, after which they are buried in certain sacred repositories.

Source: Herodotus. Excerpts from *The Histories*. Book II. In *The Library of Original Sources*. Vol. I, *The Ancient World*. Edited by Oliver J. Thatcher. Milwaukee: University Research Extension Co., 1907, p. 96.

TIMELINE   2000 1900 1800 1700 1600 1500 1400 1300 1200 1100 1000 900 800 700 600 500 400 300 200 100 1 BCE

What You Need to Know

In this excerpt, Greek historian Herodotus describes the treatment of cats in Egyptian society.

Popular culture has it that the Egyptians of the time of the pharaohs, who venerated the cat, were the first to domesticate it. In fact, archaeologists have found evidence of cats living with humans that predate Egyptian civilization by thousands of years, stretching back to the early Neolithic period around 9000 BCE. What most scholars agree on, however, is that today's household cat is a descendant of the African wild cat, that, despite its name, was endemic to both Africa and the Middle East, and that the prehistoric inhabitants of the Nile may have played an important role in the animal's domestication.

As with dogs, some archaeologists believe that the cat, in a sense, domesticated itself, in locales such as Egypt. The development of agriculture and the grain surpluses it produced attracted rats to storage facilities. The African wild cat, which preys on small rodents, among other animals, may have sensed this. Although normally skittish around humans, those individual animals that showed less fear were rewarded with healthier diets, which led to higher reproductive rates.

A Closer Look

The domesticated cat entered into Egyptian life in prehistoric times. When Herodotus visited Egypt in the fifth century BCE, the animal had developed into an important and even revered member of the Egyptian household. According to Herodotus, Egypt was full of domestic animals, of which the cat was perhaps the most common. Although Herodotus's claim that Egyptian cats had a propensity to "rush headlong into the flames" of house fires seems inexplicable, his description of the reaction of Egyptians to this loss reveals much about their attitudes toward cats. He notes that they suffer "deep affliction." He also says that when a cat dies naturally, every member of the household shaves their eyebrows, presumably as a form of mourning. Of course, one must take Herodotus's observations with a grain of salt, as he saw everything through Greek eyes and thus sometimes exaggerated the exoticism and alienness of the cultures, such as Egypt's, that he encountered in his wanderings.

This reverence clearly goes beyond any appreciation for the benefits cats bring, such as vermin hunting. In fact, the cat was worshipped as a god, known as Bast, which represented fertility and motherhood. That may have been the source of Herodotus's observations about how female cats so desired being mothers that they returned to the male cats that had killed their kittens. Bubastis, a city in the Nile delta dedicated to Bast, was the site of perhaps the best-attended religious celebration in ancient Egypt. It was not until the late fourth century CE that cat worship faded away, after a decree by the newly Christianized Roman Empire, which controlled Egypt, called for its halt.

1 100 200 300 400 500 600 700 800 900 1000 1100 1200 1300 1400 1500 1600 1700 1800 1900 2000 CE

1.2.18 The Egyptian Practice of Embalming

Egypt
Fifth Century BCE

86. There are a set of men in Egypt who practise the art of embalming, and make it their proper business. These persons, when a body is brought to them, show the bearers various models of corpses, made in wood, and painted so as to resemble nature. The most perfect is said to be after the manner of him whom I do not think it religious to name in connection with such a matter; the second sort is inferior to the first, and less costly; the third is the cheapest of all. All this the embalmers explain, and then ask in which way it is wished that the corpse should be prepared. The bearers tell them, and having concluded their bargain, take their departure, while the embalming, according to the most perfect process, is the following: They take first a crooked piece of iron, and with it draw out the brain through the nostrils, thus getting rid of a portion, while the skull is cleared of the rest by rinsing with drugs; next they make a cut along the flank with a sharp Ethiopian stone, and take out the whole contents of the abdomen, which they then cleanse, washing it thoroughly with palm-wine, and again frequently with an infusion of pounded aromatics. After this they fill the cavity with the purest bruised myrrh, with cassia, and every other sort of spicery except frankincense, and sew up the opening. Then the body is placed in natrum for seventy days, and covered entirely over. After the expiration of that space of time, which must not be exceeded, the body is washed, and wrapped round, from head to foot, with bandages of fine linen cloth, smeared over with gum, which is used generally by the Egyptians in the place of glue, and in this state it is given back to the relations, who enclose it in a wooden case which they have had made for the purpose, shaped into the figure of a man. Then fastening the case, they place it in a sepulchral chamber, upright against the wall. Such is the most costly way of embalming the dead.

87. If persons wish to avoid expense, and choose the second process, the following is the method pursued: Syringes are filled with oil made from the cedar-tree, which is then, without any incision or disembowelling, injected into the abdomen. The passage by which it might be likely to return is stopped, and the body laid in natrum the prescribed number of days. At the end of the time the cedar-oil is allowed to make its escape; and such is its power that it brings with it the whole stomach and intestines in a liquid state. The natrum meanwhile has dissolved the flesh, and so nothing is left of the dead body but the skin and the bones. It is returned in this condition to the relatives, without any further trouble being bestowed upon it.

88. The third method of embalming, which is practised in the case of the poorer classes, is to clear out the intestines with a clyster, and let the body lie in natrum the seventy days, after which it is at once given to those who come to fetch it away.

Source: Herodotus. Excerpt from *The Histories*. Book II. In *The Library of Original Sources*. Vol. I, *The Ancient World*. Edited by Oliver J. Thatcher. Milwaukee: University Research Extension Co., 1907, pp. 101–102.

TIMELINE   · 2000 1900 1800 1700 1600 1500 1400 1300 1200 1100 1000 900 800 700 600 500 400 300 200 100 1 BCE

What You Need to Know

The primary document presented here was written by fifth-century BCE Greek historian Herodotus and describes how Egyptians embalmed their dead.

The ancient Egyptians had complicated beliefs about the afterlife. These differed from many of the beliefs held by the world's major faiths today, most of which hold that the soul lives on after the body dies. The Egyptians, however, believed that the body played an important element in the afterlife, helping the *ka,* or soul, transit to the underworld. Thus, it was important that the body be preserved. Various embalming methods were employed to this end. In the case of a pharaoh's death, an exact likeness was carved and placed in the tomb, just in case the embalmed body should decay. It was also believed that the soul of the dead required all of the same things that the body required when it was among the living. Thus, the pharaoh and many nobles were buried with great treasures. In prehistoric Egypt, livestock and even servants were sacrificed and buried with their masters to wait on them in the afterlife. But by about 3000 BCE and the beginnings of Egyptian civilization, statues were substituted for human sacrifices.

A Closer Look

Egypt's arid, Saharan climate means that organic matter decays very slowly. This, say Egyptologists, is one of the reasons the ancients believed that the body as well as the soul lived on after death. Egyptians, however, did not leave the process to nature alone; they developed sophisticated methods for preserving the body. Thus evolved embalming, or the use of organic and inorganic substances to preserve human remains. So important was preserving the body after death that a veritable industry grew up in Egypt around it, as Herodotus, who traveled to Egypt, notes. These craftsmen even offered embalming deals for every pocketbook.

All of these began with the washing of the body in palm wine, and then a rinse in water from the Nile. For the wealthiest clients, the organs would be cut out of the body and then covered in natrum, or sodium carbonate, to dry them out and preserve them. The two exceptions were the brains, which were extracted and tossed aside, and the heart, which Egyptians believed was where the soul dwelled and was left in inside the body. Meanwhile, the body cavity was treated with other compounds. After about six weeks, the organs were wrapped in linen infused with natrum. In early Egyptian history, the organs would then be placed in canopic jars; later, as embalming methods improved, the organs were returned to the body wrapped in linen infused with natrum. Then, the entire body was wrapped in such linen, creating the mummy. For the less wealthy, the organs, other than the brain, were left inside and preserved by injected natrum and other substances. For the poorest clients, a simpler method of injecting sodium carbonate was used.

1 100 200 300 400 500 600 700 800 900 1000 1100 1200 1300 1400 1500 1600 1700 1800 1900 2000 CE

1.2.19 Health and Hygiene in Ancient Egypt

Egypt
Fifth Century BCE

36. In other countries the priests have long hair, in Egypt their heads are shaven; elsewhere it is customary, in mourning, for near relations to cut their hair close; the Egyptians, who wear no hair at any other time, when they lose a relative, let their beards and the hair of their heads grow long. . . .

37. They are religious to excess, far beyond any other race of men, and use the following ceremonies: They drink out of brazen cups, which they scour every day: there is no exception to this practice. They wear linen garments, which they are specially careful to have always fresh washed. They practise circumcision for the sake of cleanliness, considering it better to be cleanly than comely. The priests shave their whole body every other day, that no lice or other impure thing may adhere to them when they are engaged in the service of the gods. Their dress is entirely of linen, and their shoes of the papyrus plant: it is not lawful for them to wear either dress or shoes of any other material. They bathe twice every day in cold water, and twice each night. . . .

The following is the mode of life habitual to them: For three successive days in each month they purge the body by means of emetics and clysters, which is done out of a regard for their health, since they have a persuasion that every disease to which men are liable is occasioned by the substances whereon they feed. Apart from any such precautions, they are, I believe, next to the Libyans, the healthiest people in the world an effect of their climate, in my opinion, which has no sudden changes. Diseases almost always attack men when they are exposed to a change, and never more than during changes of the weather. . . .

84. Medicine is practised among them on a plan of separation; each physician treats a single disorder, and no more: thus the country swarms with medical practitioners, some undertaking to cure diseases of the eye, others of the head, others again of the teeth, others of the intestines, and some those which are not local.

Source: Herodotus. Excerpts from *The Histories*. Book II. In *The Library of Original Sources*. Vol. I, *The Ancient World*. Edited by Oliver J. Thatcher. Milwaukee: University Research Extension Co., 1907, pp. 84–85, 101.

TIMELINE   2000 1900 1800 1700 1600 1500 1400 1300 1200 1100 1000 900 800 700 600 500 400 300 200 100 1 BCE

What You Need to Know

Herodotus, the Greek historian who traveled to Egypt in the fifth century CE, wrote down his observations on Egyptian hygiene, which are excerpted here.

Keeping clean in ancient Egypt was not an easy task. The typical Egyptian went about barefoot and lived in homes with compacted earth floors. There was, of course, no indoor plumbing or running water. And heating water for bathing was a labor-intensive task few had the time or resources to do. Indeed, archaeologists have uncovered few evidences of bathing facilities, even in the palaces of royals, before the Hellenistic and Roman eras from the fourth century BCE onward. There is evidence, however, that simple washbasins were plentiful and that people probably did basic ablutions in the morning and evening. For full immersion bathing, they most likely bathed in the Nile River or in irrigation canals. There were, however, other methods for keeping hygienic. Natrum, or sodium bicarbonate, mixed into water was widely used, both for the exterior of the body and to wash out the mouth.

A Closer Look

Despite the lack of bathing facilities, the Egyptians appeared to be relatively healthy, at least by the standards of the time. According to Herodotus, the Egyptians were, aside from their neighbors the Libyans, "the healthiest people in the world." Herodotus credits this fact to their unchanging desert climate. "Diseases," he argues, "almost always attack men when they are exposed to a change, and never more than during changes of the weather."

But he also notes active measures the Egyptians took to sustain their well-being. He notes that both priests and ordinary persons shaved their heads regularly to prevent infestation by lice. They laundered their simple garments frequently, and they purged their digestive systems monthly, believing that one's health—for good and ill—was the result of what one ate. Whether this helped or not, the Egyptians lived in a land of bounty, so they rarely knew famine, and their diet consisted of whole grains and a wide assortment of fruits and vegetables.

The country was also, he notes, "swarm[ing] with doctors," a result of excessive specialization among practitioners, each of whom treated but one malady or one anatomical system. Egyptian medicine was particularly adept at surgery, a fact related to their complex funerary practices. Properly embalming a body for the afterlife gave Egyptians a solid understanding of human anatomy.

1.2.20 Religious Rituals in the Nile Delta

Bubastis, Egypt
Fifth Century BCE

Moreover, it is true also that the Egyptians were the first of men who made solemn assemblies and processions and approaches to the temples, and from them the Hellenes have learnt them, and my evidence for this is that the Egyptian celebrations of these have been held from a very ancient time, whereas the Hellenic were introduced but lately.

The Egyptians hold their solemn assemblies not once in the year but often, especially and with the greatest zeal and devotion at the city of Bubastis for Artemis, and next at Busiris for Isis; for in this last-named city there is a very great temple of Isis, and this city stands in the middle of the Delta of Egypt; now Isis is in the tongue of the Hellenes Demeter: thirdly, they have a solemn assembly at the city of Saïs for Athene, fourthly at Heliopolis for the Sun (Helios), fifthly at the city of Buto in honor of Leto, and sixthly at the city of Papremis for Ares.

Now, when they are coming to the city of Bubastis they do as follows:—they sail men and women together, and a great multitude of each sex in every boat; and some of the women have rattles and rattle with them, while some of the men play the flute during the whole time of the voyage, and the rest, both women and men, sing and clap their hands; and when as they sail they come opposite to any city on the way they bring the boat to land, and some of the women continue to do as I have said, others cry aloud and jeer at the women in that city, some dance, and some stand up and pull up their garments. This they do by every city along the riverbank; and when they come to Bubastis they hold festival celebrating great sacrifices, and more wine of grapes is consumed upon that festival than during the whole of the rest of the year. To this place (so say the natives) they come together year by year even to the number of seventy myriads of men and women, besides children.

Thus it is done here; and how they celebrate the festival in honor of Isis at the city of Busiris has been told by me before: for, as I said, they beat themselves in mourning after the sacrifice, all of them both men and women, very many myriads of people; but for whom they beat themselves it is not permitted to me by religion to say: and so many as there are of the Carians dwelling in Egypt do this even more than the Egyptians themselves, inasmuch as they cut their foreheads also with knives; and by this it is manifested that they are strangers and not Egyptians.

Source: Herodotus. *The History of Herodotus*. Vol. I. Excerpt from Book II. Translated by G. C. Macaulay. London and New York: MacMillan and Co., 1890, pp. 142–144.

TIMELINE   2000 1900 1800 1700 1600 1500 1400 1300 1200 1100 1000 900 800 700 600 500 400 300 200 100 1 BCE

What You Need to Know

In this passage, the Greek historian Herodotus, who traveled to Egypt in the fifth century, offers his observations of a religious ritual that took place at Bubastis and Busiris, two cities in the Nile delta. Both were the administrative capitals of *nomes,* or subdistricts within the Egyptian kingdom.

Surrounded by nearly impassable desert and with the navigable Nile running its length, ancient Egypt was one of the first places that centrally administered government over large numbers of people emerged in human history. It was that government that commanded the wealth of the state and maintained the elaborate irrigation system on which Egyptian civilization and Egyptian livelihoods depended. Not surprisingly, Egyptians revered the dynastic head of that government, the pharaoh, who was not just ancient Egypt's political leader but the focal point of its religion.

In many ancient civilizations, the leader was the mediator between the gods and humanity. But in Egypt he was something more; he was a god—the falcon-headed Horus, specifically— incarnate. After death, he became one with Horus's father, Osiris, god of the underworld. Thus, in the person of the pharaoh, the gods and humans were linked, and nature and society harmonized, all for the purposes of providing peace and prosperity to the kingdom.

A Closer Look

At Bubastis, Egyptians worshipped the cat-goddess, Bast. (The prefix "bu" means "house of.") Early in Egyptian religious history, Bast was a lion-goddess and a goddess of war and hunting. (The reference to Artemis in Herodotus's account refers to the fact that the Greeks likened Bast to their own goddess of the hunt.) By Herodotus's time, however, the god had been, in effect, domesticated as a cat and had lost much of her power. Still, she remained important to the Egyptians of the delta as a protector god for the people of the region, hence the elaborate ceremony Herodotus describes. Indeed, the annual celebration at Bubastis was perhaps the most important in Egypt.

Second to the festival of Bubastis was that of Busiris, considered to be the birthplace of Isis, the goddess consort of Osiris, the god of the underworld. Isis was also considered to the goddess of motherhood and nature. In its description of the festival in honor of Isis, Herodotus notes the presence of Carians, a pre-Hellenic people of southwestern Anatolia, or Turkey today. Indeed, Isis was not just worshipped in Egypt but by peoples around the Mediterranean Basin.

1 100 200 300   400   500   600   700   800   900   1000 1100 1200 1300   1400   1500   1600   1700 1800 1900 2000 CE

1.2.21 Phoenician Law Concerning Sacrifices

Carthage
ca. Fifth or Fourth Century BCE

Temple of Baal[zephon]. Tar[iff of d]ues, which [the superintendents of d]ues fixed in the time [of our rulers, Khalasjbaal, the judge, son of Bodtanith son of Bod[eshmun, and of Khalasbaal], the judge, son of Bodeshmun, son of Khalasbaal, and their colleagues.

For an ox as a whole burnt-offering or a prayer-offering, or a whole peace-offering, the priests shall have 10 (shekels) of silver for each; and in case of a whole burnt-offering, they shall have in addition to this fee [300 shekels of fle]sh; and in case of a prayer-offering, the trimmings, the joints; but the skin and the fat of the inwards and the feet and the rest of the flesh the owner of the sacrifice shall have.

For a calf whose horns are wanting, in case of one not castrated (?), or in case of a ram as a whole burnt-offering, the priests shall have 5 shekels of silver [for each; and in case of a whole burnt-offering they shall have in addit]ion to this fee 150 shekels of flesh; and, in case of a prayer-offering, the trimmings and the joints; but the skin and the fat of the inwards and the fe[et and the rest of the flesh the owner of the sacrifice shall have].

In case of a ram or a goat as a whole burnt-offering, or a prayer-offering, or a whole peace-offering, the priests shall have 1 shekel of silver and 2 zars for each; and, in case of a prayer-offering, they shall [have in addition to this fee the trimmings] and the joints; but the skin and the fat of the inwards and the feet and the rest of the flesh the owner of the sacrifice shall have.

For a lamb, or a kid, or the young (?) of a hart, as a whole burnt-offering, or a prayer-offering, or a whole peace-offering, the priests shall have 3/4 (of a shekel) and . . . *zars* of silver [for each; and, in case of a prayer-offering, they shall have in addition] to this fee the trimmings and the joints; but the skin and the fat of the inwards and the feet and the rest of the flesh the own[er of the sacrifice] shall have. . . .

In case of every prayer-offering that is presented before the gods, the priests shall have the trimmings and the joints; and in the case of a prayer-offering . . .

For every sacrifice which a man may offer who is poor in cattle, or poor in birds, the priests shall not have anything. . . .

Every freeman and every slave and every dependent of the gods and all men who may sacrifice, these men [shall give] for the sacrifice at the rate prescribed in the regulations . . .

Every payment which is not prescribed in this table shall be made according to the regulations which [the superintendents of the dues fixed in the time of Khalasbaal, son of Bodtanijth, and Khalasbaal, son of Bodeshmun, and their colleagues. Every priest who shall accept payment beyond what is prescribed in this table shall be fi[ned].

Source: Barton, George A., trans. *Archaeology and the Bible*. Philadelphia: American Sunday School, 1916, pp. 342–343.

TIMELINE　　2000 1900 1800 1700 1600 1500 1400 1300 1200 1100 1000 900 800 700 600 500 400 300 200 100 1 BCE

What You Need to Know

This excerpt is from a Carthaginian document, perhaps from the fifth or fourth century BCE, describing animal sacrifice.

The Phoenicians were a Semitic people who originated in the Levant, in what is now southern Lebanon. A largely urban-based culture, their greatest legacy was in the realm of language, for it was the Phoenicians who first came up with the idea of the phonetic alphabet, which, modified by the Greeks and the Romans, serves as the basis of our script today.

The Phoenicians were also some of the greatest seafarers and traders of the ancient Western world. They established commercial centers and ports far from their homeland in the western Mediterranean, as far away as Spain. Perhaps their most significant outpost was Carthage, situated on the North African coast in what is now Tunisia. Founded in 813 BCE, Carthage became a great power of its own, controlling much of the North African coast, southern Spain, Sardinia, and Corsica by the third century BCE, before being conquered by the Romans during the various Punic wars of the third and second century BCE.

A Closer Look

Given their trading and seafaring ways, which put them into contact with peoples throughout the Mediterranean world, the Phoenicians were eclectic in their religion, readily borrowing gods from the pantheons of the peoples they encountered. In their religious practices, rituals, and beliefs, they invoked Canaanite gods—Canaan being the land from which they came—such as Baal, as well as Greek gods. The Phoenicians' goddess of fertility, Ashtarte, bore a remarkable resemblance in behavior to Aphrodite, for example. As with many other ancient Mediterranean peoples, but very different from their Hebrew neighbors, the Phoenician gods were anthropomorphic and had the same emotions and behaviors as mortals. These beliefs, of course, were anathema to the Hebrews, who denounced them frequently in the Old Testament.

But the Phoenicians, and their offshoots, the Carthaginians, did have one thing in common with the Jews—the practice of animal sacrifice to the gods or God. Both peoples practiced "whole burnt offerings" (burning of the animal carcass) and "meal offerings" (nonflesh foods), and both understood those offerings as a means of atonement, to placate an angry deity or deities for the sins of humankind. Sacrifices of male animals only were made by priests on the altars of Carthaginian temples.

One difference between the two peoples was how the priests were compensated for their role in overseeing the sacrifice. The Phoenicians paid their priests, whereas the Hebrews did not, giving him instead a part of the sacrifice.

1.2.22 Persian Customs as Witnessed by Herodotus

Persia
ca. 440 BCE

The customs which I know the Persians to observe are the following. They have no images of the gods, no temples nor altars, and consider the use of them a sign of folly. This comes, I think, from their not believing the gods to have the same nature with men, as the Greeks imagine. Their wont, however, is to ascend to the summits of the loftiest mountains and there to offer sacrifice to Zeus [= Ahura-Mazda], which is the name they give to the whole circuit of the firmament.

To these gods the Persians offer sacrifice in the following manner: they raise no altar, light no fire, pour no libations; there is no sound of the flute, no putting on of chaplets, no consecrated barley cake; but the man who wishes to sacrifice brings his victim to a spot of ground which is free from pollution, and then calls upon the name of the god to whom he intends to offer. It is usual to have the turban encircled with a wreath, most commonly of myrtle. The sacrificer is not allowed to pray for blessings on himself alone, but he prays for the welfare of the king and of the whole Persian people, among whom he is of necessity included. He cuts the victim in pieces, and having boiled the flesh, he lays it out upon the tenderest herbage he can find, trefoil especially. When all is ready, one of the Magi comes forward and chants a hymn, which they say recounts the origin of the gods. It is not lawful to offer a sacrifice unless there is a Magus present. After waiting a short time the sacrificer carries the flesh of the victim away with him, and makes whatever use of it he may please. . . .

Of nations, they honor most their nearest neighbors, whom they esteem next to themselves; those who live beyond these they honor in the second degree; and so with the remainder, the further they are removed, the less the esteem in which they hold them. The reason is, that they look upon themselves as very greatly superior in all respects to the rest of mankind, regarding others as approaching in excellence in proportion as they dwell nearer to them; whence it comes to pass that those who are the farthest off must be the most degraded of mankind.

There is no nation which so readily adopts foreign customs as the Persians. Thus, they have taken the dress of the Medes, considering it superior to their own; and in war they wear the Egyptian breastplate. As soon as they hear of any luxury, they instantly make it their own. Each of them has several wives, and a still larger number of concubines.

Source: Herodotus. Excerpts from *The Histories*. Book I. In *Readings in Ancient History: Illustrative Extracts from the Sources*. Vol. I. Edited by William Stearns Davis. Boston: Allyn and Bacon, 1912, pp. 58–60.

TIMELINE   2000 1900 1800 1700 1600 1500 1400 1300 1200 1100 1000 900 800 700 600 500 400 300 200 100 1 BCE

What You Need to Know

This excerpt on Persia, from Herodotus's work *The Histories* begins with an account of the religion of the Persians.

The Persians were the most important of a number of Iranian peoples, a branch of the Indo-European family of cultures, who moved out of what is now eastern Europe and Russia and into the central Iranian plateau and surrounding lands sometime around the beginning of the first millennium BCE. Three aspects of their new lands shaped their culture. One is its abiding harshness. High and snowy mountain ranges dominate the north, and much of the south is given over to some of the most forbidding deserts in the world. This led the Persians to seek more hospitable lands elsewhere through conquest. The second is the fact that fertile oases are scattered about the country, leading to a diversity of cultures. The final defining characteristic of Iran was its location, situated roughly halfway between the great civilizations of Mesopotamia and the Indus Valley of northwest India, which encouraged trade and an openness to outside ideas.

A Closer Look

Herodotus was born in the city of Halicarnassus, located on the southwest coast of Anatolia, in what is now Turkey. At the time of his birth in 484 BCE, the city was under the control of the Persian Empire, having been conquered by Cyrus the Great several decades earlier. Much of what he wrote about Persia may have come from his own youthful experiences within the empire and the eyewitness accounts he collected as part of his effort to document the various cultures of the world, as then known to the Greeks.

Herodotus notes that the Persians have "no images of the gods, no temples, nor altars." Indeed, Persian religion was a straightforward one with little ritual and not much myth. In it, the good Ahura-Mazda and the evil Ahriman, battled for the souls of humans, though people had the power to choose between them.

Herodotus also notes the contradictions within Persian culture when it came to outsiders. He notes that "there is not nation which so readily adopts foreign customs as the Persians." In fact, their enlightened kings, particularly Cyrus, recognized that his people could learn much from the well-established civilizations of Mesopotamia and the Indus valley. But at the same, says Herodotus, the Persians believe themselves to be a superior people, a not unexpected result of their extraordinary success on the battlefield.

1.2.23 Josephus on Jewish Marriage and Family Law

Israel
First Century CE

And further, no one ought to marry a harlot, whose matrimonial oblations, arising from the prostitution of her body, God will not receive; for by these means the dispositions of the children will be liberal and virtuous; I mean, when they are not born of base parents, and of the lustful conjunction of such as marry women that are not free.

If any one has been espoused to a woman as to a virgin, and does not afterward find her so to be, let him bring his action, and accuse her, and let him make use of such indications to prove his accusation as he is furnished withal; and let the father or the brother of the damsel, or some one that is after them nearest of kin to her, defend her. If the damsel obtain a sentence in her favor, that she had not been guilty, let her live with her husband that accused her; and let him not have any further power at all to put her away, unless she give him very great occasions of suspicion, and such as can be no way contradicted. But for him that brings an accusation and calumny against his wife in an impudent and rash manner, let him be punished by receiving forty stripes save one, and let him pay fifty shekels to her father: but if the damsel be convicted, as having been corrupted, and is one of the common people, let her be stoned, because she did not preserve her virginity till she were lawfully married; but if she were the daughter of a priest, let her be burnt alive.

He that hath corrupted a damsel espoused to another man, in case he had her consent, let both him and her be put to death, for they are both equally guilty; the man, because he persuaded the woman willingly to submit to a most impure action, and to prefer it to lawful wedlock; the woman, because she was persuaded to yield herself to be corrupted, either for pleasure or for gain. However, if a man light on a woman when she is alone, and forces her, where nobody was present to come to her assistance, let him only be put to death. Let him that hath corrupted a virgin not yet espoused marry her; but if the father of the damsel be not willing that she should be his wife, let him pay fifty shekels as the price of her prostitution. . . .

Now if the insolence of young men be thus cured, let them escape the reproach which their former errors deserved; for by this means the lawgiver will appear to be good, and parents happy, while they never behold either a son or a daughter brought to punishment. But if it happen that these words and instructions, conveyed by them in order to reclaim the man, appear to be useless, then the offender renders the laws implacable enemies to the insolence he has offered his parents; let him therefore be brought forth by these very parents out of the city, with a multitude following him, and there let him be stoned; and when he has continued there for one whole day, that all the people may see him, let him be buried in the night.

Source: Josephus, Flavius. Excerpts from *Antiquities of the Jews*. Book IV, Ch. VIII. In *The Complete Works of Flavius Josephus the Celebrated Jewish Historian*. Translated by William Whiston. Auburn and Buffalo, NY: John E. Beardsley, 1895, pp. 111–113.

TIMELINE	40,000	35,000	30,000	25,000	20,000	15,000	10,000	5000	1 BCE

What You Need to Know

This selection is from the book *Jewish Antiquities*, penned in the first century CE by Josephus, a Jewish scholar who wrote in Latin and ultimately defected to the Roman side during the first Jewish-Roman War of 66 to 73. In this excerpt, Josephus discusses Jewish laws on marriage and families.

Through much of their early history, the Hebrews were a nomadic people, originating in northern Mesopotamia. Indeed, the word "Hebrew" is derived from Akkadian (the language of Babylon in Mesopotamia) and Egyptian words for *nomads*. Sometime in the late second millennium BCE, however, the Hebrews came to settle in lands they controlled, in what is now Israel and Palestine.

As nomads settling down to pursue agriculture on their own land for the first time, they continued old customs of communal labor and control of common property. Gradually, however, common land was divided up into families. That transition enhanced the role of the head of the household who was inevitably a male. Women became increasingly subservient, viewed as a form of property, to be segregated in the home. This delegation to inferior status also affected women's role in religion. Where once they had participated in the ceremonies as priestesses, they were now considered unclean—due to menstruation and childbirth—and hence less worthy of being in God's presence. And so they became relegated to segregated worshipping space by the men who came to control religious ceremonies.

A Closer Look

In *Jewish Antiquities,* Josephus notes that the laws placed great importance on the purity of the bride. Harlots, or prostitutes, are simply not permitted to marry, as God will not accept such a union. For others, their virginity is their primary asset. If a woman claims to be a virgin and is proved not to be, then she should be stoned. Almost as disturbing is that the woman is afforded almost no say in her own defense; her male relatives are given the charge of proving the accusation wrong. After marriage, a woman's chastity is paramount; should she commit adultery, she will be put to death, though at least in this case her paramour is similarly punished. Indeed, the law did distinguish between adultery and rape and said that if a wife did not give her consent to sex, she was to remain as wife and the rapist should be punished by death.

As for children, the law's paramount concern, says Josephus, is for their obedience to—and respect for—their parents. Just as God looks on humankind as his children and demands obedience from them, so parents should have the same from their offspring. If they do not, society itself is imperiled. Indeed, so great is the threat of "insolent" children that the law dictates unrepentant ones be taken from the city and stoned to death.

1.2.24 Josephus on Rules of War

Israel
First Century CE

Let all sort of warlike operations, whether they befall you now in your own time, or hereafter in the times of your posterity, be done out of your own borders: but when you are about to go to war, send embassages and heralds to those who are your voluntary enemies, for it is a right thing to make use of words to them before you come to your weapons of war; and assure them thereby, that although you have a numerous army, with horses and weapons, and, above these, a God merciful to you, and ready to assist you, you do however desire them not to compel you to fight against them, nor to take from them what they have, which will indeed be our gain, but what they will have no reason to wish we should take to ourselves. And if they hearken to you, it will be proper for you to keep peace with them; but if they trust in their own strength, as superior to yours, and will not do you justice, lead your army against them, making use of God as your supreme Commander, but ordaining for a lieutenant under him one that is of the greatest courage among you; for these different commanders, besides their being an obstacle to actions that are to be done on the sudden, are a disadvantage to those that make use of them. Lead an army pure, and of chosen men, composed of all such as have extraordinary strength of body and hardiness of soul; but do you send away the timorous part, lest they run away in the time of action, and so afford an advantage to your enemies. Do you also give leave to those that have lately built them houses, and have not yet lived in them a year's time; and to those that have planted them vineyards, and have not yet been partakers of their fruits, to continue in their own country; as well as those also who have betrothed, or lately married them wives, lest they have such an affection for these things that they he too sparing of their lives, and, by reserving themselves for these enjoyments, they become voluntary cowards, on account of their wives.

When you have pitched your camp, take care that you do nothing that is cruel. And when you are engaged in a siege; and want timber for the making of warlike engines, do not you render the land naked by cutting down trees that bear fruit, but spare them, as considering that they were made for the benefit of men; and that if they could speak, they would have a just plea against you, because, though they are not occasions of the war, they are unjustly treated, and suffer in it, and would, if they were able, remove themselves into another land. When you have beaten your enemies in battle, slay those that have fought against you; but preserve the others alive, that they may pay you tribute, excepting the nation of the Canaanites; for as to that people, you must entirely destroy them.

Source: Josephus, Flavius. Excerpt from *Antiquities of the Jews*. Book IV, Ch. VIII. In *The Complete Works of Flavius Josephus the Celebrated Jewish Historian*. Translated by William Whiston. Auburn and Buffalo: John E. Beardsley, 1895, p. 115.

TIMELINE   40,000   35,000   30,000   25,000   20,000   15,000   10,000   5000   1 BCE

What You Need to Know

This excerpt from the writings of Josephus, a Jewish scholar, discusses the rules of war in the first century CE.

As with their descendants today, the ancient Israelites, or Hebrews, lived in a dangerous neighborhood, surrounded by civilizations with far greater numbers of people and often with martial inclinations. Similarly, their bitterest foes were closer at hand. When the Hebrews moved into what was called the land of Canaan—what is now Israel/Palestine, as well as parts of Jordan and Lebanon—they came into contact with the Philistines. The latter were a formidable people, with superior weapons technology and a more disciplined and organized fighting force. Under the leadership of Saul, a member of one of the larger Hebrew tribes, the Israelites tried to conquer the Philistines. Although Saul ultimately failed, his efforts helped unite the tribes under his leadership, turning a disparate group of formerly nomadic tribes into a centrally administered kingdom, ruled from the captured Canaanite city of Jerusalem.

A Closer Look

The book of Deuteronomy in the Old Testament of the Hebrews contains some of the earliest examples of rules of war in the history of Western Civilization. Today rules of war are codified in international law and applicable to all signatory states, but for the ancient Hebrews, they were self-imposed codes of conduct or, rather, codes of conduct believed to be ordered by God, as part of His covenant with the Jewish people. To violate these codes meant to offend God and bring His wrath down upon His chosen people.

In the first century CE, Josephus, a Jewish writer who wrote in Latin, attempted to explain the Israelites rules of war to the larger Greco-Roman world. At the time, the Romans were battling to subdue the rebellious Jewish inhabitants of the imperial province of Judea. The rules Josephus describes would be familiar to modern international legal experts: who is eligible to fight, how to treat enemy combatants and civilians, why one should spare the resources of the lands to be conquered, and why it is necessary to pursue diplomacy before going to war. Notably, the latter involves first warning the enemy that an omnipotent God is on the Israelites' side, which might come across more as a threat than a legitimate effort to find a negotiated settlement to the conflict. Also noteworthy is Josephus's remark that although God tells the Jews to spare the lives of those who surrender, the rule does not apply to Canaanites, "for as to that people, you must entirely destroy them."

1 100 200 300 400 500 600 700 800 900 1000 1100 1200 1300 1400 1500 1600 1700 1800 1900 2000 CE

1.2.25 Travel and Trade around the Red Sea

Northwest Africa
First Century CE

4. Below Ptolemais of the Hunts, at a distance of about 3000 stadia [roughly 340 miles; a stadia was an ancient measure of about 600 feet], there is Adulis, a port established by law, lying at the inner end of a bay that runs in toward the south. Before the harbor lies the so-called Mountain Island, about 200 stadia seaward from the very head of the bay, with the shores of the mainland close to it on both sides. Ships bound for this port now anchor here because of attacks from the land. They used formerly to anchor at the very head of the bay, by an island called Diodorus, close to the shore, which could be reached on foot from the land; by which means the barbarous natives attacked the island. Opposite Mountain Island, on the mainland 20 stadia from shore, lies Adulis, a fair-sized village, from which there is a three-days' journey to Coloe, an inland town and the first market for ivory. From that place to the city of the people called Auxumites there is a five days' journey more; to that place all the ivory is brought from the country beyond the Nile through the district called Cyeneum, and thence to Adulis. Practically the whole number of elephants and rhinoceros that are killed live in the places inland, although at rare intervals they are hunted on the seacoast even near Adulis. Before the harbor of that market-town, out at sea on the right hand, there lie a great many little sandy islands called Alalaei, yielding tortoise-shell, which is brought to market there by the Fish-Eaters.

5. And about 800 stadia beyond there is another very deep bay, with a great mound of sand piled up at the right of the entrance; at the bottom of which the opsian stone is found, and this is the only place where it is produced. These places, from the Calf-Eaters to the other Berber country, are governed by Zoscales; who is miserly in his ways and always striving for more, but otherwise upright, and acquainted with Greek literature.

6. There are imported into these places, undressed cloth made in Egypt for the Berbers; robes from Arsinoe; cloaks of poor quality dyed in colors; double-fringed linen mantles; many articles of flint glass, and others of murrhine, made in Diospolis; and brass, which is used for ornament and in cut pieces instead of coin; sheets of soft copper, used for cooking-utensils and cut up for bracelets and anklets for the women; iron, which is made into spears used against the elephants and other wild beasts, and in their wars. Besides these, small axes are imported, and adzes and swords; copper drinking-cups, round and large; a little coin for those coming to the market; wine of Laodicea and Italy, not much; olive oil, not much; for the king, gold and silver plate made after the fashion of the country, and for clothing, military cloaks, and thin coats of skin, of no great value. Likewise from the district of Ariaca across this sea, there are imported Indian iron, and steel, and Indian cotton cloth; the broad cloth called *monachê* and that called *sagmatogênê*, and girdles, and coats of skin and mallow-colored cloth, and a few muslins, and colored lac. There are exported from these places ivory, and tortoiseshell and rhinoceros-horn. The most from Egypt is brought to this market from the month of January to September, that is, from Tybi to Thoth; but seasonably they put to sea about the month of September.

Source: Schoff, Wilfred H., trans. *The Periplus of the Erythraean Sea: Travel and Trade in the Indian Ocean by a Merchant of the First Century*. New York: Longmans, Green, and Co., 1912, pp. 22–24.

TIMELINE   40,000   35,000   30,000   25,000   20,000   15,000   10,000   5000   1 BCE

What You Need to Know

This passage is from a first century CE Roman text by an unknown author, titled *Periplous Maris Erythraei*, or Voyage around the Red Sea.

By the first century CE, virtually all of the great civilizations of the Western World had been incorporated into the Roman Empire, barring the Parthians of Persia. Under this *Pax Romana,* or peace of Rome, the Roman navy cleared the seas of pirates, making seagoing voyages around the Mediterranean World much safer. This encouraged not only trade but tourist travel as well, as well-to-do Romans flocked to Greece and Egypt to see the sites. For those without the means or inclination to undertake such travel, which could still be quite arduous, there was travel writing. One particularly popular genre was the so-called *periplous,* which translates as a "voyage around." Seagoing travel in the ancient world tended not to be long extended voyages across open seas but journeys that hugged the coastline, with frequent stops along the way for trade and reoutfitting. This allowed those on board, including writers, to make many observations on the places and peoples they encountered.

A Closer Look

The Red Sea is the vast inlet of the Indian Ocean that separates Egypt and northeast Africa from the Arabian Peninsula. *Maris* was Latin for "sea," and *Erythraei* was the Greek word for "red." The name is believed to have come from an algae that periodically blooms in its waters.

The sea had been explored by the Egyptians as early as the third millennium BCE and was well known to the Persians, the Greeks, and of course, the Romans. By the time of Augustus, when this text was written, the Red Sea had become part of a vital trade route connecting Rome with Nubia, Ethiopia, and ultimately India. Indeed, goods from as far away as China came to the West via the Red Sea. The *periplous* spends much time discussing the many goods made and traded in the region.

Although well traveled, the *Maris Erythraei* was still at the edge of the known Roman world, filled with hostile peoples and exotic animals. In one observation, the writer of the *periplous* notes the trade in ivory at the Ethiopian trading port of Adulis—in modern-day Eritrea—which was obtained from the elephants and rhinoceroses of the interior. The writer also talks of the native Berber people. Although the name is now given to the non-Arab speaking inhabitants of North Africa, it was used in Roman times to signify the Arabic-speaking peoples of the Red Sea littoral.

1 100 200 300 400 500 600 700 800 900 1000 1100 1200 1300 1400 1500 1600 1700 1800 1900 2000 CE

Part 3:
Ancient Asia

Fourth Millennium BCE–Third Century CE

1.3.1 Harappan Seal

Mohenjo-daro, Indus Valley
ca. 2500 BCE

Credit: DEA/G. Nimatallah/DeAgostini/Getty Images

TIMELINE   40,000   35,000   30,000   25,000   20,000   15,000   10,000   5000   1 BCE

What You Need to Know

The seal shown here was probably used to authenticate government or commercial documents; it comes from the Indus valley of India and dates to the third millennium BCE. Among cradles of human civilization is the Indus River valley, situated in what is now Pakistan and northwest India. There, around the year 2500 BCE, arose a Bronze Age culture known to archaeologists as the Harappan civilization, after one of its major cities. (It is also sometimes referred to as Mohenjo-daro, this name coming from the archaeological site where it was first discovered in the early twentieth century.)

The civilization was immense, by ancient standards, covering around 500,000 square miles at its height in the late third millennium BCE, about twice the size of either Mesopotamia or Egypt. It was also strikingly uniform across its great breadth, with similar architecture and a common script found throughout. While most of its inhabitants were rural, it boasted a vibrant urban culture and many great cities. For all its majesty, however, it seems to have collapsed early in the second millennium BCE, for reasons yet to be determined. Theories for its demise include climate change, a buildup of salt or alkali in irrigated fields, or disease. Whatever the reason, the decline of the Harappans was followed by nearly 1,000 years in which the subcontinent of India had no literate civilization.

A Closer Look

The cities of the first civilization of the Indus valley were marvels of the ancient world. Both Harappa and Mohenjo-daro appeared to have been planned from the beginning, rather than growing up haphazardly around older villages. The streets followed a grid, and underlying them was one of the most sophisticated sewage systems of the time. Above ground were palaces, immense citadels, and homes of all sizes, most of which centered on courtyards.

Unfortunately, we know comparatively little about the material and cultural life of the Harappans. Their script has yet to be deciphered, and they burned their dead rather than burying them with luxury objects or the artifacts of everyday life. What we do know about their cities was that they were centers of both crafts and commerce. Indeed, they served as the hubs of trading networks that stretched across northern India and as far away as Mesopotamia and the Mediterranean world. Massive granaries and bead-making factories have been unearthed at the port of Lothal, in modern-day Gujarat. In addition, archaeologists have dug up numerous seals, probably used to authenticate documents, either governmental or commercial in nature. One of them is shown in the accompanying image.

1 100 200 300   400   500   600   700   800   900   1000 1100 1200 1300   1400   1500   1600   1700 1800 1900 2000 CE

1.3.2 Jomon-Period *Fukabachi* Cup

Japan
3000–2000 BCE

Credit: DeAgostini/Getty Images

What You Need to Know

This terracotta *fukabachi* cup is from the middle Jomon period in prehistoric Japan, between 3000 and 2000 BCE.

As with many ancient cultures, Japan's was heavily determined by its geography. Specifically, Japan is composed of four main islands and a number of smaller ones, separated from the Korean Peninsula and the Asian mainland by the Strait of Korea. While allowing for cultural influences to penetrate, the 100-mile-wide strait was broad enough to hinder invaders, allowing Japanese culture to develop with little direct external interference, although borrowing from Asia was rife.

Foundation myths of the Japanese people place the time of creation in the Jomon period, with written records from later times placing it around the year 660 BCE. Archaeologists believe that many aspects of later Japanese culture—including the Shinto religion, technology, social customs, and types of architecture—existed in embryonic form during the Jomon period, which was also marked by the influx of peoples from northern Asia and various islands of the western Pacific, including what is now Taiwan.

A Closer Look

Archaeologists surmise that people have inhabited the Japanese archipelago since roughly 38,000 BCE, the date of the earliest authenticated artifacts. It is also believed that the transition from the Paleolithic era of hunting and gathering to the Neolithic era, when agriculture and more complex tools were developed, began around 14,000 BCE. The date marks the beginning of the Jomon period, which lasted until about 300 BCE.

The 4,000- to 5,000-year-old terracotta *fukabachi*, or deep-bowl, cup from the Jomon period shown here is decorated with applied strips of clay and etched lines. Indeed, the term *Jomon* in Japanese means "cord pattern" and comes from the practice of Jomon-era potters adorning their work with what looks like cords shaped out of clay. A close look at the cup here reveals such a pattern.

Although called a cup by archaeologists, the vessel was in fact probably used as a storage or cooking vessel. The artifact attests to the fact that by the time it was made, the people who shaped it had a food supply secure enough to allow some people to engage in crafts and the food surpluses that needed to be stored. Unlike most hunter-gatherers, the Jomon lived a semisedentary lifestyle and developed a high degree of social complexity.

1 100 200 300 400 500 600 700 800 900 1000 1100 1200 1300 1400 1500 1600 1700 1800 1900 2000 CE

1.3.3 Bronze Dagger from Shang Dynasty

China
ca. 1766–1122 BCE

Credit: DEA/L. De Masi/DeAgostini/Getty Images

TIMELINE   2000 1900 1800 1700 1600 1500 1400 1300 1200 1100 1000 900 800 700 600 500 400 300 200 100 1 BCE

What You Need to Know

A bronze dagger from Shang dynasty, which ruled China from 1766 to 1122 BCE, is shown here.

The Neolithic age—that is, the period in which people transitioned from the nomadic hunting and gathering life of the Paleolithic age to sedentary life and agriculture—occurred in China a couple of thousand years after it did in Mesopotamia, around 8000 BCE. It took another 6,000 years, however, until the various Neolithic cultures of the North China Plain and the Yellow River valley coalesced into a more unified Bronze Age kingdom.

Chinese history, until the early twentieth century, is divided into various dynasties, or royal lineages, and the first of these is believed to be the Xia, although almost nothing is known about it. The first dynasty for which there is an extensive archaeological record is the Shang dynasty, which began around 1500 BCE and lasted almost until the end of the second millennium BCE. It stretched across much of northern China, from the Yellow Sea in the northeast to present-day Xi'an in the west and as far south as the Yangtze River, although most of its great cities were along the more northerly Yellow River.

A Closer Look

Iron weapons did not appear in any significant numbers until the early Han dynasty of the third century BCE. This dagger was not held in a soldier's hand but was part of a larger weapon known as a dagger-axe, similar to the halberd of medieval European armory. The square end at the top was attached to a long shaft. The hole in what looks like the handle held another blade. This allowed the wielder of the weapon to employ it in both a thrusting and swinging motion.

The Chinese have unusual myths about their origins. Rather than ascribing their civilization to the work of gods, they cite great inventors of the mythical past. Among these was Huang Di, the Yellow Lord, who it is said invented weaponry, such as this dagger.

The Shang dynasty was an expansive one, with much of its territory claimed through military conquest. Based out of Anyang, the first of five Shang capitals, armies of warriors, which sometimes numbered upward of 5,000 men, used bronze-tipped spears and halberds against their enemies, forcing them into political subservience and economic tributary status to their king. By about 1200 BCE, the Shang armies began to employ chariots, which were coming into use in civilizations across the Eurasian landmass at that time, to expand ever further.

1 100 200 300 400 500 600 700 800 900 1000 1100 1200 1300 1400 1500 1600 1700 1800 1900 2000 CE

1.3.4 Shang Dynasty Oracle Bone

China
ca. 1766–1122 BCE

Credit: DeAgostini/Getty Images

TIMELINE   2000 1900 1800 1700 1600 1500 1400 1300 1200 1100 1000 900 800 700 600 500 400 300 200 100 1 BCE

What You Need to Know

Shown here is an oracle bone used to divine the future by fortune-tellers to advise emperors and lesser persons on actions they should take that would result in the most auspicious outcomes. It dates from Shang dynasty, which ruled China from 1766 to 1122 BCE.

The religions and religious philosophies we associate with Chinese civilization today—Confucianism, Taoism, and Buddhism—did not yet exist during the Shang dynasty of the second millennium BCE. But, of course, there was worship, centered on a pantheon of gods, the most important of which was Shang Ti, which translates roughly as "lord on high."

But Shang Ti was a remote god. People had to seek his favor through intermediaries. This is where a person's ancestors came into play. Shang Ti made sure that the living descendants of the ancestors performed the proper rituals and made the appropriate sacrifices. If these were done, the information was then passed on by Shang Ti in the form of instructions to ancestors to intercede with good fortune—or bad—for those living descendants. If the ancestors were pleased, life went well for the individual and the household; if displeased, bad fortune would befall them.

A Closer Look

As the high gods and ancestors controlled the fortunes of living souls—so Shang dynasty Chinese believed—it was very important for people to be able to communicate with them. This was especially so for the kings, who guided the course of civilization and the lives of millions. One of the means through which they did so was oracle bones; an example of one from the fourteenth or thirteenth century BCE is shown here.

Shang dynasty kings employed diviners, who would read the will of the gods and ancestors in any number of forms, including oracle bones. When a king had an important question to decide, he would pose it to the diviner in the form of a yes-no question. The diviner would then apply a hot metal point to the oracle bone, which was typically a cattle scapula bone, although the one pictured here came from a turtle. The burning would make cracks in the bone that the diviner would then read to answer the king's question. The writing on the bone shown here consists of various questions asked by the king. Many of the questions from surviving oracle bones concern events such as weather, disease, travel, and the meaning dreams.

The writing itself is of significance, as it was during the Shang dynasty that the beginning of modern Chinese script emerged. As in many early civilizations, Chinese writing was logographic—that is, each word was represented by a character. In the West, such writing systems were replaced by the first millennium BCE with phonetic systems. But the Chinese retained their logographic. Although more cumbersome, it meant that ancient texts could be read more easily because the written word would remain the same even after the spoken word had changed, creating a stronger tie with the ancestral past.

1 100 200 300 400 500 600 700 800 900 1000 1100 1200 1300 1400 1500 1600 1700 1800 1900 2000 CE

1.3.5 Moral Precepts from the Mahabharata

India
ca. 1000 BCE

Conquer a man who never gives by gifts;
Subdue untruthful men by truthfulness;
Vanquish an angry man by gentleness;
And overcome the evil man by goodness. (iii. 13253.)

To injure none by thought or word or deed,
To give to others, and be kind to all
This is the constant duty of the good.
High-minded men delight in doing good,
Without a thought of their own interest;
When they confer a benefit on others,
They reckon not on favours in return. (iii. 16782, 16796)

Bear railing words with patience, never meet
An angry man with anger, nor return
Reviling for reviling, smite not him
Who smites thee; let thy speech and acts be gentle. (v. 1270, 9972)

If thou art wise, seek ease and happiness
In deeds of virtue and of usefulness;
And ever act in such a way by day
That in the night thy sleep may tranquil be;
And so comport thyself when thou art young,
That when thou art grown old, thine age may pass
In calm serenity. So ply thy task
Throughout thy life, that when thy days are ended,
Thou mayst enjoy eternal bliss hereafter. (v. 1248)

Esteem that gain a loss which ends in harm;
Account that loss a gain which brings advantage. (v. 1451)

Do naught to others which if done to thee
Would cause thee pain; this is the sum of duty. (v. 1517)

Source: Excerpts from the *Mahabharata*. Translated by Sir Monier Monier-Williams. In *A Multitude of Counsellors*. Edited by J. N. Larned. Boston: Houghton, Mifflin and Co., 1901, pp. 95–97.

TIMELINE   2000 1900 1800 1700 1600 1500 1400 1300 1200 1100 1000 900 800 700 600 500 400 300 200 100 1 BCE

What You Need to Know

This passage from the Mahabharata includes a series of moral precepts. They all aimed at maintaining dharma, a concept shared by Buddhists and Jains as well, which says that proper behavior not only provided for the saving of the individual worshipper's soul but upholds the cosmic order of things.

The Mahabharata is one of two epic poems—the other is the Ramayana—written in Sanskrit by the Aryan peoples who descended from central Asia and what is now Russia to conquer north India early in the second millennium BCE. This was part of a general migration of preliterate warrior peoples from the north that included the Achaeans, who moved into Greece, and the Hittites, who came to occupy Anatolia and Mesopotamia, around the same time.

A Closer Look

The Mahabharata is the world's longest epic poem. Scholars dispute what ancient texts should be included in it, so its precise length varies between 100,000 and 200,000 *shlokas*, or couplet verses. Scholars are also unsure exactly when it was composed, although it is believed that the first verses were written early in the first millennium BCE while the last date from around the fourth century BCE. Like the Greek epics of Homer, it is believed that the tales in the Mahabharata were orally transmitted for centuries before being written down.

At the core of the Mahabharata is the story of a semimythic struggle among the Aryan peoples after they had occupied India. It is known as the Kurukshetra War, and it pitted two branches of a single family fighting for dynastic rights in an Indo-Aryan kingdom called Kuru.

But the Mahabharata is much more than a war story. It contains within it lessons and guidance on how to live as a good Hindu. The Hindu religion derived from preliterate Aryan beliefs, known as Brahmanism, which emphasized sacrifice as a way to appease the gods and grant the worshipper a good life. Gradually, the late in the first millennium BCE, the Brahmanism came to resemble what we know as Hinduism today, with its focus on believers directly worshipping the gods without priestly intermediaries.

1 100 200 300 400 500 600 700 800 900 1000 1100 1200 1300 1400 1500 1600 1700 1800 1900 2000 CE

1.3.6 The Laws of Manu on Hindu Women

India
ca. 400 BCE–100 CE

By a girl, by a young woman, or even by an aged one, nothing must be done independently, even in her own house.

In childhood a female must be subject to her father, in youth to her husband, when her lord is dead to her sons; a woman must never be independent. . . .

Him to whom her father may give her, or her brother with the father's permission, she shall obey as long as he lives, and when he is dead, she must not insult (his memory). . . .

Though destitute of virtue, or seeking pleasure (elsewhere), or devoid of good qualities (yet) a husband must be constantly worshipped as a god by a faithful wife. . . .

A faithful wife, who desires to dwell (after death) with her husband, must never do anything that might displease him who took her hand, whether he be alive or dead.

Until death let her be patient (of hardships), self-controlled, and chaste, and strive (to fulfil) that most excellent duty which (is prescribed) for wives who have one husband only. . . .

A virtuous wife who after the death of her husband constantly remains chaste, reaches heaven, though she have no son, just like those chaste men.

But a woman who from a desire to have offspring violates her duty towards her (deceased) husband, brings on herself disgrace in this world, and loses her place with her husband (in heaven).

Offspring begotten by another man is here not (considered lawful), nor (does offspring begotten) on another man's wife (belong to the begetter), nor is a second husband anywhere prescribed for virtuous women.

She who cohabits with a man of higher caste, forsaking her own husband who belongs to a lower one, will become contemptible in this world, and is called a remarried woman.

By violating her duty towards her husband, a wife is disgraced in this world, (after death) she enters the womb of a jackal, and is tormented by diseases (the punishment of) her sin.

She who, controlling her thoughts, words, and deeds, never slights her lord, resides (after death) with her husband (in heaven), and is called a virtuous (wife).

In reward of such conduct, a female who controls her thoughts, speech, and actions, gains in this (life) highest renown, and in the next (world) a place near her husband.

Source: Excerpt from *The Laws of Manu*. Translated by Georg Bühler. In *The Sacred Books of the East*. Vol. XXV. Edited by F. Max Müller. Oxford, UK: Clarendon Press, 1886, pp. 195–197.

TIMELINE   2000 1900 1800 1700 1600 1500 1400 1300 1200 1100 1000 900 800 700 600 500 400 300 200 100 1 BCE

What You Need to Know

This selection comes from the *Manusmriti*, known in English as the Law of Manu. A text in the Dharmashastra tradition of Hindu sacred texts, it focuses on the legal and religious duties and obligations of a good Hindu.

Much of what we know about the life of women in ancient India comes from religious texts, known as *vedas*, and from artistic renderings. According to these sources, women were highly prized for their beauty, particularly if that beauty was evinced through signs of health and fertility, such as ample thighs and broad, childbearing hips. They were also expected to adorn and perfume their bodies so as to make themselves more attractive to men.

As in many patriarchal cultures, women were expected to be obedient and subservient to men and, when financial circumstances allowed, to refrain from work outside the home. At the same time, women did have a certain amount of say over who their marriage partner would be, although the ultimate choice was up to their parents. Above all else, a bride was expected to be a virgin and, once married, to be completely chaste.

A Closer Look

Scholars dispute when the codes of the *Manusmriti* were written down, some saying as early as the fifth century BCE while others putting the final transcription as late as 200 CE. According to Hindu tradition, Manu is the first man, the progenitor of humankind, and the laws he laid down are sanctioned by the gods themselves.

As with all legal codes, it is unclear whether the Laws of Manu define the ideal or the actual. Whatever the case, they clearly intend women to be the servants of their men. They must obey their fathers in childhood and their husbands in marriage. Indeed, the law says, it does not matter how terrible the husband is, he "must be constantly worshipped as a god by a faithful wife." There is also no sanctification for divorce. In addition, the women is said to disgrace herself and violate the law should she remarry and have children with another man after her first husband's death.

As a sacred text, the Laws of Manu ties the proper behavior of women to divine purpose. "If a wife obeys her husband," it reads, "she will for that (reason alone) be exalted in heaven." The laws also reinforce the caste system of social stratification, insisting that a women who leaves her husband for a man of a higher caste will be considered a remarried women, that is, a disgraced women in an illegal marital relationship.

1 100 200 300   400   500   600   700   800   900   1000 1100 1200 1300   1400   1500   1600   1700 1800 1900 2000 CE

1.3.7 Mourning for Parents during the Zhou Dynasty

China
350–200 BCE

The Master said, "When a filial son is mourning for a parent, he wails, but not with a prolonged sobbing; in the movements of ceremony he pays no attention to his appearance; his words are without elegance of phrase; he cannot bear to wear fine clothes; when he hears music, he feels no delight; when he eats a delicacy, he is not conscious of its flavor:—such is the nature of grief and sorrow.

"After three days he may partake of food; for thus the people are taught that the living should not be injured on account of the dead, and that emaciation must not be carried to the extinction of life:—such is the rule of the sages. The period of mourning does not go beyond three years, to show the people that it must have an end.

"An inner and outer coffin are made; the grave-clothes also are put on, and the shroud; and (the body) is lifted (into the coffin). The sacrificial vessels, round and square, are (regularly) set forth, and (the sight of them) fills (the mourners) with (fresh) distress. The women beat their breasts, and the men stamp with their feet, wailing and weeping, while they sorrowfully escort the coffin to the grave. They consult the tortoise-shell to determine the grave and the ground about it, and there they lay the body in peace. They prepare the ancestral temple (to receive the tablet of the departed), and there present offerings to the disembodied spirit. In spring and autumn they offer sacrifices, thinking of the deceased as the seasons come round.

"The services of love and reverence to parents when alive, and those of grief and sorrow to them when dead:—these completely discharge the fundamental duty of living men. The righteous claims of life and death are all satisfied, and the filial son's service of his parents is completed."

Source: Misc. (Confucian School). "Filial Piety in Mourning for Parents." Ch. 18 of *The Hsiao King or Classic of Filial Piety*. In *The Sacred Books of China: The Texts of Confucianism. Part I: The Shu King, the Religious Portions of the Shih King, the Hsiao King*. Translated by James Legge. Edited by F. Max Müller. Oxford, UK: Clarendon Press, 1879, pp. 487–488.

TIMELINE   2000 1900 1800 1700 1600 1500 1400 1300 1200 1100 1000 900 800 700 600 500 400 300 200 100 1 BCE

What You Need to Know

The accompanying excerpt is from *Classic of Filial Piety*, a Confucian text by an unknown author, penned sometime between 350 and 200 BCE; it deals with the proper behavior of children upon the death of a parent.

As with all Chinese dynasties, the Zhou dynasty, which lasted from 1050 to 256 BCE, ended in chaos and internecine warfare. The social unrest and insecurity of the period led many to search for ways out of the mess. Indeed, the final centuries of the Zhou saw an unprecedented intellectual flowering, as various philosophers vied to promote their ideas during a period known as the "hundred schools of thought."

Among them, and ultimately the most influential, was an adviser to the court of Lu, a small state in Shandong Province on the Yellow Sea in northeast China. His name was Confucius, and after failing to win over the court at Lu to his ideas, he wandered the countryside, with a number of students in tow, seeking out a ruler who would accept his precepts. On his journeys, he encountered much that upset him about human behavior, and so he sought ways to inspire people to do good. His ideas were then written down by his students in a series of sayings, collected in the *Analects*.

A Closer Look

Confucius, who lived from 551 to 479 BCE, was roughly a contemporary of the philosophers of Greece's Golden Age, although, of course, he knew nothing about them or their ideas. But rather than focusing on metaphysics, as they did, he concentrated on ethics. Much of his thought was on the proper ordering of society, which, he said, was based on each member of that society fulfilling the duties and obligations he or she was supposed to fulfill. Those lower on the social ladder were to show respect for, and obedience to, those above them, while those on top were supposed to treat those beneath them with care and dignity.

The basic and most important unit of society was the family. Thus, nothing mattered more to social order than filial piety, the respect children should show to their parents. The excerpt from *Classic of Filial Piety* goes into detail about how children should act when a parent dies. The text lays out types of behavior appropriate in mourning and even the lengths of time that should occur for the various stages of mourning. But the author also, in very Confucian fashion, appeals for moderation. Wailing is appropriate, he argues, but not for too long. And, although it is proper to limit food intake, "emaciation must not be carried to the point of extinction of life." Indeed, the author is saying that Confucius's appeal to filial piety might prompt some followers to go to dangerous extremes, which would violate the spirit of the great philosopher's thinking.

1 100 200 300 400 500 600 700 800 900 1000 1100 1200 1300 1400 1500 1600 1700 1800 1900 2000 CE

1.3.8 The *Arthashastra* on an Ideal Mauryan Leader

India
321–296 BCE

Hence by overthrowing the aggregate of the six enemies (lust, anger, greed, vanity, haughtiness, and too much joy), he shall restrain the organs of sense; acquire wisdom by keeping company with the aged; see through his spies; establish safety and security by being ever active; maintain his subjects in the observance of their respective duties by exercising authority; keep up his personal discipline by receiving lessons in the sciences; and endear himself to the people by bringing them in contact with wealth and doing good to them. Thus, with his organs of sense under control, he shall keep away from hurting the women and property of others; avoid falsehood, haughtiness, and evil proclivities; and keep away from unrighteous and uneconomical transactions.

Not violating righteousness and economy, he shall enjoy his desires. He shall never be devoid of happiness. He may enjoy in an equal degree the three pursuits of life: charity, wealth, and desire, which are interdependent on each other. Any one of these three, when enjoyed to an excess, hurts not only the other two, but also itself. Kautilya holds that wealth, and wealth alone, is important, inasmuch as charity and desire depend upon wealth for their realization. . . .

If a king is energetic, his subjects will be equally energetic. If he is reckless, they will not only be reckless likewise, but also eat into his works. Besides, a reckless king will easily fall into the hands of his enemies. Hence the king shall ever be wakeful. He shall divide both the day and the night. . . . Of these divisions, during the first one-eighth part of the day, he shall post watchmen and attend to the accounts of receipts and expenditure; during the second part, he shall look to the affairs of both citizens and country people; during the third, he shall not only receive revenue in gold, but also attend to the appointments of superintendents; during the fifth, he shall correspond in writs with the assembly of his ministers, and receive the secret information gathered by his spies; during the sixth, he may engage himself in his favorite amusements or in self-deliberation; during the seventh, he shall superintend elephants, horses, chariots and infantry; and during the eighth part, he shall consider various plans of military operations with his commander-in-chief. At the close of the day he shall observe the evening prayer.

During the first one-eighth part of the night, he shall receive secret emissaries; during the second, he shall attend to bathing and supper and study; during the third, he shall enter the bed chamber amid the sound of trumpets and enjoy sleep during the fourth and fifth parts; having been awakened by the sound of trumpets during the sixth part, he shall recall to his mind the injunctions of sciences as well as the day's duties; during the seventh, he shall sit considering administrative measures and send out spies; and during the eighth division of the night he shall receive benedictions from sacrificial priests, teachers and the high priest, and having seen his physician, chief cook and astrologer, and having saluted both a cow with its calf and a bull by circumambulating around them, he shall get into his court. Or in conformity to his capacity, he may alter the time-table and attend to his duties.

Source: Kautilya. *Arthashastra*. Book I ("Concerning Discipline"), Ch. 7 ("Restraint of the Organs of Sense: The Life of a Saintly King"), Ch. 19 ("The Duties of a King"). Translated by R. Shamasastry. Bangalore: Government Press, 1915, pp. 17, 50–51.

TIMELINE   2000 1900 1800 1700 1600 1500 1400 1300 1200 1100 1000 900 800 700 600 500 400 300 200 100 1 BCE

What You Need to Know

This passage comes from the *Arthashastra*, a kind of economic and political primer for the rulers of the Mauryan Empire, which ruled over parts of India in the fourth and third centuries BCE.

In 326 BCE, the Macedonian conqueror Alexander the Great marched his army over the Khyber Pass into the Indus valley of northwest India, seizing control over much of the region. The impact of the invasion reverberated across the various states of north India. Taking advantage of the momentary chaos was Chandragupta Maurya, who ruled a small state in the Ganges River valley. By the final years of the fourth century BCE, he had come to control most of north India as head of the Mauryan Empire. For the first time, much of the subcontinent of India was under the rule of a single state.

Chandragupta proved as able an administrator as he was a general. Borrowing from the Persians, he divided his realm into provinces, each with its own governor. But he also maintained a tight grip over them. He usually picked his governors from his own extended family and frequently sent agents into the provinces to make sure his will was being carried out. At his capital in Patalliputra, site of the modern day city of Patna, he created a bureaucratized central state, with various departments overseeing taxation and other activities of government.

A Closer Look

To design his system of government, Chandragupta relied on the expertise of his chief minister, a man named Kautilya, who is also sometimes referred to as Chanakya or Vishnu Gupta. According to legend, Kautilya, who was of *Brahmin* birth and educated as a philosopher, was an advisor to the court of one of the kingdoms conquered by Chandragupta and then recruited by him to serve the new Mauryan Empire.

Kautilya is famous for two texts: the *Neetishashtra*, a philosophical treatise, and the political, military, and economic primer, the *Arthashastra*. The *Arthashastra* is part of a tradition of ancient writings, common to both Western and Asian civilizations, that illustrated the essence and doings of an ideal leader. The excerpt here deals with some of these attributes: avoiding moral pitfalls, such as greed, vanity, and lust; being energetic but not reckless; and paying attention to the economy. The treatise even lays out how the ideal ruler should spend his day. In short, the *Arthashastra* is a guide to not just good governance but moral governance.

At the same time, the text hints of the need for more Machiavellian techniques of governance. He mentions the use of spies and, although not cited in this excerpt, he emphasizes the need a ruler has for propaganda to control his subjects. He even advises Chandragupta to surround himself with agents dressed up as gods to lend divine sanction to his regime.

1 100 200 300 400 500 600 700 800 900 1000 1100 1200 1300 1400 1500 1600 1700 1800 1900 2000 CE

1.3.9 Bronze *Dotaku* Ritual Bell

Japan
300 BCE–300 CE

Credit: DEA/L. De Masi/De Agostini/Getty Images

What You Need to Know

The accompanying image is of a Japanese *dotaku* bell from the Yayoi period.

Although Japanese legend and myth emphasizes the uniqueness of Japanese culture and its indigenous origins in the Japanese archipelago, that culture was in fact heavily influenced in its early years by the societies of the mainland, particularly that of nearby Korea. Japanese farmers, for example, are understood to have learned wet-field rice cultivation—the source of the islands' staple food ever since—by learning from the Koreans sometime in the fourth century BCE.

Nevertheless, by the so-called Yayoi period, which lasted from around 300 BCE to 300 CE, Japanese society had developed along its own lines, dominated by aristocratic-warrior clans who controlled small regions around the islands and forced local farmers to pay financial tribute to them. The clans also fought bitterly amongst themselves. Over time, their numbers were gradually reduced as some came to hold sway over larger regions. Ultimately, the Yamato clan, whose ancestral lands were in the plain that bears their name, near the modern-day city of Osaka, came to dominate much of southern Honshu island, which served as the center of Japanese culture for centuries to come.

A Closer Look

Along with wet-field rice cultivation, the Japanese also got most of their domesticated animals from the Asian mainland, via Korea, including horses, cattle, pigs, and poultry. The *dotaku* bells are variants of smaller Korean bells and were tied around the necks of large domesticated animals for adornment and for practical purposes. They could be used to keep track of animals and, by banging on them, to spur the beasts on.

Most were made of bronze and were shaped in sandstone molds. They came in the shape of truncated cones, with loops on top for ropes to be tied through and ranged in size from a few inches to several feet in length, though most, like the one shown here, were about a foot long. Some had clappers inside and others had to be struck to make a sound.

Most of the *dotaku* bells have been dug up from the Yamato Plain region. Some have been unearthed by themselves, others in clusters, sometimes accompanied by bronze weapons and mirrors. Because they have not been found in gravesites, it is believed that they and the animals they adorned may have been communally owned. If they were in graves, archaeologists believe, then that would have signified they belonged to the deceased individual. They are also found primarily on hilltops, which suggests the bells have held a ritualistic significance and may have been an offering by local people to the deities responsible for fertility.

1 100 200 300   400   500   600   700   800   900   1000 1100 1200 1300   1400   1500   1600   1700   1800 1900 2000 CE

1.3.10 Clay Model of a Han Dynasty House

China
200 BCE–200 CE

Credit: DeAgostini/Getty Images

What You Need to Know

This clay model of a house was created sometime during the Han dynasty. Although the location of the house it modeled is unknown, it was probably from an urban area.

Until the modern age, Chinese history followed a familiar pattern. A great king or, later, emperor, would arise to unify warring states and bring order to the Middle Kingdom. The Chinese referred to their civilization as the Middle Kingdom because they believed it was at the center of the world. His descendants would rule over the land for several centuries until either decadence within or forces from without shattered their rule, leading to decades and even centuries of disunity and chaos, until a new great warlord unified the land and established a new dynasty.

Arguably the most important of these transitions from chaos to order occurred in 221 BCE, when the small state of Qin defeated the last of its enemies to found what came to be known as the Han dynasty, named for the family that established it. The Han dynasty established what is known as Legalist policies, by which is meant the replacement of rule by warrior-aristocrats with a central bureaucratic state, the essence of all later Chinese dynasties. The Han also inaugurated one of the greatest flowerings of civilization in the ancient world, bringing peace, prosperity, and unparalleled cultural and artistic output. Indeed, so central is the Han dynasty to subsequent Chinese history that it is used by the majority of Chinese citizens today to distinguish themselves ethnically from the many minority cultures of their country.

A Closer Look

As with China today, the land in the time of the Han dynasty was starkly divided between a prosperous urban civilization and an economically undeveloped and more subjugated countryside. Most farmers barely had enough to eat and lived in simple mud houses, typically under thatched roofs.

With its two windows, arched walls, tiled roof, and sturdy cupola above, which served as a vent for cooking and heating fires within, this house was probably beyond the means of most peasants, though it might have been the residence of a more prosperous, landowning farmer. If so, its mud walls would have been plastered over for a smooth surface and then painted. Urban or rural, most Han homes were built around central courtyards, where animals may have been kept, religious altars maintained, and cooking done in dry weather. Around the courtyard was a slightly elevated walkway that entered onto the various rooms. Oftentimes multiple families—especially more impoverished ones—would live in the same structure.

1 100 200 300 400 500 600 700 800 900 1000 1100 1200 1300 1400 1500 1600 1700 1800 1900 2000 CE

1.3.11 *Tirukural* on Renunciation of Flesh

India
ca. 30 BCE

How can the wont of "kindly grace" to him be known,
Who other creatures' flesh consumes to feed his own?
How can he be possessed of kindness, who to increase his own flesh, eats the flesh of other
    creatures.

No use of wealth have they who guard not their estate;
No use of grace have they with flesh who hunger sate.
As those possess no property who do not take care of it, so those possess no kindness who
    feed on flesh.
Like heart of them that murderous weapons bear, his mind,
Who eats of savoury meat, no joy in good can find.
Like the (murderous) mind of him who carries a weapon (in his hand), the mind of him who
    feasts with pleasure on the body of another (creature), has no regard for goodness.

"What's grace, or lack of grace"? "To kill" is this, that "not to kill";
To eat dead flesh can never worthy end fulfil.
If it be asked what is kindness and what its opposite, the answer would be preservation and
    destruction of life; and therefore it is not right to feed on the flesh (obtained by taking
    away life).

If flesh you eat not, life's abodes unharmed remain;
Who eats, hell swallows him, and renders not again.
Not to eat flesh contributes to the continuance of life; therefore if a man eat flesh, hell will not
    open its mouth (to let him escape out, after he has once fallen in).

"We eat the slain," you say, by us no living creatures die;
Who'd kill and sell, I pray, if none came there the flesh to buy?
If the world does not destroy life for the purpose of eating, then no one would sell flesh for the
    sake of money . . .

Whose souls the vision pure and passionless perceive,
Eat not the bodies men of life bereave.
The wise, who have freed themselves from mental delusion, will not eat the flesh which has
    been severed from an animal.

Than thousand rich oblations, with libations rare,
Better the flesh of slaughtered beings not to share.
Not to kill and eat (the flesh of) an animal, is better than the pouring forth of ghee etc., in a
    thousand sacrifices. . . .

Source: Tiruvalluvar. *Tirukural*. Ch. 26. Kurals 251–260. Translated by George Uglow Pope, W. H. Drew, John Lazarus, and F. W. Ellis. London: W. H. Allen, and Co., 1886, pp. 31–32.

TIMELINE   2000 1900 1800 1700 1600 1500 1400 1300 1200 1100 1000 900 800 700 600 500 400 300 200 100 1 BCE

What You Need to Know

This selection from the *Tirukural* relates to abstaining from the consumption of animal flesh—that is, vegetarianism. It dates to the first century BCE.

In prehistoric times and up through the beginnings of civilization in the Indus valley in the third millennium BCE, the Indian subcontinent was largely inhabited by so-called Dravidian peoples. In the second millennium BCE, the northern half of the region was invaded by the Aryans, a people from central and western Eurasia, who brought with them their Indo-European language, Brahmanist faith—which served as the foundation for Hinduism—and their caste system of social stratification.

But south of the Deccan Plateau of central India, the Dravidian peoples remained separate, keeping their own languages and cultures, though gradually Hinduism and the caste system penetrated there as well. Among these South Indian peoples were the Tamil speakers of the southeast. Even after Hinduism came to dominate the region, they held to their local gods and religious ideas, among which was a strong belief in the sacredness of all nature, which led many to renounce the eating of animal flesh.

A Closer Look

The *Tirukural* is a series of couplets, known as Kural, written in the Tamil language. Its author was a poet named Thiruvalluvar, whom the historical consensus says lived in the first century BCE and probably wrote down the poem around 30 BCE. It is considered an ancient law text by the Tamil people down to the present-day, although what it really is, is a collection of aphorisms.

The poem is influenced by Hindu ideas. Hindu scripture lays out three justifications for vegetarianism. First, it upholds the principle of *ahimsa*, or nonviolence, applying it beyond human society to the animal kingdom. The third verse of the excerpt equates the eating of "savoury meat" to murder. Second, Hindus are expected to offer sacrifices to the deities. By offering them only plant-based foods, the devotee is respecting their purity of spirit, which will be rewarded by a *prasad*, or gift from the gods. The ninth verse of the excerpt says that the gods honor no sacrifice higher than that which contains no meat. Finally, many Hindus believe that the eating of flesh hinders the mind's capacity for spiritual growth. "The wise, who have freed themselves from mental delusion" says the eighth verse, "will not eat the flesh which has been severed from an animal."

Although vegetarianism is practiced today by millions of Hindus across India and the Indian diaspora, the principle is held to with special devotion even today by the Tamils and other peoples of south India.

1   100   200   300   400   500   600   700   800   900   1000   1100   1200   1300   1400   1500   1600   1700   1800   1900   2000 CE

1.3.12 Strabo's Observations on Urban Life in India

India
100 BCE–100 CE

51. Those who have charge of the city are divided into six bodies of five each. The first has the inspection of everything relating to the mechanical arts; the second entertain strangers, assign lodgings, observe their mode of life, by means of attendants whom they attach to them, escort them out of the country on their departure; if they die, take charge of their property, have the care of them when sick, and when they die, bury them. The third class consists of those who inquire at what time and in what manner births and deaths take place, which is done with a view to tar (on these occasions), and in order that the deaths and births of persons both of good and bad character should not be concealed. The fourth division consists of those who are occupied in sales and exchanges; they have the charge of measures, and of the sale of the products in season, by a signal. The same person is not allowed to exchange various kinds of articles, except he pays a double tax. The fifth division presides over works of artisans, and disposes of articles by public notice. The new are sold apart from the old, and there is a fine imposed for mixing them together. The sixth and last comprises those who collect the tenth of the price of the articles sold. Death is the punishment for committing a fraud with regard to the tax. These are the peculiar duties performed by each class, but in their collective capacity they have the charge both of their own peculiar province and of civil affairs, the repairs of public works, prices of articles, of markets, harbours, and temples.

53. All the Indians are frugal in their mode of life, and especially in camp. They do not tolerate useless and undisciplined multitudes, and consequently observe good order. . . .

54. As an exercise of the body they prefer friction in various ways, but particularly by making use of smooth sticks of ebony, which they pass over the surface of the body. Their sepulchres are plain, and the tumuli of earth low. In contrast to their parsimony in other things, they indulge in ornament. They wear dresses worked with gold and precious stones, and flowered (variegated) robes, and are attended by persons following them with umbrellas; for as they highly esteem beauty, everything is attended to, which can improve their looks. They respect alike truth and virtue; therefore they do not assign any privilege to the old, unless they possess superior wisdom. They marry many wives, who are purchased from their parents, and give in exchange for them a yoke of oxen. Some marry wives to possess obedient attendants, others with a view to pleasure and numerous offspring, and the wives prostitute themselves, unless chastity is enforced by compulsion. No one wears a garland when sacrificing, or burning incense, or pouring out a libation. They do not stab, but strangle the victim, that nothing mutilated, but that which is entire, may be offered to the Deity. A person convicted of bearing false testimony suffers a mutilation of his extremities. He who has maimed another not only undergoes in return the loss of the same limb, but his hand also is cut off. If he has caused a workman to lose his hand or his eye, he is put to death. . . .

Source: *The Geography of Strabo*, Vol. 3. Literally Translated, with Notes by H. C. Hamilton and W. Falconer. London: Henry G. Bohn, 1857, pp. 104–106.

What You Need to Know

Strabo was a Greek philosopher, historian, and geographer of the first century BCE and the first century CE, who traveled widely around the ancient world, noting down his observations in his work *Geographica.* In this excerpt, he describes urban life in India.

As in other ancient civilizations, the vast majority of Indians lived in the countryside, working the land. At the same time, India also supported numerous towns and cities, which served as centers of governance, religious observance, learning, artisan manufacturing, and trade. Some of them grew out of existing villages, while others were planned from the ground up. Many of them, particularly of the latter type, enjoyed sophisticated infrastructure. Archaeological digs have revealed street grids, granaries, sewage systems, and large public baths used for both hygiene and ritualistic cleansing.

During periods in which India was politically unified, cities were largely governed by commissioners assigned their duties by a central administration. At other times, they largely functioned as independent city-states, ruling over varying expanses of surrounding countryside.

A Closer Look

Strabo has much to praise about Indian cities. First, he discusses governance, noting that city officials have well-defined portfolios, regulating various types of people and various kinds of activities. Indeed, he notes elaborate bureaucracies that make sure laws are carried out and taxes are paid. All in all, he says, Indians towns and cities are notable for their domestic peace. This, he attributes, not just to good governance but to the nature of Indian society itself, which, he notes positively, is based on simplicity, although he does contradict himself somewhat in his description of their propensity toward elaborate self-adornment. Indians, he points out, practice polygamy, taking some wives for service and others for sex and procreation. Finally, Strabo also discusses Indian legal codes, which he notes are quite strict. Those who bear witness, he observes, have their hands and feet cut off while those who maim another have the same injury visited upon them.

At the heart of Indian urban life—as in life generally in the subcontinent —was the caste system, a highly stratified social order that maintained tight restrictions on what kinds of occupations people could have and whom they could associate with, although in cities the strictures were sometimes looser than in the countryside, as it was more difficult, amid masses of people, to always know to which caste a person belonged.

1 100 200 300 400 500 600 700 800 900 1000 1100 1200 1300 1400 1500 1600 1700 1800 1900 2000 CE

1.3.13 The Instruction of Children in Han China

China
First Century CE

Families generally have both boys and girls. When they are three or four years old, it is important to begin their instruction. This work is truly the mother's.

When old enough to have teachers, the boys and the girls may not study together, but in different rooms, with different teachers. First let them learn politeness; afterward their respective duties in life. Then they may learn to compose both poetry and prose. Their teacher let them obey and reverence, and carefully present to him the usual gifts. When first he is invited to teach, let great politeness be observed, and no confusion occur. When the spring flowers open, and the moon shines at night, let children play in the garden, and let wine be brought to the teacher; ever regard him as one of the family. The women on meeting the teacher may only speak one sentence in salutation, then immediately retire to the inner apartments.

Girls must dwell in the secluded rooms; seldom permit them to go outside. When they are called they must come; when told to go, let them obey. If disobedient in the least, use small switches and punish them. The inner rooms' [girls'] instructions most carefully observe. Sweeping the rooms, burning the incense, and all the duties of women, let the girls thoroughly learn. Teach them the courtesies to guests, that they may know how to present salutations, and to restrain their voices; to carry tea and refreshments to guests, walking steadily and with grace. Let them not be petted and spoiled, causing other people to talk about them. Let them not go to other houses, lest they cease to respect strangers. Let them not sing songs, lest their voices be heard outside, and evil words be spoken of them. Let them not play here, there, and everywhere, lest their deeds become evil.

The present generation's children are very bad; they have learned nothing. Boys know not how to read; they grow up following their own wills, drinking wine, and seeking only amusements, living idle and useless lives, singing songs and dancing, disregarding their family duties, and fearing not their country's laws. Girls, too, are unwilling to learn; they are stubborn and talkative; they know little of women's duties, thus they injure themselves and their superiors. When grown, they find themselves disgraced. Then they are displeased with their parents, and think not to blame themselves; their evil words hurt their parents' ears. Such girls are worse than wild cats!

Source: Ban Zhao. *The Chinese Book of Etiquette and Conduct for Women and Girls, Entitled, Instruction for Chinese Women and Girls*. Translated by S. L. Baldwin. New York: Easton and Mains, 1900.

TIMELINE   2000 1900 1800 1700 1600 1500 1400 1300 1200 1100 1000 900 800 700 600 500 400 300 200 100 1 BCE

What You Need to Know

Ban Zhao, who lived from 45 to 116 CE and is considered China's first great female scholar, was one of those who revered the philosophical idea of Confucius, China's most influential philosopher. Confucius's writings focused on ethnics. In her most famous text, *Lessons for Women*, written sometime in the last decade of the first century CE, she provided specific instructions to women on how to live by Confucian principle. The excerpt here concerns how women should oversee their children's education.

Confucius, the most influential of ancient Chinese philosophers, responded to the chaos of his time—the sixth and fifth century BCE, toward the end of the Zhou dynasty—by setting forth a philosophy of ethics, based on the duties and obligations that all virtuous people should respect and practice. Doing this would ensure a social harmony then missing from Chinese life.

Following the return to strong central rule under the early Han dynasty in the third century BCE, many of Confucius's writings were destroyed by the so-called First Emperor, who believed that scholars were using those writings to question his own dictatorial policies.

But some Confucian texts were saved and experienced a revival under later Han emperors. Confucius was now revered as an almost godlike figure, and his writings became canonical texts, held sacred by the ancestors. Prime among his precepts was the filial duties children owed their parents and elders.

A Closer Look

In Han China, men were the unquestioned heads of their households, to be respected and obeyed by their wives. Still, women had much say over domestic matters, unless their husband overruled them, including the education their children received. The excerpt begins by saying that women might choose their children's teacher but then should get out of the way. It should be noted here that Ban is addressing women of means because only they could afford a private tutor in the home. Although women were supposed to allow the tutor control over their children's education, mothers were expected to provide instructions on behavior and domestic duties to their daughters.

Women of means in Han China were expected to be subservient and self-effacing. To achieve this, Ban advises mothers not to indulge their daughters, lest they become spoiled, and to teach them to be courteous and keep their voices low. A girl's reputation is paramount, and so she must not sing, which would be the sign of a too carefree soul, and must not go out of the home. In the Confucian tradition, Ban warns that failure to properly educate girls—and boys—will lead to lives of dissolution and dishonor.

1 100 200 300 400 500 600 700 800 900 1000 1100 1200 1300 1400 1500 1600 1700 1800 1900 2000 CE

1.3.14 Ban Zhao on Reverencing the Husband

China
First Century CE

When a girl leaves her father's house, her husband thereafter is her nearest relative. In her former state, before she was born, her relations in the present world were fixed. *Her husband is to her as heaven!* How dare she fail to reverence him?

The husband commands, the wife obeys; yet let there be mutual grace and love. Let them be *to each other as guests in politeness*; but whenever the husband speaks, let the wife give careful attention. If her husband does wrong, let her only exhort and persuade him, and not imitate stupid women who call down calamities on bad husbands.

When the husband goes out, the wife should respectfully ask how far he must walk. If by the middle of the night he has not returned home, she may not sleep but must still wait for him, keep the light burning and his food hot until she hears his knock at the door. Do not imitate lazy women who go to bed before it is dark.

If the husband is sick, let the wife, with careful hand, administer all the medicine, exhausting every means to restore him, and failing not to beseech the gods that his life may be prolonged. Imitate not stupid women who at such times know not sorrow.

If the husband is angry, let not the wife be angry in return, but meekly yield to him, and *press down* her angry feelings. Do not imitate bad women who are ready to quarrel with their husbands.

The winter and summer clothing for the husband wash carefully and mend neatly. Let him not be either too cold or too hot, to the injury of his bodily health. His daily food carefully prepare; let not his stomach be empty, nor his mouth thirsty, lest his body become thin and his heart sorrowful!

If your husband is sweet, be you sweet; if sorrowful, be you sorrowful. If he is rich, you are rich; if he is poor, you also are poor. In life you are one; in death let the same grave cover you.

Following these instructions, you will live with your husband in joyous accord, as perfect as that of the sweetest music, and many will sound abroad your fame.

Source: Ban Zhao. *The Chinese Book of Etiquette and Conduct for Women and Girls, Entitled, Instruction for Chinese Women and Girls*. Translated by S. L. Baldwin. New York: Easton and Mains, 1900.

TIMELINE   2000 1900 1800 1700 1600 1500 1400 1300 1200 1100 1000 900 800 700 600 500 400 300 200 100 1 BCE

What You Need to Know

The accompanying excerpt is from *Lessons for Women*, by Ban Zhao, a female scholar of first and second century CE China. It concerns how women should interact with their husbands and the duties of a proper wife.

One of the most significant achievements of the great Han dynasty from the third century BCE to the third century CE was the development of historical writing. And no family was more important to this than the Ban family, which included Ban Zhao (the Chinese always put the family name first), China's first known woman historian and scholar.

Born in Shaanxi Province in north central China to the famous historian Ban Biao, she married young, at age 14, not an unusual age for a girl of her time, and was widowed young. Rather than remarrying, she devoted herself to scholarship at the local royal court. Among her efforts were contributions to her family's history of the Han dynasty but also poems and essays. Among the best known of the latter writings was a Confucian-inspired text titled *Lessons for Women*, finished sometime in the 90s CE.

A Closer Look

Ban Zhao was inspired by the writings of Confucius, the greatest of ancient Chinese philosophers, who lived in the sixth and fifth centuries BCE. Confucius emphasized ethical matters in his teachings, specifically the duties and obligations various members of society owed each other. If people followed his precepts, personal virtue and social harmony would ensue. Prime among the duties and obligations were those between family members, especially of children for their parents but also wives for their husbands.

In Han China, the father had great authority over the family, and brides generally joined their husband's households upon marriage. Ban Zhao combined these traditions with Confucian teachings to develop a list of attributes of virtuous women. These were humility, resignation to the will of men, subservience, self-effacement, obedience, cleanliness, and industry.

The excerpt fleshes out these attributes with careful instructions on behavior and duties. What is most striking is how the women should subsume her own proclivities—her daily activities, her behavior, even her emotions—to those of her husband. "If your husband is sweet," she writes, "be you sweet; if sorrowful, be you sorrowful." Still, Ban Zhao does say that the husband should be loving and graceful to a dutiful wife. "Let them be to each other as guests in politeness," she advises.

1 100 200 300   400   500   600   700   800   900   1000 1100 1200 1300   1400   1500   1600   1700 1800 1900 2000 CE

93

1.3.15 The Indian Caste System in the *Vishnu Purana*

India
Third Century CE

Parasara—Formerly, oh best of Brahmans, when the truth-meditating Brahma was desirous of creating the world, there sprang from his mouth beings especially endowed with the quality of goodness; others from his breast, pervaded by the quality of foulness; others from his thighs, in whom foulness and darkness prevailed; and others from his feet, in whom the quality of darkness predominated. These were, in succession, beings of the several castes, Brahmans, Kshetriyas, Vaisyas, and Sudras, produced from the mouth, the breast, the thighs, and the feet of Brahma. These he created for the performance of sacrifices, the four castes being the fit instruments of their celebration. By sacrifices, oh thou who knowest the truth, the gods are nourished; and by the rain which they bestow, mankind are supported: and thus sacrifices, the source of happiness, are performed by pious men, attached to their duties, attentive to prescribed obligations, and walking in the paths of virtue. Men acquire (by them) heavenly fruition, or final felicity: they go, after death, to whatever sphere they aspire to, as the consequence of their human nature.

The beings who were created by Brahma, of these four castes, were at first endowed with righteousness and perfect faith; they abode wherever they pleased, unchecked by any impediment; their hearts were free from guile; they were pure, made free from soil, by observance of sacred institutes. In their sanctified minds Hari dwelt; and they were filled with perfect wisdom, by which they contemplated the glory of Vishnu. After a while (after the Treta age had continued for some period), that portion of Hari which has been described as one with Kala (time) infused into created beings sin, as yet feeble though formidable, or passion and the like: the impediment of soul's liberation, the seed of iniquity, sprung from darkness and desire. The innate perfectness of human nature was then no more evolved: the eight kinds of perfection, Rasollasa and the rest, were impaired; and these being enfeebled, and sin gaining strength, mortals were afflicted with pain, arising from susceptibility to contrasts, as heat and cold, and the like. They therefore constructed places of refuge, protected by trees, by mountains, or by water; surrounded them by a ditch or a wall, and formed villages and cities; and in them erected appropriate dwellings, as defences against the sun and the cold.

Source: *The Vishnu Purana.* Ch. VI. Translated by Horace Hayman Wilson. London: J. Murray, 1840, pp. 44–45.

What You Need to Know

This passage from the *Vishnu Purana* actually focuses on Brahma, the creator, and, specifically, how he created the caste system.

The puranas are sacred texts that eulogize the various deities of the Hindu pantheon by means of stories in the lives of those gods. Written at various times in the first millennium CE, most are devoted to the Trimurti God, who can be conceptualized as a single divine force of the cosmos in three distinct godly manifestations: Brahma, who embodies creation; Vishnu whose functions include maintenance and preservation of the universe; and Shiva, who is both a force of destruction and transformation.

As its name implies, the *Vishnu Purana* focuses on the second of these manifestations and is considered by many Hindus to be the most important of the puranas. (It is also called *Puranaratna*, or "gem of the puranas.") As with the other puranas, the *Vishnu Purana* is in the form of a narrative, which describes Vishnu's existence from the beginning of the universe to its ultimate destruction.

A Closer Look

As this excerpt illustrates, the caste system was given divine sanction by the vedas, or Sanskrit texts, which not surprisingly were written and maintained by the *Brahmin* caste, which did so well by the system.

The caste system evolved out of earlier Aryan beliefs. As Aryan peoples grouped themselves into ever-larger political units, the kings that ruled over them began to be invested with more authority, which they claimed was divinely sanctioned. This sanctioning came from the *Brahmins*, or priests, who also came to be royal advisors. The *Brahmins* were thus at the top of an Aryan social hierarchy, which also included—in descending order of purity, privilege, and rights—warriors and state officials, ordinary tribes peoples, and conquered peoples. This social structure eventually became highly stratified into the basic castes of the Hindu social system: the *Brahmin* (priests), *Kshatriya* (warriors and officials), *Vaishyas* (merchants, artisans, and landowners), and *Shudra* (peasants and workers). Moreover, the rights and privileges evolved into the notion that members of each caste must not intermingle too much with others. Thus, *Brahmin* would not marry—or even eat with—members of lower castes. When the Aryans conquered the native peoples of north India, they imposed this structure on them, with the Aryans at the top and the conquered peoples at the bottom. Race also came into play, as the Aryans tended to be lighter skinned than the Dravidian natives of India.

1 100 200 300 400 500 600 700 800 900 1000 1100 1200 1300 1400 1500 1600 1700 1800 1900 2000 CE

Part 4:
Ancient Greece

2000 BCE–Second Century BCE

1.4.1 Minoan Boxers Fresco

Akrotiri (Santorini)
Sixteenth Century BCE

Credit: DEA/G. Nimatallah/DeAgostini/Getty Images

What You Need to Know

This fresco comes from the settlement of Akrotiri, on the Greek island of Thera, now known as Santorini, in the Sea of Crete, some 100 miles southeast of Athens. Frescoes are paintings made from water-based pigments on freshly laid plaster. The earliest examples of frescoes, of which this is one, come from Crete and its environs. This one dates from the sixteenth century BCE, shortly before a massive volcanic eruption destroyed the island. At that time, the Mycenaeans and Minoans coexisted peacefully in the region. Roughly a century after the fresco was made, the Mycenaeans would attack Crete and destroy the Minoan civilization.

The fresco depicts two young male boxers engaged in combat. Despite the blemishes, the boxers appear to be naked, other than a cloth belt around the waste and a glove of some sort on their right hands. Boxing was popular among many peoples of the Mediterranean and among Near Eastern civilizations, including the Egyptians, the Babylonians, and the Hittites. The Greeks probably adopted it from one of these civilizations, most likely Egypt, because this was the early civilization with which they had much trade and cultural contact.

A Closer Look

Sports were an integral part of Greek life, dating back to its origins among the proto-Greek civilizations of the Mycenaeans, on the Peloponnesian Peninsula, and the Minoans of the island of Crete, in the early centuries of the second millennium BCE. Greek sports largely consisted of athletic competitions pitting one athlete against another. Hence, there were almost no team sports nor were records, against which athletes could compete, kept.

Most of what we now know about Greek athletics, however, dates from a later time, after the inauguration of the Olympic Games in 776 BCE. Games such as the Olympics, which pitted athletes from the various cities of ancient Greece, were typically part of celebrations to honor the gods. The one at Olympus was held for Zeus, the head of the Greek pantheon of gods. The Olympic Games, and other local games like it, featured footraces, long jump, discus and javelin throw, wrestling, and the pentathlon, which combined all five. Other sports included horse and chariot racing, as well as the *pankration*, a contest combining elements of boxing and wrestling. The Greeks were great aficionados of boxing and believed it was practiced among the gods on Mount Olympus.

1 100 200 300   400   500   600   700   800   900   1000 1100 1200 1300   1400   1500   1600   1700 1800 1900 2000 CE

99

1.4.2 Minoan *Pithoi*

Knossos, Crete
Sixteenth Century BCE

Credit: George Cairns/iStockPhoto.com

What You Need to Know

This large ceramic jar, known by the ancient Greek word *pithoi*, comes from the largest of the Minoan structures, the king's palace complex at Knossos.

From the middle of the eighteenth century BCE, there flourished on the island of Crete a civilization known as the Minoan. The name derives from the mythical king Minos of Crete; it was not used by the Minoans themselves but was applied to the culture by the archaeologists who began uncovering Minoan ruins in the early twentieth century. What the Minoans called themselves is not known because we have yet to decipher their script, known simply as Linear A. What we do know about them comes from their artifacts and the ruins of their architecture.

From that, scholars have discerned that the Minoans had built a prosperous, creative, and peaceful civilization, as evidenced by a lack of fortified castles and an abundance of huge residences, dominated by the king's palace at Knossos. Why this civilization came to an end has been much debated by historians but the general consensus is that it fell to the Mycenaeans of the Greek mainland in the mid-fifteenth century BCE.

A Closer Look

The lack of a readable literary record makes it difficult to know the precise nature of the political order, culture, and economy of the Minoan civilization. From the various palace complexes around the island, it appears that it may have been ruled over by an aristocracy. Evidence, in the form of *pithoi* found in and around the palaces, seems to point to those palaces being centers of economic production as well. The pithoi could hold both dry and wet goods, including wine, oil, grain, and precious metals.

The Minoans were great seafarers and traders, having contacts, largely peaceful, with civilizations across the eastern Mediterranean, including the Mycenaeans of Greece. The pithoi pictured might have been destined for an overseas trading expedition.

The pithoi reveal to archaeologists the growing sophistication of Minoan manufacturing techniques and art. Early on, they were turned by hand but later were manufactured on potter's wheels. Also, in the early period, the decorations largely consisted of simple patterns repeated around their surface, as shown here. Later, they featured naturalistic depictions of flowers, plants, and sea life. Other art forms were even more elaborate. In particular, Minoan frescoes are renowned for their naturalistic depictions of religious scenes, funerals, and the activities of daily life.

1 100 200 300 400 500 600 700 800 900 1000 1100 1200 1300 1400 1500 1600 1700 1800 1900 2000 CE

1.4.3 Late Bronze Age Copper Oxhide Ingot

Crete
ca. 1600–1200 BCE

Credit: DEA/M. Carrier/DeAgostini/Getty Images

What You Need to Know

The accompanying image shows a copper ingot, or block of smelted metal—in this case, in the so-called oxhide shape, common at the time, from the island of Crete. It dates to sometime during the Late Aegean Bronze Age, from the fifteenth to the thirteenth century BCE.

Archaeologists and historians divide the development of human technology into three general periods, based on the elements used in the construction of tools. The first is the Stone Age, dating from the early the early Neolithic period of prehistory around 10,000 BCE. The second is the Bronze Age, dating from roughly 3000 to 1000 BCE. And the third is the Iron (and later, steel) Age, which continues to the present day.

Bronze, an alloy of copper and tin, was far superior to stone, as it was harder, of lighter weight, and did not break when struck hard. On the other hand, copper, the main ingredient of bronze, constituting between 85 and 90 percent of the alloy, is relatively rare, limiting the number of objects that could be manufactured from it. Iron, by comparison, is ubiquitous. Nevertheless, bronze was widely used by early civilizations throughout the eastern Mediterranean for daily objects, ceremonial items, and weapons well into the first millennium BCE.

A Closer Look

Copper is essential for the making of bronze, which is harder and tougher than either the copper or tin that make up the alloy. Also, copper is a relatively rare substance, especially compared to iron, which largely replaced bronze as the metal of choice in the Greek world after the classical age in the fifth century BCE. Moreover, copper was rarely located near tin deposits. This meant that to make bronze the two metals had to be brought to the same smelting site. Thus, the manufacturing of bronze was one of the main spurs to long-distance trade at the dawn of Western Civilization. The only known source of copper for the Greeks during the so-called Bronze Age, beginning around the year 3000 BCE, was on the island of Cyprus in the eastern Mediterranean.

From Cyprus, the ingots were typically shipped to settlements on the Greek mainland, sometimes as tribute (a tax paid in goods) and sometimes as trade goods, where they would have been melted down and turned into any number of items, from weaponry to jewelry to household goods, such as dishware or cooking implements. Whatever the item, they would have been too expensive for an ordinary household's budget.

1 100 200 300 400 500 600 700 800 900 1000 1100 1200 1300 1400 1500 1600 1700 1800 1900 2000 CE

1.4.4 A Scene of the Trojan War from the *Iliad*

Troy (Turkey)
Eighth Century BCE

And the son of Atreus cried aloud and bade the Argives
arm them, and himself amid them did on the flashing bronze.
First he fastened fair greaves about his legs, fitted with ankle
clasps of silver, next, again, he did his breastplate about his
breast. . . . And round his shoulders he cast his sword wherein
shone studs of gold, but the scabbard about it was silver fitted
with golden chains. And he took the richly dight shield of his
valor that covereth all the body of a man, a fair shield, and round
about it were ten circles of bronze and thereon were twenty white
bosses of tin and one in the midst of black Cyanus, . . . and on his
head Agamemnon set a sturdy helm with a fourfold crest and a
plume of horsehair, and terribly the crest nodded from above.
And he grasped two strong spears shod with bronze and keen. . . .

Then each man gave in charge his horses to his charioteer to
hold them in by the fosse, well and orderly, and themselves as
heavy men at arms were hasting about being harnessed in their
gear. . . .

Source: Homer. Excerpts from *Iliad*, Book XI. In *A Source Book of Greek History*. Edited by Fred Fling. Boston: D. C. Heath, 1907, p. 17.

TIMELINE   2000 1900 1800 1700 1600 1500 1400 1300 1200 1100 1000 900 800 700 600 500 400 300 200 100 1 BCE

What You Need to Know

This passage from Homer's *Iliad* describes a scene from the Trojan War.

It is not known exactly what the Trojan War was fought over, who the combatants were, or whether it even occurred at all. Archaeologists have unearthed on the northwest coast of the Anatolian Peninsula what appears to be a walled settlement that may have been destroyed in warfare. If there was a Trojan War then it probably occurred late in the Bronze Age, perhaps in the thirteenth or twelfth centuries BCE, and may have been between the Mycenaeans and the Hittites, a people who had inhabited much of what is now Turkey since about 2000 BCE.

Instead of hard facts about the war what we and, for that matter, the ancient Greeks before us, had is the *Iliad*, an epic poem by a semilegendary poet named Homer. According to him, the war was about vengeance, an expedition to reclaim Helen, the beautiful wife of the Spartan king Menelaos, who had been abducted by a Trojan prince named Paris. After a 10-year siege, marked by numerous battles, the Greeks triumphed through deception, stealing their soldiers into the city inside a giant wooden horse presented to the Trojans as a gift.

A Closer Look

As this excerpt from the *Iliad* reveals, the Greeks were, for their era, well versed in the art of war and had some of the most sophisticated weaponry of their day. Although, as noted, the war may be legendary, the details Homer provides of Greek armament is based on the real weapons of his day.

As Homer states, the armor the son of Atreus, the king of the Mycenaeans, and the Argives, or soldiers of Argos, put on is made of bronze, an alloy formed from copper and tin. The armor consists of a breastplate, which fit around the torso with holes for arms and neck, and greaves, which covered the leg from knee to ankle, a part of the body left exposed by the wooden shield that Greek soldiers, known as hoplites, carried into battle. Befitting a king's son, Atreus's shield appears to be lengthier than that and to be made of bronze, embossed with tin. The helmet, which would also have been made of bronze, is topped with a plume of horsehair, which served as both decoration and an additional layer of protection.

The chariots he describes were actually rarely used in Greek warfare because they were unsuited for the land's mountainous terrain. But as Troy was described as sitting on a flat plain, it may have been employed in any war that occurred there. If so, it was a simple vehicle made of bronze-plated wood with a single axle and drawn by a team of two horses. It typically carried a driver and an archer or a spear carrier.

1 100 200 300   400   500   600   700   800   900   1000 1100 1200 1300   1400   1500   1600   1700 1800 1900 2000 CE

1.4.5 Building a Boat in Homer's *Odyssey*

Ionia, Anatolia
Eighth Century BCE

She gave him a great axe, fitted to his grasp, an axe of bronze, double-edged, and with a goodly handle of olive wood, fastened well. Next she gave him a polished adze, and she led the way to the border of the isle where tall trees grew, alder and poplar, and pine that reacheth unto heaven, seasoned long since and sere, that might lightly float for him. Now after she had shown him where the tall trees grew, Calypso, the fair goddess, departed homeward. And he set to cutting timber, and his work went busily. Twenty trees in all he felled, and then trimmed them with the axe of bronze, and deftly smoothed them, and over them made straight the line. Meanwhile Calypso, the fair goddess, brought him augers, so he bored each piece and joined them together, and then made all fast with trenails and dowels. Wide as is the floor of a broad ship of burden, which some man well skilled in carpentry may trace him out, of such beam did Odysseus fashion his broad raft. And thereat he wrought, and set up the deckings, fitting them to the close-set uprights, and finished them off with long gunwales, and therein he set a mast, and a yard-arm fitted thereto, and moreover he made him a rudder to guide the craft. And he fenced it with wattled osier withes from stem to stem, to be a bulwark against the wave, and piled wood to back them. Meanwhile Calypso, the fair goddess, brought him web of cloth to make him sails; and these too he fashioned skillfully. And he made fast therein braces and halyards and sheets, and at last he pushed the raft with levers down to the fair salt sea.

Source: Homer. Excerpts from *Odyssey*, Book V. In *A Source Book of Greek History*. Edited by Fred Fling. Boston: D. C. Heath, 1907, pp. 11–12.

TIMELINE   2000 1900 1800 1700 1600 1500 1400 1300 1200 1100 1000 900 800 700 600 500 400 300 200 100 1 BCE

What You Need to Know

Unlike their contemporaries in the Levant, the Hebrews, the Greeks did not have a text that told of their history as a manifestation of the divine. Instead, they had tales from their Heroic Age, a legendary era from about 1100 to 800 BCE when gods coexisted with men on Earth. The source of these tales, the Greeks believed, was an epic poet named Homer, but the *Iliad* and the *Odyssey*, the two epic poems attributed to him, were probably the work of many chroniclers. The former tells the story of when the Mycenaeans, the earliest Greeks, besieged and conquered the city of Troy in what is now Turkey. The *Odyssey* relates the trials and tribulations of the architect of the victory over Troy, as he struggles against the whims and animus of capricious gods to find his way back to his home and family in Ithaca.

A Closer Look

It was probably inevitable that the Greeks took to the seas early on. Their homeland was mountainous and the soil relatively infertile, making agriculture difficult. But it was also dotted with numerous inlets that made for natural harbors and was surrounded by seas that led to far more fertile lands and the great civilizations of the East. As early as 1450 BCE, the Mycenaeans had launched a seaborne invasion of the island of Crete, which led to the conquest and destruction of the Minoan civilization. To achieve this naval supremacy, the Greeks became expert shipbuilders. In this passage from Homer's *Odyssey*, the eponymous hero builds a ship after being marooned and imprisoned for many years on the island of Calypso, with a beautiful nymph, or nature spirit, who had fallen in love with Odysseus but then was ordered to free him by Zeus.

The sheer detail offered by the poet as to materials and techniques indicates the depth of shipbuilding knowledge possessed by the Greeks. In the poem, Odysseus is now alone, having long lost his crew, and so the ship he builds is probably much smaller than the vessel in which he initially sailed to Troy, which was probably 100 feet in length, equipped with sails and 50-oar gallery. Trading ships with smaller crews often had fewer oars, relying more on the wind to carry them.

Trade among the Greeks was typically conducted at emporia, independent trading sites, established around the Aegean and Mediterranean Seas. There, all matter of goods were traded, including prepared foods, such as cheese and olive oil, tools, household goods, perfumes and medicines, pottery, and even works of art. But sea trading was not for the fainthearted. Dangers included storms, pirates, and doldrums—periods of no wind that strand a ship at sea and lead to thirst and starvation for the crew.

1 100 200 300 400 500 600 700 800 900 1000 1100 1200 1300 1400 1500 1600 1700 1800 1900 2000 CE

1.4.6 Hesiod's Notes on Farming and Harvesting

Boetia, Greece
ca. 700 BCE

Avoid the month Lenaeon [late January and early February], wretched days, all of them fit to skin an ox, and the frosts which are cruel when Boreas blows over the earth. He blows across horse-breeding Thrace upon the wide sea and stirs it up, while earth and the forest howl. On many a high-leafed oak and thick pine he falls and brings them to the bounteous earth in mountain glens: then all the immense wood roars and the beasts shudder and put their tails between their legs, even those whose hide is covered with fur; for with his bitter blast he blows even through them although they are shaggy-breasted. He goes even through an ox's hide; it does not stop him. Also he blows through the goat's fine hair. But through the fleeces of sheep, because their wool is abundant, the keen wind Boreas pierces not at all; but it makes the old man curved as a wheel. And it does not blow through the tender maiden who stays indoors with her dear mother, unlearned as yet in the works of golden Aphrodite, and who washes her soft body and anoints herself with oil and lies down in an inner room within the house, on a winter's day when the Boneless One [the octopus or cuttlefish] gnaws his foot in his fireless house and wretched home; for the sun shows him no pastures to make for, but goes to and fro over the land and city of dusky men [Egyptians or Ethiopians], and shines more sluggishly upon the whole race of the Hellenes. . . .

When Zeus has finished sixty wintry days after the solstice, then the star Arcturus [February to March] leaves the holy stream of Ocean and first rises brilliant at dusk. After him the shrilly wailing daughter of Pandion, the swallow, appears to men when spring is just beginning. Before she comes, prune the vines, for it is best so.

But when [in mid-May] the House-carrier [the snail] climbs up the plants from the earth to escape the Pleiades, then it is no longer the season for digging vineyards, but to whet your sickles and rouse up your slaves. Avoid shady seats and sleeping until dawn in the harvest season, when the sun scorches the body. Then be busy, and bring home your fruits, getting up early to make your livelihood sure. For dawn takes away a third part of your work, dawn advances a man on his journey and advances him in his work—dawn which appears and sets many men on their road, and puts yokes on many oxen. . . .

Set your slaves to winnow Demeter's holy grain, when strong Orion [in July] first appears, on a smooth threshing-floor in an airy place. Then measure it and store it in jars. And so soon as you have safely stored all your stuff indoors, I bid you put your bondman out of doors and look out for a servant-girl with no children—for a servant with a child to nurse is troublesome. And look after the dog with jagged teeth; do not grudge him his food, or some time the Day-sleeper [a robber] may take your stuff. Bring in fodder and litter so as to have enough for your oxen and mules. After that, let your men rest their poor knees and unyoke your pair of oxen.

Source: Hesiod. Excerpts from *Works and Days*. In *The Homeric Hymns and Homerica*. Translated by Hugh G. Evelyn-White. London and New York: Loeb Classical Library, 1914, pp. 41, 43, 45, 47.

What You Need to Know

The accompanying document is from Hesiod, a Greek poet who is believed to have lived sometime in the late eighth and early seventh century BCE.

Farming was not an easy task for ancient Greeks. Beyond the fact that metal tools were few and far between—a dearth of understanding about basic agricultural understanding, such as fertilization techniques, and near absence of draft animals—their homeland was mountainous, the landscape often rocky, and the soil of low fertility. The few valleys and plains offered little arable land and the climate was arid through much of the year. Greek farms produced little surplus and most farmers produced just enough for themselves and their families to live on with little surplus to support craftsmen, nobles, and other nonagriculturalists. Indeed, in most Greek city-states, the majority of inhabitants farmed, leaving their urban dwellings behind each morning to work their fields or tend their flocks. Barley, which better suited the arid climate and poor quality soil than wheat, was the basic staple food of the Greek diet, although olives, which produced the main cooking oil, and grape vines, for wine, were also widely cultivated.

A Closer Look

Hesiod is remembered for his two great pedagogical poems: *The Theogony* and *Works and Days*. The first is a theological work, offering a kind of history of the gods. The second, excerpted here, is more down to earth. In it, he describes, among other things, daily life in his native Boetia, a region of Greece located west of Athens at the eastern end of the Gulf of Corinth. To the north lie the mountains of central Greece, covered through much of the winter in snow.

In this excerpt, Hesiod describes many of the difficulties of farming in ancient Greece, beginning with cold and wind-swept winters. When spring comes, he advises, one must work very hard indeed to earn the livelihood that will get a person through the rest of the year. Getting up at dawn, he says, is too late, for doing so "takes away a third part of your work." By afternoon, the sun is so intense that it "scorches the body." He also spends much time on everyday matters, describing farming techniques and methods for putting away crops.

But the poem also contains larger meanings. Human beings are destined to hard toil and for little reward. Fortune, as dished out by the gods, weighs heavily on them. Thus, they must live lives that appease the god's sense of righteousness.

1 100 200 300 400 500 600 700 800 900 1000 1100 1200 1300 1400 1500 1600 1700 1800 1900 2000 CE

1.4.7 Solon's Legal Reforms for Athens

Athens, Greece
ca. 594 BCE

Among his other laws there is a very peculiar and surprising one which ordains that he shall be disenfranchised who, in time of factionalism, takes neither side. He wishes, probably, that a man should not be insensible or indifferent to the common weal, arranging his private affairs securely and glorying in the fact that he has no share in the distempers and distresses of his country, but should rather espouse promptly the better and more righteous cause, share its perils, and give it his aid, instead of waiting in safety to see which cause prevails. . . .

In all other marriages [other than those involving wealthy heiresses], he prohibited dowries; the bride was to bring with her three changes of raiment, household stuff of small value, and nothing else. For he did not wish that marriage should be a matter of profit or price, but that man and wife should dwell together for the delights of love and the getting of children.

Praise is given also to that law of Solon which forbids speaking ill of the dead. For it is piety to regard the deceased as sacred, justice to spare the absent, and good policy to rob hatred of its perpetuity. He also forbade speaking ill of the living in temples, courts of law, public offices, and at festivals; the transgressor must pay three drachmas to the person injured, and two more into the public treasury. For never to master one's anger is a mark of intemperance and lack of training; but always to do so is difficult, and for some, impossible. . . .

He was highly esteemed also for his law concerning wills. Before his time, no will could be made, but the entire estate of the deceased must remain in his family. Whereas he, by permitting a man who had no children to give his property to whom he wished, ranked friendship above kinship, and favor above necessity, and made a man's possessions his own property. . . .

He also subjected the public appearances of the women, their mourning and their festivals, to a law which did away with disorder and license. . . . [Another of his laws] relieved the sons who were born out of wedlock from the necessity of supporting their fathers at all. For he that avoids the honorable state of marriage, clearly takes a woman to himself not for the sake of children, but of pleasure; and he has his reward, in that he robs himself of all right to upbraid his sons for neglecting him, since he has made their very existence a reproach to them.

But in general, Solon's laws concerning women seem very absurd. For instance, he permitted an adulterer caught in the act to be killed; but if a man committed rape upon a free woman, he was merely to be fined a hundred drachmas; and if he gained his end by persuasion, twenty drachmas. . . . Still further, no man is allowed to sell a daughter or a sister, unless he finds that she is no longer a virgin.

Source: Plutarch. Excerpts from *Solon*. In *Plutarch's Lives*. Vol. I. Translated by Bernadotte Perrin. London and Cambridge: Loeb Classical Library, 1914, pp. 457, 459, 461, 463, 467.

TIMELINE   2000 1900 1800 1700 1600 1500 1400 1300 1200 1100 1000 900 800 700 600 500 400 300 200 100 1 BCE

What You Need to Know

Following a period of political strife in the early sixth century BCE, Solon, an Athenian politician who attained near dictatorial powers, passed a series of laws to bring social order in the city-state and codify traditional practices. Plutarch, a Greco-Roman historian of the first century CE, discusses the laws concerning marriage and property in this excerpt.

The ancient Greek poleis, or city-states, were governed in a variety of ways. Indeed, the same polis typically experienced various forms of government over the course of its history. Some were ruled as monarchies, literally the rule of one man, who inherited the position. There were also tyrannies, also ruled by a single individual but one who had come to power not as an inheritance but through force or the threat of force. Others poleis were governed by aristocracies, where nobles held sway. Oligarchies also consisted of a rule by a select few who, regardless of their birth, controlled the offices and decision-making power of government. And, finally, of course, a polis might be ruled democratically, that is, by all of the (male) citizens regardless of wealth and birth status but which excluded slaves and foreigners.

A Closer Look

In his laws, Solon distributed power among the various classes of Athenian citizens, although reserving most of it for his fellow aristocrats. To ensure social peace, he passed laws against speaking ill of others and ensuring property rights and set fines for various transgressions (the fines are given in drachma, which were the equivalent of an average worker's daily wage).

Among the laws were those concerning women. Under the law, only the children of free women could become citizens. Typically, the fathers of free women provided them dowries upon marriage. Although the husband had administrative control over the possessions given in the dowry, he was not given legal ownership. And almost always, should the couple divorce, the dowry reverted to the now ex-wife.

Women also had control over the raising of children, and she was given the day-to-day task of running the household and giving the servants instructions. However, given that all but the wealthiest Greeks did not possess vast fortunes, even free women of means did a lot of domestic chores, including spinning, weaving, laundering, and cooking. Such chores, as well as social custom, kept wealthier women inside the home for much of their lives. Although poorer women had to help their husbands in the fields, such work at least allowed them to escape the confines of the home for much of the day.

1.4.8 Education in Solon's Athens

Athens, Greece
ca. Sixth Century BCE

We entrust the early upbringing of children to mothers, nurses and tutors, to train and rear them with liberal teachings. But when at length they become able to understand what it right, when modesty, shame, fear and ambition spring up in them, and when at length their bodies seem well-fitted for hard work as they get more muscular and become more strongly compacted, then we take them in hand and teach them, not only prescribing for them certain disciplines and exercises for the mind, but in certain other ways acclimatizing their bodies to hard work. We have not thought it sufficient for each person to be as he was born, either in mind or in body, but we want education and disciplines for them by which their good traits may be much improved, and their bad traits changed for the better. We take farmers as an example, who shelter and enclose their plants while they are small and young, so that they may not be injured by the breeze. But when the stalk at last begins to thicken, they prune away the excessive growth and expose them to the winds to be shaken and tossed, in that way making them more productive.

We fan into flame their minds with music and arithmetic at first, and we teach them to write and read their letters. As they progress, we recite for them sayings of wise men, deeds of long ago times, and helpful fictions, which we have put into meter to help them remember them better. Hearing of certain feats of arms and famous events, little by little they become envious, and are motivated to imitate them, in order that they, too, may be praised and admired by future generations. Both Hesiod and Homer have composed poetry of that sort for us.

Source: *Lucian*. Vol. IV. Translated by A. M. Harmon. London and New York: Loeb Classical Library, 1925.

TIMELINE   2000 1900 1800 1700 1600 1500 1400 1300 1200 1100 1000 900 800 700 600 500 400 300 200 100 1 BCE

What You Need to Know

In this excerpt, Lucian, a Hellenized Assyrian satirist and rhetorician who wrote in Greek and lived in the second century CE, claims to be speaking in the voice of Solon, a sixth-century BCE Greek famed for the laws he wrote for Athens. Here Lucian describes Solon's views on education in ancient Athens.

Education was important to the ancient Greeks, and there were some commonalities in the approach they took to it among the various city-states. Formal education was generally reserved for male citizens; slaves, girls, and sometimes even foreigners were excluded. Indeed, in some city-states, such proscriptions were written into the law. Typically, Greek children began a formal education around the age of seven in which they were taught the values and wisdom of their particular society. Physical education was also emphasized as Greeks believed that a sound body was as important as a sound mind.

But beyond that, education in ancient Greece varied widely among city-states and between classes of citizens. Education in Sparta, for example, did not focus on the arts, sciences, and letters—which were considered effete pursuits—but on military training, as the city was essentially a garrison state in which foreigners did all of the work under the control of Spartan citizens. While Athens did provided military training for its boys, the emphasis was more on math, letters, philosophy, and the arts.

A Closer Look

Early education in ancient Greece was typically left to the womenfolk—either the mothers or hired nurses. The emphasis at that early age was on inculcating morals and proper behavior. Around the age of seven, formal education began, at least for middling and upper-class boys. Few girls went to school, although in Sparta, they, too, received a limited military education. Boys from poor families seldom had the money for tuition and were needed on the farm or in the workshop.

According to Solon, says Lucian, the ancient Greeks did not necessarily view children in the way moderns do, as innocent or as clean slates ready to be written on. Instead, "we want . . . their good traits . . . improved, and their bad traits changed for the better." Later in the passage, Lucian has Solon listing the elements of a proper education. These include the basics such as reading and writing; although not mentioned, math was also emphasized. But the education should also feature a grounding in history and literature, "helpful fictions, which we have put into meter to help them remember them better." Great deeds of great men are important because, he writes, they inculcate in the young a healthy envy, so that they want to emulate the heroes of the past.

1.4.9 *Ostraka*, or Classical Greek Voting Ballots

Athens, Greece
508–322 BCE

Credit: DEA/G. Nimatallah/DeAgostini/Getty Images

What You Need to Know

The pottery shards shown here were used as a form of ballots in Athens of the classical age from the sixth to fourth centuries BCE.

Ancient Greece is widely considered to be the birthplace of democracy, at least in its Western incarnation. Between roughly 800 and 500 BCE, the different poleis, or city-states of the Greek realm, established varying forms of representative government. In this, Athens led the way, but it was a rough journey from kingship to democracy. In the seventh century BCE, many ordinary Athenians found themselves in debt to rich landowners and threatened with slavery, which led to much civil turmoil. Out of this emerged Solon, a poet and aristocrat who barred debt slavery and gave most Athenian males a role in the affairs of state. Still, tyrants—typically aristocrats who used their wealth to gain power—returned, leading to more turmoil. In 508 BCE, an aristocrat named Cleisthenes won the approval of the Athenian people to establish democratic rule. The word *democracy* means rule by the *deme*, a unit of voters equivalent to a ward or precinct today. Under Cleisthenes's system, the central government included an assembly of all citizens and a council of 500 members. Still, Athenian democracy was different from our own, as it excluded more people—women, slaves, and most immigrants—than it included. And virtually all of the major officials of the polis were aristocrats.

A Closer Look

Unlike our own democracy, Athenians did not vote for the members of the council; instead, every year the council was chosen by lottery because it was believed this would prevent the council from being dominated by aristocrats who could use their wealth to buy votes.

Under the democratic system established by Cleisthenes and approved by the Athenian people, the council prepared the legislation that the assembly of citizens voted on. The actual process of the voting was quite simple. Urns would be set up in the assembly meeting place atop the *acropolis*, the high ground and civic center of the polis, or in the various demes. The urns would be in pairs, one for a yeah vote and one for a nay vote. Voters would then place pebbles into one of the urns, and after the vote was completed, the pebbles would be counted. As these pottery shards, or *ostraka*, used in balloting show, Athenians were not fastidious about what was actually used to mark a vote. Interestingly, the word *ostraka* gives us the word "ostracism." Under Athenian democracy, the assembly could vote to expel particularly troublesome persons—usually, power-hungry aristocrats—from the city, as a way to safeguard the polis from tyranny.

1 100 200 300 400 500 600 700 800 900 1000 1100 1200 1300 1400 1500 1600 1700 1800 1900 2000 CE

1.4.10 Bronze Corinthian Helmet

Greece
ca. Fifth Century BCE

Credit: Christie's Images/Corbis

What You Need to Know

This helmet pictured here was for a Greek soldier in fifth-century Corinth, a major city-state on the Peloponnesian Peninsula. Warfare in ancient Greece had evolved a great deal by the time it was manufactured.

The topography of Greece did much to shape the civilization that inhabited it. Greece consists of a large peninsula descending from the Balkan region of eastern Europe and is divided itself into many smaller peninsulas, as well as numerous islands. The terrain is largely rocky and mountainous. These features made for poor agricultural output, meaning that Greeks had to turn to the sea for their livelihoods and in search of more fertile lands. The mountains also made communication between the various inhabited valleys and plains difficult. Thus, the Greeks, although masters of political innovation, having largely invented the Western tradition of democracy, found it impossible to unite themselves under a single government nor development the administrative tools to effectively rule larger realms or disparate peoples. Instead, Greek civilization was marked by trade, colonization, and warfare—against other peoples but just as often among themselves.

A Closer Look

At the beginning of Greek civilization around the turn of the first millennium BCE, warfare was largely conducted by armed bands under a warrior chief. Gradually war became more institutionalized, as the governments of various city-states set up mechanisms for declaring and launching wars. Various city-states had different kinds of armies, although most moved gradually from voluntary citizen forces to professional armies by the time of the Peloponnesian and Corinthian wars of the fifth and fourth centuries BCE.

The defensive protection evolved as well, from the simple leather coverings of earlier times, as this helmet attests. Made of bronze, it was both lightweight and protective. Originally from Corinth, it was soon adopted by other city-states, including the warlike Spartans, and used through the end of the classical period in the fifth century BCE. Combined with a bronze shield, the helmet was worn by the hoplites, the citizen soldiers of the various city-states, as they warred for survival against the Persians in the early fifth century BCE and among each other in the Peloponnesian wars of the late fifth century.

Although eventually replaced by fuller helmets that protected the neck as well, the Corinthian helmet remained a symbol for many later Greeks of a more heroic age. Indeed, it is more often featured in ancient Greek art, even after it had been superseded on the field of battle, than any other piece of armature.

1   100   200   300   400   500   600   700   800   900   1000   1100   1200   1300   1400   1500   1600   1700   1800   1900   2000 CE

1.4.11 The Essentials of Effective Oratory According to Plato

Athens, Greece
Fifth Century BCE

Since it is the function of speech to lead souls by persuasion, he who is to be a rhetorician must know the various forms of soul. Now, they are so and so many, and of such and such kinds; therefore, people also are of different kinds, and we must classify these. Then, there are various classes of speeches, to one of which every speech belongs. So people of a certain sort are easily persuaded by speeches of a certain sort for a certain reason to actions or beliefs of a certain sort, and people of another sort cannot be so persuaded. The student of rhetoric must, accordingly, acquire a proper knowledge of these classes and then be able to follow them accurately with his senses when he sees them in the practical affairs of life. Otherwise, he can never have any profit from the lectures he may have heard. But when he has learned to tell what sort of person is influenced by what sort of speech, and is able, if he comes upon such a person, to recognize him and to convince himself that this is the man and this now actually before him is the nature spoken of in a certain lecture, to which he now must make a practical application of a certain kind of speech in a certain way to persuade his hearer to a certain action or belief—when he has acquired all this, and has added to it a knowledge of the times for speaking and for keeping silence, and has also distinguished the favorable occasions for brief speech or pitiful speech or intensity and all the classes of speech which he has learned, then, and not till then, will his art be fully and completely finished.

Source: Plato. Excerpt from *Phaedrus*. In *Euthyphro, Apology, Crito, Phaedo, Phaedrus*. Translated by Harold North Fowler. London and New York: Loeb Classical Library, 1914, pp. 553, 555.

TIMELINE   2000 1900 1800 1700 1600 1500 1400 1300 1200 1100 1000 900 800 700 600 500 400 300 200 100 1 BCE

What You Need to Know

This selection from Plato's *Phaedrus*, a series of dialogues between himself and his teacher, offers Socrates's thoughts on oratory.

Like so much else about society and the natural world, the Greeks were fascinated by rhetoric and offered some of humanity's first systematic thinking on the subject. What interested them most was how language could affect action—specifically, the actions of a community. In other words, the development of Greek rhetoric was intimately connected to politics, another area of study they pioneered.

Through much of its early history, the various poleis, or city-states, of Greece were largely ruled either by monarchs or aristocrats, who inherited their power and exercised it as a birthright. But as cities like Athens began to move more in the direction of participatory government after the sixth century BCE, power was no longer inherited and could not be exercised arbitrarily. Leaders had to earn it, and they had to convince others to go along with their decisions. In other words, instead of force, they had to use words to get things done. And the best way to use words to promote action became the much-studied art form of spoken rhetoric or oratory.

A Closer Look

Socrates, the great philosopher of Athens's Classical Age in the fifth century BCE, was a disciple of the Sophists, thinkers who believed it was their intellectual duty to question accepted belief and to use their rational minds to inquire into human behavior and the nature of the universe. To do this, they put great emphasis on logical thinking and precise language to convey meaning. A great teacher, Socrates believed that through continuous questioning, in the form of a dialogue between instructor and student, rational thinking and excellence in behavior could be taught to anyone. Socrates most famous and influential student was Plato.

Oratory, Socrates is quoted as saying, is essentially about persuasion, if not to action at least to accept the ideas of the orator himself. But, says Socrates, this is not a one-size-fits-all activity. Effective rhetoric has to be shaped with the specific listener in mind, for some types of rhetoric will convince some people and other kinds other people. Thus, to being an effective orator, means studying and understanding the nature of men's souls. More, effective oratory relies on an understanding of how humans collectively in the form of society operate. Thus, oratory is about more than choosing the right words; it requires an understanding of the proper times to speak, and when it is appropriate to speak at all.

Every ancient Greek city-state had its agora, or central marketplace. These locations served not only trade but as the site of public gatherings and, in more democratic times, collective decision making. Politicians and those hoping to influence them would use such gatherings to make speeches for or against particular public policies.

1 100 200 300 400 500 600 700 800 900 1000 1100 1200 1300 1400 1500 1600 1700 1800 1900 2000 CE

1.4.12 A Greek Krater Depicting a Potter at Work

Sicily, Italy
Fifth Century BCE

Credit: DeAgostini/Getty Images

TIMELINE   2000 1900 1800 1700 1600 1500 1400 1300 1200 1100 1000 900 800 700 600 500 400 300 200 100 1 BCE

What You Need to Know

Shown here is a krater, or vessel for holding a mixture of wine and water, made in the Greek colony in Sicily in the fifth century BCE. The ancient Greeks preferred to drink their wine in diluted form. The image on the side shows a Greek potter and an apprentice boy working on another vessel while being watched over by Athena, the patron goddess of potters and other artisans.

With its rocky soil, mountainous landscape, and semiarid climate, the Greek Peninsula and islands did not have much in the way of rich agricultural land. As the population of the various regions of Greece began to grow in the early years of the first millennium BCE, many people found themselves increasingly impoverished and landless. But the same geography offered an out. Living on a peninsula and islands riddled with protected coves, the Greeks had long taken to the sea, viewing the waters surrounding their homeland not as a barrier but as a path to other lands. Various Greek polities began establishing colonies on more fertile lands from the Black Sea to Spain. The Greeks spread their culture across southern and eastern Europe, laying the foundations of Western Civilization. One of the earliest places the Greeks settled was the island of Sicily. There, colonizers from the city-state, or polis, of Corinth established the colony of Syracuse in the late eighth century BCE.

A Closer Look

As the image reveals, Greek potters typically worked in small shops, usually attached to their home and employing just a few laborers and apprentices, although there were larger factories worked by slaves. To make the pots, artisans dug up clay then kneaded it into coils, which were then placed on a wheel to be shaped. To create imagery, pigments derived from iron oxide were applied before the object was fired in kilns. While early Greek pottery largely featured abstract decorations, by the Classical Age of the fifth century BCE, most depicted human or godly figures, typically enacting an episode from heroic epics, or, as in this case, scenes from everyday life.

Because modern people encounter Greek pottery in museums, this gives us a false impression about its value to its creators and how and where it was originally used. In other words, as beautiful as Greek pottery appears to us, it was in its time an item for ordinary daily usage. Kraters like this one would be found in an ordinary Greek household or aboard a Greek trading ship.

The ordinariness of Greek pottery becomes evident by the fact that the basic shapes remained the same for centuries on end. That is, they were not subject to fashion—although the designs on them were—but instead served practical purposes, which can be seen in the design elements of this particular example. The handles are thick rather than delicate, necessary because when filled the amphora could weigh a lot. The base is simple and solid, so that the vessel would not tip over when being moved and lose its contents, which could be almost as precious to the owner as the vessel itself.

1 100 200 300   400   500   600   700   800   900   1000 1100 1200 1300   1400   1500   1600   1700 1800 1900 2000 CE

1.4.13 Public Works Programs of Pericles

Athens, Greece
461–429 BCE

In his desire that the unwarlike throng of common laborers should neither have no share at all in the public receipts, nor yet get fees for laziness and idleness, he boldly suggested to the people projects for great constructions, and designs for works which would call many arts into play and involve long periods of time, in order that the stay-at-homes, no whit less than the sailors and sentinels and soldiers, might have a pretext for getting a beneficial share of the public wealth. The materials to be used were stone, bronze, ivory, gold, ebony, and cypress-wood; the arts which should elaborate and work up these materials were those of carpenter, moulder, bronze-smith, stone-cutter, dyer, worker in gold and ivory, painter, embroiderer, embosser, to say nothing of the forwarders and furnishers of the material, such as factors, sailors and pilots by sea, and, by land, wagon-makers, trainers of yoked beasts, and drivers. There were also rope-makers, weavers, leather-workers, road-builders, and miners. And since each particular art, like a general with the army under his separate command, kept its own throng of unskilled and untrained laborers in compact array, to be as an instrument unto player and as body unto soul in subordinate service, it came to pass that for every age, almost, and every capacity the city's great abundance was distributed and scattered abroad by such demands.

So then the works arose, no less towering in their grandeur than inimitable in the grace of their outlines, since the workmen eagerly strove to surpass themselves in the beauty of their handicraft.

Source: Plutarch. Excerpt from *Pericles*. In *Plutarch's Lives*. Vol. III. Translated by Bernadotte Perrin. London: William Heinemann, 1916, pp. 37, 39.

What You Need to Know

This excerpt from the writings of first century CE Greco-Roman historian Plutarch discusses the building campaign of Pericles.

In the early fifth century BCE, the Greek poleis, or city-states, faced an existential threat in the form of an expansive Persian Empire. Indeed, so grave was the threat that it forced the normally fractious Greeks to combine their forces. In 480 BCE, they finally ended the Persian threat at the naval battle of Salamis under the leadership of the Athenians.

Although it was a great victory—one historians say affected the subsequent course of Western civilization—it also had its dark side, for the Athenians came to believe that they were the first among equals in the Greek world. In 478, they solidified their supremacy at sea by forming the Delian League, named after the island of Demos, a religious center for many different Greeks. The Delian League brought great riches to Athens, both in terms of trade and the tribute smaller city-states were forced to pay to her. Such tribute allowed for the great public works projects commissioned by Pericles. In the end, however, this Athenian dominance proved a source of resentment among other city-states, which would fuel internecine Greek fighting later in the century, in a series of conflicts known as the Peloponnesian War.

A Closer Look

With trading wealth and tribute flowing into Athens, its leaders embarked on a great public works campaign, which resulted in some of the great monuments we associate with the city in its so-called Classical Age of the fifth century BCE. The greatest of these builders was Pericles, who ruled Athens from 461 BCE until his death in 429.

Born to an aristocratic family, Pericles began his career as a lawyer and a politician, becoming the leader of those Athenians pushing to end aristocratic rule and establish democracy in the city. He was instrumental in the ostracism, or forced exile, of his main political rival Cimon in 461.

In office, Pericles set out to change the face of Athens, both in terms of its architecture and its socioeconomic system. Like liberal politicians of later age, he decided to put the city-state's idle laborers to work building the city's infrastructure. The result was one of the greatest architectural outputs of the ancient world—indeed, of any civilization at any time in human history.

Pericles focused much of his attention on the Athenian acropolis, a high ground that had once served as a place of refuge in times of war but was now the city's religious and civic center. There, he built the Propylaea, the gateway to the Acropolis, the Erechtheum, a temple to Poseidon, Greek god of the seas that had brought so much wealth to city, and the pinnacle of Greek achievement, the massive and perfectly proportioned Parthenon, a temple to Athena, goddess of wisdom and the city's immortal patroness.

1 100 200 300 400 500 600 700 800 900 1000 1100 1200 1300 1400 1500 1600 1700 1800 1900 2000 CE

1.4.14 A Military Funeral Procession during the Peloponnesian Wars

Athens, Greece
ca. 431–404 BCE

During the same winter, in accordance with an old national custom, the funeral of those who first fell in this war was celebrated by the Athenians at the public charge. The ceremony is as follows: Three days before the celebration they erect a tent in which the bones of the dead are laid out, and every one brings to his own dead any offering which he pleases. At the time of the funeral the bones are placed in chests of cypress wood, which are conveyed on hearses; there is one chest for each tribe. They also carry a single empty litter decked with a pall for all whose bodies are missing, and cannot be recovered after the battle. The procession is accompanied by anyone who chooses, whether citizen or stranger, and the female relatives of the deceased are present at the place of interment, and make lamentation. The public sepulchre is situated in the most beautiful spot outside the walls; there they always bury those who fall in war; only after the battle of Marathon the dead, in recognition of their preeminent valor, were interred on the field. When the remains have been laid in the earth, some man of known ability and high reputation, chosen by the city, delivers a suitable oration over them; after which the people depart. Such is the manner of interment; and the ceremony was repeated from time to time throughout the war.

Source: Thucydides. Excerpt from *The Peloponnesian War*, Book II. In *A Source Book of Greek History*. Edited by Fred Fling. Boston: D. C. Heath, 1907, p. 178.

TIMELINE   2000 1900 1800 1700 1600 1500 1400 1300 1200 1100 1000 900 800 700 600 500 400 300 200 100 1 BCE

What You Need to Know

The accompanying passage comes from the writings of Thucydides, an Athenian general and historian who lived from 460 to 395 BCE. It describes a funeral procession for Athenians who fell in battle in the Peloponnesian War.

In the wake of the Greek victory over the invading Persians in the early fifth century BCE, the Athenians, who had led the triumphant pan-Hellenic force, became increasingly arrogant and exploitative of the Greek city-states that fell under their sway, demanding ever higher levels of tribute and obeisance. By the 430s, Athens's actions had sparked much resentment in city-states such as Corinth, which turned to Sparta, a highly militarized state increasingly fearful of Athenian power, to help them. So began the Peloponnesian War, named after the peninsula where Sparta was located, in 431, after Sparta's ally of Thebes attacked a smaller neighbor, and Athens ally, named Plataea. At the time the war began, the Spartan ambassador told the Athenians, "This will be the beginning of great evil for the Greeks." His words proved prophetic, as the war would last more than a generation, bringing untold suffering and death to virtually every city-state in Greece. Only after the Spartans had laid to siege to Athens, starving it into surrender, did the war finally end in 404 BCE.

A Closer Look

The excerpt opens by mentioning that the procession was conducted at "public charge," meaning it was paid for from the public treasury. There was good reason for this. The soldiers of Athens and most of the other city-states were citizen soldiers, known as hoplites. The term *hoplite* comes the Greek word *hopla*, a type of shield they wielded in battle.

Athens, for one, required all male citizens between 18 and 20 to serve in the military, and subjected those up to age 60 to serve in times of war. Most were from the middle rungs on the social ladder, landed farmers and artisans with their own shops, or their sons, mainly, for only they could afford their own arms.

The use of hoplites as troops had its advantages. Because those fighting in wars were both soldiers and citizens, who had a say in the decision to go to war, this may have reined in the propensity of city-states to fight with one another. And because the soldiers had a strong stake in the survival of their city-state, they were often highly motivated, a factor that contributed to their victory over the huge professional armies of the Persians. But using citizen-soldiers had a major disadvantage as well: they were typically not as well trained as professional soldiers and less willing to undergo hardships in the field.

1 100 200 300 400 500 600 700 800 900 1000 1100 1200 1300 1400 1500 1600 1700 1800 1900 2000 CE

1.4.15 Terracotta Greek Theatrical Mask

Apulia, Italy
ca. 500–200 BCE

Credit: DeAgostini/Getty Images

What You Need to Know

This theater mask from the Greek colony at Apulia, in modern-day Italy, dates from sometime between 500 and 200 BCE.

As with democracy, the art of drama, at least in the West, is widely held to be an invention of the ancient Greeks. Theater itself originated during Greece's so-called Lyric Age in the eighth century BCE, as pageants held to celebrate and honor the gods of the Greek pantheon. Among these was Dionysus, the god of wine and winemaking, and hence ecstatic celebration. At his festival in Athens, men would sing songs of praise, which eventually were transformed into dramatic presentations.

Ancient Greek dramas fell into two categories still familiar today—tragedy and comedy, along with a kind of satirical burlesque known as the satyr play. Tragedy, which derives from the words for "goat-song," because the participants would compete for sacrificial goats, were based on Greek mythology or historical events and were meant to convey what mortal life was about and why the gods did what they did. In a tragedy, the hero is typically brought to misfortune by his own moral weaknesses. Comedy's origins are more obscure but probably originated in simple mimicry of people's behavior and typically made fun of human foibles, but the drama ended happily for the characters.

A Closer Look

In its early incarnation as part of festivals to honor the gods, Greek dramas were simple enactments. Typically, the playwright, the director, and the actor were one and the same. Later, the dramas came to include up to three speaking parts and any number of nonspeaking parts. Because of the limitation on speaking roles, the chorus, consisting of a dozen or more people, became an important part of the drama. By about the fifth century BCE, considered the Golden Age of Greek drama, audiences in the thousands would attend plays in great amphitheaters, typically situated on hillsides to provide better sight lines and acoustics. The large chorus and action of the play would also require a large stage.

Masks were an integral part of Greek drama because they allowed an actor to appear in different roles, which was critical given the small casts. The masks would also reveal much about the character's gender, age, social status, and underlying personality. Typically, such masks, like the one shown here, were made with exaggerated features. In part, this was done to allow even those in the far rows to read what the mask was revealing. But the features were also meant to convey the overall mood the dramatist was trying to get across to the audience—fear and horror in the case of tragedy and absurdity and amusement in the case of comedy.

1 100 200 300 400 500 600 700 800 900 1000 1100 1200 1300 1400 1500 1600 1700 1800 1900 2000 CE

1.4.16 Funerary Stele from the Athenian Necropolis of Kerameikos

Athens, Greece
Fourth Century BCE

Credit: DeAgostini/Getty Images

What You Need to Know

A fourth century BCE carved stele from the Athenian necropolis of Kerameiko is shown here. It was used as a grave marker.

According to the ancient Greeks, the human soul descended to the underworld after death. Ruled over by Hades, a major Greek god and brother of Zeus and Poseidon, and his wife Persephone, the Greek underworld, at least in the archaic period of Greek mythology, was a grim place, where "shades" of all those who have died drifted about aimlessly. By the classical age in the fifth century BCE, it was believed that the soul was judged by three demigods, known as Rhadamanthys, Minos, and Aiakos. Originally mortals, they were given eternal life by Zeus and the right to judge others because of their work in establishing the rule of law on Earth. Once judged, the soul then entered one of the different realms of Hades. Elysium, a kind of paradise, was reserved for the righteous, the heroic, and those blessed by the gods. Tartarus, in the deepest abyss of Hades, was a place of torment reserved for the wicked, the unjust, and the immoral.

A Closer Look

The Greek word for the soul was *psyche*, which was derived from the Greek word for the verb "to blow." Thus, it was believed that breath was the manifestation of the soul. When a person died, the *psyche* left the body as a puff of wind. The body of the deceased was then prepared for burial, usually by the women of the household. It would be washed, anointed with oil, and finally dressed. A funeral procession, typically at dawn, would then take it to a necropolis, literally a city of the dead. A simple gravestone might mark the passage of a poor person, while a wealthy individual was frequently honored by a lavish funeral monument, which could feature marble columns, statues, and stele. The latter was an upright stone or marble slab, with figures carved on it in relief, and typically placed on terraces next to the actual grave, rather than over the sarcophagus that contained the body. As revealed in this fourth century BCE monument, the stele often depicted the deceased in a generalized pose from daily life. Here, the dead woman sits in contemplation as a servant stands by. Such elaborate monuments, unusual in early Greek life, became more common as Greeks grew wealthy through colonization, conquest, and trade from the sixth century BCE onward.

1.4.17 A Description of Spartan Life

Sparta, Greece
ca. 375 BCE

I wish now to explain the systems of education in fashion here and elsewhere. Throughout the rest of Hellas the custom on the part of those who claimed to educate their sons in the best way is as follows: As soon as the children are of an age to understand what is said to them they are immediately placed under the charge of paidagogoi (or tutors), who are also attendants, and sent off to the school of some teacher to be taught "grammar," "music," and the concerns of the palestra. Besides this they are given shoes to wear which tend to make their feet tender, and their bodies are enervated by various changes of clothing. And as for food, the only measure recognized is that which is fixed by appetite.

But when we turn to Lycurgus, instead of leaving it to each member of the state privately to appoint a slave to be his son's tutor, he set over the young Spartans a public guardian, the paidonomos or "pastor," to give him his proper title, with complete authority over them. This guardian was selected from those who filled the highest magistracies. He had authority to hold musters of the boys, and as their overseer, in case of any misbehavior, to chastise severely. The legislator further provided the pastor with a body of youths in the prime of life and bearing whips to inflict punishment when necessary, with this happy result, that in Sparta modesty and obedience ever go hand in hand, nor is there lack of either.

Instead of softening their feet with shoe or sandal, his rule was to make them hardy through going barefoot. This habit, if practised, would, as he believed, enable them to scale heights more easily and clamber down precipices with less danger. In fact, with his feet so trained the young Spartan would leap and spring and run faster unshod than another shod in the ordinary way.

Instead of making them effeminate with a variety of clothes, his rule was to habituate them to a single garment the whole year through, thinking that so they would be better prepared to withstand the variations of heat and cold. Again, as regards food, according to his regulation, the *eiren*, or head of the flock, must see that his messmates gather to the club meal with such moderate food as to avoid that heaviness which is engendered by repletion and yet not to remain altogether unacquainted with the pains of penurious living. His belief was that by such training in boyhood they would be better able when occasion demanded to continue toiling on an empty stomach. They would be all the fitter, if the word of command were given, to remain on the stretch for a long time without extra dieting. The craving for luxuries would be less, the readiness to take any victuals set before them greater, and, in general, the regime would be found more healthy. Under it he thought the lads would increase in stature and shape into finer men, since, as he maintained, a dietary which gave suppleness to the limbs must be more conducive to both ends than one which added thickness to the bodily parts by feeding.

Source: Xenophon. Excerpt from *The Polity of the Lacedaemonians*, Book II. In *A Source Book of Greek History*. Edited by Fred Fling. Boston: D. C. Heath, 1907, pp. 66–67.

TIMELINE   2000 1900 1800 1700 1600 1500 1400 1300 1200 1100 1000 900 800 700 600 500 400 300 200 100 1 BCE

What You Need to Know

This excerpt on Spartan life is from Xenophon, an Athenian historian and writer who lived from 430 to 354 BCE.

Like other Greek poleis, or city-states, Sparta, situated in a region of the southern Peloponnesian Peninsula, known as Laconia, faced a crisis of growth in the eighth and seven centuries BCE. That is, the population had outgrown the capacity of the land to support it. While the Athenians responded by colonizing overseas, the Spartans seized their neighbors' lands by force of arms and turned the people they conquered into helots or slaves. In the middle of the sixth century, the helots rose up in a rebellion that the Spartans only put down with great loss of life—not only that of the helots, but of themselves, too.

Virtually every male Spartan had been required to fight. And so when the battles were over, the commoners demanded a say in the running of the affairs of the state. So insistent were they that they forced the nobility to draw up a more democratic order of government, but one based on martial values.

A Closer Look

Spartans believed that the new order was brought about by a legendary lawgiver named Lycurgus— in fact, as noted, the changes were brought about by popular will—and so they called their reformed government and way of life the "Lycurgan Regimen." Under this regimen, at least theoretically, all citizens were granted equality before the law and could vote on all state matters. In fact, as in Athens, an aristocracy ran the daily affairs of government under the unique Spartan innovation of a dual monarchy.

But Sparta's economy differed much from Athens. Whereas the latter used slaves to supplement the work of citizens, in Sparta, the slaves performed virtually all of the labor, both in the fields and workshops, while the citizens trained militarily to keep Sparta secure from foreign invaders and prevent further helot uprisings. Bringing up the boys to martial life meant rigorous schooling not only in the arts of war but in the shaping of their characters, to accept disciple and disdain luxury. Boys were taken from their families at age 12 and sent to military school. As noted in this excerpt from Xenophon, they had to go barefoot, in whatever season, barely clad against the elements, and frequently hungry—all so that they would make fearless soldiers capable of withstanding great deprivation.

1 100 200 300 400 500 600 700 800 900 1000 1100 1200 1300 1400 1500 1600 1700 1800 1900 2000 CE

1.4.18 Xenophon on Teaching Obedience to Slaves

Athens, Greece
ca. 362–354 BCE

Well, now, Socrates, other creatures learn obedience in two ways—by being punished when they try to disobey, and by being rewarded when they try to serve you. Colts, for example, learn to obey the horsebreaker by getting something they like when they are obedient, and suffering inconvenience when they are disobedient, until they carry out the horsebreaker's intentions. Puppies, again, are much inferior to humans in intelligence and power of expression, and yet they learn to run in circles and turn somersaults and do many other tricks in the same way. For when they obey, they get something they want, and when they are careless, they are punished. And humans can be made more obedient by word of mouth alone, by being shown that it is good for them to obey.

But in dealing with slaves, the training thought suitable for wild animals is also a very effective way of teaching obedience. For you will do much with them by filling their bellies with the food they hanker after. Those of an ambitious disposition are also spurred on by praise, some natures being hungry for praise as others for meat and drink. Now these are precisely the things that I do myself with a view to making humans more obedient. . . . I [also] have other ways of helping them on. For the clothes that I must provide for my work-people and the shoes are not all alike. Some are better than others, some worse, in order that I may reward the better servant with the superior articles, and give the inferior things to the less deserving. For I think it is very disheartening to good servants, Socrates, when they see that they do all the work, and others who are not willing to work hard and run risks when necessary, get the same as they. For my part, then, I don't choose to put the deserving on a level with the worthless, and when I know that my bailiffs have distributed the best things to the most deserving, I commend them. And if I see that flattery or any other futile service wins special favor, I don't overlook it, but reprimand the bailiff, and try to show him, Socrates, that such favoritism is not even in his own interest.

Source: Xenophon. Excerpt from *Oeconomicus*, Book XIII. In *Memorabilia and Oeconomicus*. Translated by E. C. Marchant. Cambridge and London: Loeb Classical Library, 1923, pp. 473, 475.

TIMELINE   2000 1900 1800 1700 1600 1500 1400 1300 1200 1100 1000 900 800 700 600 500 400 300 200 100 1 BCE

What You Need to Know

In this passage from the *Oeconomicus*, one of the first texts ever written on home economics, the fifth- and fourth-century BCE historian discusses in a dialogue with the philosopher Socrates, of whom he was a student, how to teach obedience in slaves.

As with many ancient civilizations, the Greeks practiced slavery. Indeed, Greek attitudes and laws concerning slavery resembled that of other societies around them, such as those of Mesopotamia. Although the slave was the property of the master to do with as he pleased, slaves nevertheless enjoyed some protections under the law. For one, they could not be killed, and they had the right to purchase themselves out of slavery.

Different city-states of ancient Greece practiced different forms of slavery. In Sparta, they did virtually all of the farming and manual labor while citizens trained for military duties, which in part meant keeping the slave force from rebelling. In Athens, most slaves served domestically, doing chores around the homes of wealthier citizens. Still, slavery had a relatively limited place in the Athenian economy. There were no plantation gangs, as there would be in ancient Rome, and free laborers did most of the work on the farms and in the cities.

A Closer Look

Slavery in ancient Athens evolved over time, as the city-state grew in power and wealth. Early on, most slaves were fellow Athenians who had fallen victim to debts they could not pay except by selling themselves. Indeed, the frequency with which this happened led to several major revolts. Indeed, preventing such social discord was an important factor behind the development of Athens's famed experiments in democracy. But as Athens expanded outward, through colonization and then conquest, the slave force became increasingly of foreign origin.

Most slaves were used in agriculture, which was the principal source of wealth of all of the city-states, including far-trading Athens. Slaves either worked individually on a small landowner's farm or in large gangs if on the estate of an aristocrat. A few enterprises, typically mines, might have slave forces in the hundreds and even thousands. Smaller numbers of slaves worked in the crafts, some being quite skilled. Again, most worked singly or as a few together in smaller workshops, although the biggest pottery factories might employ dozens at a time.

As slaves were critical to the Greek economy, obedience was necessary. In this excerpt, Xenophon begins by saying "humans can be made more obedient by word of mouth alone" but slaves require "the training thought suitable for wild animals." But, in fact, he offers much the same advice for both free men and slaves. The latter can be taught obedience by offering them food and praise, just as free men can be appealed to. He also offers them a measure of humanity by noting that, like free men, different slaves have different temperaments. Moreover, he says, they have a sense of fairness; thus, it is important to make sure that all of one's slaves are given the same amount of work.

1 100 200 300 400 500 600 700 800 900 1000 1100 1200 1300 1400 1500 1600 1700 1800 1900 2000 CE

1.4.19 Xenophon on Managing the Household

Athens, Greece
ca. 362–354 BCE

"Now," [said Ischomachus], "after seeing [the perfect ordering and organization of a ship's cargo], I told my wife: 'Considering that sailors aboard a merchant vessel, even though it be a little one, find room for things and keep order, though tossed violently to and fro, and find what they want to get, though terror-stricken, it would be downright carelessness on our part if we, who have large storerooms in our house to keep everything separate and whose house rests on solid ground, fail to find a good and handy place for everything. Would it not be sheer stupidity on our part?

"How good it is to keep one's stock of utensils in order, and how easy to find a suitable place in a house to put each set in, I have already said. And what a beautiful sight is afforded by boots of all sorts and conditions arranged in rows! How beautiful it is to see cloaks of all sorts and conditions kept separate, or blankets, or bronze vessels, or table furniture! Yes, no serious person will smile when I claim that there is beauty in the order even of pots and pans set out in neat array, however much it may move the laughter of a wit. There is nothing, in short, that does not gain in beauty when set out in order. For each set looks like a troop of utensils, and the space between the sets is beautiful to see, when each set is kept clear of it, just as a troop of dancers about the altar is a beautiful spectacle in itself, and even the free space looks beautiful and unencumbered. . . .

"Why, I decided first to show her [the wife] the possibilities of our house. For it contains few elaborate decorations, Socrates. But the rooms are designed simply with the object of providing as convenient receptacles as possible for the things that are to fill them, and thus each room invited just what was suited to it. Thus the storeroom, by the security of its position, called for the most valuable blankets and utensils, the dry-covered rooms for the corn, the cool ones for the wine, the well-lit for those works of art and vessels that need light. I showed her decorated living rooms for the family that are cool in summer and warm in winter. I showed her that the whole house fronts south, so that it was obvious that it is sunny in winter and shady in summer. I showed her the women's quarters too, separated by a bolted door from the men's, so that nothing which ought not to be moved may be taken out. . . .

"When we had divided all the portable property . . . we arranged everything in its proper place. After that, we showed the servants who have to use them where to keep the utensils they require daily, for baking, cooking, spinning, and so forth; handed them over to their care and ordered them to see that they were safe and sound. The things that we use only for festivals or entertainments, or on rare occasions, we handed over to the housekeeper, and after showing her their places and counting and making a written list of all the items, we told her to give them out to the right servants, to remember what she gave to each of them, and when receiving them back, to put everything in the place from which she took it."

Source: *Xenophon: Memorabilia and Oeconomicus*. Translated by E. C. Marchant. Cambridge and London: Loeb Classical Library, 1923.

What You Need to Know

The accompanying selection is from the *Oeconomicus* of Xenophon, a Greek writer and historian, who lived in Athens from 430 to 354 BCE, a period of great wealth in the city's history but also a time of political discord and war.

Most Greeks in ancient times lived in towns and villages. From there, the men, and sometimes the women, too, would head out each morning to till their fields, unless they were household servants, craftsmen, or nobility. The typical Athenian household varied in size, depending on the owner's wealth and status, but they followed a similar pattern—rooms ranging around and opening onto a central courtyard. The courtyard was of singular importance, for it contained the well and the family altar. For a poorer Athenian, there might be just a few rooms, dedicated to dining, sleeping, and for domestic work, such as spinning and weaving. A main room would have a hearth, where the cooking was done. A craftsman might also have a room dedicated to manufacturing, displaying, and selling his wares; this often was the only room that opened onto the street.

A Closer Look

Written in the form of a dialogue between Socrates and one of his students, this primary source is one of the first known texts on the subject of home economics. The focus of this particular part concerns how to keep the household in order. In it, Xenophon chides people for not being able to organize their possessions, noting that sailors are able to do an excellent job of this despite the fact that their ships are both tiny and often wave tossed.

Xenophon's inventory of possessions seems quite extensive—"cloaks of all sorts and conditions . . . blankets . . . bronze vessels . . . table furniture . . . pots and pans . . . a troop of utensils." No doubt, he was describing the home of a relatively prosperous Athenian. By modern standards, however, the possessions of even a well-off Greek were few and modest. There was little furniture in an ancient Greek home and not much in the way of linens, clothing, cookware, and tableware.

At the same time, the home had to serve as a storehouse for food raised by the household during the year, and indeed, many of the rooms in a typical household were devoted to storage, though as Xenophon notes, the ancient Greeks were as likely as modern people to not put things away.

1 100 200 300 400 500 600 700 800 900 1000 1100 1200 1300 1400 1500 1600 1700 1800 1900 2000 CE

1.4.20 Strabo Describes the Wonders of Alexandria

Alexandria, Egypt
ca. 7–23 CE

The advantages of the city's site are various, for, first, the place is washed by two seas, on the north by the Egyptian Sea, as it is called, and on the south by Lake Mareia. . . . This is filled by many canals from the Nile, both from above and on the sides, and through these canals the imports are much larger than those from the sea, so that the harbor on the lake was in fact richer than that on the sea. . . . [T]he salubrity of the air is also worthy of remark. And this likewise results from the fact that the land is washed by water on both sides and because of the timeliness of the Nile's risings; for the other cities that are situated on lakes have heavy and stifling air in the heats of summer, because the lakes then become marshy along their edges because of the evaporation caused by the sun's rays, and, accordingly, when so much filth-laden moisture rises, the air inhaled is noisome, and starts pestilential diseases, whereas at Alexandria, at the beginning of summer, the Nile, being full, fills the lake also, and leaves no marshy matter to corrupt the rising vapors. At that time, also, the winds blow from the north and from a vast sea, so that the Alexandrians pass their time most pleasantly in summer.

. . . The city as a whole is intersected by streets practicable for horse-riding and chariot-driving, and by two that are very broad. . . . And the city contains most beautiful public precincts and also the royal palaces, which constitute one-fourth or even one-third of the whole circuit of the city. For just as each of the kings, from love of splendor, customarily added some adornment to the public monuments, so also he would invest himself with a residence, in addition to those already built, so that now, to quote the words of the poet [Homer], "there is building upon building." All, however, are connected with one another and the harbor, even those that lie outside the harbor. The Museum is also a part of the royal palaces. It has a public walk, an exedra with seats, and a large house, in which is the common mess-hall of the men of learning who share the Museum. . . .

Polybius, who visited the city [second century BCE], is disgusted with the state of things then existing, and he says that three classes inhabited the city: first, the Egyptian or native stock of people, who were quick-tempered and not inclined to civic life; and, secondly, the mercenary class, who were severe and numerous and intractable . . . and third, the tribe of the Alexandrians, who were also not distinctly inclined to civil life, and for the same reasons, but still they were better than those others, for even though they were a mixed people, still they were Greeks by origin and mindful of the customs common to the Greeks. . . .

Such, then, if not worse, was the state of affairs under the later kings also. But the Romans have, to the best of their ability, I might say, set most things right, having organized the city.

Source: Strabo. *The Geography of Strabo*. Vol. VIII. Book XVII. Translated by Horace Leonard Jones. London and New York: Loeb Classical Library, 1932, pp. 31–36, 50–52.

TIMELINE   2000 1900 1800 1700 1600 1500 1400 1300 1200 1100 1000 900 800 700 600 500 400 300 200 100 1 BCE

What You Need to Know

This excerpt is from the writings of Strabo, a Greek philosopher, historian, and geographer, who lived from 63 BCE to 24 CE. It describes the Hellenistic city of Alexandria.

Historians divide the history of ancient Hellas, as Greeks referred to their land, into three distinct eras. The first—the so-called Hellenic period—begins with the arrival of Greek-speaking people in the region around 2000 BCE and ends with the conquest of Greece by Philip of Macedon in 338 BCE. The second—known as the Hellenistic age—begins with that conquest and ends with the Roman take-over in the early to middle years of the second century BCE. And third period is that when Rome ruled the region.

During the first period, Greek influence was spread through much of the Mediterranean by colonization. But these were often self-contained communities with little influence or sway over local peoples. It was during the second period that Greek influence was truly felt far and wide as Philip's son and successor Alexander the Great conquered the great civilizations of the Middle East in just over a decade in the 330s and 320s BCE.

A Closer Look

Among the most important of the Greek ideas that Alexander spread across the known Western world in his conquests was the idea of the self-governing city-state or polis. In 331 BCE, Alexander founded arguably the most famous of these Hellenistic cities where the Nile River met the Mediterranean. The purpose of Alexandria, as the city was called, was to link the rich agricultural lands of the Nile valley with the larger Hellenistic world.

In this excerpt from Strabo, the reader learns just how far-seeing Alexander had been in locating the city of Alexandria where he did. The sheer breadth of the city fulfilled his goal of creating a great trading port, indeed, one of the most important metropolises of the ancient Mediterranean world.

Hellenistic cities like Alexandria differed from the city-states of Greece's Classical Age in that they were less homogenous. Different cultures comingled, each possessing its own customs. Social stratification was also greater. Whereas the city-states of the Classical Age had slaves, Hellenistic cities were typically ruled over, both politically and economically, by an elite who lived according to Greek culture and customs.

Hellenistic cities, such as Alexandria, served as cultural centers, where Greek culture dominated and included theaters and libraries. The temples, where major ceremonies, and festivals were held, were located here. The cities also served as economic hubs, with central marketplaces and neighborhoods devoted to manufacturing.

1 100 200 300 400 500 600 700 800 900 1000 1100 1200 1300 1400 1500 1600 1700 1800 1900 2000 CE

1.4.21 The Importance of Learning Philosophy According to Plutarch

Chaeronea, Greece
ca. 100 CE

§ X. Next our freeborn lad ought to go in for a course of what is called general knowledge, but a smattering of this will be sufficient, a taste as it were (for perfect knowledge of all subjects would be impossible); but he must seriously cultivate philosophy. I borrow an illustration to show my meaning: it is well to sail round many cities, but advantageous to live in the best. It was a witty remark of the philosopher Bion, that, as those suitors who could not seduce Penelope took up with her maids as a *pis aller*, so those who cannot attain philosophy wear themselves out in useless pursuits. Philosophy, therefore, ought to be regarded as the most important branch of study. For as regards the cure of the body, men have found two branches, medicine and exercise: the former of which gives health, and the latter good condition of body; but philosophy is the only cure for the maladies and disorders of the soul. For with her as ruler and guide we can know what is honourable, what is disgraceful; what is just, what unjust; generally speaking, what is to be sought after, what to be avoided; how we ought to behave to the gods, to parents, to elders, to the laws, to foreigners, to rulers, to friends, to women, to children, to slaves: viz., that we ought to worship the gods, honour parents, reverence elders, obey the laws, submit ourselves to rulers, love our friends, be chaste in our relations with women, kind to our children, and not to treat our slaves badly; and, what is of the greatest importance, to be neither over elated in prosperity nor over depressed in adversity, nor to be dissolute in pleasures, nor fierce and brutish in anger. These I regard as the principal blessings that philosophy teaches. For to enjoy prosperity nobly shows a man; and to enjoy it without exciting envy shows a moderate man; and to conquer the passions by reason argues a wise man; and it is not everybody who can keep his temper in control. And those who can unite political ability with philosophy I regard as perfect men, for I take them to attain two of the greatest blessings, serving the state in a public capacity, and living the calm and tranquil life of philosophy. For, as there are three kinds of life, the practical, the contemplative, and the life of enjoyment, and of these three the one devoted to enjoyment is a paltry and animal life, and the practical without philosophy an unlovely and harsh life, and the contemplative without the practical a useless life, so we must endeavour with all our power to combine public life with philosophy as far as circumstances will permit. Such was the life led by Pericles, by Archytas of Tarentum, by Dion of Syracuse, by Epaminondas the Theban, one of whom was a disciple of Plato (viz., Dion). And as to education, I do not know that I need dwell any more on it. But in addition to what I have said, it is useful, if not necessary, not to neglect to procure old books, and to make a collection of them, as is usual in agriculture. For the use of books is an instrument in education, and it is profitable in learning to go to the fountain head.

Source: Plutarch. *Plutarch's Morals*. Translated by Arthur Richard Shilleto. London: George Bell and Sons, 1898, pp. 10–12.

TIMELINE   2000 1900 1800 1700 1600 1500 1400 1300 1200 1100 1000 900 800 700 600 500 400 300 200 100 1 BCE

What You Need to Know

The accompanying text is from the first and second century CE Greco-Roman historian and philosopher Lucius Mestrius Plutarchus, better known as Plutarch. In this excerpt, Plutarch discusses the role of philosophy in Greek life.

As evident in the art and writings of all great civilizations before the Greeks, humans have long wondered about where the universe came from and what was the meaning of humanity's role in it. But this inquiry was anchored in mythology and understood as the doings of divine beings. The great contribution of the Greeks was to examine these questions in rational terms, based on natural evidence, with man (and woman) himself as the focus of study. For that reason, the Greeks are considered the inventors of Western philosophy.

Greek philosophy, at least from the time of the Sophists and Socrates in the late sixth and fifth centuries BCE—the so-called Classical Age of Greek arts and science—was based on experimentation, the stating of a general principle and then the observation of natural phenomenon to provide the facts that upheld the principle. The Classical Age philosophers held that nothing was sacred and that thinking persons should question everything—myth, religion, social norms, and laws.

A Closer Look

Philosophy for the Greeks was not some academic enterprise, with little importance to everyday life. Rather, in coming to understand the universe and humanity's place in it, people could find happiness and fulfillment in life. Indeed, the very act of intellectual philosophical pursuit ennobled those who engaged in it. As this excerpt from Plutarch notes, philosophy is the highest form of self-understanding. That is, he writes in his work *Moralia*, or *Morals*, whereas medicine and physical education serve the body, "philosophy is the only cure for the maladies and disorders of the soul." He says that philosophy teaches people how to live a proper life and be a good citizen. It teaches them how to live with each other, how to honor the divine, and how to respond to good fortune and misfortune. It advises moderation—the source of individual happiness—in all things.

In the tradition of Socrates, Plutarch also emphasizes the need to think philosophically, an ability that can and must be taught. For, as he says, there are three kinds of life—the practical, the sensual, and the contemplative. Only with the latter can a person reach his or her highest potential and achieve the truest satisfaction in life as a sentient being.

1 100 200 300 400 500 600 700 800 900 1000 1100 1200 1300 1400 1500 1600 1700 1800 1900 2000 CE

1.4.22 Plutarch's Views on Physical Education

Chaeronea, Greece
ca. 100 CE

§ XI. Exercise also ought not to be neglected, but we ought to send our boys to the master of the gymnasium to train them duly, partly with a view to carrying the body well, partly with a view to strength. For good habit of body in boys is the foundation of a good old age. For as in fine weather we ought to lay up for winter, so in youth one ought to form good habits and live soberly so as to have a reserve stock of strength for old age. Yet ought we to husband the exertions of the body, so as not to be wearied out by them and rendered unfit for study. For, as Plato says, excessive sleep and fatigue are enemies to learning. But why dwell on this? For I am in a hurry to pass to the most important point. Our lads must be trained for warlike encounters, making themselves efficient in hurling the javelin and darts, and in the chase. For the possessions of those who are defeated in battle belong to the conquerors as booty of war; and war is not the place for delicately brought up bodies: it is the spare warrior that makes the best combatant, who as an athlete cuts his way through the ranks of the enemies. Supposing anyone objects: "How so? As you undertook to give advice on the education of freeborn children, do you now neglect the poor and plebeian ones, and give instructions only suitable to the rich?" It is easy enough to meet such critics. I should prefer to make my teaching general and suitable to all; but if any, through their poverty, shall be unable to follow up my precepts, let them blame fortune, and not the author of these hints. We must try with all our might to procure the best education for the poor as well as the rich, but if that is impossible, then we must put up with the practicable. I inserted those matters into my discourse here, that I might hereafter confine myself to all that appertains to the right education of the young.

Source: Plutarch. *Plutarch's Morals*. Translated by Arthur Richard Shilleto. London: George Bell and Sons, 1898, p. 12.

TIMELINE   2000 1900 1800 1700 1600 1500 1400 1300 1200 1100 1000 900 800 700 600 500 400 300 200 100 1 BCE

What You Need to Know

The writings of the Greco-Roman historian Plutarch of the first and second century CE are excerpted here. In this selection, he emphasizes the importance of physical education in his work *Moralia*, or *Morals*.

Arguably no civilization in history has valued physical fitness more than that of the ancient Greeks. Perhaps, it was because they placed humans at the center of the universe, that humans should be the chief focus of their philosophy. The Greek gods were not utterly unworldly, like the God of the Hebrews, nor anthropomorphized beings, like those of ancient Egypt. Instead, they looked like men and women, in idealized form.

Greek art reflects this emphasis on the human force. Indeed, it was the Greek artists and sculptors of the Classical Age of the fifth century BCE, who first offered a realistic portrait of human anatomy in their freestanding statuary, frieze work, and in the paintings on their pottery. And the body—often depicted in motion—was the focus of the work. The faces on Greek art were largely expressionless, revealing very little of the life of the mind.

A Closer Look

Given the importance the Greeks placed on the body and physical fitness, it is not surprising that they placed emphasis on physical education for the young. Even the great philosophers of Greece, who emphasized that an inquiring mind and a contemplative life were the main sources of happiness, believed that the development of the body was as important as the development of the mind. Indeed, mental health was dependent on physical health. The great doctors in the Greek tradition—Herodicus, Hippocrates, and Galen—all made physical fitness an important part of the medical teaching and writing.

Although alive long after the Classical Age, Plutarch emphasizes three very practical reasons for the importance of a physical education. First, citing the great Classical Age philosopher Plato, he writes, "excessive sleep and fatigue are enemies to learning." Next, he argues, developing good physical habits in the young will provide the foundation for good health into old age. Finally, the teaching of physical fitness and athletics is essential for the makings of a good soldier.

Indeed, so important is physical education that society should do everything in its power to make sure that all boys—regardless of birth and wealth—be provided the best physical (and mental) education possible. Two institutions, the palaestra, or wrestling school, and gymnasium were key parts of Greek schools. The former was reserved for young boys and the latter for teenagers. Gymnasia, for one, focused on physical exercise and training, often in connection with the various games that were celebrated across Greece. But they were also places where scholars came to lecture on philosophy, the natural sciences, politics, the arts, and other subjects. And many were located near public libraries, giving students and instructors access to the accumulated wisdom of Greek civilization.

1.4.23 How to Choose a Teacher in Ancient Greece

Chaeronea, Greece
ca. 100 CE

§ VII. Next, when our boys are old enough to be put into the hands of tutors, great care must be taken that we do not hand them over to slaves, or foreigners, or flighty persons. For what happens nowadays in many cases is highly ridiculous: good slaves are made farmers, or sailors, or merchants, or stewards, or money-lenders; but if they find a winebibbing, greedy, and utterly useless slave, to him parents commit the charge of their sons, whereas the good tutor ought to be such a one as was Phœnix, the tutor of Achilles. The point also which I am now going to speak about is of the utmost importance. The schoolmasters we ought to select for our boys should be of blameless life, of pure character, and of great experience. For a good training is the source and root of gentlemanly behaviour. . . . How one must despise, therefore, some fathers, who, whether from ignorance or inexperience, before putting the intended teachers to the test, commit their sons to the charge of untried and untested men. If they act so through inexperience it is not so ridiculous; but it is to the remotest degree absurd when, though perfectly aware of both the inexperience and worthlessness of some schoolmasters, they yet entrust their sons to them; some overcome by flattery, others to gratify friends who solicit their favours; acting just as if anybody ill in body, passing over the experienced physician, should, to gratify his friend, call him in, and so throw away his life; or as if to gratify one's friend one should reject the best pilot and choose him instead. Zeus and all the gods! can anyone bearing the sacred name of father put obliging a petitioner before obtaining the best education for his sons? Were they not then wise words that the time-honoured Socrates used to utter, and say that he would proclaim, if he could, climbing up to the highest part of the city, "Men, what can you be thinking of, who move heaven and earth to make money, while you bestow next to no attention on the sons you are going to leave that money to?" I would add to this that such fathers act very similarly to a person who should be very careful about his shoe but care nothing about his foot. Many persons also are so niggardly about their children, and indifferent to their interests, that for the sake of a paltry saving, they prefer worthless teachers for their children, practising a vile economy at the expense of their children's ignorance. *Apropos* of this, Aristippus on one occasion rebuked an empty-headed parent neatly and wittily. For being asked how much money a parent ought to pay for his son's education, he answered, "A thousand drachmæ." And he replying, "Hercules, what a price! I could buy a slave for as much;" Aristippus answered, "You shall have two slaves then, your son and the slave you buy." And is it not altogether strange that you accustom your son to take his food in his right hand, and chide him if he offers his left, whereas you care very little about his hearing good and sound discourses? I will tell you what happens to such admirable fathers, when they have educated and brought up their sons so badly: when the sons grow to man's estate, they disregard a sober and well-ordered life, and rush headlong into disorderly and low vices; then at the last the parents are sorry they have neglected their education, bemoaning bitterly when it is too late their sons' debasement.

Source: Plutarch. *Plutarch's Morals.* Translated by Arthur Richard Shilleto. London: George Bell and Sons, 1898, pp. 5–7.

TIMELINE 2000 1900 1800 1700 1600 1500 1400 1300 1200 1100 1000 900 800 700 600 500 400 300 200 100 1 BCE

What You Need to Know

This excerpt from the writings of Plutarch, a Greco-Roman historian of the first and second century CE, gives advice on how to select a tutor.

As in many cultures, education in ancient Greece came in two forms: informal and formal. The former was provided in the home, by the parents, other relatives, the servants, and dealt with matters such as proper behavior, basic tasks, and elementary reasoning. Once a boy reached the age of about six or seven, the formal phase of education would begin, presuming the family had the resources to pay for it and the ability to spare their sons from the farm or workshop. (Girls almost never received a formal education.)

Formal education took one of two forms: school or private tutoring, the latter typically reserved for the sons of the most important and wealthiest families. In either form, Greek education took a holistic approach. It was meant to exercise and expand the imagination through the teaching of the arts, most especially music; the mind via philosophy, math, letters, oratory and the natural sciences; and the body through physical education and military training.

A Closer Look

The ancient Greeks have a well-deserved reputation for their intellectual achievements and their glorification of the life of the mind. To achieve this, of course, required education. But, as this excerpt from the writings of Plutarch reveals, the Greeks, at least of his own age, often took the education of their young lightly. First, as was the wont of many ancient Greeks, he compared his own time unfavorably to that of the Heroic Age of the misty past, noting how the great Trojan War hero Achilles had the best of tutors in Phoenix.

By comparison, says Plutarch, his contemporaries often chose slaves of the very lowest character—"winebibbing, greedy, and utterly useless"—to serve as tutors for their children. Fathers who send out their sons to school seem almost heedless in their choice of schoolmasters. Or if not exactly heedless, many refused to spend the money needed for a first-class education for their sons. It was an exceedingly shortsighted father, he argues, who practices "a vile economy at the expense of their children's ignorance." The consequences of this could be dire, as Plutarch relates by recreating a conversation between Aristippus and a father interested in having the famed philosopher teach his boy. When the father declares he could buy a good slave for the fee Aristippus wants to charge, the latter responds, then "[y]ou shall have two slaves then, your son and the slave you buy."

1 100 200 300 400 500 600 700 800 900 1000 1100 1200 1300 1400 1500 1600 1700 1800 1900 2000 CE

1.4.24 Greek Views on the Benefits of Nursing

Chaeronea, Greece
ca. 100 CE

§ V. The next point to discuss will be nutrition. In my opinion mothers ought to nurse and suckle their own children. For they will bring them up with more sympathy and care, if they love them so intimately and, as the proverb puts it, "from their first growing their nails." Whereas the affection of wet or dry nurses is spurious and counterfeit, being merely for pay. And nature itself teaches that mothers ought themselves to suckle and rear those they have given birth to. And for that purpose she has supplied every female parent with milk. And providence has wisely provided women with two breasts, so that if they should bear twins, they would have a breast for each. And besides this, as is natural enough, they would feel more affection and love for their children by suckling them. For this supplying them with food is as it were a tightener of love, for even the brute creation, if taken away from their young, pine away, as we constantly see. Mothers must therefore, as I said, certainly try to suckle their own children: but if they are unable to do so either through physical weakness (for this contingency sometimes occurs), or in haste to have other children, they must select wet and dry nurses with the greatest care, and not introduce into their houses any kind of women. First and foremost they must be Greeks in their habits. For just as it is necessary immediately after birth to shapen the limbs of children, so that they may grow straight and not crooked, so from the beginning must their habits be carefully attended to. For infancy is supple and easily moulded, and what children learn sinks deeply into their souls while they are young and tender, whereas everything hard is softened only with great difficulty. For just as seals are impressed on soft wax, so instruction leaves its permanent mark on the minds of those still young. And divine Plato seems to me to give excellent advice to nurses not to tell their children any kind of fables, that their souls may not in the very dawn of existence be full of folly or corruption. Phocylides the poet also seems to give admirable advice when he says, "We must teach good habits while the pupil is still a boy."

§ VI. Attention also must he given to this point, that the lads that are to wait upon and be with young people must be first and foremost of good morals, and able to speak Greek distinctly and idiomatically, that they may not by contact with foreigners of loose morals contract any of their viciousness. For as those who are fond of quoting proverbs say not amiss, "If you live with a lame man, you will learn to halt."

Source: Plutarch. *Plutarch's Morals*. Translated by Arthur Richard Shilleto. London: George Bell and Sons, 1898, pp. 4–5.

What You Need to Know

In this text, the first and second century CE Greco-Roman historian and writer Plutarch explains why he thinks mothers should nurse their children.

Due to a lack of sources, we know little about ancient Greek attitudes toward, and customs relating, to the care of infants and toddlers. What we do know is that infant mortality rates were quite high, with as many as one of two children dying before their fifth birthday, so Greek parents typically bore many children.

With no maternity hospitals or clinics, children were born at home, exclusively in the presence of women, as men were excluded from the process, and female midwives, rather than male doctors, were the professionals brought in to oversee the birth. The Greeks practiced infanticide, and it was the male head of household who decided the infant's fate. Whether for reasons of gender, deformity, or a lack of financial wherewithal, a father could choose to get rid of a newborn. This was done not by an overt act of violence but, to modern sensibilities, the equally inhumane practice of leaving the infant to die by exposure.

A Closer Look

Both the ancient Greeks and Romans believed that infants not only imbibed nutrition from a mother's breast milk but also features of the mother's soul—her character and intellectual capacity, for two things. Yet despite such beliefs, feeding by a wet nurse was a frequent custom, especially in wealthier households. Sometimes the nurse was merely a servant or slave of the household, who had recently had a child of her own, or it was professional wet nurse.

In this excerpt from his *Moralia*, or *Morals*, Plutarch offers up his own reasons why women, regardless of birth, should suckle their own young. The two most important were developing a strong bond between mother and child and passing on the traits of the mother through the milk to the child.

In fact, raising young children was largely the prerogative of women in ancient Greece. Boys received virtually all of their instruction from their mother until age seven or eight, when they went off to learn a craft from fathers or more scholarly instruction from professional tutors. Because girls did not attend academies or received scholarly instruction, they remained in the company of their mothers until puberty, when they were deemed old enough for marriage.

1 100 200 300 400 500 600 700 800 900 1000 1100 1200 1300 1400 1500 1600 1700 1800 1900 2000 CE

1.4.25 The Requisite Physical Attributes for Greek Athletes

Athens, Greece
Third Century CE

The contestant in the pentathlon [the five events were javelin and discus throwing, long jumping, wrestling, and racing] should be heavy rather than light, slender, of good build, tall, not excessively muscular, but not light, either. He should have long legs, rather than in proportion to his body, and hips that are flexible and limber, on account of bending backward in throwing the javelin, and the discus, as well as on account of the jump. He will jump with less jolting, and will break nothing in his body, if he gains a firm footing, letting his hips down gradually. His hands should be long and his fingers also, for he will throw the discus far better if the discus rim is sped upwards from the hollow of his hand because of the length of his fingers. And he will throw the javelin with less trouble if his fingers do not barely reach the strap, as will be the case if they are short.

The best candidate for the long distance race should have a powerful neck and shoulders just as for the pentathlon, but he should have light, slender legs just like the runners in the stade [220 yards] race. The latter, with the help of their hands, stir their legs into the quick run as if their hands were wings. The runners in the long distance race do this near the goal but the rest of the time they move almost as if they were walking, holding up their hands in front of them, with the result that they need stronger shoulders. . . .

Let us proceed to those aspiring to wrestle. The regulation wrestler should be tall rather than in proportion, but built like those in proportion, with neither a long neck, nor yet one set down on the shoulders. The latter type of neck is not ill-adapted but looks rather deformed than athletic, and to anyone who is familiar with the two kinds of statues of Hercules, ever so much more pleasing and godlike are the high-born types and those without short necks. The neck should stand straight as in a handsome horse that is conscious of its own worth, and the throat should extend down to each collar bone. The shoulder blades should be drawn together, and the tips of the shoulders erect, thus lending to the wrestler size, nobility of aspect, force, and superiority in wrestling. A well-marked arm [i.e., with broad veins] is an advantage in wrestling. . . . It is better to have a chest which is prominent and curved outward, for the organs rest in it as though in a firm, well-shaped room. . . . In my opinion, persons with hollow, sunken chests should neither strip nor engage in exercises, for they suffer from stomach trouble, and they have unsound organs, and are short-winded.

Source: *Philostratus Gymnastics*. Translated by Rachel Sargent Robinson. In *Sources for the History of Greek Athletics*. Urbana: University of Illinois Press, 1927.

TIMELINE   2000 1900 1800 1700 1600 1500 1400 1300 1200 1100 1000 900 800 700 600 500 400 300 200 100 1 BCE

What You Need to Know

This passage comes from the writing of someone named Philostratus in the third century CE. (There were several ancient Greek authors of that name and at that time, and historians cannot determine which of them penned this piece.) In it, he describes the physical attributes best suited for each sport.

The ancient Greeks of Hellas, as they called their homeland, were a fractionalized lot, living in tiny city-states isolated from one another by a mountainous landscape. Their religious customs reflected these divisions, with each city-state, or polis, experiencing the divine in their own way. But from time to time, the Greeks would come together in religious festivals to celebrate and pay obeisance to their pan-Hellenic gods.

The most important of these was the festival in honor of Zeus, the king of the gods, held at Olympia, near the isolated western edge of the Peloponnesian Peninsula. Held every four years, the festival is now best known for the athletic contests held there. The games attracted Greeks from far and wide, even from the colonies in the western Mediterranean and, after Alexander the Great's conquests, the Levant and Egypt as well. So popular were the games that they lasted centuries after the Roman conquest of Greece in the early second century BCE. Indeed, it was only with the rise of Christianity that this pagan festival came to an end in the late fourth century CE, not to be revived again, stripped of its religious component, until modern times in 1896.

A Closer Look

The sheer detail of the descriptions Philostratus offers reveals the importance with which the Greeks held the games. Indeed, it reminds the modern reader of the all-too-familiar obsessions of contemporary sports fans.

While the ancient games at Olympia were part of a religious festival, the competitions were, like today's games, more about celebrating the physical achievements of which mortal men were capable. Then, as now, athletic competition was seen in heroic terms, as a less sanguine alternative of war. But the ancient games were also intimately tied to martial life. The training the athletes underwent was not only similar to what soldiers of the day experienced but were also preparation for the rigor and skills—think of the javelin throw—needed in ancient combat. The winners in the competitions were given awards at ceremonies, where a palm branch was placed in their outstretched hands as thousands of fans watched and cheered. They would also return to much acclaim in their home polis and be granted various privileges and gifts.

1   100   200   300   400   500   600   700   800   900   1000   1100   1200   1300   1400   1500   1600   1700   1800   1900   2000 CE

Part 5:
Ancient Rome

Second Century BCE–460 CE

1.5.1 A Roman Senator on Living With, and Without, Matrimony

Rome
Second Century BCE

A number of learned men were listening to the reading of the speech which Metellus Numidicus, an earnest and eloquent man, delivered to the people when he was censor, *On Marriage*, urging them to be ready to undertake its obligations. In that speech these words were written: "If we could get on without a wife, Romans, we would all avoid that annoyance; but since nature has ordained that we can neither live very comfortably with them nor at all without them, we must take thought for our lasting well-being rather than for the pleasure of the moment."

It seemed to some of the company that Quintus Metellus . . . ought not to have admitted the annoyance and constant inconveniences of the married state; that to do this was not so much to encourage, as to dissuade and deter [people from marrying]. But they said that his speech ought rather to have taken just the opposite tone, insisting that as a rule there were no annoyances in matrimony, and if after all they seemed sometimes to arise, they were slight, insignificant and easily endured, and were completely forgotten in its greater pleasures and advantages; furthermore, that even these annoyances did not fall to the lot of all or from any fault natural to matrimony, but as the result of the misconduct and injustice of some husbands and wives.

Source: *The Attic Nights of Aulus Gellius.* Translated by John C. Rolfe. Cambridge, MA: Harvard University Press; London, William Heinemann, Ltd. 1927.

TIMELINE   2000 1900 1800 1700 1600 1500 1400 1300 1200 1100 1000 900 800 700 600 500 400 300 200 100 1 BCE

What You Need to Know

This passage is from the speech *On Marriage* by the Roman senator Quintus Caecilius Metellus Numidicus. It was written down by Roman author Autius Gellius *Attic Nights*, an almanac published more than two centuries after Metellus's death. Metellus argues on behalf of matrimony but after the manner of damning with faint praise. Speaking from an obviously male point of view, he assumes that Roman men "would all avoid" the "annoyance" of matrimony if they could get on without their wives. But he says, wives are a necessity for our "lasting well-being," that is, a necessity rather than a want or a comfort.

Metellus was a well-known social conservative and contrarian, later becoming a censor, or a Roman official with the duty of enforcing public morality as well government finance. His speech is roundly criticized by his listeners, according to Gellius, who recognize that Metellus has, in effect, contradicted himself by praising marriage while condemning it. In fact, they argue that matrimony was not the problem, "misconduct and injustice of some husbands and wives were," a statement that underlines how matrimony was viewed less as a union of felicitous partners and more as an institution to uphold society.

A Closer Look

The Romans were monogamous; legally, a man could only have one wife at a time. The Romans, despite the actions of some of their emperors, were also not allowed by custom and law to marry close relatives. But beyond those things, Roman marriage was a very different institution from what we know today. For one thing, there were many legal restrictions on whom one could marry. Only citizens could marry one another, although others could do so if they received special permission, called a *conubium.*

For another, Roman marriage was rarely about romantic love. As youths reached the age for marriage—mid-20s for a man; midteens for a girl—their parents would search out suitable partners, based only in part on the shared temperament of the potential betrothed. Instead, the parents would consider political and economic factors, for marriage was not simply the wedding of two young people but an agreement and alliance between families. These factors became more important in wealthier and more powerful families. This led to a paradox in which the more privileged the young person was, the less say he or she had in his or her matrimonial choices.

1   100   200   300   400   500   600   700   800   900   1000   1100   1200   1300   1400   1500   1600   1700   1800   1900   2000 CE

1.5.2 Cato the Elder on Uppity Women

Rome
195 BCE

"If each of us, citizens, had determined to assert his rights and dignity as a husband with respect to his own spouse, we should have less trouble with the sex as a whole; as it is, our liberty, destroyed at home by female violence, even here in the Forum is crushed and trodden underfoot, and because we have not kept them individually under control, we dread them collectively . . . from no class is there not the greatest danger if you permit them meetings and gatherings and secret consultations. And I can scarcely decide in my own mind whether the act itself or the precedent it sets is worse; the act concerns us consuls and other magistrates; the example, citizens, rather concerns you. For whether the proposal which is laid before you is in the public interest or not is a question for you who are soon to cast your votes; but this female madness . . . brings discredit upon the magistrates. . . .

For myself, I could not conceal my blushes a while ago, when I had to make my way to the Forum through a crowd of women. Had not respect for the dignity and modesty of some individuals among them rather than of the sex as a whole kept me silent, lest they should seem to have been rebuked by a consul, I should have said, 'What sort of practice is this, of running out into the streets and blocking the roads and speaking to other women's husbands? Could you not have made the same requests, each of your own husband, at home? Or are you more attractive outside and to other women's husbands than to your own? And yet, not even at home, if modesty would keep matrons within the limits of their proper rights, did it become you to concern yourselves with the question of what laws should be adopted in this place or repealed. . . .

If they win in this, what will they not attempt? Review all the laws with which your forefathers restrained their license and made them subject to their husbands; even with all these bonds you can scarcely control them. What of this? If you suffer them to seize these bonds one by one and wrench themselves free and finally to be placed on a parity with their husbands, do you think that you will be able to endure them? The moment they begin to be your equals, they will be your superiors. But, by Hercules, they object to the passage of any new law against them, they complain not of law but of wrongs done them; what they want, rather, is that you repeal this law which you have approved and ratified and which in the trial and experience of so many years you have found good: in other words, that by abolishing this one law you weaken the force of all the rest. No law is entirely convenient for everyone; this alone is asked, whether it is good for the majority and on the whole. If every law which harms anyone in his private affairs is to be repealed and discarded, what good will it do for all the citizens to pass laws which those at whom they are aimed will at once annul?"

Source: Titus Livius (Livy). *The History of Rome*. Book 34:2-3. Translated by Evan T. Sage. Cambridge, MA: Harvard University Press; London, William Heinemann, Ltd. 1935.

TIMELINE 2000 1900 1800 1700 1600 1500 1400 1300 1200 1100 1000 900 800 700 600 500 400 300 200 100 1 BCE

What You Need to Know

The Roman statesman and author, Cato the Elder, who lived from 234 to 149 BCE, was known for his conservative values, as this excerpt from a speech he delivered in 195 BCE against the repeal of the Lex Oppia, a sumptuary law, makes clear. The speech comes to us from the *History of Rome*, written roughly 200 years later by Titus Livius, better known in English as Livy. The Lex Oppia, passed in 215 BCE, restricted the amount of gold and dyed clothes a woman could wear.

Cato's tirade reflected his views that Roman society was being slowly corrupted by its new found wealth, a result of its military conquests abroad, which was turning its citizens away from the virtues of simplicity and sacrifice. But it also reveals much about his views on women and, by implication, the views of many other Roman thinkers of his day. Cato believed that Roman women should be chaste, faithful, dedicated to home and family, and modest. Their presence in public, bedecked in gold and finery, violated those values, he said. And, since Roman women were responsible for inculcating Roman values in the young, their turn toward luxury and indulgence was a threat to the Roman polity as well. But Cato's views were clearly in a minority, at least within the Roman senate, for the legislative body ignored his compelling plea and overturned the law.

A Closer Look

Cato the Elder's speech demonstrates the conservative viewpoint at that time regarding women in Roman society. Because they were largely excluded from public life, we know far less about the lives of Roman women than we do of the men. What is clear from the record, however, is that women were largely confined to the domestic sphere and were legally, at least, appendages of the men in their lives—fathers, husbands, and, in the case of slaves and servants, the male head of the household where they worked.

Women were also confined to domestic chores, for which much of the education they received in their younger years was dedicated. Women were in charge of the cooking, cleaning, weaving, and making of clothes, although wealthier women usually had servants to do much of this for them.

Although women were expected to play a subservient role by law and custom, reality could be quite different. Women were typically in charge of household affairs, and in Roman times, as today, the wives of powerful men oftentimes served as counselors to their husbands.

1 100 200 300 400 500 600 700 800 900 1000 1100 1200 1300 1400 1500 1600 1700 1800 1900 2000 CE

1.5.3 Roman Perfume Vases

Syria
64 BCE–31 CE

Credit: Werner Forman/Universal Images Group/Getty Images

What You Need to Know

This trio of perfume flasks was manufactured sometime in the first century BCE or the first century CE. They come from present-day Syria, which was then a province of the Roman Empire.

In the early years of the Roman Republic, perfume was largely used for ceremonial purposes, typically those connected with religious festivals. But as the Roman Republic gave way to the empire, and as the society grew wealthier and more sensually indulgent, perfume came into more widespread use. Contact with the more ancient civilizations of the eastern Mediterranean, many of which used perfume in daily life, also contributed to the growing Roman appreciation of perfume. Thus, by the first century CE, the perfumes were being used profligately. Wealthy persons regularly had their servants rub perfume onto the walls and floors of their houses. At parties, perfume was added to the water of the fountains that graced people's homes. Perfumes were even splashed on household pets, such as dogs, and the horses the household's patriarch or matriarch rode on.

A Closer Look

Perfumes were widely used by Roman women throughout the empire. There were several reasons for this. The first was that Romans believed that the odors exuded by the body reflected a person's health. A perfume that enhanced a woman's own body odor made it seem as if she was healthy, and therefore attractive. Second, many Roman women wore cosmetics. This was especially the case with upper-class women and prostitutes. But Roman cosmetics often contained animal by-products that produced a foul odor. Perfume covered up the stench. Finally, by dousing themselves in perfume, Roman women shrouded themselves in a protective cocoon of sweet-smelling scent that kept some of the foul odors of Roman streets at bay.

Finally, perfumes were also used in anointing the dead. Roman funerary practice dictated that the body lay in the atrium of the home for a period of time before being buried. But perfume did more than merely cover up the smell of a putrefying corpse; it was also part of the ritual of preparing for the deceased on his or her journey into the underworld. An improperly prepared body might not be accepted by Charon, ferryman to the underworld, thus leaving the deceased in a state of limbo, where it might haunt the living.

1 100 200 300   400   500   600   700   800   900   1000 1100 1200 1300   1400   1500   1600   1700 1800 1900 2000 CE

1.5.4 Cicero on Professions and Social Status

Roman Republic
44 BCE

Now in regard to trades and other means of livelihood, which ones are to be considered becoming to a gentleman and which ones are not, we have been taught, in general, as follows: First, those means of livelihood are rejected as undesirable, and which incur people's ill-will, as those of tax-gatherers and usurers. Unbecoming to a gentleman, too . . . are the means of livelihood of all hired workmen whom we pay for mere manual labor, not for artistic skill; for in their case, the very wages they receive is a pledge of their slavery. We must consider inappropriate those also who buy from wholesale merchants to retail immediately; for they would get no profits without a great deal of downright lying; and certainly there is no action that is lower than misrepresentation. And all mechanics are engaged in vulgar trades; for no workshop can have anything liberal about it. Least respectable of all are those trades which cater to sensual pleasures. . . .

But the professions in which either a higher degree of intelligence is required or from which no small benefit to society is derived—medicine and architecture, for example, and teaching—these are proper for those whose social position they are appropriate. Trade, if it is on a small scale, is to be considered inappropriate; but if wholesome and on a large scale, importing large quantities from all parts of the world and distributing to many without misrepresentation, it is not to be greatly disparaged. It even seems to deserve the highest respect, if those who are engaged in it [are] . . . satisfied with the fortunes they have made, and make their way from the port to a country estate, as they have often made it from the sea into port. But of all the occupations by which gain is secured, none is better than agriculture, none more profitable, none more delightful, none more becoming to a freeman.

Source: Cicero. *De Officiis*. Book I, Ch. 42. Translated by Walter Miller. Loeb Classical Library. London: William Heinemann, 1913, pp.153, 155.

What You Need to Know

The accompanying document comes from the essay *De Officiis*, or *On Duties*, by Marcus Tulius Cicero, written in 44 BCE. Cicero was both a high-ranking politician and a political theorist. Although the excerpt here explores the professions Cicero deems appropriate for a "gentleman," it says much about the nature of money, professions, and social status in ancient Rome.

For Cicero and gentleman like him, money, status, and honor existed in a complex relationship with each other. Being a gentleman was not so much about how much money one had but how one obtained it. To put it simply, gentlemen earned their money by their brains and not their brawn. And they made sure that the economic activity they engaged in was appropriately virtuous.

Upper-class Romans were also suspicious of trade. For Cicero, retailing was akin to cheating and even those who made great fortunes through long-distance trade gained a greater deal of dignity and, hence social status, when they retired from money-making to take up the leisurely and intellectual pursuits of the country gentleman.

A Closer Look

Cicero's own life revealed much about how social status operated in the higher reaches of Roman society. He was born outside Rome itself to a family of equestrian rank, meaning he came from a socially distinguished lineage but not one suitable for the exalted rank of senator to which he eventually rose. Most senators, despite their claims to being simple farmers, were in fact the inheritors or owners of vast slave-worked plantations, known as *latifundia*, in the Italian countryside.

But Cicero was ambitious and brilliant. After receiving the best education Rome afforded and serving in the military, he took up a variety of posts across the empire, rising through the ranks of the imperial administration, until entering the senate. Cicero was what Romans called a *novus homo*, or "new man." That term referred to those who, by dint of their talents and intelligence, rose from relatively humble origins to the highest ranks of society.

Rome's elite were of two minds on the subject of "new men." On the one hand, they publicly praised the idea of social mobility; on the other, they often did everything they could to monopolize power and prestige in their own hands. But because Cicero's oratorical skills were so undeniably exceptional and, equally important, because he used them in defense of conservative values, he was permitted entrée into the ranks of senator.

1 100 200 300 400 500 600 700 800 900 1000 1100 1200 1300 1400 1500 1600 1700 1800 1900 2000 CE

1.5.5 A Good Roman Father's Responsibilities

Roman Empire
First Century CE

He was a good father, a kind husband, and a most capable manager of his own household, since he was far from regarding this side of his affairs as trivial, or allowing it to suffer from neglect. For this reason I think I should give some examples of his conduct in his private life.

He chose his wife for her family rather than her fortune, for he believed that while people of great wealth or high position cherish their own pride and self-esteem, nevertheless women of noble birth are by nature more ashamed of any disgraceful action and so are more obedient to their husbands in everything that is honorable. He used to say that a man who beats his wife or child is laying sacrilegious hands on the most sacred thing in the world. He considered that it was more praiseworthy to be a good husband than a great senator, and also was of the opinion that there was nothing much else to admire in Socrates, except for the fact that he was always gentle and considerate in his dealings with his wife, who was ill-tempered, and his children, who were half-witted.

When his son was born, Cato thought that nothing but the most important business should prevent him from being present when his wife gave the baby its bath and wrapped it in swaddling clothes. His wife suckled the child herself and often did the same for her slaves' children, so as to encourage brotherly feelings in them towards her own son. As soon as the boy was able to learn, his father took charge of his schooling and taught him to read, although he had in the household an educated slave named Chilo, who was a schoolmaster and taught many other boys. However, Cato did not think it right, so he tells us, that his son should be scolded or disciplined by a slave, if he were slow to learn, and still less that he should be indebted to his slave in such a vital matter as his education.

So he took it upon himself to teach the boy, not only his letters, but also the principles of Roman law. He also trained him in athletics, and taught him how to throw the javelin, fight in armor, ride a horse, use his fists in boxing, endure the extremes of heat and cold, and swim across the roughest and most swiftly flowing stretches of the Tiber. He tells us that he composed his history of Rome, writing it out with his own hand and in large characters, so that his son should possess in his own home the means of acquainting himself with the ancient annals and traditions of his country. He also mentions that he was just as careful not to use any indecent expression before his son. . . .

Such was Cato's approach to the noble task of forming and molding his son for the pursuit of virtue. The boy was an exemplary student in his readiness to learn, and his spirit was a match for his natural goodness of disposition.

Source: *Seneca: Moral Essays*. Vol. I. Translated by John W. Basore. Cambridge and London: Loeb Classical Library, 1928.

TIMELINE   2000 1900 1800 1700 1600 1500 1400 1300 1200 1100 1000 900 800 700 600 500 400 300 200 100 1 BCE

What You Need to Know

Roman fathers enjoyed absolute power and were expected to be authoritarian figures within the family and household. But, as this excerpt from Greek historian and Roman citizen Plutarch's biography of Cato the Elder illustrates, fathers could also be fair and nurturing figures. This is especially noteworthy as the statesman Cato, who lived from 234 to 149 BCE, during the formative years of Roman culture, has been remembered as a stern and disciplined soldier and politician.

Plutarch, who lived about 200 years after Cato, at the height of the Roman Empire's greatness, indulged in a bit of nostalgia in his biography. Romans of his day often looked upon their ancestors, who lived a simpler life, less obsessed with luxury and entertainment, as possessing nobler virtues than later generations. That is evident in his evocation of an idealized Cato as a "good father, a kind husband, and a most capable manager of his own household." He made sure to be present at the birth of his sons; he considered corporal punishment of his wife or his children to be "sacrilegious"; and he spent much effort and time in making sure his sons were brought up well educated, physically fit, and ready to take up the duties and responsibilities of a good Roman citizen.

A Closer Look

As with state affairs, family life in ancient Rome was dominated by men. Roman households were headed by the father or oldest living male relative, who was known as the *paterfamilias*, literally "father of the family." The *paterfamilias* owned all of the family's property and made all financial decisions. He also conducted the household religious services and was in charge of the family altar to the spirits, which protected the family.

The father even had power over the life and death of his children. When a baby was born, it was the father who decided whether the newborn lived, died, or became a slave. A deformed child was often abandoned; if the father deemed another child too much to support, the baby might be sold into slavery. The father also had the right to legally disown or even kill disobedient children.

While the father had absolute power, mothers exercised authority behind the scenes. It was they who managed the household on a daily basis and could intercede when they felt a father was acting too sternly with his children.

1 100 200 300 400 500 600 700 800 900 1000 1100 1200 1300 1400 1500 1600 1700 1800 1900 2000 CE

1.5.6 Cato the Elder's Philosophy on Slave Ownership

Roman Empire
First Century CE

Cato possessed a large number of slaves, whom he usually bought from among the prisoners captured in war, but it was his practice to choose those who, like puppies or colts, were young enough to be trained and taught their duties. None of them ever entered any house but his own, unless they were sent on an errand by Cato or his wife, and if they were asked what Cato was doing, the reply was always that they did not know. It was a rule of his establishment that a slave must either be doing something about the house, or else be asleep. He much preferred the slaves who slept well, because he believed that they were more even-tempered than the wakeful ones, and that those who had had enough sleep produced better results at any task than those who were short of it. And as he was convinced that slaves were led into mischief more often on account of love affairs than for any other reason, he made it a rule that the men could sleep with the women slaves of the establishment for a fixed price, but must have nothing to do with any others.

At the beginning of his career, when he was a poor man and was frequently on active service, he never complained of anything that he ate, and he used to say that it was ignoble to find fault with a servant for the food that he prepared. But in later life, when he had become more prosperous, he used to invite his friends and colleagues to dinner, and immediately after the meal he would beat with a leather thong any of the slaves who had been careless in preparing or serving it. He constantly contrived to provoke quarrels and dissensions among his slaves, and if they ever arrived at an understanding with one another, he became alarmed and suspicious. If ever any of his slaves was suspected of committing a capital offense, he gave the culprit a formal trial in the presence of the rest, and if he was found guilty, he had him put to death. . . .

He would also lend money to any of his slaves who wished it. They used these sums to buy young slaves, and after training them and teaching them a trade for a year at Cato's expense, they would sell them again. Often Cato would keep these boys for himself, and he would then credit to the slave the price offered by the highest bidder.

Source: Balsdon, J. P. V. D. *Life and Leisure in Ancient Rome*. Translated by J. P. V. D. Balsdon. New York: Phoenix Press, 1969.

What You Need to Know

This passage from the historian Plutarch's biography of Cato the Elder discusses the Roman statesman's treatment of his slaves.

Slaves were a common feature of Roman life, as they were in civilizations across the ancient world. This was true of Rome both in its republican and imperial eras. Although male slaves worked in small numbers in the fields of small, landholding farmers, most were situated on the great latifundia, or plantations, which were owned by some of the wealthiest and most powerful people in Rome. Indeed, many Roman senators owned latifundia throughout the countryside surrounding Rome. Latifundia dominated the agriculture in many of Rome's provinces, especially around the Mediterranean littoral. These plantations were worked not only by slaves but by freemen, who rented land from the *latifundia*'s owners in exchange for their labor and part of their crop.

Aside from agricultural work, slaves remained critical both to the overall economy of Rome and to the lifestyle of its better-off citizens, working in mines, shops and industry, and as servants in households. Indeed, so common were slaves that many in the middling classes of Roman citizens might have one or two to work for them.

A Closer Look

Under Roman law, slaves were the property of their masters, and the status of the slave passed to his or her children. Slaves could be treated with care or great cruelty, depending on the personality and attitudes of their master. A little of the former and much of the latter is seen in the behavior of the soldier, statesman, and author Cato the Elder toward the slaves in his own household. Cato, who lived from 234 to 149 BCE and was well known for his stoicism and conservative values, owned a large farm in Italy, worked by slaves. In Plutarch's biography, Cato is seen as a strict disciplinarian but one who understands that treating slaves well meant they were more content and worked harder. Thus, he made sure they always got enough sleep.

At the same time, Cato felt that slaves required a firm hand. He kept them constantly working during waking hours and frequently beat those who he felt had not met his exacting standards. A common practice in his household was his whipping of those slaves he held responsible for a poorly prepared or served meal.

Interestingly, Cato tried to provide incentives for his slaves by lending them money to buy other slaves, who they would train and then sell back to Cato, or to pay for the right to have sex with other slaves in the household.

1 100 200 300 400 500 600 700 800 900 1000 1100 1200 1300 1400 1500 1600 1700 1800 1900 2000 CE

1.5.7 Quintilian on How an Orator Should Dress

Rome
First Century CE

With regard to dress, there is no special clothing peculiar to the orator, but his dress comes more under the public eye than that of other people. It should, therefore, be distinguished and manly, as, indeed, it ought to be with all prominent individuals. For excessive care with regard to the cut of the toga, the style of the shoes, or the arrangement of the hair, is just as reprehensible as excessive carelessness. There are also details of dress which are altered to some extent by successive changes in fashion. The ancients, for example, wore no folds, and their successors wore them very short. Consequently it follows that in view of the fact that their arms were, like those of the Greeks, covered by the garment, they must have employed a different form of gesture . . . from that which is now in use.

However, I am speaking of our own day. The speaker who has not the right to wear the broad stripe [indicating senatorial status] will wear his girdle in such a way that the front edges of the tunic fall a little below his knees, while the edges in rear reach to the middle of the backs of his legs. For only women draw them lower, and only centurions higher. If we wear the purple [i.e., senatorial] stripe, it requires little care to see that it falls becomingly; negligence in this respect sometimes generates criticism. . . .

A portion of the tunic also should be drawn back in order that it may not fall over the arm when we are arguing a case, and the fold should be thrown over the shoulder, while it will not be unbecoming if the edge is turned back. On the other hand, we should not cover the shoulder and the whole of the throat; otherwise, our clothing will be unduly narrowed and will lose the impressive effect produced by breadth at the chest. The left arm should only be raised so far as to form a right angle at the elbow, while the edge of the toga should fall in equal lengths on either side. . . .

When, however, our speech draws near its close, more especially if fortune shows herself kind, practically everything is appropriate. We may stream with sweat, show signs of fatigue, and let our clothing fall in careless disorder, and the toga slip loose from us on every side. . . . On the other hand, if the toga falls down at the beginning of our speech, or when we have only proceeded a little way, the failure to replace it is a sign of indifference, or laziness, or sheer ignorance of the way in which clothes should be worn.

Source: Quintilian. *The Institutio Oratoria of Quintilian*. Vol. IV. Book XI. Translated by H. E. Butler. Loeb Classical Library. London: William Heinemann, 1922, pp. 317, 319, 325. Text slightly modified.

TIMELINE   2000 1900 1800 1700 1600 1500 1400 1300 1200 1100 1000 900 800 700 600 500 400 300 200 100 1 BCE

What You Need to Know

In this excerpt from *Institutio Oratoria*, or Instructions on Oratory, the first century CE philosopher and orator Quintilian describes the appropriate clothing for an orator.

For several reasons, clothing in ancient Rome was rather simple. First, there were not a lot of materials to choose from. Virtually all garments were made of wool or linen. Second, sewing needles were quite unwieldy, keeping stitching to a minimum. Romans, for example, did not use buttons because it was too difficult to stitch buttonholes. Instead, they used various types of broaches or clasps to fasten garments together.

The tunic, a loose and shapeless garment that was usually sleeveless and went down to the knees, was the most common form of clothing in ancient Rome. In cold weather, a person might don a second or third tunic to keep warm. The toga, which was effectively a blanket wrapped around the wearer's body and held in place by a cloth belt, was usually worn by higher-status Romans. Partly, this was because the toga entailed more material and thus was more expensive. But there were also sumptuary laws, which restricted the wearing of togas to free citizens of Rome.

A Closer Look

Ancient Rome was a highly hierarchical society, marked by numerous customs and laws meant to distinguish those of noble birth from plebeians, or the common masses, and slaves. Nowhere was this more obvious than in garments, which at a glance were meant to show the status of the wearer. For example, Quintilian notes the broad purple stripe reserved for the garb of senators.

But such distinctions are not the main focus of Quintillian's discussion of the dress proper for an orator. Instead, he emphasizes that the clothing should reflect the dignity of the profession of oration, as well as address its practical needs. He emphasizes that clothes of an orator should be both "distinguished and manly," both highly regarded attributes in the patriarchal and hierarchical society that was Rome. Men were considered the more rational sex, so no orator would want to appear feminine in appearance. At the same time, Quintillian warns against fastidiousness, or "excessive care," in one's appearance, which might project the image of someone more concerned with appearance than substance. Yet he also seems to belie his own recommendation in the detail he goes into. To the modern reader, some of it may even appear a bit arbitrary but then again, that is how people 2,000 years from now may view our business culture's attention to the right tie and lapel.

1 100 200 300 400 500 600 700 800 900 1000 1100 1200 1300 1400 1500 1600 1700 1800 1900 2000 CE

1.5.8 Recipes from a Roman Cookbook

Rome
First Century CE

To keep grapes:

Take perfect grapes from the vines, place them in a vessel, and pour rain water over them that has been boiled down one third of its volume. The vessel must be pitched and sealed with plaster, and must be kept in a cool place to which the sun has no access. Treated in this manner, the grapes will be fresh whenever you need them. You can also serve this water as honey mead to the sick. Also, if you cover the grapes with barley, you will find them sound and uninjured.

Supreme style cooked peas:

Cook the peas with oil and a piece of sow's belly. Put in a sauce pan broth, leek heads, green coriander, and put on the fire to be cooked. Of tid-bits [i.e., finely chopped meats or seasonings] cut little dice. Similarly cook thrushes or other small [game] birds, or take sliced chicken and diced brain, properly cooked. Further cook, in the available liquor or broth, Lucanian sausage and bacon; cook leeks in water. Crush a pint of toasted pignolia nuts. Also crush pepper, lovage, origany, and ginger, dilute with the broth of pork, tie. Take a square baking dish, suitable for turning over; oil it well. Sprinkle [on the bottom] a layer of crushed nuts, upon which put some peas, fully covering the bottom of the squash dish. On top of this, arrange slices of the bacon, leeks, and sliced Lucanian sausage. Again cover with a layer of peas and alternate all the rest of the available edibles in the manner described until the dish is filled, concluding at last with a layer of peas, utilizing everything. Bake this dish in the oven, or put it into a slow fire [covering it with live coals], so that it may be baked thoroughly. [Next make a sauce of the following]: Put yolks of hard-boiled eggs in the mortar with white pepper, nuts, honey, white wine, and a little broth. Mix, and put it into a sauce pan to be cooked. When [the sauce is] done, turn out the peas into a large [silver dish], and mask them with this sauce, which is called white sauce.

Pig's paunch:

Clean the paunch of a suckling pig well with salt and vinegar, and presently wash with water. Then fill it with the following dressing: pieces of pork pounded in the mortar, three brains—the nerves removed—mix with raw eggs, add nuts, whole pepper, and sauce to taste. Crush pepper, lovage, silphium, anise, ginger, a little rue; fill the paunch with it, not too much, though, leaving plenty of room for expansion, so that it does not burst while being cooked. Put it in a pot with boiling water, retire and prick with a needle so that it does not burst. When half done, take it out and hang it into the smoke to take on color. Now boil it over again and finish it leisurely. Next take the broth, some pure wine, and a little oil, open the paunch with a small knife. Sprinkle with the broth and lovage; place the pig near the fire to heat it, turn it around in bran [or bread crumbs], immerse it in brine, and finish [the outer crust to a golden brown].

Source: Apicius. *Cookery and Dining in Imperial Rome.* Translated by Joseph Dommers Vehling. New York: Dover Publications, Inc., 1936, pp. 51, 129, 168.

What You Need to Know

The accompanying recipes are from a cookbook written by the first century CE gourmet Apicius.

The Roman Empire covered a vast expanse, encompassing virtually every climate on Earth, barring the tropics and the Arctic. Aside from being a political entity, the empire was also an economic unit, with goods traded far and wide. Rome's government had built a network of roads capable of transporting troops, communications, and goods of all kinds, including crops and foodstuffs. All of these factors meant that Romans, if they had the means and were so inclined, could enjoy numerous ingredients in their cuisine. This included a wide variety of vegetables, aside from the cruciferous ones, such as broccoli and cauliflower; many of the same stone fruits and berries we enjoy today, although citrus fruits were rare; herbs and spices of all types (although more exotic ones from the tropics, such as cinnamon and black pepper, were virtually unknown); a variety of hard and soft cheeses; and animal protein from meat, poultry, and especially seafood. A particular favorite of Romans was *garum*, a fish-flavored sauce often used as a substitute for salt.

A Closer Look

As these three recipes make clear, Romans made good use of the many food ingredients that life in an expansive and prosperous empire provided them. These recipes also indicate that Romans, at least those with some wealth, had access to utensils and kitchenware of great variety.

The recipes here are remarkably detailed. The recipe for cooked peas, for example, required the use of various pans and baking dishes, as well as an oven and an open fire for what we would call stove-top cooking. The recipe for pig's paunch, or stomach, is even more complex, and reveals the many varieties of preparing and cooking foods known to the Romans, as it involves brining, boiling, smoking, and roasting.

In an age before refrigeration, much thought had to go into the preserving of foods. In the recipe for keeping grapes, the author suggests boiling them in rain water, which was probably purer and better tasting than the water provided by wells and aqueducts, and then sealing them up in a container with plaster.

1 100 200 300 400 500 600 700 800 900 1000 1100 1200 1300 1400 1500 1600 1700 1800 1900 2000 CE

1.5.9 Seneca's Advice on Treating the Help Kindly

Rome
First Century CE

I smile at those who think it degrading for a man to share a meal with his slave. But why should they think it degrading? It is only because a purse-proud etiquette surrounds a householder at his dinner with a mob of standing slaves. The master eats more than he can hold, and with monstrous greed loads his belly until it is stretched and at length ceases to do the work of a belly, so that he is at greater pains to discharge all the food than he was to stuff it down. All this time, the poor slaves may not move their lips, even to speak. . . .

When we recline at a banquet, one slave mops up the disgorged food, another crouches beneath the table and gathers up the leftovers of the tipsy guests. Another carves the priceless game birds. With unerring strokes and skilled hand, he cuts the choice morsels along the breast or the rump. Poor fellow, to live only for the purpose of cutting fat capons correctly, unless the other man is still more unhappy than he, who teaches this art for pleasure's sake, rather than he who learns it because he must.

Another, who serves the wine, must dress like a woman and wrestle with his advancing years. . . . Another, whose duty it is to put a valuation on the guests, must stick to his task, unlucky man, and watch to see whose flattery and whose immodesty, whether of appetite or of language, is to get them an invitation for tomorrow. Think also of the poor purveyors of food, who note their masters' tastes with delicate skill, who know what special flavors will sharpen their appetite, what will please their eyes, what new combinations will rouse their cloyed stomachs, what food will excite their disgust through sheer superabundance, and what will stir them to hunger on that particular day.

The master cannot bear to dine with slaves like these. He would think it beneath his dignity to associate with his slave at the same table! God forbid!

Source: Seneca, Lucius Annaeus. *Ad Lucilium Epistulae Morales*. Vol. I. Epistle XLVII. Translated by Richard M. Gummere. Loeb Classical Library. London: William Heinemann, 1917, pp. 303, 305.

TIMELINE   2000 1900 1800 1700 1600 1500 1400 1300 1200 1100 1000 900 800 700 600 500 400 300 200 100 1 BCE

What You Need to Know

This selection from the writing of Lucius Annaeus Seneca, written sometime in the first century CE, discusses the proper treatment of slaves.

As in most ancient civilizations, slavery was ubiquitous in ancient Rome. It is estimated that roughly 30 to 40 percent of the eight million or so inhabitants of the Italian heartland of Rome were slaves. For the empire as a whole, the figures are 10 to 15 percent of the 50 million total population. With these kind of numbers, slaves were critical to the smooth functioning of Roman society and the Roman economy. Most became slaves from war, debt, being sold by their parents, or by inheriting that status.

Slaves worked in any number of occupations; some, serving as advisors to powerful men, could be quite influential and wealthy themselves. Most, however, found themselves in one of five economic sectors: public project work, such as the building of roads; mining; crafts and services in cities and towns; labor on farms or *latifundia* (plantations); and domestic service.

A Closer Look

Roman slavery differed in several ways from its counterpart of more modern times. One of the most important of these was in the attitude Romans held toward their slaves. Romans were ecumenical in whom they enslaved; any conquered people could become slaves and, thus, one could find in Rome blonde slaves from Germany working alongside black slaves from Nubia (modern-day Sudan), and every group in between. Thus, Romans did not see slaves as belonging to an inferior group but as persons who had suffered misfortune.

That, of course, did not necessarily raise their status. Slaves were the mere property of their masters and had virtually no legal rights, although they could buy themselves out of slavery. As this excerpt from Seneca hints, slaves were widely denigrated by free Romans, who, he notes, "think it degrading to share a meal with . . . slaves." This comes, he says, from the fact that they are used to seeing them in subservient positions. But Seneca, a Stoic philosopher and statesman, felt that Romans of his day had forgotten the values that had built their civilization—one of which was the dignity of ordinary labor. As Seneca notes, many of the slaves surrounding a master at table had great talents, among which were the ability to anticipate the every need of their owner, to "note their masters' tastes with delicate skill." Well known as a humorist, Seneca concludes with a well chosen bit of sarcasm: "The master cannot bear to dine with slaves like these. . . . God forbid!"

1 100 200 300 400 500 600 700 800 900 1000 1100 1200 1300 1400 1500 1600 1700 1800 1900 2000 CE

1.5.10 Buying a Farm in the Country

Roman Empire
ca. First Century CE

My friend Suetonius has an inclination to purchase a small farm, of which, I am informed, an acquaintance of yours intends to sell. I ask that you would try to see to it that he may buy it on reasonable terms, a circumstance which will add to his satisfaction in obtaining it. An expensive sale price is always disagreeable, especially since it is a reflection upon the purchaser's judgment. There are several circumstances pertaining to this farm which—supposing my friend had no objection to the price—are appealing to him: the convenient distance from Rome, the goodness of the roads, the small size of the building, and the very few acres of land around it, which is just enough to amuse him, but not to overwork him. To a man of the studious inclination that Suetonius is, it is sufficient if he has a small place to relieve the mind and divert the eye, where he can amble around his grounds, traverse his single path, become familiar with his two or three vines, and count his little saplings. I mention these details to let you see how much he will be obliged to me, as I will to you, if you can help him towards the purchase of this little getaway, so agreeable to his taste, upon terms of which he will have no reason to regret. Farewell.

Source: Pliny the Younger. *Letters*. Vol. I. Book I. Letter XXIV. Translated by William Melmoth, with revisions by W. M. L. Hutchinson. Loeb Classical Library. London: William Heinemann, 1915, p. 87.

TIMELINE   2000 1900 1800 1700 1600 1500 1400 1300 1200 1100 1000 900 800 700 600 500 400 300 200 100 1 BCE

What You Need to Know

The accompanying document consists of a letter that Pliny the Younger, a Roman official and author of the first and second century CE, wrote to his friend Baebius on behalf of another friend, the biographer Suetonius. In it, Pliny praises the simple rural life as a means for a man of letters to "relieve the mind and divert the eye."

Roman farms generally produced low yields. This meant—the great Roman cities and urban culture notwithstanding—that the vast majority of the inhabitants of both the republic and empire were required to live and work on the land, for there was relatively little surplus to support a large nonfarming population. Still, the Romans did understand and employ a basic understanding of effective agriculture. They knew to rotate their crops and fertilize to maximize the fertility of the soil and to practice polyculture to avoid the perils that climate and plant disease could wreak on a farm entirely devoted to one crop. Given the semidry Mediterranean climate that constituted much of their realm, with its short, wet cool seasons and long, dry summers, Romans became adept at irrigation. A number of major rural aqueduct systems have been unearthed by archaeologists, which were used not only to bring water to farms but to provide the hydraulic energy needed for running mills.

A Closer Look

In the very early years of the Roman society, land was largely controlled by the aristocracy, with most everyone else a dependent laborer. That began to change beginning in the sixth and fifth centuries BCE with the advent of widespread private land ownership. The Roman state, such as it was, promoted the idea of a large, self-armed fighting force of small farmers, known as the *assidui*, or "hardworking ones." The plan was successful, and as Rome conquered nearby peoples, more land became available for settlement by small farmers and soldiers.

With Rome's great expansion in the first and second centuries CE came large numbers of slaves and wealth, as well as a need to feed Rome's vast army and growing urban population. The trend toward a citizenry of armed, small farmers gave way to great *latifundia*, or plantations, owned by elites and worked by slaves.

But the ideals of an earlier Rome survived. Philosophers and politicians, such as Cicero and Cato praised the values of farm life and rural living—hard work, frugality, and the avoidance of self-indulgent luxury. Many Romans looked to the example of Cincinnatus, an aristocrat and statesman from the fifth century BCE. Living a simple life on a small farm, Cincinnatus assumed power over the republic when it was threatened and then returned to humble life of a farmer once the threat was lifted. As Romans of a later era had it, Cincinnatus showed how the pastoral life inculcated a virtuous character.

1 100 200 300 400 500 600 700 800 900 1000 1100 1200 1300 1400 1500 1600 1700 1800 1900 2000 CE

1.5.11 An Ideal Retirement according to Pliny the Younger

Roman Empire
ca. First Century CE

I never spent my time more agreeably, I think, than I did lately with Spurinna. I was so much pleased with his way of life, that if ever I should arrive at old age, there is no man whom I would sooner choose for my model. I look upon order in human actions, especially at that advanced period, with the same sort of pleasure as I behold the settled course of the heavenly bodies. In youth, indeed, a certain irregularity and agitation is by no means unbecoming; but in age, when business is unseasonable, and ambition indecent, all should be calm and uniform.

Spurinna religiously pursues the above rule of life; . . . he observes a certain periodical season and method. The first part of the morning he keeps his bed; at eight he calls for his shoes, and walks three miles, in which he enjoys at once contemplation and exercise. Meanwhile, if he has any friends with him in his house, he enters upon some polite and useful topic of conversation; if he is alone, somebody reads to him; and sometimes, too, when he is not, if it is agreeable to his company. When this is over, he reposes himself, and again takes up a book, or else falls into discourse more improving than a book. . . .

When the baths are ready, which in winter is about three o'clock, and in summer about two, he undresses himself; and if there happens to be no wind, he walks about in the sun. After this he puts himself into prolonged and violent motion at playing ball; for by this sort of exercise, he combats the effect of old age. When he has bathed, he throws himself on his couch and waits dinner a little while, and in the meanwhile, some agreeable and entertaining author is read to him. In this, as in all the rest, his friends are at full liberty to partake; or to employ themselves in any other manner more suitable to their taste. You sit down to an elegant yet frugal repast, which is served up in plain and antique plate. He uses likewise dishes of Corinthian bronze, which is his hobby, not his passion. At intervals of the repast, he is frequently entertained with comedians, that even his very pleasures may be seasoned with letters; and though he continues there, even in summer, till the night is somewhat advanced, yet he prolongs the sitting over the wine with so much affability and politeness, that none of his guests ever think it tedious. By this method of living, he has preserved his sight and hearing entire, and his body active and vigorous to his 78th year, without discovering any appearance of old age, but the wisdom.

This is the sort of life which I ardently aspire after.

Source: Pliny the Younger. *Letters*. Vol. I. Book III. Letter I. Translated by William Melmoth, with revisions by W. M. L. Hutchinson. Loeb Classical Library. London: William Heinemann, 1915, pp. 181–183, 185.

TIMELINE   2000 1900 1800 1700 1600 1500 1400 1300 1200 1100 1000 900 800 700 600 500 400 300 200 100 1 BCE

What You Need to Know

The preceding passage is from one of the famed letters of Pliny the Younger, a Roman lawyer, magistrate, and author who lived from 62 to 114 CE. In this letter, Pliny describes his encounter with an elderly man named Spurinna.

Although extant official records on life expectancy are somewhat complete for the nobility living in the Italian heartland of the empire, little is known of the provinces and almost nothing about the poor and slaves, who, of course, made up the vast majority of the empire's inhabitants. Among higher-class families, life expectancy was about 35, but this is misleading because it factors in high child mortality rates. Roughly one-quarter of children died in their first year, and another 25 percent died before their tenth birthday. For those who survived childhood, however, they could expect to live between 60 and 70 years. This meant that a good deal of adults would live beyond their prime working years, given that most labor in ancient times demanded great physical exertion. In an age without public pensions, this meant that most elderly Romans lived in dire poverty, especially if they did not have family members to support them. For the economically better off, however, there was the opportunity for a retirement filled with leisure and contemplation.

A Closer Look

In this excerpt, Pliny is describing the activities of an elderly man enjoying his retirement. Pliny, who is clearly much younger than Spurinna, envies the latter's lifestyle as well, hoping that his elderly years would be passed in a similar fashion. He notes that the old man's retirement is marked by quiet reading, conversation, exercise, and a simple daily regimen. But in describing the man's lifestyle, he also notes his wealth—baths prepared for him and meals on dishes of "Corinthian bronze"—a fact that no doubt allowed Spurinna such a luxurious retirement, one unlikely to have been enjoyed by ordinary elderly Romans.

As evidenced by Pliny, Romans engaged in a variety of leisure activities. In addition to athletic activities and board games, the Romans enjoyed public entertainments of various sorts, including theatrical and musical performances. In the amphitheaters of major cities, they could view gladiatorial combats, staged animal hunts, and most popular of all, chariot races. Communal bathing was popular as well, and most Roman cities and towns featured public baths, where residents could go to soak, be massaged, and intermingle socially.

1 100 200 300 400 500 600 700 800 900 1000 1100 1200 1300 1400 1500 1600 1700 1800 1900 2000 CE

1.5.12 Pliny the Younger on Being Stood Up for Dinner

Roman Empire
ca. First Century CE

How happened it, my friend, that you did not keep your engagement the other night to sup with me? Now take notice, the court is sitting, and you shall fully reimburse me the expense I was at to treat you—which, let me tell you, was no small sum. I had prepared, you must know, a lettuce and three snails apiece; with two eggs, barley-water, some sweet wine and snow (the snow most certainly I shall charge to your account, and at a high rate, as 'twas spoiled in serving). Besides all these curious dishes, there were olives, beets, gourds, shallots, and a hundred other dainties equally sumptuous. You should likewise have been entertained either with an interlude, the rehearsal of a poem, or a piece of music, as you like best; or (such was my liberality) with all three. But the oysters, chitterlings, sea-urchins and Spanish dancers of a certain—I know not who, were, it seems, more to your taste. However I shall have my revenge of you depend upon it;—in what manner, shall at present be a secret. In good truth it was not kind thus to mortify your friend, I had almost said yourself;—and upon second thoughts I do say so: for how agreeably should we have spent the evening, in laughing, trifling, and instruction! You may sup, I confess, at many places more splendidly; but you can be treated no where, believe me, with more unconstrained cheerfulness, simplicity and freedom: only make the experiment; and if you do not ever afterwards prefer my table to any other, never favour me with your company again. Farewell.

Source: *Pliny Letters*. Vol. I. Translated by William Melmoth, with revisions by W. M. L. Hutchinson. Cambridge and London: Loeb Classical Library, 1915, pp. 53–55.

TIMELINE   2000 1900 1800 1700 1600 1500 1400 1300 1200 1100 1000 900 800 700 600 500 400 300 200 100 1 BCE

What You Need to Know

This note was sent by Pliny the Younger, a writer and government official of first and second CE Rome, to his friend Septicius Clarus, reprimanding him for failing to show up for a dinner Pliny had planned for him. Writing half in jest, Pliny suggests Septicius pay him back for the food and entertainment he arranged and promises to exact "revenge."

Dinner parties were one of the most popular forms of entertainment in Rome, at least among the economically well-to-do, and often involved numerous guests, although this dinner appears to have been for one friend only. As with more formal dinner parties today, Roman guests were often seated in carefully prearranged order, with higher-ranking people seated or, rather, laid closer to the host. Unlike Greek symposia, which were exclusively male affairs, the banquet, or *convivium*, was open to both sexes.

Hosted dinners featured three courses—an appetizer, main course, and dessert—although each course could feature numerous dishes, chosen not just to satiate the guests' appetites but to give them a sense of spectacle. The latter usually included the meat of exotic animals or even foods, such as pig's udders, forbidden by Rome's sumptuary laws. Feasts also featured entertainment, usually of a type appropriate for both men and women but sometimes of a lascivious nature. In his note, Pliny suggests what he proposed for the latter—a poem or a piece of music—was more high-minded than that of the dinner party Septicius chose to go to instead, which included dancing girls from Spain.

A Closer Look

Given the importance of banquets and dinner parties in Roman social life, it is not surprising that the dining room was among the more elaborate spaces in a Roman home. First, it was usually kept far from the kitchen, so as to minimize noise and fumes. Guests typically reclined rather than sat at the table. In some homes, dining rooms had built in concrete platforms, rising slightly toward the table so as to position the diner to better access the food. The typical dining room featured three broad couches, which seated three persons each, allowing for nine at table. Thus, the dining room was also known as the *triclinium*, or three-sofa room.

Dining rooms in better homes included many decorative features, including stucco reliefs, wall paintings, and mosaics, on both the floors and the walls. There might also be sculpture in the room and the furniture was typically highly decorated and made of the finest wood or even more luxurious materials, such as ivory and bronze.

1.5.13 Pliny the Younger's Tuscan Villa

Roman Empire
ca. First Century CE

The exposure of the main part of the house is full south; thus, it seems to invite the sun . . . into a wide and proportionably long portico, containing many divisions, one of which is an atrium. . . . In front of the portico is a terrace divided into a great number of geometrical figures, and bounded with a box-hedge. . . .

At the extremity of the portico stands a grand dining room, which through its folding doors looks upon one end of the terrace; while beyond there is a very extensive view over the meadows up into the country. From the windows, you see on the one hand the side of the terrace and such parts of the house which project forward; on the other, with the woods enclosing the adjacent hippodrome. Opposite almost to the center of the portico stands a suite of apartments . . . which encompasses a small court, shaded by four plane trees, in the midst of which a fountain rises, from whence the water running over the edges of a marble basin gently refreshes the surrounding plane trees and the ground underneath them. This suite contains a bedroom free from every kind of noise, and which the light itself cannot penetrate, together with my ordinary dining room that I use when I have none but close friends with me. . . .

From a wing of the portico, you enter into a very spacious chamber opposite to the grand dining room, which, from some of its windows, has a view of the terrace. . . .

From here, you pass through a spacious and pleasant dressing room into the cold-bath room, in which is a large, gloomy bath. But if you prefer to swim more at large, or in warmer water, there is a pool for that purpose in the courtyard, and near it a reservoir from which you may be supplied with cold water to brace yourself again, if you should perceive that you are too much relaxed by the warm. Contiguous to the cold bath is a lukewarm one, which enjoys the kindly warmth of the sun, but not so intensely as that of the hot bath, which projects from the house. . . .

Over the dressing room is built the ball court, which is large enough to allow several different kinds of games being played at once, each with its own circle of spectators. Not far from the baths is a staircase which leads to a gallery, and to three apartments on the way. One of these looks out upon the little court with the four plane trees around it; another has a view of the meadows; the third abuts upon the vineyard. . . . At one end of the gallery . . . is a chamber that overlooks the hippodrome . . . adjoining is a room which has a full exposure to the sun, especially in winter. . . .

I have now informed you why I prefer my Tuscan villa to those which I possess at Tusculum, Tibur, and Praeneste. Besides the advantages already mentioned, I there enjoy a securer, as it is a more profound leisure. I never need to put on full dress; nobody calls from next door on urgent business. All is calm and composed which contributes no less than its clear air and unclouded sky to the healthfulness of the spot.

Source: Pliny the Younger. *Letters*. Vol. I. Book V. Letter VI. Translated by William Melmoth, with revisions by W. M. L. Hutchinson. Loeb Classical Library. London: William Heinemann, 1915, pp. 381, 383, 385, 387, 395. Text slightly modified.

TIMELINE   2000 1900 1800 1700 1600 1500 1400 1300 1200 1100 1000 900 800 700 600 500 400 300 200 100 1 BCE

What You Need to Know

Gaius Plinius Caecilius Secundus, or Pliny the Younger, as he is better known, was a lawyer, a government official, an author, and a quite wealthy man. He wrote to his friends about his villa in the countryside of what is now Tuscany, in Italy, late in the first or early in the second century CE.

Most ancient Romans were poor, and their housing reflected this. The typical urbanite lived in a tiny apartment, often in poorly constructed masonry buildings that were prone to collapse. The apartments, or *insulae*, usually consisting of but two rooms, were largely used for sleeping. With no indoor plumbing, residents used public baths for washing up. Similarly, the hazards and noxious smoke of cooking had most poor Romans eating at street stalls and commercial establishments. In rural areas, most people inhabited small stone cottages of a couple of rooms, with water available at communal pumps and cooking done out of doors.

If one had wealth, however, living arrangements were very different. The urban rich lived in sumptuous townhouses, when they were not retreating to the countryside to expansive and well-appointed villas. The extensive size of both was made necessary by large staffs of servants and slaves who lived on the premises, usually in wings containing numerous small apartments.

A Closer Look

Pliny the Younger came from a wealthy family. His father was a Roman senator and owner of vast lands. And while Pliny the Younger was respected for living by the ancient Roman values of simplicity and moderation, he nevertheless enjoyed a life of ease, as evident in the accompanying letter.

Pliny the Younger's description of his villa almost sounds like it was written by a real estate agent, describing a high-end property today. The villa features beautiful views of the nearby countryside. There is a pool, "a ball court," or horse track, a "grand dining room" for entertaining, a master suite "free from every kind of noise," a southern exposure, lots of cross-ventilation in every room, and a "hippodrome," The latter was used to stage horse and chariot races. Pliny also praises a feature that we take for granted today but was a luxury for a Roman of his day—plentiful running water inside and out. Indeed, Pliny speaks at length of the many bathing facilities in his home, bathing being an important element of a Roman's daily life. Roman bathing practices could be quite elaborate, with bathers moving from hot to lukewarm to cold baths in various sequences that were said to promote better blood circulation and overall health. Equally revealing of Pliny's wealth is his rather casual mention that he owns three other villa in regions around Rome, although, he admits, the one in Tuscany was his favorite.

1 100 200 300 400 500 600 700 800 900 1000 1100 1200 1300 1400 1500 1600 1700 1800 1900 2000 CE

1.5.14 Seneca on the Benefits of Fasting

Rome
64 CE

I am so firmly determined to test the constancy of your mind that, drawing from the teachings of great men, I will give you also a lesson: Set aside a certain number of days, during which you will be content with the scantiest and cheapest food, with coarse and rough clothing, saying to yourself all the while: "Is this the condition that I feared?" It is precisely in times of immunity from care that the soul should toughen itself beforehand for occasions of greater stress, and it is while Fortune is kind that it should fortify itself against her violence. . . .

You need not suppose that I mean meals [of complete deprivation]. Let the dish be a real one, and the coarse cloak. Let the bread be hard and grimy. Endure all this for three or four days at a time, sometimes for more, so that it may be a test of yourself instead of a mere hobby. Then, I assure you, my dear Lucilius, you will leap for joy when filled with a penny's worth of food, and you will understand that a person's peace of mind does not depend on Fortune. For, even when angry, she grants enough for our needs.

There is no reason, however, why you should think that you are doing anything great. For you will merely be doing what many thousands of slaves and many thousands of poor men are doing every day. But you may credit yourself with this item: that you will not be doing it under compulsion, and that it will be as easy for you to endure it permanently as to make the experiment from time to time. . . .

Even Epicurus, the teacher of pleasure, used to observe stated intervals, during which he satisfied his hunger in scanty fashion. He wished to see whether he thereby fell short of full and complete happiness, and if so, by what amount he fell short. . . . Do you think that there can be fullness on such food? Yes, and there is pleasure also—not that shifty and fleeting pleasure . . . but a pleasure that is steadfast and sure. For although water, barley meal, and crusts of barley bread are not a cheerful diet, yet it is the highest kind of pleasure to be able to derive pleasure from this sort of food, and to have reduced one's needs to that modicum which no unfairness of Fortune can snatch away. Even prison food is more generous, and those who have been set apart for capital punishment are not so poorly fed by the man who is to execute them.

Therefore, what a noble soul one must have, to descend of one's own free will to a diet which even those who have been sentenced to death have not to fear! This is indeed forestalling the spear-thrusts of Fortune.

So begin, my dear Lucilius, to follow the custom of these people, and set apart certain days on which you will withdraw from your business, and make yourself at home with the scantiest food. Establish business relations with poverty.

Source: Seneca, Lucius Annaeus. *Ad Lucilium Epistulae Morales*. Vol. I. Epistle XVIII. Translated by Richard M. Gummere. Loeb Classical Library. London: William Heinemann, 1917, pp. 119, 121, 123.

TIMELINE   2000 1900 1800 1700 1600 1500 1400 1300 1200 1100 1000 900 800 700 600 500 400 300 200 100 1 BCE

What You Need to Know

In one of his epistles from the first century CE, the Roman philosopher and statesman Lucius Annaeus Seneca, better known as Seneca the Younger, outlines the practice of fasting as well as the benefits that came from it. Seneca does not advocate a total fast but one confined to the "scantiest and cheapest food . . . for three or four days at a time." This, he says, makes of the fast "a test of yourself instead of a mere hobby."

More interesting, however, are the reasons Seneca gives for practice. It is not for the health of the person's body but of his or her soul. Fasting, he says, helps one "understand that a person's peace of mind does not depend on Fortune. For even angry, she grants enough for our needs." Seneca was a follower of Stoicism, first developed by the fourth and third century BCE Greek philosopher Zeno. Stoics argued that fortune was beyond any mortal's control; thus, a wise person accepted fate as it was and found true happiness in being a virtuous person. Fasting, then, allowed the practitioner a way to understand this essential truth.

A Closer Look

As Seneca relates, Romans occasionally fasted, which sometimes meant a complete cessation of eating but usually implied a diet restricted both in terms of quantity and quality of food. However, wealthy Romans are deservedly remembered for their extravagant feasts and, among some, out-and-out gluttony.

By the time Rome reached its apogee in the first century CE, its wealthier inhabits could enjoy much that an empire spanning most of the known Western world could provide. Perhaps the most popular of indulgences was eating. The dining gallery in a noble Roman's home was among the largest and most opulently appointed, with luxurious furnishings and table settings. A large part, if not a majority, of the domestic slaves in such an abode were devoted to the preparation and serving of food, often at large banquets, which were one of the most popular forms of social interaction in Roman elite life. There, hosts and hostesses would try to outdo each other, providing dishes with the rarest of ingredients, most complicated of recipes, and most elaborate of presentations. Lying down on couches and served by teams of servants, hosts and guests alike would dine for hours at a time, indulging in the latest gossip and being entertained by singers, dancers, and other performers.

1 100 200 300 400 500 600 700 800 900 1000 1100 1200 1300 1400 1500 1600 1700 1800 1900 2000 CE

1.5.15 Great Buildings of Rome

Rome
ca. 77 CE

But it is now time to pass on to the marvels in building displayed by our own City . . . and so prove that here, as well, the rest of the world has been outdone by us. . . .

Not to mention among our great works the Circus Maximus, that was constructed by the Dictator Caesar, one stadium broad and three in length, and occupying with the adjacent buildings, no less than four jugera with room for no less than 160,000 spectators seated; am I not to include in the number of our magnificent constructions, the Basilica of Paulus, with its admirable Phrygian columns; the Forum of the late Emperor Augustus; the Temple of Peace erected by the Emperor Vespasian Augustus—some of the finest work the world has ever beheld . . . ?

We behold with admiration pyramids that were built by kings, while the very ground alone, that was purchased by the Dictator Caesar, for the construction of his Forum, cost 100,000,000 sesterces! . . .

For this purpose [the sewer system of Rome] there are seven rivers, made, by artificial channels, to flow beneath the city. Rushing onward, like so many impetuous torrents, they are compelled to carry off and sweep away all the sewerage. . . . Occasionally, too, the Tiber, overflowing, is thrown backward in its course, and discharges itself by these outlets. . . .

But let us now turn our attention to some marvels which, justly appreciated, may be truthfully pronounced to remain unsurpassed. Quintus Marcius Rex, upon, being commanded by the Senate to repair the Appian Aqueduct and those of the Anio and Tepula, constructed during his praetorship a new aqueduct which bore his name, and was brought hither by a channel pierced through the sides of mountains. . . .

The preceding aqueducts, however, have all been surpassed by the costly work which was more recently commenced by the Emperor Gaius, and completed by Claudius. Under these princes, the Curtian and the Caerulean Waters with the New Anio, were brought a distance of forty miles, and at so high a level that all the hills were supplied with water, on which the City is built. The sum expended on these works was 350,000,000 sesterces. If we only take into consideration the abundant supply of water to the public, for baths, ponds, canals, household purposes, gardens, places in the suburbs and country houses; and then reflect upon the distances that are traversed, the arches that have been constructed, the mountains that have been pierced, the valleys that have leveled, we must of necessity admit that there is nothing to be found more worthy of our admiration throughout the whole universe.

Source: Pliny the Elder. *Natural History*. Vol. VI. Book XXXVI, Ch. 24. Translated by John Bostock and Henry T. Riley. London: H. G. Bohn, 1857, pp. 345–347, 352–354.

TIMELINE   2000 1900 1800 1700 1600 1500 1400 1300 1200 1100 1000 900 800 700 600 500 400 300 200 100 1 BCE

What You Need to Know

In his *Naturalis Historia*, or Natural History, an encyclopedia published between 77 and 79 CE, Gaius Plinius Secundus or, as he is better known to modern readers, Pliny the Elder provides a description of the imperial capital of Rome.

Romans were among the ancient world's greatest urban planners and builders. Their ability to plan and construct large and elaborate buildings and urban centers was due to several factors—wealth, circumstance, and technological ingenuity. Great riches and power, achieved through imperials expansion, allowed Romans to put armies of laborers together to work on public projects. The Romans were also a heavily urbanized people, which meant that they had to come up with engineering solutions for the problems of providing adequate services for thousands of people and to fit buildings and infrastructure into confined spaces, usually by building upward and, in the case of water supply and sewage, downward as well. This spurred ingenuity, in the development of construction materials, such as hydraulic cement, which could harden in wet conditions, and construction techniques. The Romans, for example, perfected the arch, which can support loads evenly from one end to the other, allowing for greater height and the ability to enclose vast spaces without interior columns.

A Closer Look

Some of Rome's greatest architectural and urban planning accomplishments are outlined in this description of some of the great buildings of the Roman capital, offered by Pliny the Elder. In *Naturalis Historia*, Pliny reveals the enormous costs that went into building some of Rome's greatest monuments during the first century BCE and the first century CE, during a time of great imperial expansion. He notes that Augustus Caesar's upgrades to the Forum, or central plaza of the Roman capital, cost upward of 100 million sesterces. To put that into context, a typical unskilled laborer earned about six sesterce a day.

As great as such buildings as the Circus Maximus—a chariot racing stadium, which seated 160,000 spectators—were, Pliny reserves his highest accolades for Rome's civil engineering projects, such as the huge sewage and storm drainage system that he calls the "seven 'rivers.'" Equally worthy of his praise are the giants aqueducts, the newest of which, he notes, cost upward to 350 million sesterce. Not only of huge scale, these projects, he says, are perhaps even more noteworthy for their solid construction. While lesser buildings collapse, he says, these monuments of Roman engineering survive floods, fire, and earthquake. There is nothing, he argues in this panegyric, "more worthy of our admiration throughout the whole universe." For this, he praises Rome's great and farseeing emperors.

1.5.16 Bronze Extraction Forceps

Pompeii
ca. 79 CE

Credit: DEA/L. Pedicini/DeAgostini/Getty Images

What You Need to Know

Shown here is a pair bronze forceps from the first century CE. In the early years of Roman civilization, there was in fact little in the way of a medical profession. The heads of households or their wives were expected to know the basic herbal remedies and medical treatments and to apply those skills to the sick and injured. But as Rome expanded so, too, did medical knowledge and practice, particular after the conquest of Greece in the middle of the second century BCE. Many wealthy Romans imported Greek physicians into their households, typically as prisoners of war and slaves.

Rome's greatest contribution to medicine came through public health measures. The Romans were great administrators, engineers, and urban planners. They put these interrelated skills to good use in providing clean water, effective sewage, and bathing facilities in their cities. No doubt, these projects did more to save human life than the rudimentary medicine of the day, even that practiced by the renowned physicians of ancient Greece.

A Closer Look

The Greek physicians, and their Roman imitators, were adept at surgery. Based largely on anatomical research done by the Greeks, the Roman surgeons had a relatively good understanding of gross human anatomy. Common operations included the removal of hernias and tumors, trepanation (a procedure involving the drilling of holes in the skull to remove pressure and relieve headaches), and even cataract surgery. In the latter, a thin and hollow needle would pierce the surface of the eye to break up the cataract, the pieces of which would be then sucked out through the needle.

To conduct various forms of surgery, the Romans used a number of instruments. As with the techniques they employed, most of these were borrowed from earlier civilizations. Among these was extraction forceps, such as the bronze set in the accompanying image unearthed from Pompeii, the southern Italian city buried in ash from the eruption of Mount Vesuvius in 79 CE. These forceps were used for a number of procedures, such as removing foreign objects or pieces of broken bone in the flesh. The forceps were also used for tooth extraction. Of course, the Romans knew nothing of the germ theory of medicine; failing to sterilize equipment no doubt led to infections that probably did as much, if not more, harm than the surgery helped.

1 100 200 300 400 500 600 700 800 900 1000 1100 1200 1300 1400 1500 1600 1700 1800 1900 2000 CE

1.5.17 Bronze Sistrum

Pompeii
ca. 79 CE

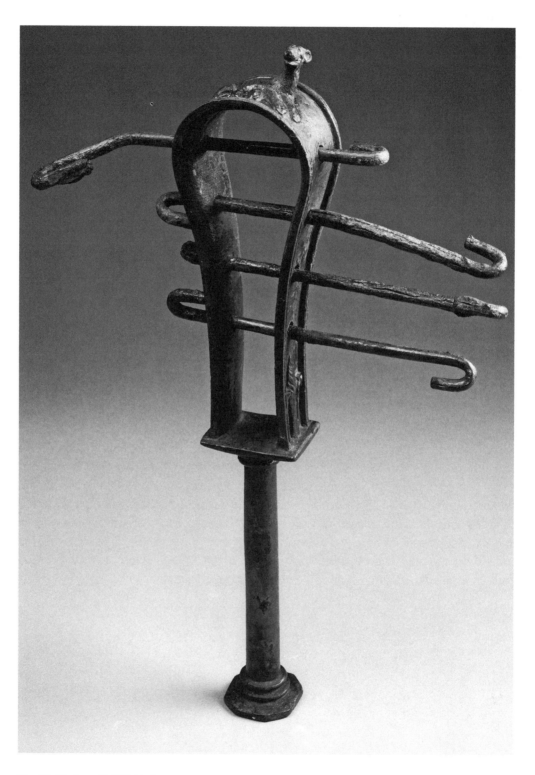

Credit: DeAgostini/Getty Images

What You Need to Know

This bronze sistrum was uncovered from the ruins of Pompeii, the famed southern Italian city destroyed by an erupting Mount Vesuvius in 79 CE.

Music was an integral part of the culture of the ancient Roman Empire, played in both ceremonial and popular settings. Music was used to help convey the souls of the dead to the underworld in funeral ceremonies. It heralded the great games of the Roman circus. It was played at important civic events, such as the triumphal parades following a conquest by the Roman legions. Music was also used in theater, particularly in a genre known as the *pantomimus*, an early form of ballet. And, of course, it was an integral part of daily life, played in taverns and squares wherever Romans came together. Music was also an important part of a cultured Roman's education, and competitions were a frequent occurrence in Roman life. What Roman music actually sounded like is impossible to determine precisely, but it is known that they used a Greek method for writing down compositions, based on a four-tone scale.

A Closer Look

Encompassing much of the Western world at its peak in the first centuries CE, the Roman Empire was a mix of cross-pollinating cultures, with Roman ideas, art forms, and artifacts traveling outward and provincial trends flowing toward the empire's Italian heartland. Among this material culture were musical instruments, which fell into four basic types: wind, string, a form of organ, and percussion.

The sistrum was in fact an Egyptian and Mesopotamian percussion instrument. It was somewhat similar to a modern tambourine in that it produced its sound by shaking, specifically by means of the tiny hoops that dangled from the crossbars. To the ancient Egyptians, it was a sacred instrument, used in religious dances and other ceremonies, but among the Romans, it lost its connection to faith.

Atop the sistrum was a bronze figurine of a mother dog nursing her pups. Dogs were common in Roman culture. They signified some of the same things and played many of the same roles as they do today. They were a symbol of loyalty and were used in hunting, herding, guarding, and warfare, as well as being, among the wealthier classes who could afford to keep them, much loved members of the household.

1 100 200 300 400 500 600 700 800 900 1000 1100 1200 1300 1400 1500 1600 1700 1800 1900 2000 CE

1.5.18 Portable Terracotta Stove

Pompeii
ca. 79 CE

Credit: DEA/A. Dagli Orti/DeAgostini/Getty Images

What You Need to Know

This terracotta stove is from Pompeii, in southern Italy, and dates to the first century CE. Such stoves could be used for both cooking and heating.

Wealthier Roman households usually had large built in ovens, necessary for cooking the large amounts of food needed to feed households that contained numerous occupants, including a large servant staff. In addition, wealthy Romans frequently entertained in their homes, which usually involved multicourse meals. The portability of the stove would have come in handy, as Romans, particularly in small towns and the countryside, tended to cook outdoors in courtyards, when weather permitted, and indoors when it did not. In the big cities, courtyards were rarer, so people usually cooked in their living quarters on small braziers.

Whether in wealthy or more modest households, kitchens tended to be small, hidden, and kept away from living and entertaining areas. This was done for reasons of fire safety, heat—the Mediterranean heartland of the empire was usually quite hot in summers—and odors.

A Closer Look

Like us, Romans typically consumed three meals a day, although, among the rich, these could be quite extended affairs. The three included a breakfast or *jentaculum*, served at dawn; a small lunch eaten in late morning; and the *cena*, the main meal of the day served in the early to late evening.

Wealthy Romans did not, of course, cook for themselves but had slaves or servants do it for them. The poor, on the other hand, had to cook for themselves, although in urban areas, many got their food from what we today would call takeout restaurants or street food stalls. Bread, the staple for most Romans, was typically baked in public kitchens, often provided free or at subsidized prices by the state. Other foods, such as fish and meat, were cooked on small open braziers, made of metal, or small ovens made of terracotta, a fired clay material that could be glazed or not. The stove shown here, from first century CE Pompeii, is portable. Romans typically prepared and cooked their food in outdoor courtyards, when weather permitted, which was often the case in the Mediterranean climate they enjoyed, and indoors when it did not, hence the need for portable stoves.

1 100 200 300   400   500   600   700   800   900   1000 1100 1200 1300   1400   1500   1600   1700 1800 1900 2000 CE

185

1.5.19 Scale for Bronze Coins

Pompeii
ca. 79 CE

Credit: DeAgostini/Getty Images

What You Need to Know

This scale from first-century Pompeii, which was used to weigh bronze coins, was buried in the lava that destroyed the southern Italian city in 79 CE.

At its height under the Emperor Augustus Caesar and his successors, the Roman Empire covered a vast expanse, from Mesopotamia to Britain, and from North Africa to the Black Sea. Although it was the Roman legions that initially conquered these realms, Roman traders helped maintain the bonds of empire among diverse peoples. Once-isolated economies were woven into a vast imperial one. Grain came from as far away as Egypt and Gaul (modern-day France); Britain grew and spun wool; olive oil and wine were produced around much of the Mediterranean basin. Roman coins were used across the empire as currency for many of these transactions.

And wherever towns and cities emerged, so did industry. In the first century of the Roman Empire, the Italian heartland was the source of most of the manufactured goods. But by the second century CE, the cities of Italy were in decline, industrially speaking, eclipsed by more efficient and productive enterprises in the provinces of northwest Europe. Gaul, Britain, and Germany all became centers of pottery production and glassmaking, producing for their own markets and those of the Mediterranean region as well.

A Closer Look

To facilitate trade across the empire, the Roman Empire both minted money and enforced monetary laws to prevent the debasement of currency. The Romans used three types of metals for coins—gold, silver, and bronze. Gold coins, being rare and precious, were not generally used for daily transactions. Also, in the early centuries of the empire, gold coins, as well as silver ones, could only be produced by the central Roman authorities, which enhanced their value beyond the intrinsic worth of the precious metals they contained. The origin of bronze coins, which being of lesser value were the most frequently used; these could be minted by both local and central authorities.

The scale shown here used the coin on the right, embossed with the profile of the emperor, as a counterweight to measure bronze coins, which would have been placed in the dish on the left. The weight of coins was important because "shaving" was a common practice in Roman times. People devalued coins by slicing away at the edges for the precious metals they contained. By having a fixed coin of predetermined weight at one end of the scale, the person assessing the value of the coins could be assured that they had not been shaved.

1 100 200 300   400   500   600   700   800   900   1000 1100 1200 1300   1400   1500   1600   1700 1800 1900 2000 CE

1.5.20 Roman Terracotta Oil Lamp

Pompeii
ca. 79 CE

Credit: DeAgostini/Getty Images

What You Need to Know

This terracotta oil lamp was unearthed at Pompeii, a small Roman city buried by the eruption of nearby Mount Vesuvius in 79 CE.

Oil lamps were the primary source of illumination in ancient Roman times, as evidenced by the sheer volume of them found in ruins across the length of what was once the empire. They were used in households, workshops, stores, and virtually every other indoor space. They were also used extensively at public events as well, including religious festival. Placed into sconces on walls and above doorways, they provided illumination along well-traveled streets.

Besides providing illumination, lamps served ritualistic purposes. They were often used in temples, where priests lit them as offerings to the gods. They have been found in numerous Roman tombs. They were placed there not only as part of a collection of items from deceased's property but as a way to illuminate his or her path to the underworld.

A Closer Look

This type of lamp, made of commonplace terracotta, was manufactured in large quantities from a common mold made from gypsum or other malleable materials. The lamps were made in two halves and then fitted together, before being fired in an oven and given a glaze. Mass-produced, terracotta lamps were inexpensive and so could be destined for a poor person's home or in the service rooms of a rich person's dwelling. Costlier lamps were usually made of various forms of metal and would feature far more intricate and elaborate decoration.

The lamp pictured here featured just one wick hole, for a single flame, (the larger hole at the bottom was for pouring the oil in), thereby saving on oil—which was usually made from olives or other vegetable matter—but providing less light.

The image on the bowl of the lamp depicts two winged figures holding a wreath. Both the wreath and the palm fronds beneath were Roman symbols of victory in war. Lamps frequently included decorations depicting commemorations, religious symbolism, scenes from everyday life, or simply abstract decoration.

1 100 200 300 400 500 600 700 800 900 1000 1100 1200 1300 1400 1500 1600 1700 1800 1900 2000 CE

1.5.21 Quintilian's Prescription for Educating a Child

Rome
ca. 95 CE

There is one point which I must emphasize before I begin, which is this. Without natural gifts, technical rules are useless. Consequently, the student who is devoid of talent will derive no more profit from this work than barren soil from a treatise on agriculture. There are, it is true, other natural aids, such as the possession of a good voice and robust lungs, sound health, powers of endurance and grace, and if these are possessed only to a moderate extent, they may be improved by methodical training. . . .

I would, therefore, have a father conceive the highest hopes of his son from the moment of his birth. If he does so, he will be more careful about the groundwork of his education. For there is absolutely no foundation for the complaint that but few men have the power to take in the knowledge that is imparted to them, and that the majority are so slow of understanding that education is a waste of time and labor. On the contrary, you will find that most are quick to reason and ready to learn. Reasoning comes as naturally to human beings as flying to birds, speed to horses and ferocity to beasts of prey; our minds are endowed by nature with such activity and sagacity that the soul is believed to proceed from heaven. . . .

Above all, see that the child's nurse speaks correctly. The ideal . . . would be that she should be a philosopher. Failing that . . . the best should be chosen, as far as possible. No doubt the most important point is that they should be of good character, but they should speak correctly as well. It is the nurse that the child first hears, and her words that he will first attempt to imitate. . . .

As regards parents, I should like to see them as highly educated as possible, and I do not restrict this remark to fathers alone. We are told that the eloquence of the Gracchi owed much to their mother Cornelia, whose letters even today testify to the cultivation of her style. . . .

If any of my readers regards me as somewhat exacting in my demands, I would ask that reader to reflect that it is no easy task to create an orator, even though his education be carried out under the most favorable circumstances, and that further and greater difficulties are still before us. For continuous application, the very best of teachers, and a variety of experiences are necessary. Therefore, the rules which we lay down for the education of our pupil must be of the best.

Source: Quintilian. *The Institutio Oratoria of Quintilian*. Book I. Vol. I. Translated by H. E. Butler. Loeb Classical Library. London: William Heinemann, 1920, pp. 19, 21, 23, 25.

TIMELINE   2000 1900 1800 1700 1600 1500 1400 1300 1200 1100 1000 900 800 700 600 500 400 300 200 100 1 BCE

What You Need to Know

The excerpt is from the *Institutes of Oratory*, which as its name implies was a primer for the teaching of oration, a highly prized skill among ancient Romans, who viewed great practitioners of the art as among the noblest of men. The author was educator and philosopher Quintillian, who lived from 35 to 100 CE.

The underlying philosophy behind Quintillian's writings, as he notes in the beginning of his excerpt, is that most children are capable of learning quickly and well, although he does note that some are better equipped physically—"robust lungs, sound health, powers of endurance and grace"—for the demands of oratory in an age before artificial amplification of sound.

But if preparation for oration places a burden on the child, it requires an extra effort of the father, who is expected to spend much time and effort on his son's training. Quintillian also notes that fathers alone are not responsible for the raising of an educated child. As head of the household, the father should make sure that his youngest children are placed in the care of a nurse who "speaks correctly." He also says that mothers have an important role as well, noting that two of Rome's greatest statesmen, the brothers Tiberius and Gaius Gracchi, owed much of their oratorical skill to their mother.

A Closer Look

Most Roman children were educated in the home, although there were schools of various sorts in urban centers. Until the age of about six or seven, the main influence came from the mother, who taught both sons and daughters to speak proper Latin and to respect Roman customs and traditions—moral rectitude, respect for their elders, reverence for the gods, and devotion to the state.

After that early period, sons and daughters went in two different directions. The latter remained under the tutelage of the mother, who trained them in domestic duties such as sewing, weaving, and spinning. In wealthier households, cleaning and food preparation were the tasks of servants and slaves. Most daughters were not educated academically, some not even to read and write.

Sons, meanwhile, were turned over to their fathers, who educated them in their letters, history, philosophy, and other arts and sciences, as well in physical activities, usually with a martial bent. Fathers also educated their sons to their duties as future fathers, heads of households, and citizens.

1 100 200 300   400   500   600   700   800   900   1000 1100 1200 1300   1400   1500   1600   1700 1800 1900 2000 CE

1.5.22 Roman Ivory Dice

Volubilis, Morocco
First–Third Centuries CE

Credit: DEA/G. Dagli Orti/DeAgostini/Getty Images

What You Need to Know

The ivory *tesserae*, or gaming pieces, pictured here were made in the first to third centuries CE and originating in the Roman city of Volubilis in modern-day Morocco.

Romans had mixed attitudes about gambling. On one hand, Roman law very much frowned on the activity. Indeed, there were a series of laws passed to prevent all forms of gambling, other than betting on officially sanctioned contests of the Roman circus, including chariot races and gladiatorial combat. Penalties could also be quite stiff, including significant fines, the amount frequently matching how much had been bet and even prison time. The law also did not recognize gambling winnings or losses in the laws concerning property and debt.

But as is often the case in history, we do not know whether the law reflected the popular will or was written by authorities to try and control something that was widespread. Much of the evidence we have points to the latter. Archaeologists have found dice among the artifacts in countless digs. They have even found evidence of casinos or, at least, storefronts devoted to gambling.

A Closer Look

Dice games were popular among Romans, who used two types of dice. These were the *tali*, which had four marked faces (1, 3, 4, and 6), plus two sides, one concave and one convex with a hole through the middle, and the *tesserae*, which like our own had six marked sides. Also like today, Romans tended to play gambling games that featured more than one die, often tossed from a cup by a croupier. When dice were not available, marked stones, sticks, or animal bones might be used in games of chance.

Dice games were played in any number of settings, including not just gambling houses but brothels as well. Under Roman law, using dice to gamble for money was illegal, which led those who sponsored games to offer winnings in chips, or *roundels* as they were called, which could then be converted to money. Whether government officials were bothered by the fact that roundels had specific amounts on them is unclear. In fact, money itself could be used for gambling as Romans had a number of games of chance based on the flipping or tossing of coins.

1 100 200 300   400   500   600   700   800   900   1000 1100 1200 1300   1400   1500   1600   1700 1800 1900 2000 CE

1.5.23 Roman Ivory Toiletries

Volubilis, Morocco
First–Third Centuries CE

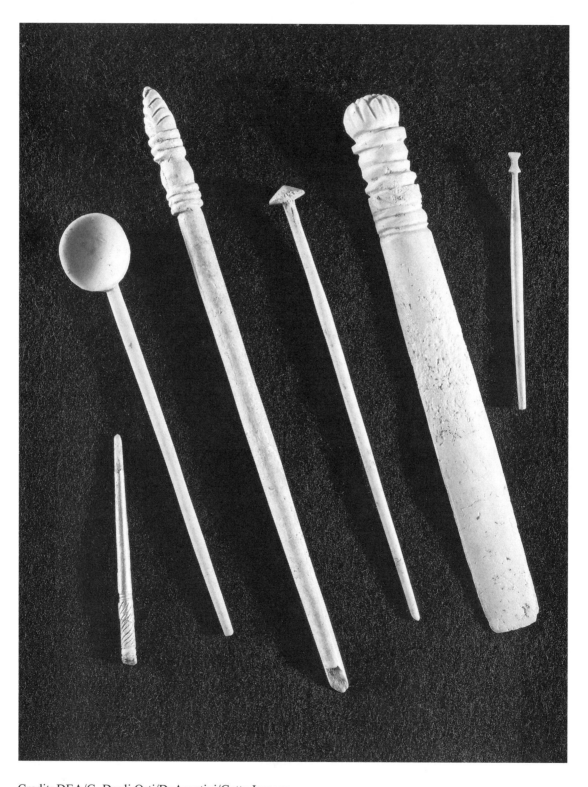

Credit: DEA/G. Dagli Orti/DeAgostini/Getty Images

What You Need to Know

This set of ivory toiletries from Volubilis, in what is now Morocco, date from between the first and third century CE, at the height of the Roman Empire's power and reach.

As the numerous ruins of public and private baths reveal to us, Romans valued personal hygiene and grooming. But while Romans took great care of their personal appearance, Roman culture—with its roots in the virtues and martial values of the civilization's republican era—frowned on both putting too much emphasis on how one appeared or on using extravagant means to improve how one looked.

But, of course, what the culture frowned up and what people indulged in were two different matters. During the republican era before the first century CE, officials of the government attempted to impose restrictions on personal adornment, either through outright prohibition or taxation. But as the empire became increasingly rich and powerful, cultural and legal restraints fell to the wayside. Extensive trading networks, some stretching all the way to China, brought in materials for the manufacture of luxurious personal grooming tools and compounds for making cosmetics.

A Closer Look

In this photo we see a number of cosmetic tools and accessories, including hair pins and a spoon-like palette for holding cosmetics while they were being applied. The objects are all made of ivory, a rare and expensive substance that had to be imported from across the Sahara. Hence, these objects were most likely in the inventory of a wealthy household.

Cosmetics were widely used among all classes and both sexes. Made of compounds from distant lands, these could be quite expensive, although poorer Romans made do with locally derived materials.

Roman women often wore their hair long—it was considered then, as now, to be a sign of a woman's fertility and sexuality; the men tended to prize short hair and clean-shaven faces, although fashions changed. For example, when the bearded Hadrian came to power in 117 CE, a more hirsute look became popular. Simpler hairstyles of the republican and early imperial periods gave way by the late first and early second century to extravagant braided coils piled high atop the head. Such complicated hairdos required lengthy sessions beneath the hands of an expert servant. In a hurry, a Roman matron might don a prestyled wig. Blonde hair from Germany and black hair from Asia were particularly prized.

1 100 200 300   400   500   600   700   800   900   1000 1100 1200 1300   1400   1500   1600   1700 1800 1900 2000 CE

1.5.24 Tasks of the Priests of Jupiter

Rome
Second Century CE

Ceremonies in great number are imposed upon the priest of Jupiter and also many abstentions of which we read in the books written On Public Priests. . . . Of these, the following are in general what I remember:

It is unlawful for the priest of Jupiter to ride upon a horse. It is also unlawful for him to see the classes arrayed outside the religious boundaries of the city, that is, the army in battle array. Hence the priest of Jupiter is rarely made consul, since wars were entrusted to the consuls. Also, it is always unlawful for the priest to take an oath, and likewise to wear a ring, unless it be perforated and without a gem. It is against the law for fire to be taken from the *flaminia*, that is, from the home of the *flamen Dialis* [priest of Jupiter], except for a sacred rite. If a person in chains enters his house, he must be freed, the bonds must be drawn up through a skylight in the ceiling to the roof and from there let down into the street. He has no knot in his head-dress, girdle, or any other part of his clothing. If anyone is being taken to be flogged, and falls at his feet as a suppliant, it is unlawful for the man to be flogged on that day. Only a free man may cut the hair of the priest. It is not customary for the priest to touch, or even name, a she-goat, raw flesh, ivy, and beans.

The priest of Jupiter must not pass under an arbor of vines. The feet of the couch on which he sleeps must be smeared with a thin coating of clay, and he must not sleep away from this bed for three nights in succession, and no other person must sleep in that bed. At the foot of his bed, there should be a box with sacrificial cakes. The cuttings of the nails and hair of the priest must be buried in the earth under a fruitful tree. Every day is a holy day for the priest. He must not be in the open air without his cap; that he may go without it in the house only recently has been decided by the pontiffs [the highest-ranking priests] . . . and it is said that some other ceremonies have been remitted, and he has been excused from observing them.

The priest of Jupiter must not touch any bread fermented with yeast. He does not remove his inner tunic except under cover, in order that he may not be naked in the open air, as it were under the eye of Jupiter. No other person has a place at the table above the priest of Jupiter, except for the priest who presides over sacrifices. If the priest has lost his wife, he abdicates his office. The marriage of the priest cannot be dissolved except by death. He never enters a place of burial, he never touches a dead body, but he is not forbidden to attend a funeral.

The ceremonies of the priestess of Jupiter are about the same. They say that she observes other separate ones. For example, she wears a dyed robe, that she has a twig from a fruitful tree in her head-dress, that it is forbidden for her to go up more than three rounds of a ladder. Also, when she goes to a chapel, that she neither combs her head nor dresses her hair.

Source: Gellius, Aulus. *The Attic Nights of Aulus Gellius*. Vol. II. Book X. Translated by John C. Rolfe. Loeb Classical Library. Cambridge, MA: Harvard University Press, 1927, pp. 249, 251, 253.

TIMELINE   2000 1900 1800 1700 1600 1500 1400 1300 1200 1100 1000 900 800 700 600 500 400 300 200 100 1 BCE

What You Need to Know

The accompanying excerpt is from Attic Nights, a kind of almanac penned by the Roman author Aulus Gellius sometime in the middle of the second century CE. In it, the writer describes the duties and rituals of the priests and priestesses of Jupiter, the king of the gods and the chief deity of the Roman public religion pantheon.

The English word "religion" is derived from the Latin *religio*, meaning "something that ties things together." And, in fact, in ancient Rome, religion tied people together—family members, subjects and state, humanity and the gods. Roman worship in pagan times involved a kind of covenant between worshippers and their deities. Unlike these other faiths, however, the covenant was not based on moral behavior in exchange for God's grant of salvation. Instead, the Romans believed that if practitioners or, in the case of more public worship, the state followed the laws of religious observance, they or it would win the favor of the gods.

A Closer Look

Roman religion also operated in two realms—personal and public. In the former, heads of households officiated in rituals invoking the protection of spirits. Such invocation ceremonies, usually performed in the presence of a household altar holding small statues of guardian spirits, were the most common form of worship. The point of the worship was to gain the favor of the gods and therefore good fortune in the lives of practitioners.

Public worship was a more elaborate affair. Conducted in large and elaborate temples, it was dedicated to invoking the favor of the major gods, such as Jupiter, Poseidon, and Mars, in state affairs. Maintaining the temples and officiating at the public ceremonies were groups of priests, whose spiritual task was to mediate between the Roman state and the gods.

Many of the duties described by Gellius involve prescriptions and proscription about how to dress, what to eat, what actions can be taken, and how to behave. In other words, the priests and priestesses had to obey these rules and thereby remain in the good graces of Jupiter, thereby assuring the emperor that these religious officials could invoke the favor of the gods. Some of the rules seem rather arbitrary to the modern reader, for example, the requirement that a priest not pass under an arbor of vines. But then, the gods of ancient Rome could be capricious, a reflection of existence itself. Collectively, the rules were intended to maintain an aura of mystery and spirituality around the priests and priestesses.

1 100 200 300 400 500 600 700 800 900 1000 1100 1200 1300 1400 1500 1600 1700 1800 1900 2000 CE

1.5.25 Juvenal's View on Urban Life in Rome

Rome
ca. 100 CE

But here we inhabit a city supported for the most part by slender props: for that is how the bailiff patches up the cracks in the old wall, bidding the inmates sleep at ease under a roof ready to tumble about their ears. No, no, I must live where there are no fires, no nightly alarms. . . . If you can tear yourself away from the games of the Circus, you can buy an excellent house at Sora, at Fabrateria, or Fursino, for what you pay now in Rome to rent a dark garret for one year.

Most sick people here in Rome perish for want of sleep, the illness itself having been produced by food lying undigested on a fevered stomach. For what sleep is possible in a lodging? Who but the wealthy get sleep in Rome? There lies the root of the disorder. The crossing of wagons in the narrow winding streets, the slanging of drovers when brought to a stand, would make sleep impossible for a Drusus—or a sea-calf. When the rich man has a call of social duty, the mob makes way for him as he is borne swiftly over their heads in a huge Liburnian car. He writes or reads or sleeps inside as he goes along, for the closed window of the litter induces slumber. Yet he will arrive before us; hurry as we may, we are blocked by a surging crowd in front, and by a dense mass of people pressing in on us from behind: one man digs an elbow into me, another a hard sedan-pole; one bangs a beam, another a wine-cask, against my head. My legs are plastered with mud; soon huge feet trample on me from every side, and a soldier plants his hobnails firmly on my toe.

See now the smoke rising from that crowd which hurries as if to a dole: there are a hundred guests, each followed by a cook of his own. Corbulo himself could scarce bear the weight of all the big vessels and other gear which that poor little slave is carrying with head erect, fanning the flame as he runs along. Newly-patched tunics are torn in two; up comes a huge fir-log swaying on a wagon, and then a second dray carrying a whole pine-tree; they tower aloft and threaten the people. For if that axle with its load of Ligurian marble breaks down, and pours an overturned mountain on to the crowd, what is left of their bodies? Who can identify the limbs, who the bones? 'The poor man's crushed corpse wholly disappears, just like his soul. At home meanwhile the folk, unwitting, are washing the dishes, blowing up the fire with distended cheek, clattering over the greasy flesh-scrapers, filling the oil-flasks and laying out the towels. And while each of them is thus busy over his own task, their master is already sitting, a new arrival, upon the bank, and shuddering at the grim ferryman: he has no copper in his mouth to tender for his fare, and no hope of a passage over the murky flood, poor wretch.

And now regard the different and diverse perils of the night. See what a height it is to that towering roof from which a potsherd comes crack upon my head every time that some broken or leaky vessel is pitched out of the window! See with what a smash it strikes and dints the pavement! There's death in every open window as you pass along at night; you may well be deemed a fool, improvident of sudden accident, if you go out to dinner without having made your will. You can but hope, and put up a piteous prayer in your heart, that they may be content to pour down on you the contents of their slop-basins!

Source: Juvenal. Excerpt from the *Third Satire*. In *Juvenal and Persius*. Translated by G. G. Ramsay. Loeb Classical Library. London: William Heinemann, 1918 (reprint 1928), pp. 47–55.

TIMELINE   2000 1900 1800 1700 1600 1500 1400 1300 1200 1100 1000 900 800 700 600 500 400 300 200 100 1 BCE

What You Need to Know

This satirical description of life in Rome, penned around 100 CE, is from the poet Juvenal's *Satires*.

The city of Rome was a wonder of the ancient Western world. Roman myth has it that the city was founded in the eighth century BCE by the orphan twin brothers Romulus and Remus, sons of the war god Mars, who told them to found the city on the spot where they had been suckled by she-wolves. In fact, human habitation on and around the famed Seven Hills of Rome along the lower Tiber River in central Italy dates back to prehistoric times.

At the height of its imperial reach in the first and second century CE, the city of Rome had grown to be a behemoth, at least by ancient standards. With roughly 500,000 to 750,000, it was the largest city of its time. The Romans were the ancient world's greatest civil engineers, and their talents were well on display in their capital city, with its magnificent palaces, temples, and public baths. Most impressive of all were the aqueducts. No less than 10 served the city, bringing in fresh water from as far as 90 miles away.

A Closer Look

A modern-day visitor, too, can see the engineering and architectural wonders of ancient Rome— the Pantheon, the Forum, and the Coliseum. Built with stone, and once clad in marble, they met the highest construction standards of the day and have weathered the centuries enviably. Walking in their midst, the tourist can imagine the triumphal marches and great ceremonies they hosted. But this was not the Rome of everyday life.

As this excerpt from Juvenal's *Satires* reveals, ancient Rome had all of the problems modern urban centers face: crowded housing, fire, noise pollution, street crime, and frustrating and even life-threatening traffic. Indeed, Juvenal recommends living elsewhere, noting that for the rent of a single dark and squalid room in Rome, a person could buy a "fine house at Sora, at Fabrateria, or Fursino," all suburbs of the city.

Juvenal, of course, was writing a satire, and thus exaggerating the miseries of city life. He was trying to put forth an image popular among Romans of his day contrasting the corruption of city life with the simpler ways of an older rural life. While the specifics of his biography have been lost to history, his detailed description of Roman city life seems to indicate that he spent much time there. Perhaps this was because, as he lectured his readers, he could not live without the chariot races in the circus and the other pleasures city life provided.

1 100 200 300 400 500 600 700 800 900 1000 1100 1200 1300 1400 1500 1600 1700 1800 1900 2000 CE

1.5.26 Poverty in the Roman Capital City

Rome
ca. 100–110 CE

"And what of this, that the poor man gives food and occasion for jest if his cloak be torn and dirty; if his toga be a little soiled; if one of his shoes gapes where the leather is split, or if some fresh stitches of coarse thread reveal where not one, but many a rent has been patched? Of all the woes of luckless poverty none is harder to endure than this, that it exposes men to ridicule. 'Out you go! for very shame,' says the marshal; 'out of the Knights' stalls, all of you whose means do not satisfy the law.' Here let the sons of panders, born in any brothel, take their seats; here let the spruce son of an auctioneer clap his hands, with the smart sons of a gladiator on one side of him and the young gentlemen of a trainer on the other: such was the will of the numskull Otho who assigned to each of us his place (the law of Otho, B.C. 67, reserved the first fourteen rows in the theatre behind the *orchestra* where senators sat for knights. Knights [Latin, *equites*] were the wealthy "middle class"). Who ever was approved as a son-in-law if he was short of cash, and no match for the money-bags of the young lady? What poor man ever gets a legacy, or is appointed assessor to an *aedile* (public officials who among other duties were responsible for public buildings and the games)? Romans without money should have marched out in a body long ago!

"It is no easy matter, anywhere, for a man to rise when poverty stands in the way of his merits: but nowhere is the effort harder than in Rome, where you must pay a big rent for a wretched lodging, a big sum to fill the bellies of your slaves, and buy a frugal dinner for yourself. You are ashamed to dine off cheap pottery; but you would see no shame in it if transported suddenly to a Marsian or Sabine table, where you would be pleased enough to wear a cape of coarse Venetian blue.

"There are many parts of Italy, to tell the truth, in which no man puts on a toga until he is dead. Even on days of festival, when a brave show is made in a theatre of turf, and when the well-known afterpiece steps once more upon the boards; when the rustic babe on its mother's breast shrinks back affrighted at the gaping of the pallid masks, you will see stalls and populace all dressed alike, and the worshipful *aediles* content with white tunics as vesture for their high office. In Rome, every one dresses smartly, above his means, and sometimes something more than what is enough is taken out of another man's pocket. This failing is universal here: we all live in a state of pretentious poverty. To put it shortly, nothing can be had in Rome for nothing. How much does it cost you to be able now and then to make your bow to Cossus? Or to be vouchsafed one glance, with lip firmly closed, from Veiento? One of these great men is cutting off his beard; another is dedicating the locks of a favorite; the house is full of cakes—which you will have to pay for. Take your cake, and let this thought rankle in your heart: we clients are compelled to pay tribute and add to a sleek menial's perquisites."

Source: Juvenal. Excerpt from the *Third Satire*. In *Juvenal and Persius*. Translated by G. G. Ramsay. Loeb Classical Library. London: William Heinemann, 1918 (reprint 1928), pp. 43, 45, 47.

TIMELINE   2000 1900 1800 1700 1600 1500 1400 1300 1200 1100 1000 900 800 700 600 500 400 300 200 100 1 BCE

What You Need to Know

This passage is from the *Third Satire* of Juvenal, a poet and writer who penned this piece probably in the first decade of the second century CE. In it, Juvenal, who often wrote in an absurdist vein and thus should not be taken literally, assumes the voice of a friend named Umbricius, a once well off Roman now down on his luck.

For all of its power and glory, the Roman Empire, even at its height in the first and second centuries CE, did not have a particularly productive economy. The vast majority of people lived on the land, producing food for themselves and not much more. Industry was based on simple techniques, and output was low. The empire's commercial economy depended heavily on the labor of slaves, which, in Roman times as in more modern era, was far less efficient that free labor. Thus, with little in the way of productivity, the Roman Empire was rife with poverty. Moreover, income inequality was extremely high in ancient Rome, meaning that those on the lowest rungs of the economy were very impoverished indeed.

A Closer Look

In this passage from *Third Satire*, Umbricius discusses many of the ills of Rome, including its noise, corruption, crime, pollution, and miserable housing. Here, he discusses the poverty that is rife in the capital city of the Roman Empire. Rather than discussing economic want, however, he focuses on the indignities and injustices of poverty, how "it exposes men to ridicule."

Rome was divided into legally recognized classes of people. There were the nobility, or patricians, and the plebeians, or commoners; there were citizens and noncitizens; and, of course, there were free people and slaves. Overlapping all of this was the status that wealth or poverty brought. Successful traders or businesspeople, no matter what class they had originated in, even the slave class, could buy the symbols of status that were so much a part of Roman life. They could enjoy the same pursuits and live in the same posh neighborhoods as the nobles, even if they were not fully accepted as one of their own. At the same time, as Juvenal makes clear with the case of his friend, a high-ranking Roman could fall very far indeed, should economic fortune befall him. Moreover, he notes that while social mobility might exist, those born poor are most likely to remain poor. "What poor man ever gets a legacy, or is appointed" to a lucrative public office, he asks his readers rhetorically?

1.5.27 Pliny the Younger and Trajan Discuss How to Punish Christians

Bithynia, Anatolia
ca. 112 CE

I have never been present at an examination of Christians. Consequently, I do not know the nature or the extent of the punishments usually meted out to them, nor the grounds for starting an investigation and how far it should be pressed. Nor am I at all sure whether any distinction should be made between them on the grounds of age, or if young people and adults should be treated alike; whether a pardon ought to be granted to anyone retracting his beliefs, or if he has once professed Christianity, he will gain nothing by renouncing it, and whether it is the mere name of Christian which is punishable, even if innocent of crime, or rather the crimes associated with the name.

For the moment, this is the course of action I have taken with all persons brought before me on the charge of being Christians. I have asked them in person if they are Christians, and if they admit it, I repeat the question a second and third time, with a warning of the punishment awaiting them. If they persist, I order them to be led away for execution; for, whatever the nature of their admission, I am convinced that their stubbornness and unshakeable obstinacy ought not to go unpunished. . . .

Now that I have begun to deal with this problem, as so often happens, the charges are becoming more widespread and increasing in variety. An anonymous pamphlet has been circulated which contains the names of a number of accused persons. Among these I considered that I should dismiss any who denied that they were or ever had been Christians when they had repeated after me a formula of invocation to the gods and had made offerings of wine and incense to your statue, which I had ordered to be brought into court for this purpose along with the images of the gods, and furthermore had reviled the name of Christ. None of these things, I understand, can any genuine Christian be induced to do.

Others, whose names were given to me by an informer, first admitted the charge and then denied it. They said that they had ceased to be Christians two or more years previously, and some of them even 20 years ago. They all did reverence to your statue and the images of the gods in the same way as the others, and reviled the name of Christ. They also declared that the sum total of their guilt or error amounted to no more than this: they had met regularly before dawn on a fixed day to chant verses alternately among themselves in honor of Christ as if to a god, and also to bind themselves by oath, not for any criminal purpose, but to abstain from theft, robbery and adultery, to commit no breach of trust and not to deny a deposit when called upon to restore it. . . .

Trajan's reply:

You have followed the right course of procedure, my friend, in your examination of the cases of persons charged with being Christians, for it is impossible to lay down a general rule to a fixed formula. These people must not be hunted out; if they are brought before you and the charge against them is proved, they must be punished, but in the case of anyone who denies that he is a Christian, and makes it clear that he is not, by offering prayers to our gods, he is to be pardoned as a result of his repentance, however suspect his past conduct may be.

Source: Pliny the Younger. *Letters and Panegyricus.* Vol. II. Translated by Betty Radice. Cambridge and London: Loeb Classical Library, 1915.

What You Need to Know

This exchange of letters between Pliny the Younger to the emperor Trajan was written in 112 CE. At the time, Pliny was the governor of the Roman province of Bithynia et Pontus, a region on the Black Sea Coast of what is now Turkey. In his letter, Pliny asks for guidance on how to deal with Christians.

There was a degree of hostility toward Christians in the second century CE Rome. Many ordinary citizens of Rome, who held to their pagan beliefs as intensely as Christians did theirs, felt that Christian denial and denunciation of the pagan gods would cause the latter to turn against Rome, bringing on great misfortune. Thus, like the authors of the pamphlet Pliny mentions, they asked the authorities to take appropriate measures. In response, many Christians kept their faith a secret, conducting their rituals out of the public eye. This led to misunderstandings. Some pagans, for example, felt that the communion ritual, in which Christians ate and drank the body of Christ, was an act of cannibalism.

A Closer Look

In the first missive, Pliny the Younger says he is receiving numerous anonymous accusations about people practicing Christianity. He tells the emperor that if the accused deny the charges or indicate that they no longer practice the faith, and then swear fealty to the gods of Rome, he will not punish them. In response, Trajan not only says Pliny's lenient approach is the proper one but that the governor should not activity seek out Christians for punishment.

Although Trajan took a relatively relaxed attitude toward Christianity—indeed, Trajan is considered by historians to be one of Rome's greatest emperors, a reputation resting in part on his tolerance toward the diverse religious practices of his realm—the new faith challenged the political and religious order of the empire. As Pliny notes, no true Christian could ever accept Roman gods. This was a problem for Rome, as the authority of the emperor and, indeed, of the government itself, was based on the idea that it was sanctioned by the gods. From the perspective of those in power, to reject the Roman pantheon was to reject the existing political order, unaware that Jesus himself had told his followers to accept the power of Caesar in earthly matters.

1.5.28 Roman Gladiator Mosaic

Gallia Belgica (Germany)
Third Century CE

Credit: Ann Ronan Pictures/Print Collector/Getty Images

What You Need to Know

This third-century CE mosaic is from the Roman province of Gallia Belgica, in what is now Belgium, northern France, and western Germany. It depicts two gladiators fighting.

Provincial Roman towns and cities were an integral part of the empire. They were centers for trade, culture, and industry; they also served as military garrisons and the political administrative centers for surrounding rural areas. As such, the authorities in Rome did everything they could to secure social peace in their urban centers. The government used two means to keep the peace so as to preempt the use of force. The first was to provide "bread," shorthand for basic staples, which might include oil and wine, as well as grain. The second was the "circus," another shorthand, this time for public entertainment. This might include both theater and what today would be deemed spectator sports, most especially horse and chariot racing, as well as gladiatorial combat.

A Closer Look

Gladiatorial combat was an integral part of Roman culture and was staged not just in Rome and the Italian heartland of the empire but also in the empire's far reaches, as attested by this mosaic from the city of Saarbrucken, then a garrison town, administrative center, and trading port on the River Rhine, on the border with the barbarian-controlled lands of what is now Germany. The image shows two contestants fighting; in the middle stands a robed referee, known as a *rudis*, for the short staff, or *rudis*, he carried. The rudis was used to caution or separate contestants.

Although known in many cultures, gladiatorial combat was adopted from early Roman's Etruscan neighbors, who staged contests as part of their funeral for noble persons. For the Etruscans, they were a kind of blood sacrifice for the dead. The Romans transformed gladiatorial contests into civic and popular events. Various classes of people served as gladiators. Common criminals were often thrown into the arena, without weapons, to be brutally slaughtered. Some were prisoners of war or slaves who were armed and fought until they or their opponents were killed. A few were even women. Most fought because they had little choice, but there were free-men who entered the arena for money, fame, or simply an adrenalin rush. Although a few Roman citizens protested the brutality of this form of entertainment, most enjoyed the contests, as the sheer size of the arenas where they were held around the empire indicates.

1 100 200 300   400   500   600   700   800   900   1000 1100 1200 1300   1400   1500   1600   1700 1800 1900 2000 CE

1.5.29 Roman Gold Collar with Sardonyx Medallion

Roman Empire
Fourth Century CE

Credit: DEA/G. Dagli Orti/DeAgostini/Getty Images

What You Need to Know

The object pictured here is a gold neck collar, with a sardonyx cabochon, or gemstone that has been polished and then shaped rather than cut into facets. Sardonyx is a form of onyx, marked by dark red bands, though the piece here appears black.

At the height of the Roman Empire, trade flourished. Much of it was in agricultural products or the goods of everyday life, such as cloth and timber. But there was also a flourishing trade in precious stones and metals. Indeed, ancient Rome's mineral sources came from beyond the empire's boundaries, with gold flowing in from sub-Saharan Africa and precious gems from South Asia. The gold and onyx used to make this necklace was originally from various parts of Rome's trading sphere. Onyx was mined in various parts of Rome's trading sphere, including Persia and the Atlas Mountains of North Africa.

Although they had access to many mineral sources and were aware of the elaborate forms of jewelry worn by some of their subject peoples and neighbors, citizens of Rome generally preferred simpler forms of dress and accessories.

A Closer Look

Romans generally preferred simplicity in their dress and accessories, as this beautifully worked but understated collar indicates. The gold is minimally worked featuring only two small beads and some wire wrapping, while the sardonyx cabochon features the simple outline of a horse in full gallop. Even in the latter years of the empire—this piece comes from the fourth century CE—Romans adhered to the notion that simplicity in self-presentation evoked the values of modesty and virtue.

Although the Romans generally preferred more subdued styles of jewelry, the women of Rome nevertheless had an abundance of types of jewelry to wear. These included rings, necklaces, anklets, armbands, bracelets, broaches, and fibula, the latter used to pin together clothing. Roman women with means tended to adorn themselves with all different kinds of jewelry, especially for parties and when entertaining guests at home. But even late in the Roman era, excessive adornment was considered inappropriate for public functions, such as religious and civil ceremonies. At such events, women often left their jewelry at home, preferring a simply decorated fibula or broach and nothing else.

The clothing worn with the jewelry tended to be simple in design as well. While the poor of both sexes wore simple tunics, upper-class women clad themselves in *stolae*, or long pleated dresses—usually made of linen—tied in place with belts.

1 100 200 300 400 500 600 700 800 900 1000 1100 1200 1300 1400 1500 1600 1700 1800 1900 2000 CE

1.5.30 Character of Visigoth King Theodoric II

Septimania (southern France)
ca. 460 CE

You have often begged a description of Theodoric the Gothic King, whose gentle breeding fame commends to every nation; you want him in his quantity and quality, in his person, and the manner of his existence. I gladly accede, as far as the limits of my page allow, and highly approve so fine and ingenuous a curiosity.

Well, he is a man worth knowing, even by those who cannot enjoy his close acquaintance. So happily have Providence and Nature joined to endow him with the perfect gifts of fortune; his way of life is such that not even the envy which lies in wait for kings can rob him of his proper praise. And first as to his person. He is well set up, in height above the average man, but below the giant. . . .

Now for the routine of his public life. Before daybreak he goes with a very small suite to attend the service of his priests. He prays with assiduity, but, if I may speak in confidence, one may suspect more of habit than conviction in this piety. Administrative duties of the kingdom take up the rest of the morning. Armed nobles stand about the royal seat; the mass of guards in their garb of skins are admitted that they may be within call, but kept at the threshold for quiet's sake; only a murmur of them comes in from their post at the doors, between the curtain and the outer barrier. And now the foreign envoys are introduced. The king hears them out, and says little; if a thing needs more discussion he puts it off, but accelerates matters ripe for dispatch. The second hour arrives; he rises from the throne to inspect his treasure-chamber or stable. If the chase is the order of the day, he joins it, but never carries his bow at his side, considering this derogatory to royal state. . . .

On ordinary days, his table resembles that of a private person. The board does not groan beneath a mass of dull and unpolished silver set on by panting servitors; the weight lies rather in the conversation than in the plate; there is either sensible talk or none. . . .

About the ninth hour, the burden of government begins again. Back come the importunates, back the ushers to remove them; on all sides buzz the voices of petitioners, a sound which lasts till evening, and does not diminish till interrupted by the royal repast; even then they only disperse to attend their various patrons among the courtiers, and are astir till bedtime. Sometimes, though this is rare, supper is enlivened by sallies of mimes, but no guest is ever exposed to the wound of a biting tongue. Withal there is no noise of hydraulic organ, or choir with its conductor intoning a set piece; you will hear no players of lyre or flute, no master of the music, no girls with cithara or tabor; the king cares for no strains but those which no less charm the mind with virtue than the ear with melody. When he rises to withdraw, the treasury watch begins its vigil; armed sentries stand on guard during the first hours of slumber.

Source: Sidonius Apollinaris. *The Letters of Sidonius*. Vol. I. Translated by O. M. Dalton. Oxford: Clarendon Press, 1915, pp. 2–4, 6.

TIMELINE   2000 1900 1800 1700 1600 1500 1400 1300 1200 1100 1000 900 800 700 600 500 400 300 200 100 1 BCE

What You Need to Know

This excerpt is from a letter written sometime in the mid-fifth century by Sidonius Apollinaris, a Roman noble and diplomat to the Visigoth kingdom, to his brother Agricola, back in Italy. In it, he describes the eighth king of the Visigoths Theodoric II.

During the period of its greatest expansion in the first and second centuries CE, the Roman Empire's northern borders in Europe lay along the Rhine and Danube Rivers. Beyond those frontiers, the continent was inhabited by peoples and tribes who spoke a variety of languages. History has remembered them collectively as "barbarians," but this rubric derides their culture, denies their many accomplishments, and ignores the fact there were many differences among them. Among the Germanic tribes, the Anglo-Saxons of what is now Britain were a nomadic people largely outside the influence of Roman culture while the Visigoths and Ostrogoths of Central Europe were settled agriculturalists who accepted much of Roman culture including, in the latter years of the empire, a variant of Christianity. During the fourth century, as Rome declined, and the Huns of central Asia began to move westward and occupy Central Europe, the Visigoths and Ostrogoths moved over the Roman frontier into Gaul, Spain, and even northern Italy.

A Closer Look

By the fifth century CE, as Roman authority and military might weakened in the provinces, some of the Germanic tribes had established their own Romanized realms within the old confines of the empire. Among these were the Visigoths, who had established a kingdom in Septimania, a Roman province in what is now southern France.

Visigoth king Theodoric II rose to the throne after killing his brother in 453. Despite the bloody way he came to power—which, of course, would not have been shocking to a Roman—Sidonius describes a physically impressive, highly cultured man. The diplomat praises Theodoric for embodying the virtues of a good Roman of the fifth century—pious, dignified, and moderate in his appetites. He also depicts a court that is also highly cultured but one in which the business of government is handled efficiently and effectively.

By late in the Roman era, when this letter was written, peoples across the far-flung empire had long become assimilated to Roman culture. Many of these areas were incorporated into the imperial economy, with large *latifundia*, or slave-worked, plantations providing agricultural products for trade. In the many Roman towns that often grew up around imperial garrisons, many enjoyed the same entertainments as their compatriots in Rome itself, including chariot racing, public baths, and theater.

1 100 200 300 400   500 600 700 800 900 1000 1100 1200 1300   1400 1500 1600   1700 1800 1900 2000 CE

Part 6:
Byzantine Empire and Russia

Fourth–Mid-Twelfth Century CE

1.6.1 Byzantine Pilgrimage Flask

Egypt
ca. Fourth–Seventh Centuries CE

Credit: Corbis

What You Need to Know

This is a terracotta pilgrimage flask from the early centuries of the Byzantine Empire.

Life in the Byzantine Empire was much dominated by the Christian faith it had inherited from the waning days of the Roman Empire. For most, it was also difficult; peasants of the Byzantine Empire lived short lives, prone to disease, crop failure, famine, and occasionally foreign invasion. Not surprisingly, they consoled themselves with faith. They also lived constricted lives, rarely leaving the vicinity of where they were born, grew up, and died.

For these reasons, pilgrimages were not only appealing but common undertakings by Byzantine Christians, as they were in Western Europe. They offered the pilgrim a chance to see and experience things beyond his or her own narrow orbit, even as they offered spiritual solace. Most pilgrimages were short-distance affairs to nearby sites. But sometimes, they could involve journeys of hundreds of miles, especially if the pilgrim was seeking intercession with God from a saint associated with a given ailment, for which the pilgrim was seeking relief, or class of persons to which the pilgrim belonged.

A Closer Look

The flask features an image of Saint Menas, an Egyptian soldier of the early fourth-century Roman army martyred for his Christian faith. He is surrounded by church imagery and objects, including, on the right, an oversized censer, for dispending incense, and on the left, a miniature shrine with a hanging lamp. The figure is in orant, or praying position, and the words above his head read: "Blessing of Saint Menas, Amen."

The flask was the possession of a pilgrim, who most likely used it to hold holy water, oil, or earth, blessed at the site of a shrine, perhaps to Saint Menas, which was located in the desert west of Alexandria, Egypt. Until the expansion of Islam in the seventh century, this region was under the control of the Byzantine Empire. Pilgrims believed that such substances carried divine powers, having been in the presence of a saint's relics and bones, and so they would bring them back from the journeys they took to pilgrimage sites.

All classes of people engaged in pilgrimages, from the wealthy to the indigent poor, although most were peasant farmers, as they made up the vast majority of the empire's population. While men were more typically represented, women went on pilgrimages, too.

1 100 200 300 400 500 600 700 800 900 1000 1100 1200 1300 1400 1500 1600 1700 1800 1900 2000 CE

1.6.2 *Digest of Justinian* on Fugitive Slaves

Constantinople
530–533 CE

Ulpianus (on the Edict 1) A man who has concealed a fugitive slave is a thief.

1. The Senate laid down that fugitive slaves are not to be admitted into parks nor to be sheltered by the overseers or agents of landowners, and it prescribed a fine; but if any persons should within twenty days have either restored such slaves to their owners or brought them up before the magistrates, it excused their previous behaviour; indeed, further on in the same enactment, impunity is promised to anyone who hands over fugitive slaves to their owners or to the magistrate within the prescribed time after finding any such on his ground.
2. The decree allowed both soldiers and civilians a right of entry on the estates of Senators or private persons for the purpose of following up a runaway slave, in fact the *lex Fabia* and a decree of the Senate passed in the consulship of Modestus were enacted with a similar object. It was further laid down that persons who wished to search for fugitive slaves should have letters given them addressed to the magistrates, a fine of a hundred solidi being prescribed at the same time to be payable by the latter, if, on receiving such letters they declined to assist the persons engaged in the search; and a similar penalty was imposed on anyone who refused to allow a search to be made on his ground. Moreover there is a rescript of the Divine Marcus and Commodus of general application by which it is expressly laid down that governors, magistrates and police are bound to assist any owner in seeking out runaway slaves and that they must give them up if they find them, also that persons on whose ground the slaves are in hiding are to be punished if any unlawful behaviour is brought home to them.
3. Every person whatever who apprehends a runaway slave is bound to bring him forward publicly.
4. And the magistrates are very properly enjoined to keep any such slaves carefully in custody, so as to prevent their escape.
5. Under the term "fugitive" must be included a slave who is given to roving. . . .
6. A slave is deemed to be brought forward publicly if he is handed over to the municipal magistrates or government officers.
7. Careful custody will allow putting the slave in irons. . . .

Callistratus (Hearings 6) Slaves who are simply runaways should be restored to their owners; but, where they affect the station of free men, the practice is to inflict severe punishment.

Source: *Digest of Justinian*. Vol. II. Book XI. Translated by Charles Henry Monro. Cambridge: Cambridge University Press, 1909, pp. 237–238.

TIMELINE   2000 1900 1800 1700 1600 1500 1400 1300 1200 1100 1000 900 800 700 600 500 400 300 200 100 1 BCE

What You Need to Know

In the early 530s, Emperor Justinian I ordered that a compendium of ancient Roman law be put together. It became known as the *Digest of Justinian* and ultimately ran to 50 volumes. The accompanying excerpt is the law on fugitive slaves, as compiled from the works of Paulus, Ulpianus, and other earlier jurists.

Early governments had tried to codify Roman law, but such efforts were not only scattered across different works, but the laws listed in one often contradicted those inscribed in another. By putting all of the laws into one digest, Justinian established a definitive legal code, although it was based on several earlier sources for the law. For example, nearly half of the *Digest of Justinian* comes from the Roman jurist Ulpinus, who lived in the second and third centuries CE.

During his long reign from 527 to 565, Justinian embarked on a series of military campaigns in Italy and North Africa, in an effort to recreate the old Roman Empire. Although the wars were ultimately a failure—not only did they not create political unify, but they nearly bankrupted the Byzantine state—they produced swelling ranks of slaves, most of whom ended up working in urban areas, as domestic servants, and in artisanal establishments.

A Closer Look

As in so many other things about the Byzantine Empire, slavery was an inheritance from the Greco-Roman world of ancient times. It was both widespread and tolerated by the Byzantine Greek Orthodox Church.

Slaves were come by in two ways, through indebtedness—although the practice of selling off children to pay off a parent's financial obligation was frowned on by the government—and war. Slaves were of almost every ethnicity within the empire; Slavery in the Byzantine Empire had no racial overtones, nor was there a social stigma attached to it. Indeed, slaves worked as craftsman, clerks, and advisers to wealthy and powerful individuals.

To modern readers, the laws seem harsh and strict. Runaways are given virtually no rights to claim their freedom and are immediately to be restored to their masters. Should they claim to be freemen, the law says, "the practice is to inflict severe punishment." Much of the law concerns the duties of free persons in returning fugitive slaves to their masters. All people of the empire were bound, the code declares, to actively participate in such efforts and anyone who succored or hid a runaway faced an unnamed punishment.

1   100   200   300   400   500   600   700   800   900   1000   1100   1200   1300   1400   1500   1600   1700   1800   1900   2000 CE

1.6.3 The Institutes of Justinian on Marriage

Constantinople
533 CE

Roman citizens are joined together in lawful marriage when they unite themselves according to the rules of law, the males having reached the time of puberty, and the females being of the age of child-bearing, whether they be heads of families or subject-members of families; provided only the subject-members of families have in addition the consent of the ascendants in whose potestas they are; for both civil and natural law so strongly insist on this being needful, that the authorization of the ascendant ought further to be precedent. Hence it used to be debated whether the daughter of a madman could be married, or the son of a madman take a wife; and since opinions differed as to the son, we have ourselves published a decision whereby the son of a madman is allowed, in like manner as the daughter of a madman, to marry without his father's intervention, according to a method appointed by our constitution.

I. Again, we cannot marry any woman we please, for there are some from marriage with whom we must abstain. Thus between persons who stand to one another in the relation of ascendants and descendants marriage cannot be contracted; for instance, between father and daughter, or grandfather and granddaughter, or mother and son, or grandmother and grandson, and so for all further degrees; and if such persons cohabit, they are said to have contracted an unholy and incestuous marriage. And these rules hold so universally, that although they enter into the relation of ascendants and descendants by adoption, they cannot be united in marriage; and even after the adoption has been dissolved, the same rule stands; therefore you cannot marry a woman who has once been your daughter or granddaughter by adoption, even though you have emancipated her.

2. Also between persons who are related collaterally there is a rule of like character, but not so stringent. Marriage is absolutely forbidden between a brother and a sister, whether they be born from the same father and the same mother, or from one or other of them. But if a woman become your sister by adoption, then, so long as the adoption stands, marriage certainly cannot subsist between you and her: but when the adoption has been dissolved by emancipation, you can marry her: and so also if you have been emancipated, there is no bar to the marriage. . . .

12. If any persons cohabit in contravention of the rules we have laid down, we do not admit the existence of husband, wife, marriage-ceremonies, marriage itself, or marriage-settlement. The children therefore of such a cohabitation are not under the potestas of their father, but so far as patria potestas is concerned stand on the same footing as those conceived in prostitution. For these too are considered to have no father, since their father is uncertain: and therefore they are usually called spurious children, either from a Greek word, being as it were conceived at random, or being children without a father. Hence it results that on the dissolution of a connection of this kind no claim for restitution of the marriage settlement is allowed. Moreover persons who enter into forbidden marriages are liable to other penalties enumerated in the imperial constitutions.

Source: *The Institutes of Justinian*. Book I. Translated by John Thomas Abdy and Bryan Walker. Cambridge: Cambridge University Press, 1876, pp. 27–29, 33.

TIMELINE   2000 1900 1800 1700 1600 1500 1400 1300 1200 1100 1000 900 800 700 600 500 400 300 200 100 1 BCE

What You Need to Know

The accompanying document comes from the *Institutes of Justinian*, compiled in the early 530s and published in 533. As its name implies, the *Institutes* covered the law pertaining to institutions of Byzantine society, including marriage.

The passage here includes some of the laws concerning marriage between members of the same family. For the most part, both the Romans and the Byzantines frowned on such marriage, particularly if there was a blood relationship. Neither civilization was unique in such prohibitions. Most cultures ban the practice. One of the main reasons for this was to ensure that marriages established relations between families to create more sources of wealth, labor, and income.

The Romans and the early Byzantines had another reason for the ban. Intermarriage among family members was common in some of the civilizations of the Middle East and North Africa, such as Egypt. Banning the practice in their own realm was a way for Romans and Byzantines to assert what they felt was their own civilization's superiority.

A Closer Look

As the inheritors of the culture of the Roman Empire, Byzantines continued earlier marital practices. Arranged marriages were typical. Particularly in families with wealth or social standing, the parents on both sides sought out partners for their children who were suitable in terms of their status and the resources they brought to the two families. At the highest levels of society, arranged marriages might cement political alliances.

As in most other civilizations of the ancient and medieval world, Byzantine women or rather girls, were married off at a young age, usually shortly after entering puberty. This made sure that their most fertile years were spent having children. Given the incredibly high child mortality rates of the era, this made sense as far as preserving the family's heritage was concerned. As in ancient Rome, Byzantine society was a highly patriarchal one. Once in marriage, women were expected to transfer their allegiance from their fathers to their husbands, although they retained some say over the rearing of children and the management of household affairs. And, under Justinian's codes, they retained certain property rights, including control over their own dowry and the right to inherit and bequeath property.

1 100 200 300 400 500 600 700 800 900 1000 1100 1200 1300 1400 1500 1600 1700 1800 1900 2000 CE

1.6.4 Racing Factions in the Byzantine Capital

Constantinople
ca. 560 CE

The population in every city has for a long time been divided into two groups, the Greens and the Blues; but only recently, for the sake of these names and the places which they occupy while watching the games, have they come to spend their money, to abandon their bodies to the cruelest tortures, and to consider it a not unworthy thing to die a most disgraceful death. The members fight with their opponents not knowing for what reason they risk their lives, but realizing full well that even when they vanquish their opponents in brawls, they will be carted off to prison and that, after they have suffered the most extreme tortures, they will be killed.

Therefore, there arises in them an endless and unreasoning hatred against their fellow men, respecting neither marriage nor kinship nor bonds of friendship, even if those who support different colors might be brothers or some other kind of relatives. Neither human nor divine affairs matter to them compared to winning these fights. When some impious act is committed by one of them against God, or when the laws and the state are injured by their comrades or opponents, or perhaps when they lack the necessities of life, or their country is suffering dire need, they ignore all this as long as events turn out well for their own "faction." For this is what they call the bands of rioters. Even women participate in this abomination, not only accompanying the men but, if the occasion arises, even opposing them, although they do not go to the public spectacles nor are they motivated by any other reason. Thus I, for my part, consider them nothing else than a sickness of the soul. And this is how things are among the people of every city.

Source: Procopius. *History of the Wars*. Vol. I. Translated by H. B. Dewing. Loeb Classical Library. London: William Heinemann, 1914, pp. 219, 221. Modifications made.

TIMELINE   2000 1900 1800 1700 1600 1500 1400 1300 1200 1100 1000 900 800 700 600 500 400 300 200 100 1 BCE

What You Need to Know

Among the many legacies of ancient Rome carried on by the Byzantines was chariot racing, as this sixth century account by Procopius of Caesaria attests. Born in the Byzantine province of Palestine around the year 500, the Greek-educated Procopius is the best-known chronicler of the age of the Emperor Justinian. The excerpt here is from his *History of the Wars of Justinian*, which chronicles the emperor's efforts to retake Italy and North Africa.

With the western half of the empire was increasingly vulnerable to barbarian invasion In 330 CE, the Emperor Constantine moved the capital of the Roman Empire from Rome to the city of Byzantium in 330 CE. The city renamed the "city of Constantine," or Constantinople. Situated across the trade routes connecting Asia and Europe, Constantinople was a culturally diverse city. Although many languages were spoken, particularly in the city's many marketplaces, Greek was what most people spoke in their homes and daily transactions with each other. The city was well served institutionally, with the cityscape dotted with hospitals, homes for elderly, and orphanages. These were run by churches but received some funding from the imperial government. The city also possessed a relatively advanced infrastructure for the day, boasting one of the few functioning sewer systems in the medieval world and, of course, the largest hippodrome, or horse-racing track, in Europe, a vast U-shaped structure near the imperial palace.

A Closer Look

This excerpt from Procopius deals with chariot racing in the capital, Constantinople, and more specifically, the politics of chariot racing. Procopius notes the existence of two groups of fans— the greens and the blues. To modern readers, Procopius's description bears a resemblance to the fanaticism of modern sports fans. But, in fact, these rival camps served an important political purpose. One of the main political events of the late Roman Empire were public displays of acclamation for the emperor. The green and blue camps would vie to outperform the other in expressing their support for the emperor. Gradually, the greens and the blues came to represent not only backing for a particular chariot team but a set of views and attitudes on how the state should be run. Although these differences, as Procopius notes, could lead to rioting in the streets, they also served to notify the emperor about the will of the people. Whichever camp dominated the acclamation, he could assume, was the one in political ascendance.

1 100 200 300 400 500 | 600 700 800 900 1000 1100 1200 1300 1400 1500 1600 1700 1800 1900 2000 CE

1.6.5 A Description of the Rus from the *Risala*

Russia
Tenth Century CE

§ 80 I have seen the Rus as they came on their merchant journeys and encamped by the Volga. I have never seen more perfect physical specimens, tall as date palms, blonde and ruddy; they wear neither tunics nor caftans, but the men wear a garment which covers one side of the body and leaves a hand free.

§ 81 Each man has an axe, a sword, and a knife and keeps each by him at all times. The swords are broad and grooved, of Frankish sort. Every man is tattooed from finger nails to neck with dark green (or green or blue-black) trees, figures, etc.

§ 82 Each woman wears on either breast a box of iron, silver, copper or gold; the value of the box indicates the wealth of the husband. Each box has a ring from which depends a knife. The women wear neck rings of gold and silver, one for each 10,000 dirhems which her husband is worth; some women have many. Their most prized ornaments are beads of green glass of the same make as ceramic objects one finds on their ships. They trade beads among themselves and they pay an exaggerated price for them, for they buy them for a dirhem apiece. They string them as necklaces for their women.

§ 83 They are the filthiest of God's creatures. They have no modesty in defecation and urination, nor do they wash after pollution from orgasm, nor do they wash their hands after eating. Thus they are like wild asses. When they have come from their land and anchored on, or tied up at the shore of the Volga, which is a great river, they build big houses of wood on the shore, each holding ten to twenty persons more or less. Each man has a couch on which he sits. With them are pretty slave girls destined for sale to merchants: a man will have sexual intercourse with his slave girl while his companion looks on. Sometimes whole groups will come together in this fashion, each in the presence of others. A merchant who arrives to buy a slave girl from them may have to wait and look on while a Rus completes the act of intercourse with a slave girl.

§ 84 Every day they must wash their faces and heads and this they do in the dirtiest and filthiest fashion possible: to wit, every morning a girl servant brings a great basin of water; she offers this to her master and he washes his hands and face and his hair—he washes it and combs it out with a comb in the water; then he blows his nose and spits into the basin. When he has finished, the servant carries the basin to the next person, who does likewise. She carries the basin thus to all the household in turn, and each blows his nose, spits, and washes his face and hair in it.

§ 86 An ill person is put in a tent apart with some bread and water and people do not come to speak with him; they do not come even to see him every day, especially if his is a poor man or a slave. If he recovers, he returns to them, and if he dies, they cremate him. If he is a slave, he is left to be eaten by dogs and birds of prey. If the Rus catch a thief or robber, they hang him on a tall tree and leave him hanging until his body falls in pieces.

Source: From Ibn Fadlan, The Risala, http://www.vikinganswerlady.com/ibn_fdln.shtml.

TIMELINE   2000 1900 1800 1700 1600 1500 1400 1300 1200 1100 1000 900 800 700 600 500 400 300 200 100 1 BCE

What You Need to Know

Ahmad ibn Fadlan, who lived from during the tenth century, was a diplomat of the Muslim Abbasid Caliphate in Baghdad. At the time, Baghdad was the richest and most cultured city in the Islamic world, famed for its arts, literature, and scientific achievement. In 921, Baghdad dispatched Fadlan to serve in the caliphate's embassy in Bolghar. At the time, the state had just converted to Islam and had yet to experience the glories it was soon to achieve, as Fadlan's disparaging account of its inhabitants reveals.

In this excerpt from his collected writings, *The Risala, an Account among the People of Russia*, Fadlan praises the physiques of the Bulghars, but little else. He has particular disdain for their hygiene, a not surprising attitude given the well-practiced bathing and hygiene habits of the Muslims of Baghdad, of which Fadlan was one. This praising of the physicality but not the culture of those considered inferior by the writer was a common theme in travelers' accounts going all the way back to the ancient Greeks. But Fadlan's comments on the Bulghars are particularly harsh; he calls them the "filthiest of God's creatures."

A Closer Look

In the Middle Ages, the term *Rus* was applied by Europeans and Muslims to the people who inhabited the vast woodlands and steppes of what is now western Russia, which is a derivative of the term. Among the Rus peoples were the Volga Bulghars. They were not a Slavic-speaking people like most of the inhabitants of the region but Finno-Ugric and Turkic speakers. Their state, known as Volga Bulgaria, dated from roughly the seventh century and lasted until the Mongol conquests of the mid-thirteenth century. It was situated at the confluence of the Volga and Kama rivers, about 600 miles east of the present-day city of Moscow.

The state was a small and weak one through the beginning of the ninth century, dominated by stronger peoples, such as the Khazars, to their south. That began to change in the early ninth century when, under the leadership of Almish ibn Skilki Yiltawar, they converted to Islam and joined the larger Muslim cultural orbit. The decline of the Khazars later in the century allowed them to expand and prosper even more, turning their capital, known as Bolghar, into one of the wealthier cities in the Islamic world.

1 100 200 300   400   500   600   700   800   900   1000 1100 1200 1300   1400   1500   1600   1700   1800   1900   2000 CE

1.6.6 *The Book of the Eparch* on Economic Regulation in Constantinople

Constantinople
Tenth Century CE

2. Jewelers

1. We ordain that the jewelers may, if any one invites them, buy the things that pertain to them, such as gold, silver, pearls, or precious stones; but not bronze and woven linens or any other materials which others should purchase rather than they. . . .

3. Following the old custom, on the regular market days the jewelers shall take their seats in their shops along with their statores or attendants in charge of their sales tables. . . .

7. If any jeweler is found to have bought a sacred object, whether damaged or intact, without having shown it to the eparch, both he and the seller shall suffer confiscation.

3. Bankers

1. Anyone who wishes to be nominated as a banker must be vouched for by respected and honest men who will guarantee that he will do nothing contrary to the ordinances; to wit, that he will not pare down, or cut, or put false inscriptions on nomismata or miliarisia, or set one of his own slaves in his place at his bank if he should happen to be occupied with some temporary duties, so that no trickery may thereby enter into the business of the profession. . . .

2. The moneychangers shall report to the eparch the forgers who station themselves in the squares and streets in order to prevent them from indulging in illegal practices. . . .

17. Fishmongers

1. The fishmongers shall take their stand in the so-called Greatest Vaults of the city to sell their fish. Each vault shall have an overseer whose duty it is to observe the cost of the fish at sea and the resale price, so that he may receive a commission of one miliarision on the nomisma.

2. Those who sell fish shall not pickle them or sell them to strangers for export, unless there is a surplus, when they may do so to prevent their spoiling.

19. Tavern keepers

3. Tavern keepers are forbidden to open their shops and sell wine or food before the second hour of the day (7 a.m.) on high festivals or on Sundays. At night they shall close their shops and put out the fires when the second hour arrives (7 p.m.), in order to prevent the habitual daytime patrons, if they have the opportunity of returning at night, from becoming intoxicated and shamelessly engaging in fights, acts of violence, and brawls.

Source: Excerpts from *The Book of the Prefect*. Translated by A. E. R. Boak. In *Journal of Economic and Business History* 1 (1928–1929): 597–618. Modifications made.

What You Need to Know

The Book of the Eparch, from which this excerpt comes, was an economic manual written and promulgated by the office of the Eparch, the governor of Constantinople, who controlled both the judicial and economic affairs of the city.

To travelers from Western Europe, then just emerging from centuries of economic and cultural stagnation, the Byzantine Empire appeared awash in wealth and luxury. That is because, unlike Western Europe, where the state had shriveled to near irrelevance in the second half of the first millennium, Byzantium had a strong central government.

Constantinople, the empire's capital, located on the strategic waterway between the Black and Mediterranean Seas, was a center of trade, linking the Muslim world of the Middle East with European Christendom. Its merchant houses, many of them owned by Jews and Muslims, were replete with goods from around the world. The mansions of Byzantine nobles, many of whom owned vast tracts of land in the countryside but preferred to spend much of their time in the city, were filled with the finest luxury goods and most exquisite art of the day.

A Closer Look

Through assessors and inspectors, the Eparch made sure the book's rules were carried out to the letter. Some of these regulations were intended for the larger good of the public. There were zoning rules, dictating where fishmongers could sell their wares, and requirements that those wishing to become bankers "be vouchsafed for by respected and honest men." Others were designed to meet the needs of guilds, which were set up to establish high standards for a particular trade to prevent competition.

Among the government's main preoccupations was ensuring the smooth running of the imperial economy. It had a monopoly on the minting of coinage, set interest rates, and established tariffs and rules on foreign trade. During food shortages, it even set prices on staples and requisitioned supplies from the countryside to ensure social peace in the capital.

Even in ordinary times, it issued all kinds of rules about how different professions and businesses could be run. It usually did this by setting minimum standards for the many trade and merchant guilds that operated throughout the empire. These regulations and standards could be quite exacting and dealt with what seems to modern readers the most trivial of details, as this excerpt from the *Book of the Eparch* makes clear.

1.6.7 Icon of Saint Eudocia

Constantinople
Tenth Century CE

Credit: DeAgostini/Getty Images

What You Need to Know

The artifact shown here is a Byzantine icon. Icons are representational images of religious personages, Jesus, or God, rendered in various media.

Faith and imagery have a long and tortured history. Muslims, famously, ban all representative imagery from their holy places and even frown on the use of it in secular life. One of the factors behind the Protestant Reformation of the early modern era in European history was the extensive use of imagery, particularly of saints, within the Catholic Church, which was viewed as a kind of idolatry. The Eastern Orthodox Church of the Byzantine Empire experienced a great paroxysm over representative imagery in the eighth century, when several emperors attempted to ban most imagery in churches and monasteries.

The reason for this attitude is that, according to Christian and Muslim doctrine, all divine power rests with God, although sometimes channeled through saints. Uneducated and unsophisticated worshippers, various theologians have argued, may come to worship the images of saints, believing that they actually contained the divine spirit rather than merely being representations of the divine.

A Closer Look

The icon here shows a multicolored mosaic made from marble. It depicts Saint Eudocia. In life, she was the wife of Theodosius II, the fifth-century Roman emperor who ruled from Constantinople, later the capital of the Byzantine Empire, and helped spread the Christian faith and codify early Christian writings. Eudocia, herself, was seen by Byzantine Christians as playing a critical role in her husband's Christian work.

Icons were central to the Byzantine Church. Typically, the icons would be in various sanctuaries of churches. Before or after masses, as well as at other times, worshippers would kneel down in front of the icons and pray to them. As early as the third century, church officials had permitted the faithful to venerate, but not worship, images of God, Jesus, the Virgin, and saints. They felt that while all prayers must be directed to God the Father, icons encouraged reverence. Early church officials also allowed worshippers to ask Jesus, the Virgin, or the saints to intercede on their behalf with God.

But, as noted, such veneration became heresy if the believer began to worship the image, seeing it as holy in and of itself. In 730, the Byzantine emperor Leo III became convinced this was in fact happening and ordered all church icons destroyed. Leo was an iconoclast, or destroyer of icons. (The word today means anybody who attacks orthodox or popular ideas or institutions.) His actions led to an uproar throughout the empire that lasted until a successor restored icons in 843.

1   100   200   300   400   500   600   700   800   900   1000   1100   1200   1300   1400   1500   1600   1700   1800   1900   2000 CE

1.6.8 Gold Solidus

Byzantine Empire
Eleventh Century CE

Credit: DeAgostini/Getty Images

What You Need to Know

This Byzantine coin from the eleventh century is known as a solidus. The face of the coin shown here depicts two persons. On the right is the Emperor Romanus III Argyros, who ruled Byzantium from 1028 to 1034. To his left is the Patriarch of Constantinople, the head of the Eastern Orthodox Church. His left hand is extended, holding the crown atop Romanus's head, to show that the emperor has divine blessing.

The Byzantine Empire had one of the most robust economies in the world in the eleventh century. At its foundation was agriculture, which was the occupation that engaged the vast majority of its subjects. But in urban areas, trade was also important. Cities throughout the empire, as well as rural fairs, were centers of trade. The Byzantine Empire straddled the divide between East and West, between the vibrant Islamic world of the Middle East—as well as India beyond—and the growing economies of Christian Europe, which were just emerging from the so-called Dark Ages, when little long-distance trade was conducted.

A Closer Look

First minted in ancient Rome and made of gold, the solidus was the basic unit of currency throughout Europe, west and east, during the Middle Ages. As with the Roman Empire that preceded it, the Byzantine Empire's trade was facilitated by specie—specifically, bronze, silver, and gold coins of various values. The government issued the coins, and attested to their value, although their intrinsic worth was established by the metal they contained.

Much of the empire's trade was actually controlled by foreign merchants, and because long-distance trade was usually more valuable, it often required the use of gold coins, like this solidus. As in Western Europe, the economy of the Byzantine aristocracy and church rested largely on agriculture. Virtually all urban trade was under the control of Jewish, Muslim, and later, Italian merchants. The Byzantines themselves disdained trade as an economic pursuit. The aristocracy considered it unworthy of their nobility, while church officials, who controlled much land in the empire, saw it as bordering on sinful usury.

However, coins that featured the emperor and the head of the Church sent a message to ordinary people of the Byzantine Empire that the government officials they had to deal with in their daily life were, in fact, doing the work of a divinely appointed emperor. This gave the government a legitimacy it might not have otherwise enjoyed, especially when it came to collect taxes or punish people for committing crimes.

1 100 200 300 400 500 600 700 800 900 1000 1100 1200 1300 1400 1500 1600 1700 1800 1900 2000 CE

1.6.9 Illuminated Illustration from *Homilies on the Virgin*

Constantinople
Twelfth Century CE

Credit: Universal History Archive/Getty Images

What You Need to Know

While the Byzantines considered themselves the political heirs of the Roman world and the inheritors of the cultural heritage of ancient Greece, their representational art differed much from these earlier civilizations, as revealed in the accompanying image of a page from a twelfth-century illuminated manuscript known as the *Homilies of the Virgin*. In Christian terminology, a homily is a brief sermon or writing aimed at educating the worshipper. The illustration depicts the ascension of the resurrected Christ into heaven. The central figure at the bottom is the Virgin Mary, while on the far left bottom is depicted the Prophet Isaiah and the on right, with a crown, King David. According to Christian scripture, Isaiah predicted the birth of Jesus and King David was the Son of God's forbearer.

Illustrated manuscripts were typically made in monasteries but held in churches opened to the lay public. These elaborate books would be brought out at mass or during holy day celebrations. Although the vast majority of worshippers could not literally read from them, they could in a sense "read" the imagery, especially as they would be well acquainted with stories from the Gospels or the lives of saints that were being illustrated. This reinforced the power of the Christian message of the text, which would be read to them by priests.

A Closer Look

Illuminated manuscripts are religious texts supplemented with illustrations and often sumptuous decorations. The earliest Byzantine manuscripts date to the fifth and sixth centuries. As noted, most manuscripts were produced in monasteries, often after they had received a commission from a wealthy individual who would ask the monks to pray for him in exchange for the donation. The wealthier the commission the more elaborate the manuscript.

The larger monasteries had dedicated rooms for the production of illuminated manuscripts, known collectively as scriptoriums, where monks were able to labor in silence and contemplation of the divine as they copied the gospels and etched the illustrations and decorations. In smaller monasteries, monks might work on the manuscripts in their own cells.

At first manuscript books were rather simple and made by a single author. By the twelfth century, however, they were made on production lines, as it were. With monks, specializing in a certain aspect of production, adding their element, before passing the manuscript on to the next monk.

1 100 200 300 400 500 600 700 800 900 1000 1100 1200 1300 1400 1500 1600 1700 1800 1900 2000 CE

1.6.10 The Great Fair at Thessalonica

Thessalonica, Greece
Mid-Twelfth Century CE

The Demetria is a festival . . . and it is at the same time the most important fair held in Macedonia. Not only do the natives of the country flock together to it in great numbers, but multitudes also come from all lands and of every race—Greeks, wherever they are found, the various tribes of Mysians [i.e., people of Moesia] who dwell on our borders as far as the Ister and Scythia, Campanians and other Italians, Iberians, Lusitanians, and Transalpine Celts—this is the Byzantine way of describing the Bulgarians, &c., Neapolitans, Spaniards, Portuguese, and French; and, to make a long story short, the shores of the ocean send pilgrims and suppliants to visit the martyr [Saint Demetrius], so widely extended is his fame throughout Europe. For myself, being a Cappadocian from beyond the boundaries of the empire,—this country was now under the Seljouk [Seljuk] sultans of Iconium—and having never before been present on the occasion, but having only heard it described, I was anxious to get a bird's eye view of the whole scene, that I might pass over nothing unnoticed.

With this object I made my way up to a height close by the scene of the fair, where I sat down and surveyed everything at my leisure. What I saw there was a number of merchants' booths, set up in parallel rows opposite one another; and these rows extended to a great length, and were sufficiently wide apart to leave a broad space in the middle, so as to give free passage for the stream of the people. Looking at the closeness of the booths to one another and the regularity of their position, one might take them for lines drawn lengthwise from two opposite points. At right angles to these, other booths were set up, also forming rows, though of no great length, so that they resembled the tiny feet that grow outside the bodies of certain reptiles. . . .

And if you are anxious to know what it contained, my inquisitive friend, as I saw it afterwards when I came down from the hills—well, there was every kind of material woven or spun by men or women, all those that come from Boeotia and the Peloponnese, and all that are brought in trading ships from Italy to Greece. Besides this, Phoenicia furnishes numerous articles, and Egypt, and Spain, and the pillars of Hercules, where the finest coverlets are manufactured. These things the merchants bring direct from their respective countries to old Macedonia and Thessalonica; but the Euxine also contributes to the splendour of the fair, by sending across its products to Constantinople, whence the cargoes are brought by numerous horses and mules. All this I went through and carefully examined afterwards when I came down; but even while I was still seated on the height above I was struck with wonder at the number and variety of the animals, and the extraordinary confusion of their noises which assailed my ears—horses neighing, oxen lowing, sheep bleating, pigs grunting, and dogs barking, for these also accompany their masters as a defence against wolves and thieves.

Source: Excerpt from *Timarion*. Translated by H. Tozer. In "Byzantine Satire." *Journal of Hellenic Studies* 52 (1881): 244–245.

TIMELINE   2000 1900 1800 1700 1600 1500 1400 1300 1200 1100 1000 900 800 700 600 500 400 300 200 100 1 BCE

What You Need to Know

The great fair at Thessaloniki, described in this passage from a twelfth-century Byzantine satire by an unknown writer, the *Timarion*, occurred annually in October, to commemorate the feast day of the local fourth-century Christian martyr, Saint Demetrius. Fairs were an outgrowth of pilgrimages, scheduled around a local saint's day and situated near that saint's burial site or reliquary.

While a lack of safe passage, poor transportation links, and low economic productivity hampered manufacturing and long-distance trade in Europe through much of the early Middle Ages, the Byzantine Empire was a haven of security and a hub of industry and trade. When commerce and manufacturing began to revive in Western Europe in the eleventh century, traders from there began to expand outward, including into the Byzantine Empire.

Emerging towns and cities in the West were critical to this early manufacturing and served as the loci of local trade; nonetheless, much long-distance exchange occurred at the great fairs of the late Middle Ages, both in Western Europe and Byzantium. Because of the great distances involved and the many dangers along the way—including bandits on land and pirates and shipwrecks at sea—small artisans rarely had the financial resources to participate in the fairs. Instead, professional merchants from a given region would amass the goods, either by buying them outright or taking them on consignment, for trade. Indeed, given the dangers, merchants would often pool their capital and thus minimize their individual financial risk.

A Closer Look

As with virtually all aspects of medieval life, the great trading fairs were intimately connected to faith, as most grew out of local religious celebrations. But by the late Middle Ages, the trade aspect of the fairs had become as important, if not more important, than the religious pilgrimages, as the *Timarion*'s description of well-organized lines of merchant booths at the Thessaloniki fair illustrates. The narrator notes the presence of traders from as far away as Lusitania (modern-day Portugal) and Egypt. He also describes the many animals at the fair, many of them driven great distances. But the fair, located in the Aegean Sea port and situated near where Europe, Asia Minor, and North Africa meet, most certainly included a wide array of other goods, including textiles of the "Transalpine Celts" (probably, northern France and what is now Belgium and the Netherlands), glass from Venice, silver from the Balkans, and silks from China, via the Levant and Egypt.

But the fairs were about more than just trade. They were places where people from every corner of the empire could mingle and pass on news to one another. Fairs were also places where new manufacturing techniques might be passed from craftsman to craftsman. Fairs were also social events. Merchants who had not seen each other in a long time could reestablish friendships. Entertainment was also an important feature. Troubadours, poets, jugglers, and other entertainers frequently traveled the fair circuit, earning their livelihood by performing for attendees, from whom they would receive tips.

1 100 200 300 400 500 600 700 800 900 1000 1100 1200 1300 1400 1500 1600 1700 1800 1900 2000 CE

Part 7:
Islamic World

Seventh–Sixteenth Centuries CE

1.7.1 Heaven and Hell According to the Koran

Arabia
Seventh Century CE

When the day that must come shall have come suddenly,
None shall treat its sudden coming as a lie:
Day that shall abase! Day that shall exalt!
When the earth shall be shaken with a shock,
And the mountains shall be crumbled with a crumbling,
And become scattered dust,
And into three bands shall ye be divided;
Then the people of the right hand—how happy the people of the right hand!
And the people of the left hand—how wretched the people of the left hand!
And they who were foremost on earth—the foremost still.
These are they who shall be brought close to God,
In gardens of delight;
A crowd from the ancients, And a few from later generations;
On inwrought couches
Reclining on them face to face:
Immortal youths go round about to them
With goblets and ewers and a cup from a fountain; . . .
And with such fruits as they shall make choice of,
And with flesh of such birds as they shall long for:
And theirs shall be the Houris with large dark eyes like close-kept pearls,
A recompense for their labours past. . . .

Verily of a rare creation have We created the Houris,
And We have made them ever virgins. . . .
But the people of the left hand—how wretched shall be the people of the left hand!
Amid pestilential winds and in scalding water, And the shadow of a black smoke,
Not cooling, not pleasant.
They truly, ere this, were blessed with worldly goods,
But persisted in heinous wickedness, And were wont to say,
"When we have died, and become dust and bones, shall we indeed be raised?
And our fathers the men of yore?"
Say: Aye, the former and the latter.
Gathered shall they surely be before the time of a known day.
Then verily you, O you the erring, the imputers of falsehood,
Shall surely eat of the tree of Zakkoum,
And fill your bellies with it,
And thereupon shall ye drink of the boiling water,
And ye shall drink as the thirsty camel drinketh.
This shall be their repast in the day of reckoning!

Source: *El Koran, or The Koran*. Sura LVI, 1–35, 40–56. Translated by J. M. Rodwell. London: Bernard Quaritch, 1876, pp. 51–53.

TIMELINE   2000 1900 1800 1700 1600 1500 1400 1300 1200 1100 1000 900 800 700 600 500 400 300 200 100 1 BCE

What You Need to Know

This excerpt consists of *suras*, or verses, from the Koran, Islam's holy book, focusing on the afterlife.

Many of the first religions of the ancient Western world and elsewhere declared that, upon death, the soul of a person was weighed by a god or gods, to be punished or rewarded depending on the deeds of the person while he or she was alive. In the Western monotheistic tradition, the judgment was of the greatest importance, for it determined where the soul would spend eternity—either in the presence of God, in a kind of paradise, or in a place where God's favor was for all intents and purposes absent, to be eternally tormented in hell. According to the Koran, which is made up of the revelations the Prophet Muhammad received from Allah, or God, in the early seventh century CE, the same applied to Muslim souls. But whereas Christian scripture is rather vague on the nature of heaven and hell, the Koran is far more descriptive and specific, as it is about so many other aspects of human existence and belief, especially concerning rules for how to live a life that will take a person to heaven upon his or her death.

A Closer Look

The Arabic word for "heaven," is *jannah*, a derivative of the term for "garden." Indeed, the Islamic heaven very much resembles a garden, which is perhaps not surprising given the harsh desert environment in which it first arose. The Islamic heaven is revealed in not only the Koran but also the Hadiths, or the sayings and deeds of the Prophet Muhammad, and the *tafsir*, or exegeses of later Muslim theologians.

Jannah, according to these various holy texts, is a place where all emotional and physical suffering is absent and where every sensual pleasure—including, food, leisure, and sex—is indulged. Notably, as the Koran excerpt says, men are rewarded with *houris*, or beautiful female companions. But these pleasures come in a distant second to the greatest joy of heaven—being in the presence of God, as noted in this excerpt from the 16th *sura*, or verse, of the Koran.

The Arabic hell resembles the Christian hell. It is a place of everlasting fire, where sinners are burnt by—and forced to drink—molten metal. It is filled with poisonous insects and snakes, each bit of which leads to 40 years of suffering. The tormented are also forced to eat the bitter fruit of the *zakkoum* tree.

The Arabic term for hell is *jahannam*, derived from the Hebrew name for a valley outside Jerusalem where idol worshippers and apostates were exiled. And, indeed, *jahannam*'s worst torments are reserved not for those who do evil but those who turn their backs on God.

1 100 200 300 400 500 600 700 800 900 1000 1100 1200 1300 1400 1500 1600 1700 1800 1900 2000 CE

1.7.2 The Koran on Women and Inheritance

Arabia
Seventh Century CE

Men ought to have a part of what their parents and kindred leave, and women a part of what their parents and kindred leave: whether it be little or much, let them have a stated portion. . . .

With regard to your children God commandeth you to give the male the portion of two females; and if they be females more than two, then they shall have two-thirds of that which their father hath left: but if she be an only daughter she shall have the half; and the father and mother of the deceased shall each of them have a sixth part of what he hath left, if he have a child; but if he have no child and his parents be his heirs, then his mother shall have the third: and if he have brethren, his mother shall have the sixth, after paying the bequests he shall have bequeathed, and his debts. As to your fathers, or your children, ye know not which of them is the most advantageous to you. This is the ordinance of God. Verily, God is Knowing, Wise!

Half of what your wives leave shall be yours, if they have no issue; but if they have issue, then a fourth of what they leave shall be yours, after paying the bequests they shall bequeath, and debts.

And your wives shall have a fourth part of what ye leave, if ye have no issue; but if ye have issue, then they shall have an eighth part of what ye leave, after paying the bequests ye shall bequeath and debts.

If a man or a woman make a distant relation their heir, and he or she have a brother or a sister, each of these two shall have a sixth; but if there are more than this, then shall they be sharers in a third, after payment of the bequests he shall have bequeathed, and debts, without loss to any one. This is the ordinance of God, and God is Knowing, Gracious!

These are the precepts of God; and whoso obeyeth God and his Prophet, him shall God bring into gardens beneath whose shades the rivers flow, therein to abide for ever: and this, the great blessedness!

And whoso shall rebel against God and his Apostle, and transgress his ordinances, him shall God cause to enter unto Hell-fire, to abide therein for ever; and this, a shameful torment!

If any of your women be guilty of whoredom, then bring four witnesses against them from among yourselves; and if they bear witness to the fact, shut them up within their houses till death release them, or God make some way for them.

Source: *El Koran, or The Koran.* Sura IV, 8–19. Translated by J. M. Rodwell. London: Bernard Quaritch, 1876, pp. 452–454.

TIMELINE   2000 1900 1800 1700 1600 1500 1400 1300 1200 1100 1000 900 800 700 600 500 400 300 200 100 1 BCE

What You Need to Know

These *suras*, or verses, from the Koran concern the inheritance rights of woman, revealing in the process the status of women in early Islamic society.

In the minds of many people in the West, women in the Muslim world have an unenviable lot, living essentially as second-class citizens within their own societies. They are subject to the will of men, have few rights and privileges, and are kept in isolation. Some of this is based in reality. In Muslim lands where a strict fundamentalism or orthodoxy holds sway—such as Afghanistan under the Taliban or Saudi Arabia today—women are kept in isolation from society, and men make most of the decisions for them. Many in the West assume that these attitudes and practices are derived from the Islamic faith prevalent in these societies. But this is flawed reasoning, for two reasons. First, aside from radical societies like Taliban-run Afghanistan, women in Muslim societies enjoy the same civil rights as men and can be as well educated and, within certain parameters, can perform almost any job a man can. The second flaw concerns the Islamic basis for this supposed second-class citizenship. Although it is true that the Koran, Islam's holy book, asserts a lesser status for women—being of the seventh century, it is hard to imagine it doing otherwise—it nevertheless offers women a number of rights and privileges largely absent through much of the civilized world at that time, including the right to inherit and hold property, which gave women a degree of economic independence.

A Closer Look

Before the seventh-century promulgation of the Koran, which Muslims believe consists of the revelations the Prophet Muhammad received from Allah, or God, the peoples of the Arabian Peninsula lived by tribal law and custom. And these did not treat women equitably. Newborn daughters could be killed by their fathers, while adolescent girls could be sold to future husbands as slaves, who could then terminate their marriage at will. Women had no real inheritance or property rights, leaving them economically dependent on men.

The Koran changed this in two ways—one abstract and the other specific. First, it declared women to be the spiritual equals of men, thereby due the respect accorded to all believers. It also gave them specific rights in this world, most notably the right to control their own property and receive an inheritance, radical notions for the world of that time. *Sura 4*, which is excerpted here, says, "Men ought to have a part of what their parents and kindred leave, and women a part of what their parents and kindred leave."

Although many of the laws in the Koran are clearly biased in favor of men, the holy book nevertheless says, implicitly, that women were to be protected by the law and should not be subjected to the mere whims of men. For example, it declares that a woman accused of "whoredom" can only be punished upon the declaration of four witnesses.

1 100 200 300 400 500 600 700 800 900 1000 1100 1200 1300 1400 1500 1600 1700 1800 1900 2000 CE

1.7.3 The *Sunnah* on Charity

Arabia
Seventh–Eighth Centuries CE

When God created the earth it began to shake and tremble; then God created mountains, and put them upon the earth, and the land became firm and fixed; and the angels were astonished at the hardness of the hills, and said, "O God, is there anything of thy creation harder than hills?" and God said, "Yes, water is harder than the hills, because it breaketh them." Then the angel said, "O Lord, is there anything of thy creation harder than water?" He said, "Yes, wind overcometh water: it doth agitate it and put it in motion." They said, "O our Lord! is there anything of thy creation harder than wind?" He said, "Yes, the children of Adam giving alms: those who give with their right hand, and conceal from their left, overcome all."

The liberal man is near the pleasure of God and is near paradise, which he shall enter into, and is near the hearts of men as a friend, and he is distant from hell; but the niggard is far from God's pleasure and from paradise, and far from the hearts of men, and near the fire; and verily a liberal ignorant man is more beloved by God than a niggardly worshiper.

A man's giving in alms one piece of silver in his lifetime is better for him than giving one hundred when about to die.

Think not that any good act is contemptible, though it be but your brother's coming to you with an open countenance and good humor.

There is alms for a man's every joint, every day in which the sun riseth; doing justice between two people is alms; and assisting a man upon his beast, and with his baggage, is alms; and pure words, for which are rewards; and answering a questioner with mildness is alms, and every step which is made toward prayer is alms, and removing that which is an inconvenience to man, such as stones and thorns, is alms.

The people of the Prophet's house killed a goat, and the Prophet said, "What remaineth of it?" They said, "Nothing but the shoulder; for they have sent the whole to the poor and neighbors, except a shoulder which remaineth." The Prophet said, "Nay, it is the whole goat that remaineth except its shoulder: that remaineth which they have given away, the rewards of which will be eternal, and what remaineth in the house is fleeting."

Feed the hungry, visit the sick, and free the captive if he be unjustly bound.

Source: "Selections from the Sunan or Sayings and Traditions of Mohammed: Of Charity." In *The Sacred Books and Early Literature of the East. Volume VI: Medieval Arabic, Moorish, and Turkish.* Edited by Charles F. Horne. New York: Parke, Austin, and Lipscomb, 1917, pp. 16–17.

TIMELINE   2000 1900 1800 1700 1600 1500 1400 1300 1200 1100 1000 900 800 700 600 500 400 300 200 100 1 BCE

What You Need to Know

This excerpt on Zakat, or charity, comes from the *Sunnah*, or collections of writings on the words and deeds of the Prophet Muhammad, which offer precepts on how pious Muslims should live their lives.

The *Zakat* is one of the Five Pillars of Islam, mandatory duties that all Muslims are required by Allah to perform. According to the *Sunnah*, it was Muhammad who set the example for *zakat*, though the *zakat* is also mentioned in the Koran, the holy book of Islam that Muslims believe is made up of the revelations Allah (God) gave to Muhammad.

But it was Abu-Bakr, the first caliph, or leader of the Muslim *umma*, or community, following Muhammad's death in 632, who set up the specific laws concerning *zakat*. Initially, these included a mandate for the state to enforce and collect the *zakat* as a kind of tax. That was soon dropped for voluntary payment. Today, in most Muslim-majority countries and in minority Muslim communities elsewhere, paying of the *zakat* remains voluntary, although in Saudi Arabia and Pakistan, it is compulsory under civil law.

A Closer Look

Although the Koran mandates payment of the *zakat* out of one's wealth, it does offer an exemption for those who lack *nisab*, or financial means, to do so. It also implies that the amount of the *zakat* should reflect the wealth of the individual believer. Beyond that, however, it is vague as to what percentage that should be and what kinds of wealth the percentage should be based on. Later, Islamic scholars established an annual figure of 2.5 percent and applied it to virtually all assets, aside from personal ones, such as clothing, furniture, and one's primary residence.

The Koran does, however, lay out who is to receive funds raised by the *zakat*. These include the absolute poor, those unable to meet their daily needs, persons whose debts were accrued trying to meet basic needs, orphan children living on the street, slaves whom the *zakat* donor is trying to free, and those doing God's work. In addition, the Koran says that charity must only go to Muslims or to those non-Muslims sympathetic to the faith. Finally, a portion of the *zakat* should be given to those who collect it on behalf of others.

Outside the early caliphate and a few jurisdictions today, the *zakat* is voluntary, but that applies only to the laws of this world. As this excerpt from the *Sunnah* attests, God looks very unfavorably on those who are capable of charity but who refuse to give it. "The liberal man is near the pleasure of God and is near paradise," it declares, "while the niggard [miser] is far from God's pleasure and from paradise."

1 100 200 300 400 500 600 700 800 900 1000 1100 1200 1300 1400 1500 1600 1700 1800 1900 2000 CE

1.7.4 The *Sunnah* on Prayer

Arabia
Seventh–Eighth Centuries CE

Angels come among you both night and day; then those of the night ascend to heaven, and God asketh them how they left his creatures: they say, We left them at prayer, and we found them at prayer.

The rewards for the prayers which are performed by people assembled together are double of those which are said at home.

Ye must not say your prayers at the rising or the setting of the sun: so when a limb of the sun appeareth, leave your prayers until her whole orb is up: and when the sun beginneth to set, quit your prayers until the whole orb hath disappeared; for, verily she riseth between the two horns of the devil.

No neglect of duty is imputable during sleep; for neglect can only take place when one is awake: therefore, when any of you forget your prayers, say them when ye recollect.

When any one of you goeth to sleep, the devil tieth three knots upon his neck; and saith over every knot, "The night is long, sleep." Therefore, if a servant awake and remember God, it openeth one knot; and if he perform the ablution, it openeth another; and if he say prayers, it openeth the other; and he riseth in the morning in gladness and purity: otherwise he riseth in a lethargic state.

When a Moslem performeth the ablution, it washeth from his face those faults which he may have cast his eyes upon; and when he washeth his hands, it removeth the faults they may have committed, and when he washeth his feet, it dispelleth the faults toward which they may have carried him: so that he will rise up in purity from the place of ablution.

Source: "Selections from the Sunan or Sayings and Traditions of Mohammed: Concerning Prayer." In *The Sacred Books and Early Literature of the East, Volume VI: Medieval Arabic, Moorish, and Turkish*. Edited by Charles F. Horne. New York: Parke, Austin, and Lipscomb, 1917, pp. 15–16.

What You Need to Know

The accompanying document includes passages of prayer from the *Sunnah*, the collection of writings about the words and deeds of the Prophet Muhammad.

According to the Holy Scripture of Islam, contained both in the Koran and the *Sunnah*, good Muslims are required to perform certain duties to God and other members of the Islamic *umma*, or community. Known as the Five Pillars, these are *shahadah*, or declaration that there is no god but Allah and that Muhammad is His messenger; the *zakat*, or giving away of a part of one's wealth to charity; the *sahm*, or fasting in daylight hours during the month of Ramadan, which marks the beginning of the process by which Allah sent down his revelations to Muhammad; the *hajj*, or pilgrimage to Mecca for those who are physically and financially able; and the *salat*, or daily ritual prayer, which can be conducted anywhere but should always be directed toward the holy of Mecca, where Muhammad was born and first preached his divine revelations.

A Closer Look

The accompanying excerpt from the *Sunnah* concerns the last of the five pillars of Islam mandatory duties, all Muslims are enjoined by the Koran to do the *salat*, or prayer. The word *salat* is derived from the Arabic term for "bowing," as Muslims prostate themselves before God in prayer. Of the five mandatory duties of a Muslim, prayer is the one that most affects his or her daily life because it must be performed five times daily at set hours, which vary depending on the time of year. As noted in the excerpt, the *Sunnah* is quite specific on those times, declaring that prayers must not be conducted when the sun is just coming up or just descending. There are exceptions and variations on this. Islamic scripture, for example, allows for exemptions from prayer for the mentally ill or those in the midst of an emergency. Also, women who are menstruating should not pray; as with traditional Jewish law, which excludes menstruating women from temple worship, Muslims consider menstruating women to be ritualistically impure and thus not fit to pray.

The purpose of the *salat* is not all that different from Jewish or Christian prayer. With its ritualistic opening verse—"There is no god but Allah, and the Prophet Muhammad is His messenger"—Muslims are reminded of God's omnipotence. Prayer also gives thanks for His blessings and reminds Muslims to lead a proper life, as revealed in Muslim scripture.

1.7.5 The *Sunnah* on Women and Slaves

Arabia
850–890 CE

The world and all things in it are valuable, but the most valuable thing in the world is a virtuous woman. . . .

A Muslim cannot obtain (after righteousness) anything better than a well-disposed, beautiful wife: such a wife as, when ordered by her husband to do anything, obeyeth; and if her husband look at her, is happy; and if her husband swear by her to do a thing, she doth it to make his oath true; and if he be absent from her, she wisheth him well in her own person by guarding herself from inchastity, and taketh care of his property.

Verily the best of women are those who are content with little.

Admonish your wives with kindness; for women were created out of a crooked rib of Adam, therefore if ye wish to straighten it, ye will break it; and if ye let it alone, it will be always crooked.

Every woman who dieth, and her husband is pleased with her, shall enter into paradise. . . .

A woman may be married by four qualifications; one, on account of her money; another, on account of the nobility of her pedigree; another, on account of her beauty; a fourth, on account of her faith; therefore look out for religious women, but if ye do it from any other consideration, may your hands be rubbed in dirt.

A widow shall not be married until she be consulted; nor shall a virgin be married until her consent be asked, whose consent is by her silence. . . .

Do not prevent your women from coming to the mosque: but their homes are better for them. . . .

God has ordained that your brothers should be your slaves: therefore him whom God hath ordained to be the slave of his brother, his brother must give him of the food which he eateth himself, and of the clothes wherewith he clotheth himself, and not order him to do anything beyond his power, and if he doth order such a work, he must himself assist him in doing it.

He who beateth his slaves without fault, or slappeth him in the face, his atonement for this is freeing him.

A man who behaveth ill to his slave will not enter into paradise.

Forgive thy servant 70 times a day.

Source: "Selections from the Sunan or Sayings and Traditions of Mohammed: Of Women and Slaves." In *The Sacred Books and Early Literature of the East, Volume VI: Medieval Arabic, Moorish, and Turkish.* Edited by Charles F. Horne. New York: Parke, Austin, and Lipscomb, 1917, pp. 21–22.

TIMELINE   2000 1900 1800 1700 1600 1500 1400 1300 1200 1100 1000 900 800 700 600 500 400 300 200 100 1 BCE

What You Need to Know

This excerpt about Muhammad's teachings on women and slaves is from the *Sunnah*. It was written down by followers and other believers in the first few generations after Muhammad's death in 632.

Islamic society of the medieval era consisted of several classes of people. As in many premodern societies, wealth was not necessarily the most important determinant of one's status. In the case of Islamic society, heritage and faith played greater roles in the hierarchy of rank. At the top were those who belonged to the household of the caliph, or ruler of the Islamic *umma*, or community, as well as other high-ranking Arab Muslims. The latter were descendants of the original inhabitants of the Arabian Peninsula where Islam began and essentially formed the aristocracy of Islamic society. Beneath them were later converts to Islam from other lands. Further down the ladder were the *dhimmi*, or "people of the book," essentially those who followed the monotheistic faiths—Judaism and Christianity—whose holy books were deemed scripture by Muslims. At the bottom were slaves. Like the Old and New Testaments, the Koran, or holy book of Islam, offers no objection to slavery, although it does declare that Muslims and other "protected people" cannot be enslaved. And, of course, like the scripture of Jews and Christians, Islamic law and tradition declared that men were the superiors of women, although women were afforded certain rights and privileges.

A Closer Look

The *Sunnah* is a collection of writings based on the life of the Prophet Muhammad, which includes what he said, the deeds he performed, and examples from how he lived his life. It serves as a set of precepts by which all good Muslims should live. It also offers rules about how society should be governed and organized.

The accompanying document consists of excerpts from the *Sunnah* that concern the proper treatment of lowly classes of people—namely, women and slaves. As to the former, the *Sunnah* offers a rather enlightened set of precepts, at least for its time. It declares that women—specifically, virtuous women—have a right to veto a marriage partner arranged by others. It instructs husband's to "admonish your wives with kindness" but in a rather patronizing fashion. Being made of Adam's rib, women, it declares, are naturally "crooked," so trying to straighten them may instead break them.

On slavery, the *Sunnah* is quite explicit: God ordained slavery. But it also tells masters to feed their slaves the same food they eat. In addition, it declares that if one beats his slave, then he must set that slave free for "a man who behaveth ill to his slave will not enter into paradise."

1.7.6 Koran Scroll Fragment

Baghdad, Abbasid Caliphate
750–1258 CE

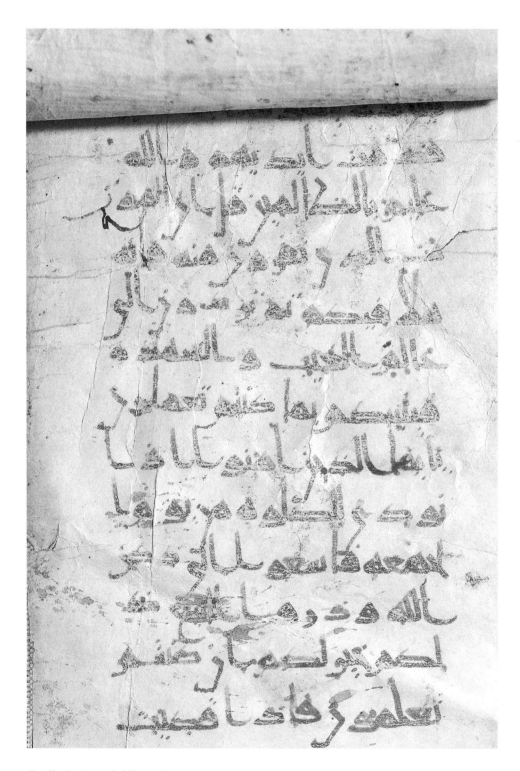

Credit: DeAgostini/Getty Images

What You Need to Know

This scroll fragment of the Koran is from the Abbasid Caliphate, which ruled over parts of the Arabic world from its capital in Baghdad from the middle of the eighth century to the middle of the thirteenth century. Muslims then, and today, not only revere the holy book for its spiritual teachings but also for the beauty of its classical Arabic.

Arabic is not only the language of the Arab people, it also serves as the language of scripture for the entire Muslim world. Indeed, Muslims believe that no language expresses the will of God better as that was the language God chose to speak to humankind through the Prophet Muhammad. Arabic is the most commonly spoken of the Semitic languages—others are Hebrew and the archaic Aramaic, the language of Palestine in the time of Christ—which are part of a broader Afro-Asiatic family of languages.

In fact, Arabic today, and even as far back as medieval times, was really two languages, a feature known to linguists as diglossia. That is, there was and is a formal Arabic, based on the classical language of the Koran, which even in Muhammad's time was somewhat different from the colloquial Arabic spoken on the streets of Mecca in everyday conversation. Today, the difference between the two is even greater. Although most Arabs revere classical Arabic, as the appropriate language for poetry, sacred writing, and formal oration, no one actually speaks it as their first language.

A Closer Look

Until the nineteenth century, printing was largely unknown in the Islamic world. Thus, most of the early copies of the Koran were written by hand by calligraphers. Such production methods meant that few private homes, others than those of high government officials and the richest of private citizens, had their own copies of the holy book. Most were, in fact, in the possession of mosques, and most Muslim faithful, who were largely illiterate, were only acquainted with Islamic scripture through oral recitation.

There were many rules and rituals about how the Koran could be written and read. As to the former, the holy book could only be written in certain types of script, although these changed over the centuries. As for oral recitation, religious scholars had established guides to pronunciation, down to the very letters and syllables of the Arabic language. Such guides were especially useful for the many Muslims for whom Arabic was not their native tongue.

1 100 200 300 400 500 600 700 800 900 1000 1100 1200 1300 1400 1500 1600 1700 1800 1900 2000 CE

1.7.7 Laws Governing Mecca

Arabia
Ninth Century CE

Amr an-Nakid from Mujahid: "Makkah is inviolable," said the Prophet, "It is not legal either to sell its dwellings or to rent its houses."...

Khalaf ibn-Hisham al-Bazzar from ibh-Juraij who said, "I have read a letter written by Umar ibn-Abd-al-Azziz in which the renting of houses in Makkah is prohibited."

Abu-Ubaid from ibn-Umar; the latter said: "The whole of al-Haram is a place of worship.."...

The following tradition regarding the text, "Alike for those who abide therein and for the stranger" was communicated to us by Uthman ibn-abi-Shaibah from Abd-ar-Rahman ibn-Sabit: By the stranger is meant the pilgrims and visitors who go there and who have equal right in the buildings, being entitled to live wherever they want, provided none of the natives of Makkah goes out of his home.

The following tradition regarding the same text was communicated to us by Uthman on the authority of Mujahid: The inhabitants of Makkah and other people are alike so far as the dwellings are concerned.

Uthman and Amr from Mujahid: Umar ibn-al-Khattab once said to the people of Makkah, "Make no doors for your houses that the stranger may live wherever he wants."

Uthman ibn-abi-Shaibah and Bakr ibn-al-Haitham from abu-Hasin—The latter said, "I once told Said ibn-Jubair in Makkah that I wanted to 'abide therein' to which he replied, 'Thou art already "abiding therein"' and he read 'Alike for those who abide therein and for the stranger.'"...

Said Sufyan ibn-Said ath-Thauri: "To rent a house in Makkah is illegal"; and he insisted on that.

According to Al-Auza I, ibn-abi-Laila and abu-Hanifah, if the rent is made during the nights of the Pilgrimage it is void, but if it is in other nights, whether the one who hires is a neighbor or not, it is all right.

According to certain followers of abu-Yusuf, its rent is absolutely legal. The one "abiding therein" and the "stranger" are alike only as regards making the circuit of the "House."

Source: al-Baladhuri, Abbas Ahmad ibn-Jabir. "Makkah." In *The Origins of the Islamic State*. Translated by Philip Hitti. New York: Columbia University Press, 1916, pp. 69–72.

TIMELINE   2000 1900 1800 1700 1600 1500 1400 1300 1200 1100 1000 900 800 700 600 500 400 300 200 100 1 BCE

What You Need to Know

This excerpt on the laws for Mecca is from the ninth-century Persian poet Ahmad al-Baladhuri's *Kitab Futuh al-Buldan*, or Book of the Conquests of Lands—that is, the conquests of Islam.

Mecca is a city in the western part of the Arabian Peninsula, known as the Heraz. It was the birthplace of the Prophet Muhammad in the year 570 and where he lived most of his life. Around the age of 40, he left Mecca to seek spiritual solace in the wilderness. There, according to Muslims, he received revelations from Allah. Upon his return to Mecca, he preached this message, gathering a small band of followers. But his sermons calling for the destruction of the pagan idols in the pre-Islamic shrine known as the Kaaba upset authorities, who drove him and his followers from the city in 622, an event known as the *hijra*. It is in that year that the Islamic era and calendar begins. In exile in Medina, another trading city about 100 miles north of Mecca, he gathered many more followers. Together, they returned to Mecca in 630 and took the city without a fight. Ever since, Mecca has been the holiest city of Islam and the Kaaba, minus its idols, the faith's holiest shrine. Muslims show their reverence for the city by praying in its direction five times daily.

A Closer Look

In this excerpt from the *Book of the Conquests of Lands*, Ahmad al-Baladhuri first declares that the entire city is a place of worship, which ultimately belongs to Allah, rather than the city's inhabitants. Thus, he notes, pilgrims have as much right to stay in its buildings as the owners do. Moreover, the law forbids anyone to receive rent from visitors.

According to Islamic scripture, good Muslims must do more than pray to Mecca five times daily; they must conduct a pilgrimage to it—an act known as the *hajj*—at least once in their lives, if they have the physical and financial means to do so. A male who undertakes such a pilgrimage has the honorific, *al-Haji*, placed after his name.

Given its sacred nature and the fact that it was the site of a massive annual pilgrimage, Muslims have developed over the centuries special laws concerning its governance. These have changed somewhat over time, reflecting social developments, political control, and technology. Where once the arduous journey to Mecca kept the number of pilgrims low, today's jet age allows hundreds of thousands to attend.

1.7.8 Al-Khwarizmi on Algebra

Baghdad, Abbasid Caliphate
ca. 820 CE

I found that these three kinds; namely, roots, squares, and numbers, may be combined together, and thus three compound species arise; that is, "squares and roots equal to numbers;" "squares and numbers equal to roots;" "roots and numbers equal to squares."

Roots and Squares are equal to Numbers; for instance, "1 square, and 10 roots of the same, amount to 39 dirhems;" that is to say, what must be the square which, when increased by 10 of its own roots, amount to 39? The solution is this: you halve the number 3 of the roots, which in the present instance yields 5. This you multiply by itself; the product is 25. Add this to 39; the sum is 64. Now take the root of this, which is 8, and subtract from it half the number of the roots, which is 5; the remainder is 3. This is the root of the square which you sought for; the square itself is 9.

Squares and Number are equal to Roots; for instance, "a square and 21 in number are equal to 10 roots of the same square." That is to say, what must be the amount of a square, which, when 21 dirhems are added to it, becomes equal to the equivalent of 10 roots of that square? Solution: Halve the number of the roots; the moiety is 5. Multiply this by itself; the product is 25. Subtract from this the 21 which are connected with the square; the remainder is 4. Extract its root; it is 2. Subtract this from the moiety of the roots, which is 5; the remainder is 3. This is the root of the square which you required, and the square is 9. Or you may add the root to the moiety of the roots; the sum is 7; this is the root of the square which you sought for, and the square itself is 49.

When you meet with an instance which refers you to this case, try its solution by addition, and if that do not serve, then subtraction certainly will. For in this case both addition and subtraction may be employed, which will not answer in any other of the three cases in which the number of the roots must be halved. And know, that, when in a question belonging to this case you have halved the number of the roots and multiplied the moiety by itself, if the product be less than the number of dirhems connected with the square, then the instance is impossible; but if the product be equal to the dirhems by themselves, then the root of the square is equal to the moiety of the roots alone, without either addition or subtraction.

In every instance where you have two squares, or more or less, reduce them to one entire square, as I have explained under the first case.

Source: Khwarizmi, Muhammad Ibn-Musa al. *The Algebra of Mohammed ben Musa*. Edited and translated by Frederic Rosen. London: J. Murray, 1831, 1986, pp. 8, 11–13.

What You Need to Know

This excerpt comes from Muhammad ibn Musa Al-Khwarizmi's *Compendiuous Book on Calculation by Completion and Balancing* on various aspects of algebra.

Algebra is a branch of mathematics in which symbols are used to represent numbers, quantities, or members of a specified set; the symbols are then manipulated to express relationships that apply to all members of the set. The English term *algebra* comes from the Arabic word *al-jebr*, meaning "reuniting of broken parts." There is a good reason for this linguistic heritage. The Arab world of the Middle Ages was renowned for its advances in mathematics.

As in many other fields of scientific inquiry, Islamic mathematicians both preserved the work of ancient scholars in the field—at a time when European learning and scholarship was at a nadir—and added to it. Historians of science offer various theories as to why the Islamic world was so adept at mathematics. One of these is Islam's emphasis on an abstract deity, whose work is rendered concrete through the injunctions of the Koran and other holy writings. This pushed Islamic scholars toward abstract thinking that explains the real world, the essence of mathematics. Also, Islam's injunction against representational art led to elaborate abstract design, which rested on a foundation of mathematics.

A Closer Look

Historians dispute exactly who invented the branch of mathematics known as algebra and when. Some put it as far back as the third century CE and the work Diophantus, a Hellenistic scholar who lived in Alexandria, Egypt. Others contend it was a Persian scholar working in Baghdad in the early ninth century who is sometimes given the title of "father of algebra." In fact, as with all science, there is no one figure responsible for inventing a field of study. Like his predecessor and successors, Muhammad ibn Musa al-Khwarizmi built on the work of others, most especially Indian scholars such as Brahmagupta of the seventh century.

What is not in question are al-Khwarizmi's specific contributions to the field. He is best known for his work on linear and quadratic equations. The excerpt from his ca. 820 text shown here provides a taste of his thinking on the subject. Notably, as with other Islamic scholars, his calculations are rendered rhetorically, in prose rather than numerical equations. Al-Khwarizmi is also recognized for doing much to popularize the Indian system of numeration in the West, which eventually became the Arabic-based numerals we use today.

But like many scholars of his day, al-Khwarizmi was a polymath, responsible for ideas and innovations across a broad number of fields. He was a geographer, who translated and added to the information about Africa and Asia compiled by Ptolemy, the great Hellenistic geographer and astronomer of the second century CE. Al-Khwarizmi also contributed improvements to key navigational and astronomical instruments, such as the astrolabe, a tool for measuring the location of stars, and the sundial.

1.7.9 Baghdad under the Abbasids

Baghdad
ca. 1000 CE

The city of Bagdad formed two vast semi-circles on the right and left banks of the Tigris, twelve miles in diameter. The numerous suburbs, covered with parks, gardens, villas and beautiful promenades, and plentifully supplied with rich, bazaars, and finely built mosques and baths, stretched for a considerable distance on both sides of the river.

In the days of its prosperity the population of Bagdad and its suburbs amounted to over two millions! The palace of the Kalif [Caliph] stood in the midst of a vast park "several hours in circumference" which beside a menagerie and aviary comprised an inclosure for wild animals reserved for the chase. The palace grounds were laid out with gardens, and adorned with exquisite taste with plants, flowers, and trees, reservoirs and fountains, surrounded by sculptured figures. On this side of the river stood the palaces of the great nobles. Immense streets, none less than forty cubits wide, traversed the city from one end to the other, dividing it into blocks or quarters, each under the control of an overseer or supervisor, who looked after the cleanliness, sanitation and the comfort of the inhabitants.

The water exits both on the north and the south were like the city gates, guarded night and day by relays of soldiers stationed on the watch towers on both sides of the river. Every household was plentifully supplied with water at all seasons by the numerous aqueducts which intersected the town; and the streets, gardens and parks were regularly swept and watered, and no refuse was allowed to remain within the walls.

An immense square in front of the imperial palace was used for reviews, military inspections, tournaments and races; at night the square and the streets were lighted by lamps.

There was also a vast open space where the troops whose barracks lay on the left bank of the river were paraded daily. The long wide estrades [platforms] at the different gates of the city were used by the citizens for gossip and recreation or for watching the flow of travelers and country folk into the capital. The different nationalities in the capital had each a head officer to represent their interests with the government, and to whom the stranger could appeal for counsel or help.

Bagdad was a veritable City of Palaces, not made of stucco and mortar, but of marble. The buildings were usually of several stories. The palaces and mansions were lavishly gilded and decorated, and hung with beautiful tapestry and hangings of brocade or silk. The rooms were lightly and tastefully furnished with luxurious divans, costly tables, unique Chinese vases and gold and silver ornaments.

Both sides of the river were for miles fronted by the palaces, kiosks, gardens and parks of the grandees and nobles, marble steps led down to the water's edge, and the scene on the river was animated by thousands of gondolas, decked with little flags, dancing like sunbeams on the water, and carrying the pleasure-seeking Bagdad citizens from one part of the city to the other. Along the wide-stretching quays lay whole fleets at anchor, sea and river craft of all kinds, from the Chinese junk to the old Assyrian raft resting on inflated skins.

The mosques of the city were at once vast in size and remarkably beautiful. There were also in Bagdad numerous colleges of learning, hospitals, infirmaries for both sexes, and lunatic asylums.

Source: Ali, Ameer. Excerpt from *History of the Saracens*. In *Readings in Ancient History: Illustrative Extracts from the Sources*. Vol. II, Chapter XI. Edited by William Stearns Davis. Boston: Allyn and Bacon, 1912–1913, pp. 365–367.

TIMELINE   2000 1900 1800 1700 1600 1500 1400 1300 1200 1100 1000 900 800 700 600 500 400 300 200 100 1 BCE

What You Need to Know

This passage comes from the *Geographical Encyclopedia*, by the author Yakut, written around the year 1000. It describes Baghdad under the Abbasid Caliphate or Islamic state.

With the death of the Prophet Muhammad in 632, the task of leading and expanding the *umma*, or Islamic community, fell to his successors. But who were these to be? Neither the Koran, Islam's holy book, or the *Sunnah*, accounts of the sayings and actions of the Prophet, had much to say on the topic of succession. Ultimately, Muhammad's closest followers chose what they called a *khalifa*, or caliph in English, an Arabic word meaning both leader and successor, to rule over the *umma*. His realm was known as the caliphate.

The first four caliphs were elected by their peers. But after the fourth, Ali, was assassinated in 661, a civil war broke out. In its wake, a follower of Muhammad's named Mu'awiya of the Umayyad clan assumed the role of leader of the caliphate. From that point on, the position of caliph became dynastic. For the next 80 or so years, the Umayyads ruled the caliphate from a new capital, Damascus, in Syria. In 747, a rival clan called the Abbasids seized power.

A Closer Look

The Abbasid rule differed significantly from that of the Umayyads, who ruled in dictatorial fashion. The Abbasids promoted the idea of citizenship and the rule of law. They were also more cosmopolitan and open to other cultures within the Islamic community than their predecessors, the Umayyads, who had been anchored in ancient Arab tradition. The Abbasids also decentralized power to local authorities throughout the Islamic world. By these means, they gained the allegiance of Muslims from Central Asia to Spain.

Under Abbasid rule, the Islamic world flourished both economically and culturally for a time. Trade expanded, public works were built, art flourished, and great scientific achievements were made. Nowhere was this more evident than in the Abbasid capital of Baghdad, as attested by this excerpt from the *Geographical Encyclopedia*, by the author Yakut, written around the year 1000. Baghdad became a major center of commerce, where almost any food or product known to the medieval world could be had in its many markets, and swelled in size, growing into, arguably, the largest city in the world by the end of the first millennium BCE. Patronage from the caliphs also meant that it was a leading center of art, science, education, and literature.

It was also a city where peoples from across the Islamic and non-Islamic worlds comingled and got on relatively well. On its street could be found Muslims from as far away as India and North Africa, Christians from Europe, Hindus from India, Buddhists from East Asia, and Jews from across the Western world.

1 100 200 300 400 500 600 700 800 900 1000 1100 1200 1300 1400 1500 1600 1700 1800 1900 2000 CE

1.7.10 Muslim Views on Marriage

Persia
1105 CE

Seeing that God, as the Koran says, "only created men and genii for the purpose of worshipping," the first and obvious advantage of marriage is that the worshippers of God may increase in number.
. . .

Another advantage of marriage is that, as the Prophet said, the prayers of children profit their parents when the latter are dead, and children who die before their parents intercede for them on the Day of Judgment. . . .

It is related of a certain celibate saint that he once dreamt that the Judgment Day had come. The sun had approached close to the earth and people were perishing of thirst; a crowd of boys were moving about giving them water out of gold and silver vessels. But when the saint asked for water he was repulsed, and one of the boys said to him, "Not one of us here is your son." As soon as the saint awoke he made preparations to marry.

Another advantage of marriage is that to sit with and be friendly to one's wife is a relaxation for the mind after being occupied in religious duties, and after such relaxation one may return to one's devotions with renewed zest. Thus the Prophet himself, when he found the weight of his revelations press too heavily upon him touched his wife Ayesha and said, "Speak to me, O Ayesha, speak to me!" This he did that, from that familiar human touch, he might receive strength to support fresh revelations. For a similar reason he used to bid the Muezzin Bilal give the call to prayer, and sometimes he used to smell sweet perfumes. It is a well-known saying of his, "I have loved three things in the world: perfumes, and women, and refreshment in prayer." On one occasion Omar asked the Prophet what were the things specially to be sought in the world. He answered, "A tongue occupied in the remembrance of God, a grateful heart, and a believing wife."

A further advantage of marriage is that there should be some one to take care of the house, cook the food, wash the dishes, and sweep the floor, etc. If a man is busy in such work he cannot acquire learning, or carry on his business, or engage in his devotions properly. For this reason Abu Suleiman has said, "A good wife is not a blessing of this world merely, but of the next, because she provides a man leisure in which to think of the next world"; and one of the Caliph Omar's sayings is, "After faith, no blessing is equal to a good wife."

Marriage has, moreover, this good in it, that to be patient with feminine peculiarities, to provide the necessaries which wives require, and to keep them in the path of the law, is a very important part of religion.

Source: al-Ghażālī, Abu Hamid. *The Alchemy of Happiness*. Ch. VII. Translated by Claud Field. London: John Murray, 1910, pp. 102–105.

What You Need to Know

This excerpt comes from the *Kimiya-yi Sa'adat*, or *The Alchemy of Happiness*, written by the Persian theologian Abu Hamid Muhammad al-Ghazali around the year 1105.

Like all of the world's major religions, Islam offers a template for how worshippers should lead their lives, with marriage being one of the things all the faithful should engage in. And, indeed, both the Koran, the revelations of Allah (God), and the Hadith, the deeds and sayings of the Prophet Muhammad, have much to say on the subject. Verses in the Koran liken marriage to a form of protection and comfort for the couple, much like clothing. But, of course, the main purpose of marriage is procreative. Without marriage, the Koran says, there would be no continuity to human civilization and no new worshippers of Allah. The Muslim holy book also emphasizes the importance of the family as both a social and economic unit, providing emotional and physical support to its members. These scriptural arguments for marriage are expanded on in this excerpt from al-Ghazali's *The Alchemy of Happiness*.

A Closer Look

Alchemy was a pseudoscience practiced in both Islamic and European societies in the Middle Ages. It focused on the search for catalytic substances that could transform matter and energy, such as the philosopher's stone that would turn base metals into precious ones or the elixir of life that change mortal bodies into immortal ones. By using the word in his title, al-Ghazali is saying that his book contains wisdom that can transform a life of sadness into one of happiness.

On the topic of marriage, al-Ghazali begins by reiterating the Koranic injunctions for marriage—"that the worshippers of God may increase in number." He notes that the prayers of the children that come from marriage will aid the deceased on Judgment Day. But he then goes on to list less theoretical arguments. In addition, he says, with an emphasis on the needs of men typical of al-Ghazali's day and age, that the relaxation a man finds with his wife renews his energy for more devotion to God.

But al-Ghazali also cites more worldly reasons for marriage, again with a patriarchal slant. Marriage offers a man someone to take care of the home, "cook the food, wash the dishes, and sweep the floor." At the same time, marriage allows women the benefit of being instructed in the ways of God by their husbands.

1.7.11 Small Plaques for Casket

Fatimid Caliphate
Twelfth–Thirteenth Centuries CE

Credit: DEA /G. Nimatallah/DeAgostini/Getty Images

What You Need to Know

Shown here is a plaque from a funeral casket from the twelfth or thirteenth century, during the Fatimid Calipthate, or Islamic state.

Founded in the 600s, centuries after the time of Jesus Christ and millennia since the beginning of the Judaic religion, Islam builds on both of these traditions. Indeed, the Prophet Muhammad, who received the revelations from Allah, or God, that serve as the basis of the faith, implied that the revelations he received were the culmination of God's revelations to humankind.

Not surprisingly, then, many of the tenets of Islamic faith, resemble those of the *dhimmi*, an Arab word for the so-called "peoples of the book," that is, Jews and Christians. Among these are those concerning death. According to Islam, Allah is omnipotent, with full control over everything that happens on Earth and in heaven. Nothing can happen without Allah's permission. Still, Muslims hold that God gave humankind free will to decide between right and wrong.

The Koran, or holy book of Islam, also says that Allah has set aside a judgment day for some time in the future. On that day, the world will be destroyed and all the souls of people who have ever lived are called to judgment. The good will live in Allah's presence for eternity; the evildoers will spend eternity in hell.

A Closer Look

The Sharia, or Islamic holy law, calls for simplicity in funerary ritual. First, the body must be bathed and then shrouded in cloth. After that, *salah*, or formal prayers, are said over the dead, and then the body is buried. (Cremation is forbidden under Islamic law.) Again, according to Sharia, the body should be lain perpendicular to Mecca, the holiest city of Islam, to which observant Muslims direct their prayers five times daily, but should not be put into a casket.

Yet the accompanying image shows a plaque from the Fatimid Caliphate, which ruled over much of the Western Islamic world from the tenth century onward. Not only does it includes an image of humans but was part of a casket, both forbidden under Islamic law. What, then, do we make of it? The Islamic world was a heterogenous one, containing numerous cultures and even peoples of different faiths, and there was often much leniency in following Islamic law. Moreover, the Fatimids were that part of the Islamic world geographically adjacent to the Christian world and contained the Holy Lands of the Levant, conquered by the Christians during the Crusades of the eleventh through thirteenth centuries. This plaque, which comes from either the twelfth or thirteenth century, may reflect Christian influence. Indeed, the figure on the right, which may be a depiction of the deceased, bears a resemblance to medieval European saints' portraits.

1 100 200 300 400 500 600 700 800 900 1000 1100 1200 1300 1400 1500 1600 1700 1800 1900 2000 CE

1.7.12 Bronze Ewer Inlaid with Silver

Abbasid Caliphate
Thirteenth Century CE

Credit: DeAgostini/Getty Images

What You Need to Know

This ewer, or pitcher, dates from the period of the Abbasid Caliphate, which ruled over parts of the Arab and Islamic world from its capital Baghdad from around 750 to the conquest and sacking of the city by Mongol invaders in 1258.

To understand the art of the Islamic world, it is necessary to understand the principles of the faith that underpins that world. According to Muslims, in the year 610, an Arab merchant named Muhammad received revelations from Allah or God. When he began to preach this message, he was booted from the city by officials associated with the pre-Islamic faith of the region, whose holiest site was a shrine known as the Kaaba. When Muhammad and his followers returned in triumph to the city in 630, he seized the Kaaba and destroyed all of what he considered pagan idols within. Allah, he declared, had forbidden not only religious representations but representations of humans in any form, which Muhammad said were the work of Satan.

A Closer Look

Despite Muhammad's ban on representational imagery, Muslims in subsequent centuries proved more tolerant. They tended to respect the sacred images of other faiths, especially those of Christians, and included human faces and forms in nonsacred art, especially on a small scale and as long as it was not part of a public project. Still, Islamic art is best known and appreciated for its exquisite, even ecstatic use of abstract imagery and design.

An example is the ewer shown here; although it is clearly for private use, it nevertheless eschews representational imagery. This may be because it is a three-dimensional object. Many Muslim theologians interpreted the ban on representational imagery to apply only to objects that cast a shadow. Hence, paintings and tapestries were exempt from the taboo. Some contemporary religious scholars apply the same logic to video images, because they, too, do not cast shadows.

The ewer shown here is made of bronze and is inlaid with silver. It is obviously a quite precious object and so probably came from a wealthy household. It may have been used for water or other nonalcoholic beverages, alcohol, of course, being forbidden under Islam. Islamic artisans devoted much energy to creating exquisite artifacts of this type, that is, daily movable objects, an inheritance from the ancient nomadic traditions of the Arabs.

1 100 200 300 400 500 600 700 800 900 1000 1100 1200 1300 1400 1500 1600 1700 1800 1900 2000 CE

1.7.13 Body Diagram from the *Anatomy of the Human Body*

Persia
Fifteenth and Sixteenth Centuries CE

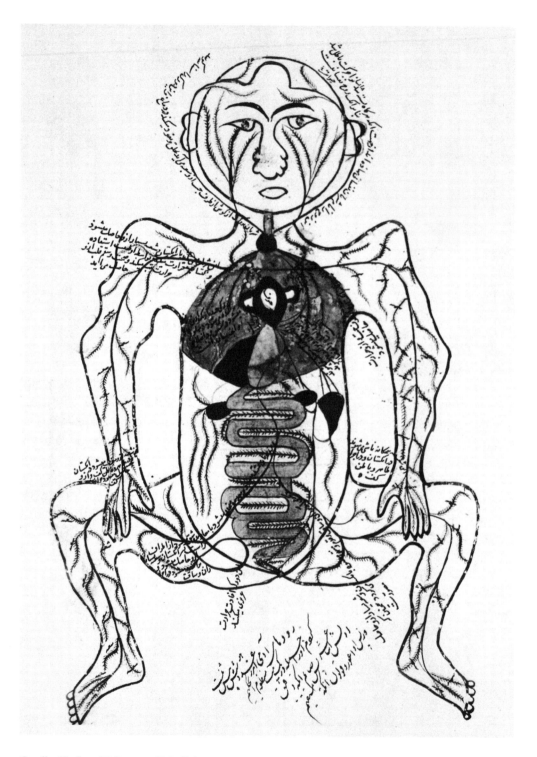

Credit: National Library of Medicine

What You Need to Know

The accompanying image shows a body diagram, first researched and drawn by Mansur ibn Ilyas, a Persian physician of the fourteenth century, though the example here is from a later copy of his manuscript published in either the late fifteenth or early sixteenth century. Of particular note is the detailed portrait of the body's venous system and of its intestinal tract.

Emerging out of the Arabian Peninsula in the early seventh century CE, Islamic armies captured most of southwest Asia, North Africa, and even Spain within a hundred years. The Islamic sphere they created was culturally diverse, but also had elements that united it. Most important was the Islamic faith, although Muslim rulers were quite tolerant toward members of other faiths adhering to the Abrahamic tradition, that is, Christians and Jews, as long as they paid tribute to their Islamic rulers. Both communities contributed much to Islamic scholarship, including in the field of medicine.

Another unifying factor was Arabic, which became the language used for administration, education, and even among the masses. Many of the great scholarly texts from around the medieval Islamic world were written in Arabic. In sum, the Islamic world was united by a common set of ethics and a common culture, even as it absorbed the teachings of other societies. This combination of cosmopolitanism, a shared outlook on religion, and a common literary tradition created one of the great flowerings of learning and scholarship of the medieval era in Western history.

A Closer Look

Perhaps nowhere did Islamic scholarship of the medieval era soar higher than in the realm of science. Arabs and other peoples of the Arab world helped preserve the teachings of ancient scholars while Europe was in chaos, but they also added much knowledge in the fields of astronomy, alchemy (then a legitimate scientific pursuit), mathematics, and medicine. Indeed, Islamic medicine far surpassed anything achieved in Christian Europe at the time.

Among the achievements were Baghdad physician al-Razi's encyclopedia on medicine, which, among other things, discerned the difference between measles and smallpox, two of the most common and deadliest diseases of the era. Al-Zahrawi of Islamic Spain produced great advances in surgery, including the cauterization of wounds. Ibn Sina, better known as Avicenna in English, of Bukhara in Central Asia was an expert in pharmacology, compiling an index of no less than 700 useful drugs.

All of this medical achievement was premised on knowledge of human anatomy, of which Islamic culture was especially adept, as this illustration shows.

1 100 200 300 400 500 600 700 800 900 1000 1100 1200 1300 1400 1500 1600 1700 1800 1900 2000 CE

1.7.14 Ceremonial Ottoman Caftan

Ottoman Empire
ca. Fifteenth and Sixteenth Centuries CE

Credit: tolgabayraktar/iStockphoto.com

What You Need to Know

A ceremonial caftan from the Ottoman Empire is shown here.

For Europeans of the early modern era, the court of the Ottoman Empire was synonymous with sensual indulgence and wealth. As to the former, the Sultan's palace was not necessarily the den of sexual iniquity that contemporary Europeans portrayed it as. The sultan's many concubines were not in the harem for sexual pleasure alone but to ensure a competent successor to the throne, as their children, under Ottoman law, gained royal status as the offspring of the sultan.

But there was a good reason for European views of Ottoman wealth, as this luxurious embroidered caftan of the kind worn by the sultan illustrates. Ruling as an absolute monarch over a realm that stretched from North Africa to Arabia and across southeastern Europe, the sultans in Istanbul had vast resources at their disposal. A productive agricultural sector and an effective taxation system, at least in the early centuries of Ottoman rule, guaranteed a steady flow of revenue into government coffers, which were, in effect, the personal treasury of the sultan.

A Closer Look

Caftans, or kaftans, as the word is sometimes spelled, are long coats buttoned in the front, usually stretching to the ankles and with sleeves that descend to the wrist. They are sometimes held in place by sashes. They can be made from any number of materials—wool, cotton, silk, and others—and have been worn for thousands of years and across cultures from the Eastern Asia to Western Africa, although they were never popular in Western Europe.

In Islamic cultures, they were often the dress of court officials and aristocrats. The fabrics they were made from and the designs incorporated into them often denoted the person's social and even political status. The more luxurious the fabric and the more elaborate the design, the higher up in the social hierarchy the wearer was. Caftans were also used in diplomacy. The sultan or his representatives often presented them to foreign dignitaries as a way to cement better relations or conclude a treaty.

As with almost any form of dress, the caftan was subject to fashion trends. As the centuries progressed from the sixteenth-century heyday of the Ottoman Empire, the caftans began to feature more intricate designs and brighter colors. Their manufacture reflected the extent of the Ottoman Empire. Originally made of Turkish fabrics, the most expensive caftans came to be made not just of Middle Eastern cotton but of fine woolens from Europe—typically for cold weather wear—and silk from distant China.

1 100 200 300   400   500   600   700   800   900   1000 1100 1200 1300   1400 1500 1600   1700 1800 1900 2000 CE

Part 8:
Africa

4000 BCE–Sixteenth Century CE

1.8.1 Saharan Prehistoric Cave Painting

Tassili n'Ajjer, Algeria
4000–2000 BCE

Credit: Patrick Gruban/Flickr

What You Need to Know

The rock art in the accompanying photo is from the site of Tassili n'Ajjer in the Sahara. It depicts a hunting scene and dates back to 4000–2000 BCE.

Today, the Sahara, the world's largest desert, is perhaps the most forbidding environment on Earth, outside the polar regions, with the highest sustained temperatures ever recorded and an average rainfall of less than an inch. But this has not always been the case. For the thousands of years after the last ice age ended around 10,000 BCE, the Sahara, if not exactly lush, enjoyed a semiarid environment, akin to that experienced along the populated Mediterranean Coast of North Africa today.

Higher rainfall watered grasslands that attracted herds of large quadrupeds, including horses, buffalo, camels, and various forms of antelope. Small bands of nomadic hunters preyed on these creatures. Later, in the first millennium BCE, these people would begin to domesticate some of these animals, practicing an early form of pastoralism along the fringes of the desert.

But even during these rainier times, the region was prone to periodic but quite lengthy droughts. Some historians suggest that it was during one of these that people began to settle in the Nile valley to eventually practice agriculture and establish one of the world's first civilizations.

A Closer Look

Rock and cave paintings, such as the one shown here from Tassili n'Ajjer, in modern-day Algeria, have been found on every continent on Earth. The creations of hunting and gathering peoples, they typically depicted animals being pursued or slain by hunters. The caves at Tassili n'Ajjer hold roughly 15,000 such paintings. Other ruins found there include habitations, burial mounds, and smaller artifacts, such as ceramic sherds. The paintings were typically made from mineral pigments—the reddish ones shown here came from ocher, an oxide of iron—and applied with fingers or simple brushes, although no cave painter implements have ever been found.

Archaeologists have developed a number of theories for why prehistoric hunting and gathering peoples painted such images. Because they are located deep in caves, where they would be protected from the elements, scholars theorize that they were more than merely decoration; they had ritualistic meaning. Perhaps by depicting the animals, the creators of the rock art believed they would gain some kind of control over them, ensuring more successful hunts. This particular cave painting seems to provide evidence for that conclusion; the animal is depicted in a still position while the hunters, some of whom are carrying bows, are shown in motion.

1   100   200   300   400   500   600   700   800   900   1000   1100   1200   1300   1400   1500   1600   1700   1800   1900   2000 CE

1.8.2 Egyptian New Kingdom Fresco Depicting Nubian Servants

Thebes, Egypt
ca. 1290–1224 BCE

Credit: DEA/G. Dagli Orti/DeAgostini/Getty Images

What You Need to Know

This fresco comes from the tomb of King Ramses II in the Valley of the Kings, a burial site for pharaohs and nobles from the sixteenth to the eleventh centuries BCE, located near the city of Thebes (present-day Luxor) in southern Egypt. Ramses, one of the longest reigning and most powerful of the pharaohs, ruled over Egypt from 1279 to 1213 BCE. He was known by the Egyptians as "Great Ancestor," for his military conquests and expansion of the kingdom outside the Nile Valley.

The term "Nubian" refers to a people of ancient times who lived along the Nile River and in surrounding deserts directly to the south of Egypt below the first cataracts, which blocked upstream navigation, at Aswan. The origins of the term are disputed. Some linguists say it is derived from the ancient Egyptian word for gold, or "nebu," because much of that precious metal in Egypt came from there. Other say it is simply a variant of Noubai, the name a nomadic people of the region gave themselves. The Egyptians themselves also referred to the Nubians as Kushites, after the name—Kush—they gave to the lands south of their kingdom.

Paleolithic peoples had been living in the region for hundreds of thousands of years. By the mid–Neolithic era, around 6000 BCE, they had begun to settle into stable agricultural communities, among the first of the world's peoples to do so. It was also around this time that they came into contact with the people of the Lower Nile, or Egypt, who would come to heavily influence Nubian culture after the rise of the pharaohs in the third millennium BCE.

A Closer Look

The fresco depicts two Nubian servants, their ancestry notable in their dark skin and haloes of curly hair. Although Egypt periodically asserted its control over Nubia through military means, including under Ramses II, the relationship between the two civilizations was typically more benign. There was much trade and cultural exchange between them, while intermarriage, particularly in southern Egypt where the two comingled, was quite common. Today, one can note the Nubian heritage in the dark skin and curly hair prevalent among many Egyptians.

Depicting Nubians as servants did not necessarily indicate an inferior status. Working in the household of the pharaoh and other nobles was often a position of high status. The figures depicted here are dressed in elaborate clothing, indicating that they were probably not simply household servants but trusted attendants.

Nubians also served in the court of the pharaoh, as advisors as well as attendants, and were represented in the elite corps of the Egyptian, serving both as soldiers and in positions of high command. And for 75 years in the eighth and seventh century BCE, Nubians even became pharaohs, after one of their own kings conquered Lower Egypt.

1 100 200 300 400 500 600 700 800 900 1000 1100 1200 1300 1400 1500 1600 1700 1800 1900 2000 CE

1.8.3 Hunters of the Horn of Africa

East Africa
ca. 23 CE

Far in the interior was a place called Endera [right about modern Aksum], inhabited by a naked tribe [the Gymnetae] who use bows and reed arrows, the points of which are hardened in the fire. They generally shoot the animals from trees, sometimes from the ground. They have numerous herds of wild cattle among them, on the flesh of which they subsist, and on that of other wild animals. When they have taken nothing in the chase, they dress dried skins upon hot coals, and are satisfied with food of this kind. It is their custom to propose trials of skill in archery for those who have not attained manhood. . . .

Further still towards the south [near modern Addis Ababa] are the Cynamolgi [Greek: "dog milkers"], called by the natives Agrii, with long hair and long beards, who keep a breed of very large dogs for hunting the Indian cattle which come into their country from the neighboring district, driven there either by wild beasts or by scarcity of pasturage. The time of their incursion is from the summer solstice to the middle of winter. . . .

Above is the city Darada, and a hunting-ground for elephants, called "At the Well." The district is inhabited by the Elephantophagi (or Elephant-eaters), who are occupied in hunting them. When they descry from the trees a herd of elephants directing their course through the forest, they do not then attack, but they approach by stealth and hamstring the hindmost stragglers from the herd. Some kill them with bows and arrows, the latter being dipped in the gall of serpents. The shooting with the bow is performed by three men, two, advancing in front, hold the bow, and one draws the string. Others remark the trees against which the elephant is accustomed to rest, and, approaching on the opposite side, cut the trunk of the tree low down. When the animal comes and leans against it, the tree and the elephant fall down together. The elephant is unable to rise, because its legs are formed of one piece of bone which is inflexible; the hunters leap down from the trees, kill it, and cut it in pieces. The nomads call the hunters Acatharti, or impure.

Above this nation is situated a small tribe---the Struthophagi (or Bird-eaters), in whose country [about modern Lake Tana] are birds of the size of deer, which are unable to fly, but run with the swiftness of the ostrich. Some hunt them with bows and arrows, others covered with the skins of birds. They hide the right hand in the neck of the skin, and move it as the birds move their necks. With the left hand they scatter grain from a bag suspended to the side; they thus entice the birds, until they drive them into pits, where the hunters despatch them with cudgels. The skins are used both as clothes and as coverings for beds. The Ethiopians called Simi are at war with these people, and use as weapons the horns of antelopes.

Source: *The Geography of Strabo: Literally Translated, with Notes.* Vol. 3. Translated by H. C. Hamilton, Esq., & W. Falconer. London: H. G. Bohn, 1857, pp. 196–197.

TIMELINE   2000 1900 1800 1700 1600 1500 1400 1300 1200 1100 1000 900 800 700 600 500 400 300 200 100 1 BCE

What You Need to Know

This passage about the people of the Horn of Africa is from Strabo's work *Geographica*, or *The Geography*, which is a compendium of information on various lands compiled during his extensive travels. Strabo was a Greek historian and geographer who lived in the first century BCE and the first century CE. Although little known in its own time, *Geographica* is one of the best sources scholars have today on the ways of life of diverse peoples of the ancient world.

Over the course of the Paleolithic era, which began 400,000 years ago and continued until the Neolithic era 10,000 years ago, humans followed a nomadic way of life, depending on the hunting of wild game and gathering of native plants for sustenance. Over the same period, humans began to fashion increasingly sophisticated tools and express themselves in rituals and artistry. Although the Neolithic era saw a transition to sedentary living and a dependence on agriculture and domesticated livestock among various peoples around the world, most of humanity remained hunters and gatherers for much longer.

A Closer Look

The excerpt here from *Geographica* is based on Strabo's observations taken during expeditions to what is now Sudan and Ethiopia and describes various hunting and gathering peoples of the region south of Egypt. The first, from a place called Endera in Axum, an Ethiopian kingdom of the time, he calls the Gynetae. They are primarily hunters, he notes, who use the most basic of weapons, bows and reed arrows. Another group he refers to as the Cynamolgi, or "dog milkers" in Greek. In the passage quoted here, he does not mention them drinking dog milk but he does note that they possess a very large type of canine for hunting. A third and fourth group are described as the Elephantophagi, or "Elephant-eaters" in Greek, and the Struthophagi, or Bird-Eaters. Although Strabo's descriptions paint a picture of very primitive peoples, as different from a cultured Greek of the era as humans could be, they were in fact incorporated into the larger Roman world. The peoples of the ancient Mediterranean world prized elephant ivory and ostrich feathers, which they obtained, if through middlemen, from these hunters and gatherers of the Horn of Africa.

1 100 200 300 400 500 600 700 800 900 1000 1100 1200 1300 1400 1500 1600 1700 1800 1900 2000 CE

1.8.4 Bronze Relief of Benin Warriors

Nigeria
Sixteenth Century CE

Credit: Library of Congress

What You Need to Know

The bronze plaque shown here is from the Benin Kingdom. It dates from the sixteenth century and depicts a nobleman, wearing a high choker necklace made from coral beads, standing next to attendants.

In the fifteenth century, there arose in the rain forests of West Africa—in what is now the Niger Delta region—the kingdom of Benin. It lasted for roughly 500 years, until absorbed by the British Empire at the end of the nineteenth century. Little is known about the kingdom at its height in the fifteenth and sixteenth centuries, although it seems to have been ruled by a king who governed in concert with local nobles. Indeed, there appears to have been frequent power struggles between the two, which weakened the kingdom and left to it be partially dismembered by other kingdoms over the centuries. The court of the king, or *oba*, was characterized by elaborate ceremony and rituals. Early European visitors describe the capital of Benin City, in what is now southwest Nigeria, as vast, well planned, and scrupulously maintained, with constant patrols to maintain domestic peace and no sign of beggars or homeless persons.

A Closer Look

The Kingdom of Benin was also a center of great artistic output. Most notable were carvings in ivory and bronze. Of special note are Benin's bronze plaques. Nearly 1,000 survive to the present day. Typically featuring front-facing, full-length portraits of important personages, they tell the story of court life and military conquests, as well as cosmological concepts. The one shown here, like most others of its kind, is believed to have decorated the walls of the *oba*'s palace complex at Benin City.

Benin society was highly structured with rigid social ranking. Craftsmen were organized into guilds, including blacksmithing, weaving, ivory carving, and so on. These were often family affairs, with fathers passing on their membership to their sons. As with European guilds, those of Benin were meant to keep the numbers of practitioners limited, and thus the price for their goods high. But they also ensured a certain level of craftsmanship and provided various services for their members, including burial insurance, in exchange for fees. Of all of the guilds, the most prestigious of these were for those who cast in bronze. Their high social status was due in part to the fact that much of their work was for the king and nobles. But it also came from their skills; the Benin process of making bronze castings, known as the lost wax method, was quite complex and difficult to learn.

1 100 200 300 400 500 600 700 800 900 1000 1100 1200 1300 1400 1500 1600 1700 1800 1900 2000 CE

1.8.5 Yoruba Ancestor Monolith

Nigeria
Sixteenth Century CE

Credit: DeAgostini/Getty Images

What You Need to Know

This sixteenth-century Yoruba monolith, rendered from basalt and standing just under six feet, thus life-size, depicts the spirit of an ancestor.

The Yoruba, who today number about 35 million, are a people united by a common language and culture who inhabit what is today southwestern Nigeria and much of the neighboring country of Benin. Origins of the Yoruba people date back to the first millennium BCE, while their recent history can be traced to the first half of the second millennium CE.

The Yoruba, of course, have their own legends explaining their origins. Oral histories state that the Yoruba people are descended from the first man created by Oduduwa, the younger brother of Obatala, the god attributed with the creation of the earth. All of creation, however, was the work of the supreme Yoruba deity, Olodumare.

The first man became king of the very first city of the Yoruba, the legendary Ile-Ife. Archaeologists believe that Ile-Ife may correspond to the real city of Ife, located in southwest Nigeria, which dates to the seventh century BCE. Meanwhile, Olduduwa also had other sons and daughters who became the founders of rival kingdoms and peoples.

A Closer Look

The Yoruba believe that human beings consist of two elements, the body and the spirit. The latter consists of two elements: the *emi*, or breath, and the *ori*, or brain. The *emi* is the spirit's vital energy, which animates the body but also can think and act independently of it. The *ori* has many more aspects to it than the *emi*. It represents the source of thought, but it also determined the person's destiny and fate. At the same time, the *ori* is also conceptualized as the person's ancestral guardian soul. The Yoruba believe in reincarnation, with the soul moving from body to body after death. By appealing to this aspect of *ori*, a person can take control of his or her destiny. In a sense, then, the *ori* embodies both the idea of predetermination and free will.

To gain control of one's fate, one must worship his own *ori*. But the Yoruba, like many peoples of sub-Saharan Africa, do not identify themselves strictly as individuals but as the sum of their relationships, particular familial ones. Thus, to have a say in one's destiny, a person has to worship all of his family's ancestral souls, who watch over him or her. The accompanying image of an *ori* incarnated as an ancestor would be prayed to regularly to determine the fate of the worshipper.

1 100 200 300 400 500 600 700 800 900 1000 1100 1200 1300 1400 1500 1600 1700 1800 1900 2000 CE

1.8.6 Tellem Rain Sculpture

Mali
Fifteenth–Seventeenth Centuries CE

Credit: DeAgostini/Getty Images

What You Need to Know

This Tellem sculpture was found in the cliff dwellings of the Bandiagara Escarpment. Made of wood, it has been dated to sometime between the years 1400 and 1700, preserved by the region's arid climate.

The Bandiagara Escarpment consists of a series of sandstone cliffs, some 1,500 feet above the plains to the south, in the Mopti Region, of present-day Mali, south of the Niger River. The cliffs were originally the home of the Tellem people, who built their homes directly onto the lower sides of the cliffs. They also dug caves high up on the cliffs to keep them safe from the flash floods that frequently strike the area. So spectacular are the ruins that they have been deemed a World Heritage Site by UNESCO, the United Nation's scientific and cultural branch. Little is known about the Tellem, although some accounts say they were of small stature, perhaps one of the pre-Bantu peoples of the region. Bantu peoples emerged out of what is now Nigeria to dominate sub-Saharan Africa in the second and first millennia BCE. One of these, the Dogon eventually took control of Bandiagara around the year 1400 CE. It is not known whether they conquered the Tellem or simply assimilated with them. In either case, the Tellem culture disappeared sometime after their arrival and little is known of it.

A Closer Look

This Tellem sculpture depicts what archaeologists believe is a figure of a woman with her arm raised in prayer for rain. The sex of the figure is significant. Females in all cultures are symbols of fertility, and rain made the world fertile.

Rain, and the lack of it, was no doubt of the greatest concern to the Tellem people. The Sahel region where they dwelled, although better watered than the Sahara to the north, was—and is—notorious for its fickle rainfall. In some years, there is an overabundance, and in others there is little.

The elaborate cliff side villages and tombs indicate that the Tellem were not nomads or hunters and gatherers. That way of life would not nearly have provided enough food to sustain such densely populated villages. It also would have made rainfall all that more important. If they were like other African peoples of the region, the Tellem would have worshipped a host of deities, many of them embodiments of natural forces, such as rain and thunder. The figure here is probably appealing to such a deity.

1 100 200 300 400 500 600 700 800 900 1000 1100 1200 1300 1400 1500 1600 1700 1800 1900 2000 CE

1.8.7 Ethiopian Orthodox Gospel Book

Ethiopia
ca. 1504–1505 CE

Credit: Getty Images

What You Need to Know

This image is from a gospel book, illuminated by an unknown artist of the early sixteenth century. It depicts Saint Mark in the act of writing his gospel, describing the life, death, and resurrection of Christ. Notably, Saint Mark is portrayed as an African, with deep brown skin and a halo of curly black hair. The inscription at the top refers to the date on which the illumination was made.

Ethiopia is the oldest independent state in Africa and among the oldest civilizations in the world. Inhabiting the highlands of the Horn of Africa, the Ethiopians are described in the ancient writings of both the Greeks—the fifth-century BCE historian Herodutus mentions them in his writings—and the Hebrews. According to the Old Testament, the Ethiopian Queen of Sheba visited Jerusalem in the time of King Solomon at the beginning of the first millennium BCE. The word *Ethiopia*, according to the Ethiopians themselves, may come either from Etiopik, a descendant of Noah. But most linguists believe the name comes from the Greek term for "men with sunburned faces."

The first great kingdom of Ethiopia was Axum, which arose around the time of Christ. Over the next 500 years, Axum and its successor states extended their political and economic sway over much of the Horn of Africa and into the Arabian Peninsula, across the Red Sea. The rise of Islam, however, diminished their power. Cast out of Arabia in the seventh century, they soon lost control of neighboring peoples in Africa. By the sixteenth century, even the heartland of Ethiopia had fallen under the sway of Islamic invaders.

A Closer Look

Today, Ethiopia is the only predominantly Christian country in the Horn of Africa. Historians believed that the faith arrived in the kingdom sometime in the fourth century, brought there by missionaries from Egypt. The Ethiopian variant of Christianity still resembles that of the Coptic Christians of Egypt. Although most peoples in northeast Africa converted to Islam in the seventh century, the peoples of the Ethiopian Highlands remained faithful to Christianity. Today, the country of Ethiopia is roughly two-thirds Christian and one-third Muslim.

Traditionally, the Ethiopian Orthodox Church was—and is—a highly structured institution. Rites and ceremonies were directed by priests, who often offered prayers to patron saints and God for his congregation as a whole. The Ethiopian church calendar was full of holy days. On such days, priests would carry the *tabot*, or ark, containing relics of the local saint through the community. Indeed, it was the tabot, rather than the church building, which was consecrated. Fasts were central to the practice of Ethiopian Christianity—not just at Lent, but for a number of holy events throughout the year.

1 100 200 300 400 500 600 700 800 900 1000 1100 1200 1300 1400 1500 1600 1700 1800 1900 2000 CE

1.8.8 Description of Timbuktu and Its People

Timbuktu
ca. 1510 CE

This name was in our times (as some think) imposed upon this kingdom from the name of a certain town so called, which (they say) king Mense Suleiman founded in the year of the Hegeira 610 [7], and it is situate within twelve miles of a certain branch of Niger, all the houses whereof are now changed into cottages built of chalk, and covered with thatch. Howbeit there is a most stately temple to be seen, the walls whereof are made of stone and lime; and a princely palace also built by a most excellent workman of Granada [8]. Here are many shops of artificers, and merchants, and especially of such as weave linen and cotton cloth. And hither do the Barbary merchants bring cloth of Europe. All the women of this region except maid-servants go with their faces covered, and sell all necessary victuals. The inhabitants, & especially strangers there residing, are exceeding rich, insomuch, that the king that now is, married both his daughters unto two rich merchants. Here are many wells, containing most sweet water; and so often as the river Niger overfloweth, they conveigh the water thereof by certain sluices into the town. Corn, cattle, milk, and butter this region yeeldeth in great abundance: but salt is very scarce here; for it is brought hither by land from Tegaza, which is five hundred miles distant. When I my self was here, I saw one camel's load of salt sold for 80 ducates. The rich king of Tombuto hath many plates and scepters of gold, some whereof weigh 1300 pounds: and he keeps a magnificent and well furnished court. When he travelleth any whither he rideth upon a camel, which is lead by some of his noblemen; and so he doth likewise when he goeth to warfare, and all his soldiers ride upon horses. Whosoever will speak unto this king must first fall down before his feet, & then taking up earth roust sprinkle it upon his own head & shoulders: which custom is ordinarily observed by them that never saluted the king before, or come as ambassadors from other princes. He hath always three thousand horsemen, and a great number of footmen that shoot poisoned arrows, attending upon him. They have often skirmishes with those that refuse to pay tribute, and so many as they take, they sell unto the merchants of Tombuto. Here are very few horses bred, and the merchants and courtiers keep certain little nags which they use to travel upon: but their best horses are brought out of Barbary. And the king so soon as he heareth that any merchants are come to town with horses, he commandeth a certain number to be brought before him, and choosing the best horse for himself, he payeth a most liberal price for him [9].

Source: *The History and Description of Africa and of the Notable Things Therein Contained, written by Al-Hassan Ibn-Mohammed al-Wezaz Al-Fasi, a Moor, Baptised as Giovanni Leone, but Better Known as Leo Africanus. Done into English in the Year 1600, by John Pory, and now edited, with an introduction and notes by Dr. Robert Brown*. Volume III. London: Hakluyt Society, 1896, pp. 824–826.

What You Need to Know

This passage is from *The History and Description of Africa and of the Notable Things Therein Contained*. The author was a diplomat and writer named Al-Hasan al-Fasi, better known to the European world as Leo Africanus.

One of the things about the city of Timbuktu, situated on the Niger River in interior West Africa, that made it so enticing to European explorers, who competed to see who could get there first in the eighteenth and nineteenth centuries, was its legendary wealth. That reputation had been firmly established in the early fourteenth century by Mansa Musa I, leader of the Malian Empire, of which Timbuktu became the cultural capital.

Musa was a devout follower of Islam who, in 1324 and 1325, made the *hajj*, or pilgrimage, to Mecca, which all good Muslims who are physically and financially able are obliged to undertake. By all accounts, Musa was more than able. Although contemporary tales of Musa's pilgrimage need to be approached skeptically—medieval chroniclers are prone to wild exaggerations—they collectively add up to a picture of a man of almost inconceivable wealth. His entourage was said to include no less than 12,000 slaves, each of whom carried four pounds of gold. In addition, some 80 camels were packed with hundreds of pounds of gold dust each. Modern economists have estimated that, if these accounts are even remotely true, Mansa Musa may have the distinction of being the richest man in history.

A Closer Look

Leo Africanus was a Moor born in Granada in Andalucia in 1494, two years after the city fell to the Christian kings of Spain, conquering this last Muslim kingdom on the Iberian Peninsula. Accompanying an uncle, he served on a diplomatic mission to Timbuktu and the Songhai Empire in 1510, taking copious notes along the way. Sixteen years later, he completed the book based on these notes, although it would not be published until 1550, shortly before his death.

Africanus describes an economically dynamic Timbuktu, with numerous merchants and artisan shops. He also describes its king as fabulously wealthy and powerful, possessing large stores of gold and controlling an army of 3,000 horsemen and innumerable foot soldiers. And, indeed, Timbuktu was among the most important trading cities at the southern end of the Trans-Sahara trade routes, where gold from the mines of West Africa was exchanged for salt from North Africa and manufactured goods from Europe.

As a center of trade, Timbuktu was one of the most cosmopolitan cities in Africa. On its tangled web of streets, one could find Tuareg warriors, Arab traders, nomads from the Sahara, and Jenne merchants. On the borderland between greener and more-watered Sahel and the arid Sahara Desert to the north, Timbuktu was not unlike a seaport. Instead of ships coming into dock, however, it was caravans of hundreds of camels lining the Niger River to drink, after having their goods unloaded in the many mud and wood warehouses lining the city's outskirts.

1 100 200 300 400 500 600 700 800 900 1000 1100 1200 1300 1400 1500 1600 1700 1800 1900 2000 CE

Part 9:
The Americas

First–Sixteenth Centuries CE

1.9.1 Nazca Trophy Head Vessel

Southern Peru
1–750 CE

Credit: DEA/G. Dagli Orti/DeAgostini/Getty Images

What You Need to Know

The vessel shown here is what archaeologists refer to as a "trophy head" vessel. It was created by the Nazca people (sometimes spelled "Nasca") of coastal Peru, sometime between 1,250 and 2,000 years ago.

The Nazca were a group of culturally related peoples, rather than a centrally governed civilization. That is, the Nazca culture, which lasted from roughly the first to eighth centuries CE, consisted of a number of independent chiefdoms, linked together by trade, language, and culture, although with what appears to be a single large ceremonial center called Cahuachi. This dispersion of authority was a direct outgrowth of the environment. The Nazca inhabited the dry coast of what is now southern Peru, between the Andes and the Pacific, concentrated in the various valleys surrounding snow-fed streams from the mountains.

The culture is best known for the so-called Nazca lines, vast and intricate etchings in the earth itself, known as geoglyphs, depicting animals and abstract shapes. Some archaeologists theorize they formed a kind of calendar, while others believe they were a means by which the Nazca communicated with their gods. Recent studies have also argued that they may have been designed for ceremonial processions, where people could "walk" the lines. Whatever the reason for them, both the etchings and Nazca civilization itself came to an end in the seventh century, probably as a result of massive flooding and the overexploitation of the fragile environment in which they lived.

A Closer Look

The vessel shown here has a double spout and was used for drinking, probably an alcoholic beverage known as corn beer. The multicolored vessels were high-status goods and may have been obtained on a pilgrimage to the ceremonial city of Cahuachi. On it is displayed a trophy head, like those obtained in battle.

Like other pre-Columbian Andean cultures, the Nazca cut off the heads of their enemies to use in ritual and display. Holes were also drilled in the foreheads to allow them to be hung from ropes. This allowed them to be displayed on one's person, either on a belt or attached to a cloak. At other times, the heads were simply held in the warrior's hands.

Most archaeologists believe that the Nazca were a warlike people, in constant struggle among themselves and with outside groups for control of water, land, and other resources. This is evidenced not only in the abundance of trophy heads found in gravesites but also in their art, including the iconography on their ceramics. Some imagery shows the very process of taking and displaying trophy heads, while others depict ritualistic ceremonies in which the trophy heads are held by shamans, or priests who sought connections between the human and spirit world. The image here shows a painted ceramic vessel formed in the shape of a trophy head, with eyes closed and the mouth sewn shut with two cactus spines, a pattern typical of many trophy heads.

1 100 200 300 400 500 600 700 800 900 1000 1100 1200 1300 1400 1500 1600 1700 1800 1900 2000 CE

1.9.2 Moche Clay Trumpets

Northern Peru
100–800 CE

Credit: DEA/G. Dagli Orti/DeAgostini/Getty Images

What You Need to Know

The trumpets shown here were made from terracotta, or fired clay. They were made by people of the Moche culture of Peru, sometime in the first millennium BCE. Archaeologists conjecture that the instruments were not for recreational playing but were employed in religious ceremonies and in military camps and battlefields. The figure on the bell of the horn at right appears to be that of a soldier or perhaps an elite.

The Moche culture embraced a number of peoples living along what is now the northern coast of Peru. It flourished from the first to the eighth centuries CE. Although the Moche region was—and is—relatively arid, its broad plains were watered by streams flowing from the Andean Mountains to the Pacific. The Moche economy was based on agriculture, which was nourished by a sophisticated irrigation complex, and the raising of domestic animals, such as llamas, guinea pigs, and ducks. Diets were also supplemented by hunting, particularly of deer, and fishing.

The numerous irrigation canals speak of highly organized societies since building and maintaining them was very labor intensive and required communal rules to operate. However, it is not believed that the Moche were united under one central government. At the same time, the output from these artificially watered lands allowed for agricultural surpluses that supported large ceremonial, administrative, and trading centers with platform pyramids and U-shaped buildings—some of them more than a hundred feet in height—for use by authorities. The tombs of these centers have revealed great treasure troves of art and artifacts, many of them rendered in precious metals.

A Closer Look

Many Moche ceremonies were connected to military triumphs. From their perches atop brightly colored temples priests and priestesses, attired in elaborate outfits of gold, intricately woven textiles, and feathers, would look down as phalanxes of soldiers marched into the central plazas of Moche settlements, carrying with them the trophies of war, including weaponry and enemy soldiers destined for sacrifice. Crowds would stand on the sidelines cheering the warriors, often accompanied by the playing of ceramic trumpets, like the ones shown here.

The trumpets reveal the Moche people's skills in ceramics. The Moche people were highly skilled at ceramics; the representational figures on the trumpets display a high skill level among Moche artisans, whose ceramics are best known for their portraiture. Various kinds of vessels were formed in the shape of human heads. The depiction of disfigurements and blemishes indicate that many of the portraits were of a specific people. Still, the sheer quantity of ceramics discovered—and the fact that much of it is not nearly as finely rendered as these trumpets—indicates that the Moche were capable of production on an industrial, rather than artisanal, scale.

1 100 200 300 400 500 600 700 800   900   1000 1100 1200 1300   1400   1500   1600   1700 1800 1900 2000 CE

1.9.3 Tiwanaku Bronze Axe and *Tupu* Pins

Tiwanaku (Bolivia)
500–1000 CE

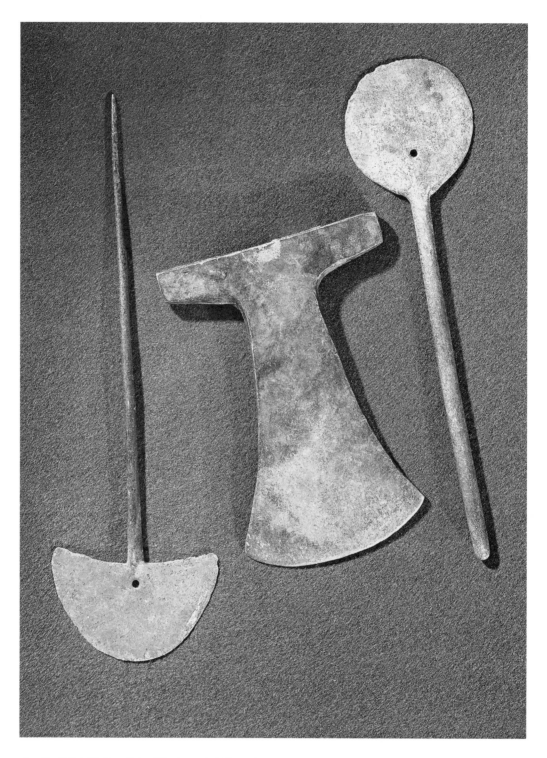

Credit: DEA/G. Dagli Orti/DeAgostini/Getty Images

What You Need to Know

This bronze axe head and two pins, known as *tupu*, are artifacts from the Tiwanaku civilization and date to the late first millennium or early second millennium CE. The *tupu* were used by women to hold their shawls together.

Stretching from the northern reaches of what is now Chile to the Altiplano, or high plains, of western Bolivia, northward into southern coastal Peru, the Tiwanaku civilization and the areas it influenced thrived for much of the first millennium and early second millennium. What the Tiwanaku called themselves is lost to history. The current name refers to the site of the greatest ruins associated with the Tiwanaku, which are located just south of Lake Titicaca in western Bolivia.

The regions the Tiwanaku inhabited varied significantly by topography and climate. The area around Lake Titicaca is fertile, well watered, and enjoys mild temperatures, allowing for an abundance of crops that supported the great urban center of Tiwanaku. The arid and cold conditions of the Altiplano required extensive irrigation and the practice of raised bed agriculture. The staple crop was the potato and the highly nutritious quinoa plant.

A Closer Look

The Tiwanaku were experts at the creation of monumental architecture built from huge stones carved to exacting measurements and then fitted together so perfectly that they required no mortar to hold them in place. Indeed, the Inca believed that the temple complex at Tiwanaku was built on the site where the world began. But as the objects in the accompanying image show, the Tiwanaku had also mastered the art of metallurgy. Along with decorative items and tools, bronze was also used in weaponry and in the implements for human sacrifice, which the Tiwanaku practiced.

The Tiwanaku also used bronze for the manufacture of I-shaped cramps, used to hold the small stones together that formed the walls of their extensive irrigation systems. The Tiwanaku were, indeed, masters of irrigation, having independently developed a system, used in other parts of the world, known as "flooded-raised field" agriculture. Ideal for regions of great temperature extremes, like the high altitude Lake Titicaca basin, where the Tiwanaku made their homes, flooded-raised field agriculture consists of planting mounds surrounded by irrigation ditches. The ditches not only supply water but retain heat from the hot daytime to warm the beds of plants during frigid nights.

1   100   200   300   400   500   600   700   800   900   1000   1100   1200   1300   1400   1500   1600   1700   1800   1900   2000 CE

1.9.4 Mississippian Stone Frog Pipe

Cahokia (Missouri)
600–1400 CE

Credit: Ira Block/National Geographic Creative/Corbis

What You Need to Know

This stone pipe made in the image of a frog was unearthed in one of the burial mounds that surrounded the ancient Mississippian city of Cahokia. The pipe was used for smoking tobacco. The bowl for the leaf is on top and the hole for drawing in the smoke is unseen in the frog's rear end. Cahokians typically made their pipes in the images of animals, either realistic, like this one, or in anthropomorphized form.

The Mississippian culture was a Native American culture that embraced various peoples living in the Mississippi River valley, between the Appalachian Mountains to the east and the Missouri River to the west, and from the Southern Great Lakes in the north to the Gulf of Mexico in the south, from around 600 to 1400 CE. While the various Mississippian people spoke different languages, they shared a culture of mound building, corn- and bean-based agriculture, complex hierarchical social structures, and centralized control of politics and religion. They shared not only culture but engaged in much long-distance trade with one another and with outsiders. Mississippian culture was anchored by a number of urban centers, many of them centered on large-scale earthen pyramids and mounds used for religious purposes and burial. The greatest of these centers was that of Cahokia, in what is now southwestern Illinois.

A Closer Look

Tobacco is, of course, indigenous to much of the Americas, north and south. It may be have been cultivated as far back as 6000 BCE. By the time of the Mississippian culture, it was widely used for any number of purposes—religious, social, medicinal, monetary, and recreational. In religion, it was used to invoke a trancelike state, and its smoke was believed to transmit prayers to heaven. Communal smoking often followed negotiations between and among different groups. Its medical uses were numerous, including as a pain-killer and a poultice, a kind of healing bandage used to relieve pain or inflammation. It also served as a medium of exchange.

But the sheer prevalence of tobacco seeds throughout the ruins of Cahokia seems to indicate that it was used primarily for recreational purposes and by all classes of this highly socially stratified civilization. Typically, it was smoked but Cahokians also chewed it, ate it, and drank it, mixed with other plants, as a tea.

1   100   200   300   400   500   600   700   800   900   1000   1100   1200   1300   1400   1500   1600   1700   1800   1900   2000 CE

1.9.5 Classic-Period Sculpture of a Maya Scribe

Copan (Honduras)
Eighth Century CE

Credit: DeAgostini/Getty Images

What You Need to Know

This sculpture of a Maya scribe from the city of Copan, in modern-day Honduras, dates to the eighth century CE. Like many such depictions, it shows the scribe seated in the writing position, a pen of some kind gripped in his right hand and a container for ink held in his left. Although this particular sculpture does not have an inscription, many did, identifying the figure as an advisor to the king or as the keeper of the royal records.

The Maya were the only pre-Columbian people to have developed a systematic script, which consisted of about 850 glyphs, or icons that stood for words. Etched in stone or written in codexes, or manuscript books, the script was used to record astronomical events, religious stories, and dynastic histories.

The archaeological evidence points to the central role of scribes in Maya culture. Virtually every Maya royal court had one and they appeared to be of high social ranking, as they are frequently depicted in both sculpture and painting. Indeed, it is theorized that they may have actually been members of the royal families, perhaps the younger son of a king who was not destined for the throne.

A Closer Look

Esteemed by many scholars to have been the most scientifically advanced civilization of the pre-Columbian Americas, the Maya culture existed on the Yucatan Peninsula and northern Central America from roughly 300 to 900 CE. Their ceremonial complexes, which also served as administrative centers and trading hubs, featured large pyramids and intricate carvings. Their calendar was more accurate than the Gregorian one used in Europe at the time.

Archaeologists divide the ancient history of the Maya peoples into three phases: preclassical, classical, and decline. In the first period, from the first millennium BCE to about 300 CE, the Maya lived in small communities, their culture heavily influenced by the Olmec, a civilization that thrived from around 1500 to 400 BCE along the eastern coast of Mexico north of the Yucatan. The classical period, from 300 to 900 CE, is noted for its script, its science, and its great temple complexes. The period of decline following the year 900 saw a cessation of building and writing. Overpopulation leading to environmental degradation, combined perhaps with climate change, is cited by most archaeologists for the collapse of Mayan civilization.

1 100 200 300   400   500   600   700   800   900   1000 1100 1200 1300   1400   1500   1600   1700 1800 1900 2000 CE

1.9.6 Ancestral Pueblo Turquoise Beads

Chaco Canyon (American Southwest)
1050–1100 CE

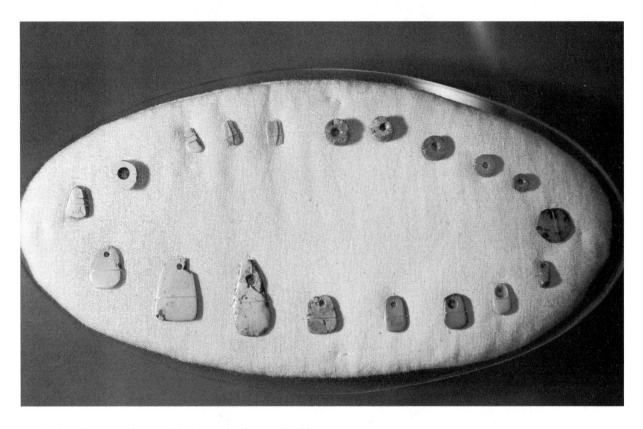

Credit: Marilyn Angel Wynn/Nativestock Pictures/Corbis

What You Need to Know

The collection of turquoise beads shown here, with holes in the middle so they could be strung together, were made by the Ancestral Pueblo people of what is now the American Southwest. Ethnically related to the modern-day Pueblo peoples of the same region, the Ancestral Pueblo existed as a unique culture for much of the first and early second millennium CE.

The Ancestral Pueblo were a group of ethnically and linguistically related people, ancestors to the current Pueblo peoples, who inhabited the Four Corners region of the American Southwest, where the current states of Arizona, Colorado, New Mexico, and Utah meet. They are believed to have originated around 1200 BCE and to have disappeared, as a distinctive civilization, in the fourteenth century CE.

The Ancestral Pueblo were masters of irrigation and architecture. While the Four Corners region was once more lush than it is now, it nevertheless required the Ancestral Pueblo to build elaborate networks of canals to bring water from streams to the mesa top fields, in which they laid pumice as mulch to hold in moisture. But it is their spectacular multistory dwellings built into the sides of cliffs for which they are best known. They remained the tallest buildings in what is now the United States through the early nineteenth century.

A Closer Look

The Ancestral Pueblo built extensive road systems that connected their various population centers. The Chaco system alone consisted of some eight major roads, some as much as 30 feet wide, that stretched for 180 miles. The roads were used largely for communication and trade, the latter including food products, pottery, beads, and precious stones, such as turquoise.

Indeed, turquoise was a key commodity of the Ancestral Pueblo. Because there are extensive deposits in the region, it became a key export to other peoples in the region, traded for metal objects, feathers, and other exotic items from distant sources.

Increasingly, evidence shows that a vast if intermittent trading network existed between the Ancestral Pueblo and the great contemporary civilizations of the Valley of Mexico and Central America. The turquoise beads, shown in the accompanying image, are some of that evidence. Turquoise was primarily mined in the American Southwest but was highly valued among the Mesoamericans for use in mosaics. Long-distance routes allowed items from the latter to be exchanged for tropical birds and feathers, masks, and cacao, the source of chocolate, for the prized blue stones obtained by the Ancestral Pueblo. However, this does not appear to have been done through direct contact. Instead, trade was conducted through intermediaries—namely, the various peoples of what is now northwest Mexico.

1   100   200   300   400   500   600   700   800   900   1000   1100   1200 1300   1400   1500   1600   1700   1800   1900   2000 CE

1.9.7 Maya Almanac from the Dresden Codex

Yucatan Peninsula
Thirteenth Century CE

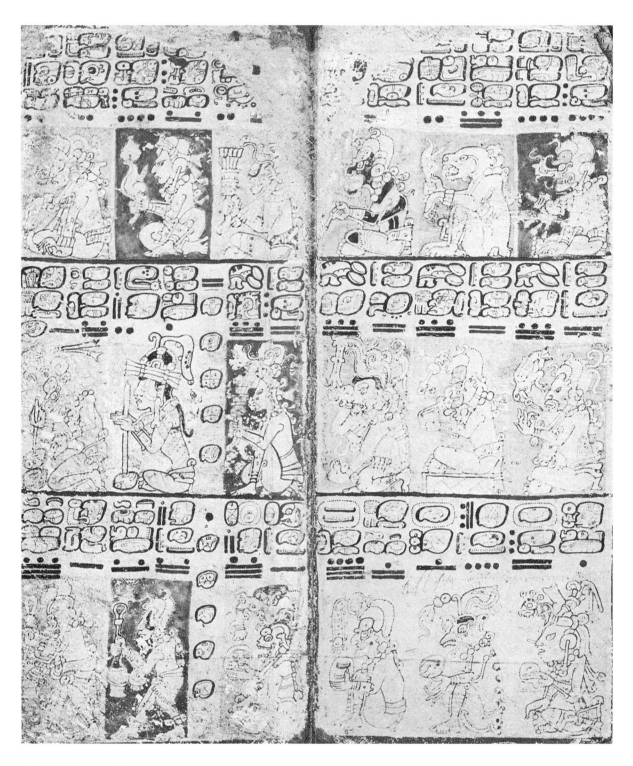

Credit: Library of Congress

What You Need to Know

The accompanying image shows a page from the Dresden Codex, which was written and illustrated in the thirteenth century. (The name comes from the fact that, after being obtained by the Spanish conquistador Hernando Cortes, it ended up in the Royal Library in Dresden, Germany.) The pages pictured here from the codex, or manuscript book, are from an almanac that explained and illustrated forms of divination. Specifically, the illustrations and text show both various gods and dates on the 260-day ritual calendar of the Maya.

The Maya are a people who have occupied the Yucatan Peninsula of Mexico and northern Central America since the second or third millennium BCE. The term Maya may be derived from Itzamna, the name of their creator deity.

The urban-based civilization of the Maya thrived from around 300 to 900 CE. Many archaeologists and historians maintain that no other civilization of the pre-Columbian Americas achieved the same level of artistic and intellectual achievement.

A Closer Look

The Dresden Codex provides evidence of the three greatest achievements of Maya civilization—their script, their calendar, and mathematics. Unfortunately, the Spanish conquistadores, determined to wipe out any vestiges of pagan religion and culture, burned most of the Maya codices.

The Dresden Codex is written in a logographic script, like that of ancient Egypt or China today, in which symbols stand for words rather than phonemes, or sounds. The Maya script consisted of roughly 850 such symbols, which were primarily used to record religious ideas, astronomical information, and historical chronologies. Some were etched into stele and other monumental architecture, while others were written down into books made from bark paper and deerskin.

The Dresden Codex is our best source of information on the Maya calendar and the astronomical observations it was based on. Such observations were used to predict celestial events and schedule religious ceremonies. The Maya calendar was a marvel of its time. Based on the cycles of the sun, the moon, and Venus, and divided into eighteen 20-day months, with an annual five-day interlude, adding it up to 365 days, it was more accurate than the contemporary Gregorian calendar of Europe.

1 100 200 300 400 500 600 700 800 900 1000 1100 1200 1300 1400 1500 1600 1700 1800 1900 2000 CE

1.9.8 Aztec Spear-Throwers

Mexico
Fifteenth Century CE

Credit: DeAgostini/Getty Images

What You Need to Know

Shown here are two spear-throwers, made by the Aztec people of central Mexico in the fifteenth century CE.

The term Aztec is an anachronism. In fact, the people we refer to as the Aztecs called themselves the Mexica, from which the modern country's name originates. The term "Aztec" derives from their legendary homeland Aztlan and did not come into widespread usage until the nineteenth century. Whatever we choose to call them, the Aztec people originated in the deserts of northern Mexico and then migrated into the agriculturally rich Valley of Mexico in the early fourteenth century. Gradually, they turned themselves into a highly militarized society, ultimately conquering the valley as well as surrounding lands.

Originally, the Aztec Empire was composed of the three city-states of Tenochtitlán, Texcoco, and Tlocapan, which were all inhabited by culturally related peoples speaking the Nahuatl language. They were gradually forged into a more integrated state, based on Tenochtitlán, by a number of powerful Mexica rulers in the fourteenth and fifteenth centuries.

The Mexica religion was as foreboding as their warriors were effective. The Aztecs worshipped the sun god Huitzilopochtli, among many other deities. They believed that history was divided into sun periods, each ending in catastrophe. The Aztecs lived in the time of the Fifth Sun. To ward off another catastrophe, they had to placate Huitzilopochtli with huge numbers of human sacrifices—5,000 alone at the coronation of the Emperor Motecuhzoma (Montezuma) II in 1502— which they obtained from their frequent military conquests.

A Closer Look

The Aztecs believed that providing Huitzilopochtli with the hearts torn from living sacrificial victims gave them great power. In fact, already a warlike people, the Aztecs systematically turned themselves into a highly organized militaristic people over the course of a century, subduing all of the surrounding peoples. The Aztec army was not a temporary militia, recruited when needed, but a vast standing army of paid professionals. At first these soldiers were Aztecs themselves but eventually the army came to include recruits from tributary states, which were also required to pay taxes to their Aztec overlords in the form of material goods, raw materials, and sacrificial victims as well.

Aztec warfare was a highly ritualized affair, aimed at capturing as many of the enemy as possible, rather than killing them. Great phalanxes of soldiers would begin their battles by hurling projectiles into the ranks of their enemy, using spear-throwers—known as *atatl*—such as the two shown in the accompanying image. This was aimed at breaking the foe's will. Aztec soldiers would then march into their opponent's ranks and strike them on their legs with sharp-edged, obsidian clubs, bringing the enemies to their knees. They would then tie up their foes to bring them back as potential recruits, slaves, or sacrificial victims. The Aztec called these engagements "flowery wars."

1 100 200 300 400 500 600 700 800 900 1000 1100 1200 1300 1400 1500 1600 1700 1800 1900 2000 CE

1.9.9 Christopher Columbus's Notes on the Carib and Taino Peoples

Caribbean
October 12, 1492 CE

As I saw that they were very friendly to us, and perceived that they could be much more easily converted to our holy faith by gentle means than by force, I presented them with some red caps, and strings of beads to wear upon the neck, and many other trifles of small value, wherewith they were much delighted, and became wonderfully attached to us. Afterwards they came swimming to the boats, bringing parrots, balls of cotton thread, javelins, and many other things which they exchanged for articles we gave them, such as glass beads, and hawk's bells; which trade was carried on with the utmost good will. But they seemed on the whole to me, to be a very poor people. They all go completely naked, even the women, though I saw but one girl. All whom I saw were young, not above thirty years of age, well made, with fine shapes and faces; their hair short, and coarse like that of a horse's tail, combed toward the forehead, except a small portion which they suffer to hang down behind, and never cut. Some paint themselves with black, which makes them appear like those of the Canaries, neither black nor white; others with white, others with red, and others with such colors as they can find. Some paint the face, and some the whole body; others only the eyes, and others the nose. Weapons they have none, nor are acquainted with them, for I showed them swords which they grasped by the blades, and cut themselves through ignorance. They have no iron, their javelins being without it, and nothing more than sticks, though some have fish-bones or other things at the ends. They are all of a good size and stature, and handsomely formed. I saw some with scars of wounds upon their bodies, and demanded by signs the of them; they answered me in the same way, that there came people from the other islands in the neighborhood who endeavored to make prisoners of them, and they defended themselves. I thought then, and still believe, that these were from the continent. It appears to me, that the people are ingenious, and would be good servants and I am of opinion that they would very readily become Christians, as they appear to have no religion.

Source: Columbus, Christopher. Excerpt from journal. In *Personal Narrative of the First Voyage of Columbus to America*. Translated by Samuel Kettell. Boston: Thomas B. Wait and Son, 1827, pp. 35–36.

What You Need to Know

This excerpt is from the journal of Christopher Columbus on the first day—October 12, 1492—he encountered the "New World."

Famously, the Italian explorer Christopher Columbus was hired by the monarchs of the newly united Spanish kingdom in 1492 to find a westward sea route to the East Indies. Instead, on October 12, he sighted the island of San Salvador in the Bahamas (Guanahani in the native Taino language), where he encountered a people he called, egregiously, Indians.

The Taino, which means "good people" in their native language, were a group of ethnically related peoples who inhabited the Bahamas and the islands of the Caribbean, before contact with European explorers in the late fifteenth and early sixteenth centuries. The Taino lived in small groups, usually clans that traced their heritage to a common ancestor. Most were led by a cacique, or chief, although he typically governed with the consent of the clan's elder members.

The Carib peoples were linguistically different from the Taino and inhabited the islands of the Lesser Antilles, having migrated there from the Orinoco River basin of what is now Venezuela. The Carib society was more egalitarian than its Taino equivalent although also more warlike, at least in the eyes of the Europeans who encountered them. However, early stories of their cannibalism— the word derives from their name—have been discounted by archaeologists and surrounding Caribs as well.

A Closer Look

As this journal excerpt relates, Columbus was impressed by the physiognomy of the Taino; the explorer was only the first of many Europeans to focus on the impressive physicality of Amerindian peoples they considered culturally inferior. Although Columbus was a careful observer, he nevertheless arrived in America with the biases of European and Christian culture, which assumed a sense of superiority over less technologically advanced cultures and which discounted pagan faiths as misguided at best and the work of the devil at worst. Still, his accounts are among the few we have of the early Taino and geographically related Carib people before European contact. In fact, Columbus and the Europeans who came in his wake would introduce diseases that, combined with the slave-like conditions in which they were forced to work for the Spaniards, effectively wiped out the Taino and reduced the Carib to a tiny number. Columbus notes that they went about naked, although by this he probably meant they merely covered their genitals. He also notes their limited material culture and lack of metallurgy.

But Columbus was also limited by his own cultural biases. He says the Taino had no weapons but in fact, they did, although not metal ones. He also said they could "readily become Christians"— conversion was one of the stipulations the king and queen of Spain put on Columbus for their financing of his expedition—because they had no religion of their own. In fact, the Taino and Carib had an elaborate animist faith, with a grand creator presiding over a natural world infused with spirits.

1 100 200 300 400 500 600 700 800 900 1000 1100 1200 1300 1400 1500 1600 1700 1800 1900 2000 CE

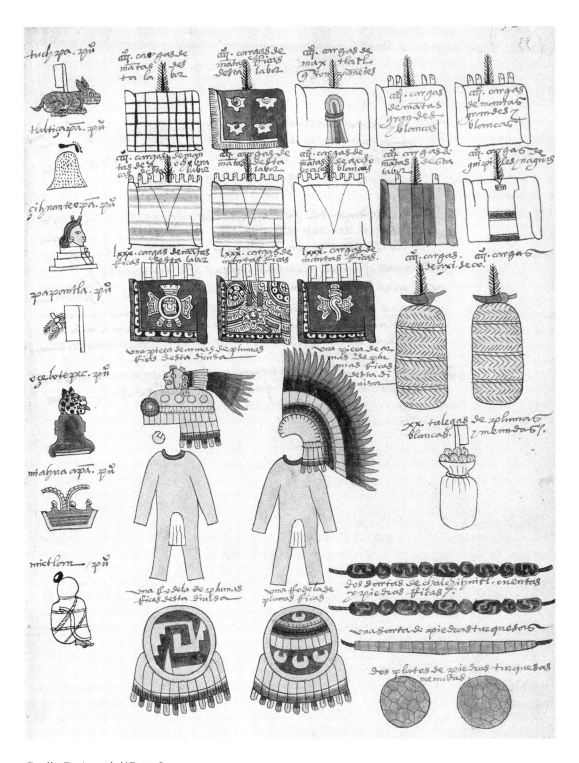

Credit: DeAgostini/Getty Images

What You Need to Know

The Codex Mendoza, a page of which is shown here, was a manuscript commissioned by Antonio de Mendoza, the viceroy of New Spain, in late 1530s, about 20 years after the Spanish conquistador Hernando de Cortes had subdued the Aztecs. The codex, or manuscript book, contained both Aztec pictograms and Spanish writing. Written to inform the Hapsburg Emperor and Spanish king Charles V of his new royal possessions in the Americas, it offers depictions of Aztec life and the history of Aztec conquests before the arrival of the Spanish, largely in the form of tribute paid by subdued peoples to the Aztecs.

At the height of their empire in the late fifteenth and early sixteenth centuries—just before the Spanish conquest—the Aztec directly ruled roughly 100,000 square miles of territory in central Mexico, and controlled tributary states that stretched from the Gulf of Mexico to the Pacific Ocean and from what is now northern Mexico to present-day Guatemala. It is estimated that some five million people lived within the empire and several million in the tributary states. Tenochtitlán itself, the Aztec capital, was home to roughly 200,000 persons, equivalent to Paris or Naples, the two largest European cities at the time.

A Closer Look

Aztec society was organized around warfare, which was also the focus of their religion. Aztec aggression against neighboring peoples was conducted for three reasons: to accrue wealth in the form of tribute, to recruit soldiers for more military campaigns, and to obtain persons for human sacrifice. Aztec leaders deemed all three crucial for the preservation of their empire, which is the main reason they engaged in aggressive warfare against their neighbors. At their height in the late fifteenth and early sixteenth centuries, the Aztec had subjugated most of the peoples of Mesoamerica to their tribute system, which included garments for both civilian and military use, feathers, weaponry, precious stones, and annual yields of beans, maize, and chocolate in thousands of tons.

The prizes of war shown here include feather headdresses, turquoise jewelry, and bags of chili peppers. The Spanish were very interested in the codex because it offered them information on how much they themselves could exact in taxes and tribute from the same peoples the Aztecs had exploited.

The vanquished were expected to supply laborers, who formed the backbone of the Aztec economy. They worked growing crops for great cities of the empire, as well as constructing the huge temples and palaces of the capital Tenochtitlán and other vast cities. They were also responsible for the construction and upkeep vast infrastructure that kept the empire functioning: roads, dikes, aqueducts, bridges, and causeways. The Codex Mendoza codex offered the Spanish a way to calculate how many laborers they themselves could recruit for their own plantations and infrastructure projects.

1 100 200 300 400 500 600 700 800 900 1000 1100 1200 1300 1400 1500 1600 1700 1800 1900 2000 CE

1.9.11 Cortes's Descriptions of the Aztec City of Tenochtitlán

Tenochtitlán (Mexico City)
1520 CE

This great city of Temixtitlan [Tenochtitlán] is situated in this salt lake, and from the main land to the denser parts of it, by whichever route one chooses to enter, the distance is two leagues. There are four avenues or entrances to the city, all of which are formed by artificial causeways, two spears' length in width. The city is as large as Seville or Cordova; its streets, I speak of the principal ones, are very wide and straight; some of these, and all the inferior ones, are half land and half water, and are navigated by canoes. All the streets at intervals have openings, through which the water flows, crossing from one street to another; and at these openings, some of which are very wide, there are also very wide bridges, composed of large pieces of timber, of great strength and well put together; on many of these bridges ten horses can go abreast. Foreseeing that if the inhabitants of the city should prove treacherous, they would possess great advantages from the manner in which the city is constructed, since by removing the bridges at the entrances, and abandoning the place, they could leave us to perish by famine without our being able to reach the main land, as soon as I had entered it, I made great haste to build four brigatines, which were soon finished, and were large enough to take ashore three hundred men and the horses, whenever it should become necessary.

This city has many public squares, in which are situated the markets and other places for buying and selling. There is one square twice as large as that of the city of Salamanca, surrounded by porticoes, where are daily assembled more than sixty thousand souls, engaged in buying and selling; and where are found all kinds of merchandise that the world affords, embracing the necessaries of life, as for instance articles of food, as well as jewels of gold and silver, lead, brass, copper, tin, precious stones, bones, shells, snails, and feathers. . . .

This great city contains a large number of temples, or houses, for their idols, very handsome edifices, which are situated in the different districts and the suburbs; in the principal ones religious persons of each particular sect are constantly residing. . . . Among these temples there is one which far surpasses all the rest, whose grandeur of architectural details no human tongue is able to describe; for within its precincts, surrounded by a lofty wall, there is room enough for a town of five hundred families. Around the interior of the enclosure there are handsome edifices, containing large halls and corridors, in which the religious persons attached to the temple reside. There are fully forty towers, which are lofty and well built, the largest of which has fifty steps leading to its main body, and is higher than the tower of the principal tower of the church at Seville. The stone and wood of which they are constructed are so well wrought in every part, that nothing could be better done, for the interior of the chapels containing the idols consists of curious imagery, wrought in stone, with plaster ceilings, and wood-work carved in relief, and painted with figures of monsters and other objects. All these towers are the burial places of the nobles, and every chapel in them is dedicated to a particular idol, to which they pay their devotions.

Source: Cortés, Hernando. Excerpts from second letter to Charles V. In *The Library of Original Sources: 9th to 16th Century*. Vol. V. Edited by Oliver Joseph Thatcher. New York: University Research Extension, 1907, pp. 318, 320.

TIMELINE   2000 1900 1800 1700 1600 1500 1400 1300 1200 1100 1000 900 800 700 600 500 400 300 200 100 1 BCE

What You Need to Know

This text comes from Hernando de Cortes's letter to Spain's King Charles V. Cortes was the Spanish officer who led a military expedition that conquered the Aztec Empire. Although the letter was written in 1520, at the time of the conquest, it sheds light on Aztec society and life before that event.

Well known is the story of how Christopher Columbus, searching for a western route to the East Indies, stumbled upon the Americas. He and the first Spaniards to follow were told stories by the peoples of the Caribbean of a great and wealthy civilization to the west, on the mainland of North America. In 1519, Cortes decided to follow up on these stories, landing near what is now the Mexican gulf port of Veracruz.

Leading his troops, and gathering recruits from among the Aztecs' tributary peoples, he marched on their great Tenochtitlán, which was not far from Teotihuacan and Tula. Possessing superior weapons, and facing a demoralized enemy, he quickly conquered the city and subjected the people of the Valley of Mexico to Spanish rule. In doing so, he was overwhelmed by what he saw of the sheer grandeur of Tenochtitlán. He notes its location at the center of the vast Lake Texcoco, the sheer scale of its urban planning, civil engineering projects, and religious structures, and the agricultural and material wealth of its marketplaces.

A Closer Look

The Valley of Mexico is an extensive high plain situated in the central part of the country, between eastern and western Sierra Madre Mountains. From early in the first millennium BCE, until the arrival of European conquerors in the early sixteenth century, it has been home to a series of centrally administered and socially hierarchical civilizations. The first was that centered on the great city of Teotihuacan, which may have housed as many as 200,000 inhabitants. Teotihuacan fell to less developed peoples from the south and west, who destroyed it around the year 700, although they could not raze its great pyramids, believed to be dedicated to the sun and the moon. After a "time of troubles," from the ninth to eleventh centuries, there arose yet another great urban center, just to the northwest of Teotihuacan, the Toltec city of Tula, which also fell to outside invaders in the early thirteenth century. Around a century later, the Aztecs arrived, who ultimately would control the greatest of the pre-Columbian empires of the Valley of Mexico.

The cities of pre-Columbian Mexico were major urban centers that served various purposes. They were the seats for governments that ruled over extensive territories and a variety of subject peoples. They were centers of trade, with huge marketplaces where a vast array of ordinary and luxury goods, purchased and extracted as tribute from surrounding areas, were bought and sold. And finally, the cities were religious centers, home to the temple complexes and priestly class that gave divine sanction to the rule of the Aztecs and other imperial peoples before them.

1 100 200 300 400 500 600 700 800 900 1000 1100 1200 1300 1400 1500 1600 1700 1800 1900 2000 CE

1.9.12 The Administration of Inca Provinces

Peru
1540 CE

[E]ach province, at the end of the year, was ordered to set down in the quipus, by means of the knots, all the men who had died in it during the year, as well as all who were born. In the beginning of the following year, the quipus were taken to Cuzco, where an account was made of the births and deaths throughout the empire. These returns were prepared with great care and accuracy, and without any fraud or deceit. When the returns had been made up, the lord and his officers knew what people were poor, the number of widows, whether they were able to pay tribute, how many men could be taken for soldiers, and many other facts which were considered, among these people, to be of great importance. As this empire was of such vast extent, a fact which I have frequently pointed out in many parts of this work, and as in each province there were a great number of storehouses for provisions and other necessaries for a campaign, and for the equipment of soldiers, if there was a war these great resources were used where the camps were formed, without touching the supplies of allies, or drawing upon the stores of different villages. . . . Then the storehouses were again filled from the obligatory tributes; and if, by chance, there came a year of great sterility, the storehouses were, in like manner, ordered to be opened, and the necessary provisions were given out to the suffering provinces. But as soon as a year of plenty came, the deficiencies so caused were made up.

In these [principal] places there were larger houses and more resources than in many of the other towns of this great empire, so that they were the central positions or capitals of the provinces; for the tribute was brought into these centres from certain distant places at so many leagues distance to one, and at so many to another. The rules were so clear that every village knew to which centre it had to send its tribute. In all these capitals the kings had temples of the Sun, and houses with great store of plate, with people whose only duty it was to work at making rich pieces of gold and great vases of silver. There were also many soldiers as a garrison, and also a principal agent or lieutenant who was over all, and to whom an account had to be rendered of all that came in, while he was expected to keep the account of all expenditure. . . .

The tribute which was paid to the central station by the natives, as well gold and silver as weapons, clothes and all other things, was delivered to the camayos who had charge of the quipus, that an account might be taken. These officers kept the records with reference to the issue of stores to the armies, or to others, respecting whom they might receive orders, or to be sent to Cuzco. When overseers came from the city of Cuzco to examine the accounts, or the officers went there to submit their quipus for inspection, it was necessary that there should be no mistake, but that the accounts should be balanced. And few years were allowed to pass without these examinations of the accounts being made.

Source: Cieza de León, Pedro de. *The Second Part of the Chronicle of Peru, translated by Clements R. Markham.* London: Hakluyt Society, 1883, pp. 57–61.

TIMELINE   2000 1900 1800 1700 1600 1500 1400 1300 1200 1100 1000 900 800 700 600 500 400 300 200 100 1 BCE

What You Need to Know

In this passage, Spanish conquistador and chronicler of Inca life Pedro de Cieza de León describes how the Inca Empire ruled its vast territory.

Since around the time of Christ, the central Andean region of South America was host to a number of civilizations, including the Moche, Nazca, Tiwanaku, and Inca, the last of these, which fell to the Spanish in the early sixteenth century. Like the contemporary Aztecs of Mexico, the Inca began as a small polity with a material culture based on items of daily use rather than the luxuries they would later come to enjoy, inhabiting some of the valleys of central Peru. Then, late in the pre-Columbian period, in the mid-fifteenth century, they turned themselves into a highly militarized society that eventually conquered the entire Andean region from Ecuador to northern Chile. The term *Inca* came from the name for their emperor. The Inca themselves formally called their empire Tawantinsuyu, or "land of the four united quarters."

Also, like the Aztec, Inca religious beliefs undergirded their military expansion. The Incas believed that their ruler descended from the sun god; if the emperor prospered, so too did the empire. When an emperor died, his successor gained all of his powers and privileges, but not his property, which passed to his family who took care of them in his name. This process is called "split inheritance." By means of this process, the new emperor came to the throne empty-handed, requiring him to conquer new lands and peoples to establish his own fortune and, by implication, the fortune of the empire.

A Closer Look

All of these conquests brought more peoples of the Andean region under the sway of the Inca and their emperor. On the eve of the Spanish conquest in the early 1530s, the Inca had expanded their realm to cover 350,000 square miles of territory, which included more than 10 million people of diverse ethnic groups. To administer the empire, the Inca divided it into 80 provinces and built an elaborate road network, which allowed the emperor in Cuzco to communicate with local governors, typically nobles who had been granted lands and tribute for their military exploits. The road system also helped facilitate trade and the paying of tribute to the emperor. As this excerpt from Pedro de Cieza de León reveals, that tribute could be quite valuable. "Gold, silver, clothing, arms and all else they gave," he notes of the subordinate peoples.

Subjugated peoples had to accept the Inca pantheon of deities and adopt the Inca language of Quechua, which remains today the most widely spoken indigenous language in the Americas. Administratively, the accountants in the local provincial governors and the emperor's palace kept close tabs of tribute paid and supplies sent on *quipus*, knotted strings used for tabulation.

1 100 200 300 400 500 600 700 800 900 1000 1100 1200 1300 1400 1500 1600 1700 1800 1900 2000 CE

1.9.13 Andean *Chuspa* Bag

Andean South America
Late Fifteenth–Sixteenth Centuries CE

Credit: DeAgostini/Getty Images

What You Need to Know

This *chuspa*, or bag for holding coca leaves, was made by peoples of the Andean region of South America sometime in the fifteenth or sixteenth century.

Among the most important crops in the ancient Andes was the coca plant, originally a wild plant indigenous to the region and from which the drug cocaine is derived. In its raw leaf form, coca has a similar, although far milder, effect on the human physiognomy as powder cocaine. It is a gentle analgesic, stimulant, and appetite suppressant, which can also produce a slight sense of euphoria. As such it is legal and widely grown in Bolivia and Peru today and is chewed, or drank as tea, by locals and travelers alike, the latter to overcome the effects of altitude sickness.

It is unclear when the peoples of the Andes discovered that the coca leaf had a pharmaceutical effect, as one experiences little effect by merely chewing it. Only by simultaneously sucking on a bit of lime (the mineral not the fruit) can the alkaloid substance that affects the body and brain be released. Traces of coca have been found in mummified bodies in burial sites dating back to about 2000 BCE.

A Closer Look

Virtually all of the great Andean civilizations of the pre-Columbian era grew and used coca leaf and considered it a gift from the gods. Still, coca had many uses beyond its medicinal effects. It was one of the items included in the burial of high-ranking people, and it was offered as a sacrifice to the gods of the various peoples of the Andes. So important and sacred was it that under the Inca of the fourteenth through sixteenth centuries, its production and distribution were a state monopoly. The government also dictated who was permitted to chew the leaf, which archaeologists believe was restricted to the ruling elite, priests and other religious officials, and those in the military.

Like the substances it carried, the *chuspa* has been in use by Andean peoples since pre-Columbian times. This particular example dates to the fifteenth or sixteenth century. Typically woven from llama wool, the patterns on the *chuspa* bag reflected both the individual artistry of the weaver as well as the region where it was made. *Chuspas*, as well as the coca they carry, continue to be used by the peoples of the Andean region.

1.9.14 Pre-Inca and Inca Religions

Andean South America
1609 CE

For the better understanding of the idolatry, mode of life, and customs of the Indians of Peru it will be necessary for us to divide those times into two epochs. We shall narrate how they lived before the time of the Incas, and afterwards we shall give an account of the government of those kingdoms by the Incas, that the one may not be confounded with the other, and that neither the customs nor the gods of the period before the Incas may be attributed to the Inca period. It must be understood, then, that in the first epoch some of the Indians were little better than tame beasts, and others much worse than wild beasts. To begin with their gods, we must relate that they were in unison with the other signs of their folly and dullness, both as regards their number and the vileness of the things they adored. . . .

[T]hey worshipped different animals, some for their fierceness, such as the tiger, lion, and bear; and as they looked upon them as gods, they did not fly from them, if they crossed their path, but went down on the ground to worship them, and these Indians allowed themselves to be killed and eaten, without attempting flight, or making any defense. They also adored other animals for their cunning, such as foxes and monkeys. They worshipped the dog for his faithfulness and noble character, the cat for its agility, the bird which they call *cuntur* [condor] for its size, and some nations adored the eagle because they thought they were descended from it, as well as the *cuntur*. Other nations worshipped falcons for their swiftness, and for their industry for procuring food. They worshipped the owl for the beauty of his eyes and head, and the bat for his quickness of sight, which caused much wonder that he could see at night. They also adored many other birds according to their caprices. They venerated the great serpents [anacondas], that are met with in the Antis, twenty-five to thirty feet in length, more or less, and thicker than a man's thigh, for their monstrous size and fierceness. They also looked upon other smaller snakes as gods, in places where they are not so large as in the Antis, as well as lizards, toads, and frogs. In fine, there was not an animal, how vile and filthy soever, that they did not look upon as a god. . . .

The Indians living to the south and west of Cuzco, in the provinces called *Colla-suyu* and *Cunti-suyu*, give another account of the origin of the Incas. They say that this great event happened after the deluge. . . . Their account is that, after the flood subsided, a man appeared in Tiahuacanu [Tiwanaku], to the southward of Cuzco who was so powerful that he divided the world into four parts, and gave them to four men who were called kings. The first was called Manco Ccapac, the second Colla, the third Tocay, and the fourth Pinahua. They say that he gave the northern part to Manco Ccapac, the southern to Colla (from whose name they afterwards called the great province Colla), the eastern to Tocay, and the western to Pinahua. He ordered each to repair to his district, to conquer it, and to govern the people he might find there. But they do not say whether the deluge had drowned the people, or whether they had been brought to life again, in order to be conquered and instructed; and so it is with respect to all that they relate touching those times.

Source: Garcilaso de la Vega, El Inga. *Royal Commentaries of the Incas and General History of Peru*. Pts. 1 and 2. Trans. H. Livermore. 1609.

TIMELINE 2000 1900 1800 1700 1600 1500 1400 1300 1200 1100 1000 900 800 700 600 500 400 300 200 100 1 BCE

What You Need to Know

This is an excerpt on the religions of the Inca and pre-Inca peoples of the Andean region of South America by Garcilaso de la Vega. The son of a Spanish conquistador and an Inca woman of noble ancestry, Garcilaso de la Vega, who lived from 1539, just seven years after the Spanish conquest of Cuzco, in 1616 wrote extensively about Inca life.

Around the turn of the second millennium CE, the Incas were a small polity inhabiting the Andean valley around what is now Cuzco, Peru. Gradually, they began to conquer their neighbors until on the eve of the Spanish conquest in the 1530s, they ruled over most of the Andean region from Ecuador in the north to northern Chile in the south. The Inca themselves traced their ancestry to the first king, Manco Capac, who reigned during the late twelfth and early thirteenth centuries. But it was in the era of Pachacuti Inca, who ruled from 1438 to 1471 that the Inca expanded their realm to truly imperial dimensions.

The Inca imposed their own values and customs on the people they had conquered, although often these social norms were not that different from those of the subordinated ethnic groups. At the same time, the Inca understood that effective rule also meant allowing subject peoples to retain some of their old customs and practices to keep them from rebelling against imperial rule. The Inca, then, would allow subject peoples to retain their gods but required them to make those gods subject to gods of the Inca, that is, putting the Inca gods on a higher level within local religious pantheons.

A Closer Look

In the excerpt printed here, Garcilaso de la Vega discusses not just the mythic origins of the Inca but the religions of the region before their conquests in the fifteenth century. Before proceeding to what he wrote, it should be remembered that de la Vega was a devout Catholic, and thus disdained what he considered pagan beliefs and religious practices. At one point, he says the gods of the pre-Inca peoples were "in unison with other signs of [the people's] folly and dullness."

De la Vega notes that pre-Inca peoples were animists, that is, they believed that spirits inhabited natural objects and phenomena and that a universal spirit infused all of nature. He says that they "adored," that is, worshipped, all kinds of animals, both domestic and wild, which he mistakenly calls their gods. Indeed, according to de la Vega, the peoples of the Andes held certain wild animals to be so sacred that they would not defend themselves against their depredations.

On the sacred origins of the Inca, de la Vega points to their account of a great flood, from which a single man emerged to found a dynasty, a frequent trope in creation myths around the world.

1 100 200 300   400   500   600   700   800   900   1000 1100 1200 1300   1400   1500 1600   1700 1800 1900 2000 CE

1.9.15 Pomo Cooking Basket

Northern California
ca. Sixteenth–Nineteenth Centuries CE

Credit: Marilyn Angel Wynn/Nativestock Pictures/Corbis

What You Need to Know

The Pomo people of what is now northern California made cooking baskets like the one shown here, in which heated rocks were placed in, atop, or beside the food to be cooked.

The Pomo are a collection of peoples sharing a similar culture and speaking related Pomoan languages, who lived—and still live—in the coastal mountain ranges between San Francisco and the Oregon border. The Pomo were not a unified people, linked through a common political system. Instead, they lived in small bands consisting of a number of extended family groups. Although they practiced a limited form of agriculture, they subsisted primarily on hunting and gathering.

Like other peoples of the region, the Pomo practiced shamanism, a form of spiritualism in which a selected member of society, deemed to have a special connection to the spiritual world, communicated the wishes of people to the spirits and vice versa. At the same time, all members of various Pomo peoples were able to directly interact with the spirit world through dances and rituals, which often led to trancelike states.

A Closer Look

Pomo baskets were woven from a number of plant sources, including swamp cane, saguaro cactus, rye grass, willow shoots, and sedge roots. They were used for any number of things in Pomo life. Aside from cooking, different kinds might be used for transportation and storage of food and other items, for fishing weirs or bird traps, in religious ceremonies, and to carry babies. Although both sexes wove the baskets, men were generally responsible for the fishing, birding, and baby-carrying vessels, while women made the others. The Pomo employed three methods for making their baskets: plaiting, coiling, and twining.

The Pomo used any number of designs in their basket making, with each having its own meaning. The most significant feature of the Pomo basket patterns is the *dau*, or spirit door. This *dau* allowed good spirits to come into the basket and bad spirits to escape. The *dau* was typically integrated in subtle fashion, as a tiny change in the stitching pattern or an opening between various stitches.

1 100 200 300 400 500 600 700 800 900 1000 1100 1200 1300 1400 1500 1600 1700 1800 1900 2000 CE

Part 10:
Central and East Asia

Sixth–Fourteenth Centuries CE

1.10.1 *Haniwa* Horse from Yayoi-Period Japan

Japan
Sixth Century CE

Credit: Christie's Images/Corbis

What You Need to Know

Haniwa are hollow cylinders or representative figures made of terracotta, or unglazed clay. One of a horse from the sixth century is depicted here.

Until about the middle of the first millennium CE, most of Japan was ruled by local aristocratic clans. These were warrior groups that controlled the nearby countryside and demanded tribute from the peasants who farmed it. By the fifth century, however, the leader of one of those clans, from the rich agricultural lands of the Yamato plain, around the present-day metropolis of Osaka, began to assert kingship over the surrounding clans.

The Yamato rulers did not have the military means to conquer other clans so they gave them much leeway over local matters. They also sought to assert their authority by religious means. They allowed the other clans to keep their gods but required that they be subordinate to their own deity, the sun-goddess. Out of this arrangement grew the indigenous Japanese faith of Shintoism, a form of nature worship, full of both joyous celebration and strict purification rituals for believers.

A Closer Look

According to Japanese legend, the origins of the *haniwa* dated back to the so-called Yayoi period in Japanese prehistory, roughly the centuries between 300 BCE and 300 CE, when they were used to substitute for human sacrificial victims, usually the deceased noble person's attendants, of earlier times.

The figures were supposed to protect the deceased in the afterlife, while the cylinders allowed the living to place ritualistic offerings for the dead. The figures came in any number of shapes— boats, houses, people, and animals, chosen to serve or accompany the person in the afterlife— but they followed set design patterns as the artisans who manufactured them were given little latitude for creativity.

Haniwa were made using the *wasumi* technique, in which clay is formed into coils and then built up in layers to make the cylinder or figure. They could be just a few inches tall or up to four or five feet in height. The *haniwa* were employed in a variety of ritualistic settings but were most often used in funerary rites for persons of noble birth. Unlike funerary artifacts in many other civilizations, however, the *haniwa* were not placed in the grave of the deceased but atop it, in rows, half embedded in the soil, to mark off the territory of the gravesite. They were often joined together by ropes or poles to better demarcate the site.

1 100 200 300 400 500 600 700 800 900 1000 1100 1200 1300 1400 1500 1600 1700 1800 1900 2000 CE

1.10.2 Sui Dynasty Flutist Figurine

China
Sixth–Seventh Centuries CE

Credit: DeAgostini/Getty Images

What You Need to Know

This small glazed terracotta statue of a flute player is from the Sui dynasty.

Although China is the world's oldest continuous civilization, with a culture spanning more than 5,000 years of history, that history has not been without its disruptions. Great dynasties, or successions of rulers from the same family lineage, have risen and fallen, with the periods in between them marked by internal strife and civil discord. The longest of these interludes was the so-called Age of Division, between the fall of the Han dynasty in 220 CE and the rise of the Sui dynasty in 581.

Under the leadership of Yang Jian, a government official, both north China, centered on the Yellow River, and south China, along the Yangtze, were united for the first time in centuries under the Sui. Led by Emperor Wen of the Sui dynasty, which he founded, China expanded into Vietnam and Korea. But expansion and great engineering projects were achieved only through ruthless leadership, which helped lead to the Sui dynasty's fall to the Tang in 618, making it the shortest-lived major dynasty in Chinese history.

A Closer Look

As in other civilizations, music was an important part of Chinese popular culture, played in virtually every setting and for both pleasure and ceremony, at weddings, funerals, and other life events. But it also had a deeper philosophical meaning. Human harmonies were the manifestation of nature's harmonies. Chinese scientific understanding of nature—its elements and its rhythms—informed the rules of musical structure.

Confucius, China's greatest philosopher, who lived more than a millennium before the Sui, added a moral dimension to music. It improved the individual soul, he said, and thereby contributed to the harmony of society, which, in turn, led to stable government. While Confucius and other philosophers promoted formal forms of music, China's emperors, including those of the Sui, also paid close attention to folk music. This was not out of any aesthetic appreciation but for political reasons. So worried were they that subversive music might undermine people's respect for their rule that they sent out government agents to report back to the court on what was being played on Chinese streets and stages. But although musicians were seen as potential agents of political dissent, they did not enjoy a particularly high social status in Chinese life.

1   100   200   300   400   500   600   700   800   900   1000   1100   1200   1300   1400   1500   1600   1700   1800   1900   2000 CE

317

1.10.3 Tang Dynasty Poem "Drinking Alone by Moonlight"

China
Eighth Century CE

A cup of wine under the flowering trees;
I drink alone, for no friend is near.
Raising my cup I beckon the bright moon,
For he, with my shadow, will make three men.
The moon, alas! is no drinker of wine;
Listless, my shadow creeps about at my side.
Yet with the moon as friend and the shadow as slave
I must make merry before the Spring is spent. . . .
While we were sober, three shared the fun;
Now we are drunk, each goes his way.
May we long share our odd, inanimate feast,
And meet at last on the Cloudy River of the Sky.

In the third month the town of Hsien-yang
Is thick-spread with a carpet of fallen flowers.
Who in Spring can bear to grieve alone?
Who, sober, look on sights like these?
Riches and Poverty, long or short life,
By the Maker of Things are portioned and disposed;
But a cup of wine levels life and death
And a thousand things obstinately hard to prove.
When I am drunk, I lose Heaven and Earth.
Motionless—I cleave to my lonely bed.
At last I forget that I exist at all,
And at that moment my joy is great indeed.

If High Heaven had no love for wine,
There would not be a Wine Star in the sky.
If Earth herself had no love for wine,
There would not be a city called Wine Springs.
Since Heaven and Earth both love wine,
I can love wine, without shame before God. . . .
At the third cup I penetrate the Great Way;
A full gallon—Nature and I are one.
But the things I feel when wine possesses my soul
I will never tell to those who are not drunk.

Source: Li Po. "Drinking Alone by Moonlight." In *More Translations from the Chinese*. Translated by Arthur Waley. New York: Alfred A. Knopf, 1919, pp. 27–28.

What You Need to Know

This poem, "Drinking Alone by Moonlight," was written by Tang dynasty poet Li Po in the eighth century.

The Tang dynasty, in power from 618 to 907, was an era of great artistic flowering in China, as its capital at Chang'an became the cultural center of East Asia. Merchants and missionaries, students and artists flocked to its centrally planned grid of streets, bringing with them ideas from across Eurasia. Rarely in Chinese history has the Middle Kingdom been so open to outside influences.

The first 150 years of the Tang was particularly well governed as a meritocracy, with a bureaucracy filled with officials recruited from the best government-run schools in China and put through a rigorous examination process before gaining any kind of power. Candidates had to demonstrate that they, under Confucian principles and ethics, aimed at ensuring social harmony. The Tang believed, however, that a well-schooled administrator must not only understand politics and governance but should be highly cultured as well. Understanding the rules of poetry was an important prerequisite for holding office.

A Closer Look

This literary requirement might seem unusual to today's readers, but educated persons of the Tang dynasty believed that rules of poetry provided a kind of mental discipline that would serve administrators well once in office, in both shaping and communicating their ideas. And indeed, the Tang era is considered by modern scholars to represent the golden age of Chinese poetry.

Of all the poets of this age, the most renowned, then and since, is Li Po (sometimes transliterated as Li Bo). He is believed to have been born in 701, somewhere in western China; some ancient sources say his family had been exiled there for some crime. At age four, his family moved to Sichuan Province, and from an early age he showed a rare gift for scholarship and poetry. As his fame spread, he became a favorite writer of the imperial family. What contemporaries appreciated most about Li's poetry was how it reflected his idiosyncratic vision of life, in evocative and, at times, even exuberant language and imagery, while hewing to the rigorous rules and structure of classic Chinese verse.

How much Li's well-documented alcoholism contributed to his unique vision can never be known. In his poems told in the first person voice, he often portrayed himself as a drunkard, as in "Drinking Alone by Moonlight," perhaps his most quoted piece. Legend has it that Li died while in a drunken stupor, falling from a boat and drowning after trying to embrace the moon.

1 100 200 300 400 500 600 700 800 900 1000 1100 1200 1300 1400 1500 1600 1700 1800 1900 2000 CE

1.10.4 The *Kojiki* on Cosmic Origins

Japan
712 CE

The Beginning of Heaven and Earth

The names of the Deities that were born in the Plain of High Heaven when the Heaven and Earth began were the Deity Master-of-the-August-Centre-of-Heaven, next the High-August-Producing-Wondrous Deity, next the Divine-Producing-Wondrous-Deity. These three Deities were all Deities born alone, and hid their persons. The names of the Deities that were born next from a thing that sprouted up like unto a reed-shoot when the earth, young and like unto floating oil, drifted about medusa-like, were the Pleasant-Reed-Shoot-Prince-Elder Deity, next the Heavenly-Eternally-Standing-Deity. These two Deities were likewise born alone, and hid their persons. . . .

The Seven Divine Generations

The names of the Deities that were born next were the Earthly-Eternally-Standing-Deity, next the Luxuriant-Integrating-Master-Deity. These two Deities were likewise Deities born alone, and hid their persons. The names of the Deities that were born next were the Deity Mud-Earth-Lord next his younger sister the Deity Mud-Earth-Lady; next the Germ-Integrating-Deity, next his younger sister the Life-Integrating-Deity; next the Deity Elder-of-the-Great-Place, next his younger sister the Deity Elder-Lady-of-the-Great-Place; next the Deity Perfect-Exterior, next his younger sister the Deity Oh-Awful-Lady; next the Deity the Male-Who-Invites, next his younger sister the Deity the Female-Who-Invites. From the Earthly-Eternally-Standing Deity down to the Deity the Female-Who-Invites in the previous list are what are termed the Seven Divine Generations.

Courtship of the Deities the Male-Who-Invites and the Female-Who-Invites

Having descended from Heaven onto this island, they saw to the erection of an heavenly august pillar, they saw to the erection of an hall of eight fathoms. Then the August Male-Who-Invites asked his younger sister the August Female-Who-Invites, "How is your body made?" She responded, "My body grew by growing, but there is one part that did not grow fully." Then the August Male-Who-Invites said, "My body grew by growing, but there is one part that grew too much. Therefore, would it be good for me to insert this part that grew too much into your part that did not grow fully, so that I will generate regions?" "It would be good." Then the August Male-Who-Invites said, "Since this is so, let us place together our august parts, running around this celestial column." Having made this agreement, the August Male-Who-Invites said, "Run around from the right, and I'll run from the left." When they had run around, the August Female-Who-Invites said, "O pleasant and lovable youth!" and the August Male-Who-Invites said, "O pleasant and lovely maiden!" When they finished, the August Male-Who-Invites said to his sister, "A woman should not speak first." Nevertheless, they began the work of creation in bed, and they produced a son named Hirudo. This child they placed in a boat of reeds, and let it float away. Next they gave birth to the Island of Aha. This likewise is not reckoned among their children.

Source: Chamberlain, Basil Hall, trans. *Translation of "Ko-ji-ki": or "Records of Ancient Matters."* Kobe: Asiatic Society of Japan, 1919, pp. 15, 17, 20–21. Chamberlain's Latin passages translated by Lawrence Morris.

What You Need to Know

This selection comes from the *Kojiki*, the oldest text in the Japanese language, which consists of myths about the origins of creation. It is the central text of the indigenous Shinto religion, which, alongside Buddhism, is one of the two major faiths of Japanese history and Japanese society today. The *Kojiki* was transcribed in the early eighth century, but it is based on stories that are much older. Indeed, the name *kojiki* means the "account of ancient doings."

Virtually all peoples through history have developed cosmogonies, or myths about how the universe began. These cosmogonies vary greatly from culture to culture, but they do share some common elements. First, they explain what preceded creation. Some put forth a picture of primordial chaos of undifferentiated matter, while others say there was nothing at all.

Deities are central to all cosmogonies. Typically, there is a primordial god who kicks off the act of creation, although where that primordial god comes from is usually left vague. Creation itself is also embodied as a deity or deities and is often divided into two essential spheres. These are the earth and the heavens, which are usually represented as deities of different sexes, with the former most often a female and the latter male. These main gods then create other deities who embody specific aspects of the universe. Finally, at some point, the deity or deities create humanity, as well as coming to embody the experiences of humanity, such as war, love, and so forth.

A Closer Look

As in many other such cosmogonies, the *Kojiki* begins with the creation of the earth and heavens, which are embodied as deities. Creation is the result of sexual intercourse between two primordial and gendered deities, the Male-Who-Invites and the Female-Who-Invites. The Shinto faith is a polytheistic one. Thus, out of these two primordial gods come other deities, who embody the various parts of nature. As in other creation myths, the *Kojiki* also explains the origins of divine justice. In this case, too, it is a highly sexualized and gendered process. The gods produce bad offspring—resulting in unfortunate or evil doings—when the woman speaks before the man and good offspring—resulting in just and fortunate doings—when the man speaks before the woman.

While people would offer prayers at Shinto shrines to the gods described in the *Kojiki*, the real influence they had was on how ordinary Japanese saw themselves and their place in nature. The *Kojiki* explained the origins of the Japanese people as part of the overall creation of nature. Thus, people would see themselves as part of their natural surroundings, which were infused with the same spirit that permeated the souls of people. In short, the Japanese saw themselves as deeply connected to the land they inhabited.

China
Ninth Century CE

On Being Sixty

Between thirty and forty, one is distracted by the Five Lusts;
Between seventy and eighty, one is a prey to a hundred diseases.
But from fifty to sixty one is free from all ills;
Calm and still—the heart enjoys rest.
I have put behind me Love and Greed; I have done with Profit and Fame;
I am still short of illness and decay and far from decrepit age.
Strength of limb I still possess to seek the rivers and hills;
Still my heart has spirit enough to listen to flutes and strings.
At leisure I open new wine and taste several cups;
Drunken I recall old poems and sing a whole volume.
Meng-te has asked for a poem and herewith I exhort him
Not to complain of three-score, "the time of obedient ears."

Last Poem

They have put my bed beside the unpainted screen;
They have shifted my stove in front of the blue curtain.
I listen to my grandchildren, reading me a book;
I watch the servants, heating up my soup.
With rapid pencil I answer the poems of friends;
I feel in my pockets and pull out medicine-money.
When this superintendence of trifling affairs is done,
I lie back on my pillows and sleep with my face to the South.

Source: Bai Juyi. "On Being Sixty," and "Last Poem." In *A Hundred and Seventy Chinese Poems*. Translated by Arthur Waley. London: Constable, 1918, pp. 161, 168.

TIMELINE   2000 1900 1800 1700 1600 1500 1400 1300 1200 1100 1000 900 800 700 600 500 400 300 200 100 1 BCE

What You Need to Know

Chinese poet Bai Juyi wrote these two poems about growing old in the ninth century.

The great philosopher Confucius, whose writings on ethics from the sixth and fifth centuries BCE have shaped China's culture ever since, had much to say on the subject of age and aging. Attempting to form an ethical system that would create social harmony out of the many interpersonal relationships within society, Confucius made it imperative that the young respect their elders. Indeed, in any family or organization, the oldest person is to receive the greatest honors and respect. They are to speak first at any social occasion and to have their voices heard before any major decision is made. Most important was filial piety. Children should not only respect their parents but live their lives in such a way as to honor them. At the same time, according to Confucius, the older person in a social relationship—such as a father or an employer—should offer benevolence to the younger, as well as the duty of instruction.

A Closer Look

Bai Juyi (sometimes written Bao Juyi or Bo Juyi) was a Chinese poet of the Tang dynasty, which lasted from 618 to 907 and is renowned as the golden age of classical Chinese literature. He was born in 772 to an impoverished family of scholars in Shanxi Province in north central China. In the year 800, he took the *jinshi*, the Confucian-based, civil service examination required for most government posts. He gradually rose through the ranks, despite the fact that some of his writings upset members of the imperial court, ultimately becoming the mayor of several towns. In 832, he retired to the Xiangshan Monastery in Henan Province, where he continued to write.

While Bai wrote a number of essays and letters that have survived, he is best known for his poetry. He was a prolific verse writer, penning some 2,800 poems in his lifetime. Two of these, on the subject of age, are printed here. In the first, titled "On Being Sixty," Bai declares one's fifties to be the ideal age, free of the lusts of youth and not yet prone to the frailties of age. He also speaks of drinking as the catalyst for creativity, a common theme in Tang poetry. In the second "Last Poem," which, despite its title, was not in fact his last attempt at verse making, he contemplates his final years, when he has put aside all concerns about "trifling affairs" and seeks simple pleasures in sleeping with his "face to the South," that is, toward the warming sun. Confucian philosophy, which influenced his work, spoke of the natural ages of man, which Bai renders evocatively in poetic imagery.

1 100 200 300 400 500 600 700 800 900 1000 1100 1200 1300 1400 1500 1600 1700 1800 1900 2000 CE

China
Ninth Century CE

The Charcoal-Seller

An old charcoal-seller
Cutting wood and burning charcoal in the forests of the Southern Mountain.
His face, stained with dust and ashes, has turned to the colour of smoke.
The hair on his temples is streaked with gray: his ten fingers are black.
The money he gets by selling charcoal, how far does it go?
It is just enough to clothe his limbs and put food in his mouth.
Although, alas, the coat on his back is a coat without a lining,
He hopes for the coming of cold weather, to send up the price of coal!
Last night, outside the city, a whole foot of snow;
At dawn he drives the charcoal wagon along the frozen ruts.
Oxen, weary; man, hungry; the sun, already high.
Outside the Gate, to the south of the Market, at last they stop in the mud.
Suddenly, a pair of prancing horsemen. Who can it be coming?
A public official in a yellow coat and a boy in a white shirt.
In their hands they hold a written warrant: on their tongues the words of an order;
They turn back the wagon and curse the oxen, leading them off to the north.
A whole wagon of charcoal!
More than a thousand pieces!
If officials choose to take it away, the woodman may not complain.
Half a piece of red silk and a single yard of damask,
The Courtiers have tied to the oxen's collar, as the price of a wagon of coal.

Source: Bai Juyi. "The Charcoal-Seller." In *A Hundred and Seventy Chinese Poems*. Translated by Arthur Waley. London: Constable, 1918, pp. 137–138.

What You Need to Know

The poem printed here, "The Charcoal-Seller," was written by Bai Juyi, a government official from the central Chinese provinces of Shanxi and Henan, who became one of the most celebrated poets of the Tang dynasty. As the name indicates, it tells the story of an aging purveyor of charcoal, a key fuel source in Chinese towns and cities.

While the Tang dynasty, which ruled China from 618 to 907, is best remembered for its extraordinary cultural output, particularly its poetry, it was also a time of much privation for the peasantry and lower classes. Population growth had reduced the amount of land people inherited from their parents. Yet each peasant still had to pay the same amount of taxes as if he owned the whole farm. This caused many to flee the land for towns and cities, where they struggled to survive in deepening poverty.

Adding to the people's woes was a rebellion led by a general named An Lushan, which embroiled much of northern China in civil conflict from 755 to 763. It was only put down when the emperor brought in ethnic Uighur troops from western China. But to keep its western flank secure, the Tang dynasty emperors had to pay extortionate amounts to Uighur leaders. This forced the government to increase tax payments from the peasantry, further adding to their financial woes.

A Closer Look

Manufacturing charcoal was a dirty and unpleasant job. Bai describes the title character as having a face "stained with dust and ashes . . . turned to the color of smoke." Meanwhile selling the stuff provided little income. Indeed, the charcoal seller of the poem is so impoverished he can barely clothe himself. So desperate for money, he actually looks forward to winter—when demand for charcoal rises, along with its price—despite the fact that he lacks a coat to keep warm.

Adding to his woes are Tang dynasty tax collectors. In the poem, one of them confiscates the charcoal seller's inventory just as the snows of winter are setting in, offering him but little compensation. Bai uses a clothing motif to evoke the injustice. The charcoal seller has no lined coat, while the government "boy" wears a white shirt and yellow coat, bright dyes being the preserve of the wealthy in Tang dynasty era China. It is for poems such as these that Bai often found himself in disfavor at the imperial court.

1.10.7 *The Tale of Genji* on Life in the Heian Imperial Court

Kyoto, Japan
978–1014 CE

In the reign of a certain Emperor, whose name is unknown to us, there was, among the Niogo and Koyi of the Imperial Court, one who, though she was not of high birth, enjoyed the full tide of Royal favor. Hence her superiors, each one of whom had always been thinking—"I shall be the one," gazed upon her disdainfully with malignant eyes, and her equals and inferiors were more indignant still.

Such being the state of affairs, the anxiety which she had to endure was great and constant, and this was probably the reason why her health was at last so much affected, that she was often compelled to absent herself from Court, and to retire to the residence of her mother. . . .

These circumstances, however, only tended to make the favor shown to her by the Emperor wax warmer and warmer, and it was even shown to such an extent as to become a warning to after-generations. . . .

In due course, and in consequence, we may suppose, of the Divine blessing on the sincerity of their affection, a jewel of a little prince was born to her. The first prince who had been born to the Emperor was the child of Koki-den-Niogo, the daughter of the Udaijin (a great officer of State). Not only was he first in point of age, but his influence on his mother's side was so great that public opinion had almost unanimously fixed upon him as heir-apparent. Of this the Emperor was fully conscious, and he only regarded the new-born child with that affection which one lavishes on a domestic favorite.

To return to her rival. Her constitution was extremely delicate, as we have seen already, and she was surrounded by those who would fain lay bare, so to say, her hidden scars. Her apartments in the palace were Kiri-Tsubo (the chamber of Kiri); so called from the trees that were planted around. In visiting her there the Emperor had to pass before several other chambers, whose occupants universally chafed when they saw it. And again, when it was her turn to attend upon the Emperor, it often happened that they played off mischievous pranks upon her, at different points in the corridor, which leads to the Imperial quarters. Sometimes they would soil the skirts of her attendants, sometimes they would shut against her the door of the covered portico, where no other passage existed; and thus, in every possible way, they one and all combined to annoy her.

The Emperor at length became aware of this, and gave her, for her special chamber, another apartment, which was in the Koro-Den, and which was quite close to those in which he himself resided. . . .

Source: Murasaki Shikibu. Excerpt from *Genji Monogatari*, Ch. 1, "The Chamber of Kiri." In *Japanese Literature*. Translated by Suyematz Kenchio. Rev. ed. World's Great Classics series. New York: Colonial, 1900, pp. 11–13.

TIMELINE   2000 1900 1800 1700 1600 1500 1400 1300 1200 1100 1000 900 800 700 600 500 400 300 200 100 1 BCE

What You Need to Know

The *Genji Monogatari*, or *Tale of Genji* in English, is considered by scholars to be the greatest piece of literature in Japanese history. It was written early in the eleventh century by a female courtier at the Heian Court who is remembered by the name Murasaki Shikibu. Like most members of the court, as well as the characters in the *Tale of Genji* itself, Murasaki was known to those around her by title, not name. Murasaki is the name of the book's heroine, while Shikibu is the name of the government post—Official in Charge of Ceremony—held by her father.

During the Heian period, which lasted from 794 to 1185, life in the imperial Japanese court at its eponymous capital, later named Kyoto, reached its apogee. Life there was filled with endless ceremony while social standing determined every aspect of one's life, from what one ate to with whom one could fall in love. Religious rites of the native Shinto religion, along with those of Buddhism, which came to Japan from China in the sixth century, occupied much of the calendar.

A Closer Look

Members of the Heian court also engaged in near constant rituals to ward off evil spirits associated with bad dreams or omens. Obsessive cleanliness led to purification rituals around a women's menstruation or the death of a friend or family member. While men had diversions, such as sports, dance, and poetry writing, women were expected to do little and were kept in virtual seclusion, spending most of their lives hidden by screens, multiple layers of clothing, and thick makeup over their faces. Still, love and even extramarital affairs were not entirely forbidden, although both were engaged in in highly stylized and ritualized ways.

The excerpt here relates the career of a courtly woman who, while young, becomes one of the emperor's mistresses. Such a position both enhances her status and triggers an intense jealousy among rival courtesans, who try to keep her away from the emperor and treat her servants badly. When she bears the emperor a son, she gains a reprieve, being moved to an apartment close to the emperor's own quarters. The boy she gives birth to becomes the title character of the book, Prince Genji.

But his tale is no war epic. Rather it consists of his sexual conquests, which are always conducted in the most elegant manner, and of his love for a young girl whom he brings into his household until she is old enough to marry him. The *Tale of Genji* is sometimes referred to as the world's first novel, in that it focuses on the emotional inner life of its characters rather than their external exploits.

1.10.8 Song Dynasty Marble Polo Ball

China
Tenth–Twelfth Centuries CE

Credit: Museum of East Asian Art/Heritage Images/Getty Images

What You Need to Know

The polo ball shown here, shaped from marble, dates to the northern Song dynasty of the tenth to twelfth centuries.

The history of sporting activity in China goes back to the very first well-documented dynasty, the Shang, some 2,500 years ago, who began the tradition of dragon boat racing. Dragon boats were long canoes propelled by teams of rowers. A sign of the sheer length of continuous civilization in China is evident in the fact that the sport is still popular there, although it is now more about tradition and ritual than athletics.

The Chinese also had ball games. One known as *cuju* that resembles modern soccer dates back to the Song dynasty era, which has led some historians to claim that the "beautiful game" was yet another of China's great contributions to world civilization.

A Closer Look

The origins of polo, a game played on horseback, in which teams of players try to drive a small ball between their opponents' goal posts, date back to the Medes, an Iranian people who invented it sometime in the second half of the first millennium BCE. Historians conjecture that it was first used as a means for training cavalry units. But all of this is the documented history. In fact, say historians, the game, which in its basics is quite simple and thus would be a natural thing for horsemen to engage in, may date back thousands of years, to the domestication of the horse and the first riders.

The historical record, however, notes that polo as a formal sport remained in Persia for roughly a millennium before it spread outward to the Middle East, Europe, and the Indian subcontinent. It is believed to have arrived in China during the Tang dynasty from 618 to 907. As in Persia, polo under the Tang and Song was primarily played by cavalry units, typically elite ones.

The polo ball here may be ceremonial, perhaps serving as some kind of trophy, rather than an object actually in the game. A marble ball would be exceptionally heavy, probably breaking any mallet used against it. In fact, most Chinese polo balls before the modern era were either made of wood or leather.

1 100 200 300 400 500 600 700 800 900 1000 1100 1200 1300 1400 1500 1600 1700 1800 1900 2000 CE

1.10.9 Song Dynasty Metal Coin

China
ca. 1102–1106 CE

Credit: Weather888/Dreamstime.com

What You Need to Know

The accompanying image is of a metal coin from Song dynasty China of the early twelfth century.

The Tang dynasty ruled China from 618 to 907. After its fall, China entered one of its periodic periods of social unrest and disunity, in which much of the country fell under the control of local warlords. In 960, a soldier named Zhao Kuangyin established the Song dynasty, which would rule China until 1279. Surrounded by formidable enemies, the Songs were forced to maintain a large standing army.

A century after the establishment of the dynasty, the Song faced an economic crisis stemming from these military expenditures. In 1069, the emperor Shenzong instituted reforms designed to increase the empire's productive output and, with it, government revenues. Understanding that his economy ultimately depended on the peasantry, he and his minister, Wang Anshi, relieved many peasants of their labor service to the empire and offered them low-interest loans to help them increase output. But such measures offended many in the vast Song bureaucracy; these officials felt that such policies would actually hurt the empire's finances. And so they resisted them, creating a rift that would weaken the Song dynasty in the twelfth century when it would face its greatest enemy yet, in the Mongols led by Genghis Khan.

A Closer Look

As social animals, humans have been engaged in barter and trade well back into prehistoric times. Barter, of course, has its limits—namely, that the buyer and seller each have to have something that the other wants. The obvious solution is an exchange medium that is universally sought after and that has an agreed-on value. Thus, one person can exchange this item for a good that he or she wants, allowing that person to then take that exchange medium to another person who has something of value the original seller wants.

Various kinds of exchange mediums have been used through history, some with inherent value, such as cattle, and some whose value rests solely in it being accepted as a form of exchange, such as cowry shells, which were used in parts of China in the second millennium BCE. Such a medium of exchange, of course, has to be hard to procure or produce so that it did not lose its value; the cowry shell met that criteria because it could only be had from certain distant sources.

Better still was a medium of exchange whose production rested in the hands of a central government, which could regulate its production and guarantee that it was not counterfeit. Early forms of money in China, dating back to the Zhou dynasty around the year 1000 BCE were essentially copper or bronze imitations of cowry shells. Later, the shells were replaced by flat round coins, such as the one pictured here. The hole in the middle allowed it to be strung together for ease of carrying and payment.

1 100 200 300   400   500   600   700   800   900   1000 1100   1200 1300   1400   1500   1600   1700   1800   1900 2000 CE

1.10.10 Samurai Behavior Described in the *Genpei Seisuiki*

Japan
ca. 1185–1333 CE

A Samurai in the service of the Heike lived in the land of Musashi and was called Nagai no Saito Betto Sanemori. One day, he reflected, "I am over 70 years old; I cannot expect more glory. I cannot escape from death. It doesn't matter where I die—it's all the same." So he put on his clothing of red silk and his armor . . . and he headed out into combat on his own, facing death. In the army of Kiso, there was a man named Tezuka no Taro Mitsumori, who lived in the land of Sinano. When he saw Sanemori, he drew close to him. Likewise, Sanemori, seeing Tezuka, strode towards him. Tezuka said, "Who are you, that you fight on your own? Are you a general or a regular samurai? You are provoking me. Say your name! Me, I am called Tezuka no Taro Kanazashi no Mitsumori, from the town of Suwa, in the land of Shinano. I am a good opponent. Tell me your name and let's begin!" They urged their horses together. "I have heard of you," said Sanemori. "I will not reveal my name, however, for various reasons, but I have no ill-feeling towards you. Strike off my head and show it to the Ghennji—you will be well rewarded. Do not cast my head into the river; the lord Kiso should recognize me. I am fighting on my own because I have renounced life. It is pleasant to fight any enemy!" . . . Sanemori, grabbing Tezuka's samurai, drew his own sword and chopped off the samurai's head. At the same time, Tezuka, keeping hold of Sanemori's right shoulder-piece, drove his sword through Sanemori all the way to the guard. He then cut off his head.

Tezuka, carrying the head of his enemy, came before the lord Kiso and said, "Mitsumori has won the head of a courageous warrior! When I asked him to tell me his name, he replied, 'I have reasons for not doing so. The lord Kiso will recognize me.' And he did not say his name. His embroidered silk, though, indicated that he was a samurai. . . . When I wondered if he were young, I saw that the wrinkles in his face suggested that he was more than 70. When I considered that he might be an old man, I realized that his black hair and beard showed him to be in full vigor. Whose head, then, is this?" Kiso exclaimed: "Oh, no! This must be Saito Betto of Musashi. Nevertheless, since I was young when I knew him, he ought to be covered by white hair by now. How can it be that his hair and beard are still black? Nevertheless, the rest of his face resembles him perfectly. It is very strange. Higutchi is a long-time friend of his; he should be able to recognize him." He then sent for Higutchi. Higutchi took the head and glanced at it, and began to cry out, "Oh, no! What a sad thing! It is Sanemori. But why this black hair and beard? Yes, I remember. Sanemori often said, 'Old men who take the bow and arrows off to combat ought to dye their hair black. If in peacetime the young mock white hair, even more do they do so in time of war. If an old man attacks, they say that he lacks wisdom; if he retreats, they insult him by calling him a coward. One doesn't dare compete with these young people. As regards the enemy, they think the old are just nothings. The white hairs of old age are a true sorrow."

Source: Excerpt from *Genpei Seisuiki*. In *Anthologie de la littérateur japonaise des origins au XXe siècle*. Edited by Michel Revon. Paris: Delagrave, 1919, pp. 241–244. Translated and modified by Lawrence Morris.

TIMELINE   2000 1900 1800 1700 1600 1500 1400 1300 1200 1100 1000 900 800 700 600 500 400 300 200 100 1 BCE

What You Need to Know

The values of the samurai are revealed in a lengthy narrative history known as the *Genpei Seisuiki*, penned sometime during Kamakura era from 1185 to 1333.

Historically, the Japanese have borrowed many aspects of their culture from the Chinese. Politically, they modeled their royal household after that of the Mainland. But there was one major difference. Whereas in China, the emperor often held real power, in Japan, it was a largely ceremonial position, with most administrative tasks turned over to the leaders of a particularly influential clan. By late in the first millennium CE, however, this system began to break down, leading to a period of social unrest in the twelfth century.

The discord gave rise to a new warrior elite, the so-called samurai, the Japanese term for "warrior." Although the Japanese imperial household resembled that of China, the new order bore a resemblance to medieval Europe. Weak central government left it to aristocrats to run local affairs and maintain peace in their areas of control. They did this by creating private armies of samurai, much like their contemporaries in Europe did with their knights. And, as in Europe, the *samurai* were expected to live by a strict code of behavior.

A Closer Look

The samurai code was known as the *Bushido*, translated as the "path of the soldier-scholar." The name of the code implies that while the *samurai* must be fierce and warlike, he must temper his power with wisdom derived from an understanding of philosophy. With this in mind, the highest purpose of the *samurai* was to gain glory, both for his feats on the battlefield but also through his understanding of life. There were eight Bushido principles: courage, mercy, courtesy to others, honesty and sincerity, honor, loyalty, and self-control. But the most important was rectitude in the pursuit of justice, to decide on a righteous path, and stay true to it, even if that meant death.

The Kamakura was a shogunate, a distinctly Japanese form of government in which one clan serves as the regents for the semidivine, although largely ceremonial, emperor. In the account offered in the accompanying excerpt, an aging *samurai* named Sanemori laments the fact that he is no longer respected by his more youthful opponents on the battlefield. He decides to challenge this disrespect by dyeing his gray hair black and going into battle against two younger warriors. It is essentially a suicide gesture and he is killed. But in dying so honorably, he has attained the glory so central to the Bushido, achieving widespread and everlasting fame.

1 100 200 300 400 500 600 700 800 900 1000 1100 1200 1300 1400 1500 1600 1700 1800 1900 2000 CE

1.10.11 Marco Polo's Description of the Mongol Capital

Hangzhou, China
Thirteenth Century CE

When you have left the city of Changan [the political capital of Mongol China] and have traveled for three days through a splendid country, passing a number of towns and villages, you arrive at the most noble city of Kinsay, a name which is as much as to say in our tongue "The City of Heaven," as I told you before.

And since we have got thither I will enter into particulars about its magnificence; and these are well worth the telling, for the city is beyond dispute the finest and the noblest in the world. In this we shall speak according to the written statement which the Queen of this Realm sent to Bayan the Conqueror of the country for transmission to the Great Khan, in order that he might be aware of the surpassing grandeur of the city and might be moved to save it from destruction or injury. I will tell you all the truth as it was set down in that document. For truth it was, as the said Marco Polo at a later date was able to witness with his own eyes. . . .

First and foremost, then, the document stated that the city of Kinsay is so great that it encompasses one hundred miles. And there are in it twelve thousand bridges of stone, for the most part so lofty that a great fleet could pass beneath them. And let no man marvel that there are so many bridges, for you see the whole city stands as it were in the water and surrounded by water, so that a great many bridges are required to give free passage about it. And though the bridges be so high the approaches are so well contrived that carts and horses do cross them. The document aforesaid also went on to state that there were in this city twelve guilds of the different crafts, and that each guild had 12,000 houses in the occupation of its workmen. Each of these houses contains at least 12 men, while some contain 20 and some 40 (not that these are all masters, but included the journeymen who work under the masters). And yet all these craftsmen had full occupation, for many other cities of the kingdom are supplied from this city with what they require.

The document aforesaid also stated that the number and wealth of the merchants, and the amount of goods that passed through their hands, were so enormous that no man could form a just estimate of them. And I should have told you with regard to those masters of the different crafts who are at the head of such houses as I have mentioned, that neither they nor their wives ever touch a piece of work with their own hands, but live as nicely and delicately as if they were kings and queens. The wives indeed are most dainty and angelical creatures! Moreover it was an ordinance laid down by the King that every man should follow his father's business and no other, no matter if he possessed 100,000 bezants [a Byzantine coin].

Inside the city there is a lake which has a compass of some 30 miles and all round it are erected beautiful palaces and mansions, of the richest and most exquisite structure that you can imagine, belonging to the nobles of the city. There are also on its shores many abbeys and churches of the Idolaters.

Source: Polo, Marco. Excerpts from *The Book of Ser Marco Polo the Venetian Concerning the Kingdoms and Marvels of the East*. Vol. II. Translated and edited by Henry Yule. 3rd ed., revised by Henri Cordier. New York: Charles Scribner's Sons, 1903, pp. 185–186.

TIMELINE   2000 1900 1800 1700 1600 1500 1400 1300 1200 1100 1000 900 800 700 600 500 400 300 200 100 1 BCE

What You Need to Know

Sometime in the late thirteenth century, the city of Hangzhou received a delegation of very unusual visitors, three merchants from the Polo family of Venice, Italy. The youngest of three, named Marco, would later write down his observations and experiences traveling across Eurasia and around the Indian Ocean in his *Book of the Marvels of World.*

Rising population in the countryside during the Tang and Song dynasties, which together ruled China from the seventh through the thirteenth centuries, led to overcrowding on the land. As farms were broken up among heirs, fewer and fewer families could be supported on the land, a situation made worse by regressive tax policies that often penalized peasant farmers. The result was a steady influx of people into Chinese cities. By the time the Mongols seized control of China in the thirteenth century under their leaders Genghis Khan and his grandson and successor Kublai Khan, the Middle Kingdom, the term the Chinese used for their land, boasted dozens of very large cities, and innumerable towns dotted the countryside. The largest of these, indeed the largest city in the world in the late thirteenth century, was Hangzhou on the central coast of China, near present-day Shanghai. Although not the capital of the Mongol Yuan dynasty, it was the commercial center of China, with a population estimated to be somewhere between half a million and 1.5 million. Today, with nearly nine million people, it is the fourth largest city in the country.

A Closer Look

In this excerpt, the young Polo describes the city of Hangzhou, which he calls Kinsay, a bastardization of the Mandarin name for the city Han Tsei. (Hangzhou is the pronunciation in the local Hangzhou dialect.) The metropolis was a marvel to Polo, although one must take his superlatives with a grain of salt. Like many medieval European chroniclers, he was prone to exaggeration and to relating inflated secondhand accounts of things. Still, several things about the city impress him. First is its size, which he describes as covering 10,000 square miles. This, of course, was a great exaggeration but the city was certainly many times larger than the largest city in Western Europe at the time, Paris. The second is its economic dynamism. He notes no less than twelve guilds, or merchant and artisan organizations, each with thousands of workshops. Guild members not only policed themselves, by making sure the quality and quantity of products produced kept prices high, but they were also responsible for some basic municipal functions, such as keeping wells in operation and making sure streets were kept clean. Polo is less impressed with the religion of the Chinese, however. At one point he calls them "Idolators," a derogative Christian term for practitioners of faiths other than Christianity, particularly those outside the Western tradition of Judaism, Christianity, and Islam.

1 100 200 300 400 500 600 700 800 900 1000 1100 1200 1300 1400 1500 1600 1700 1800 1900 2000 CE

1.10.12 Mongol Koumiss Flask

Mongolia
ca. Thirteenth Century CE

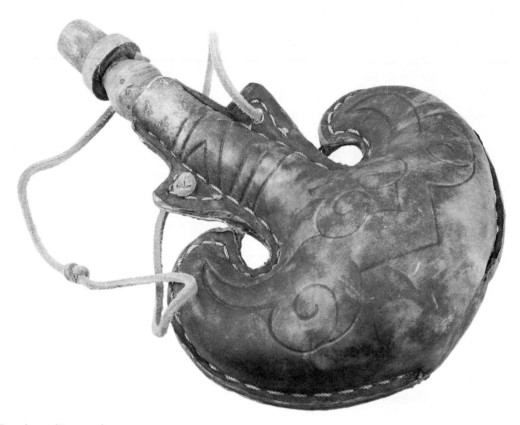

Credit: Buschmen/Dreamstime.com

What You Need to Know

Shown here is a traditional horsehide flask, still used by Mongolian herders today, meant to hold koumiss, a staple drink of the Mongols made from fermented mare's milk.

No event in the late Middle Ages had a more profound effect on the peoples and civilizations of Eurasia, from Korea to Southeast Asia to Central Europe, than the Mongol expansion of the thirteenth and fourteenth centuries.

The Mongols were a nomadic people living on the steppes, or grasslands, of central Asia. In the late twelfth century, cooling temperatures withered the grasses that the Mongols used to sustain their herds of sheep, goats, camels, yaks, and horses. Facing hunger and even starvation, the Mongols expanded outward into the great agriculture-based civilizations of Eurasia. They did this under the leadership of a man named Temujin, who later took the name Genghis Khan, a name that meant, appropriately enough, "universal sovereign." Over the course of his lifetime, from 1162 to 1227, Genghis would conquer the most expansive contiguous empire in human history. And nothing was more critical to Genghis's success than the Mongol horseman, whose ability to ride great distances, suffer terrible privations, and live off the land made him a formidable warrior.

A Closer Look

Historians and archaeologists are not actually sure who first domesticated the horse sometime in the fifth or fourth millennia BCE. But the peoples of the central Asian steppes were among the first to make them a central part of their culture. The horse gave great mobility to these people, allowing them to search out rich grassland and hunting grounds and to help them herd other domesticated animals. Later, the horse would give the Mongols, considered by many scholars to be the greatest horsemen in history, the ability to strike hard and fast against enemy armies.

The Mongols used their horses both as mounts for riders and to pull war chariots. Under Genghis, who proved to be as great an administrator as he was a military strategist, the Mongols also used the horse to control the lands they had conquered. The emperor established way stations across his realm, where fresh horses were kept so that riders could carry communications rapidly from Genghis's capital at Karakorum, in what is now Mongolia.

The horse had the added advantage of not just being a means of transport and communications for the Mongols but a source of food and material as well.

1   100 200 300   400   500   600   700   800   900   1000 1100 1200 1300   1400   1500   1600   1700   1800   1900   2000 CE

1.10.13 Marco Polo's Description of Mongol Warriors

Eurasia
Thirteenth Century CE

All their harness of war is excellent and costly. Their arms are bows and arrows, sword and mace; but above all the bow, for they are capital archers, indeed the best that are known. On their backs they wear armor of cuirbouly, prepared from buffalo and other hides, which is very strong. They are excellent soldiers, and passing valiant in battle. They are also more capable of hardships than other nations; for many a time, if need be, they will go for a month without any supply of food, living only on the milk of their mares and on such game as their bows may win them. Their horses also will subsist entirely on the grass of the plains, so that there is no need to carry store of barley or straw or oats; and they are very docile to their riders. These, in case of need, will abide on horseback the livelong night, armed at all points, while the horse will be continually grazing.

Of all troops in the world these are they which endure the greatest hardship and fatigue, and which cost the least; and they are the best of all for making wide conquests of country. And this you will perceive from what you have heard and shall hear in this book; and (as a fact) there can be no manner of doubt that now they are the masters of the biggest half of the world. Their troops are admirably ordered in the manner that I shall now relate.

When they come to an engagement with the enemy, they will gain the victory in this fashion. They never let themselves get into a regular medley, but keep perpetually riding round and shooting into the enemy. And as they do not count it any shame to run away in battle, they will sometimes pretend to do so, and in running away they turn in the saddle and shoot hard and strong at the foe, and in this way make great havoc. Their horses are trained so perfectly that they will double hither and thither, just like a dog, in a way that is quite astonishing. Thus they fight to as good purpose in running away as if they stood and faced the enemy, because of the vast volleys of arrows that they shoot in this way, turning round upon their pursuers, who are fancying that they have won the battle. But when the Tartars see that they have killed and wounded a good many horses and men, they wheel round bodily, and return to the charge in perfect order and with loud cries; and in a very short time the enemy are routed. In truth they are stout and valiant soldiers, and inured to war. And you perceive that it is just when the enemy sees them run, and imagines that he has gained the battle, that he has in reality lost it; for the Tartars wheel round in a moment when they judge the right time has come. And after this fashion they have won many a fight.

Source: Polo, Marco, and Rustichello of Pisa. *The Book of Ser Marco Polo the Venetian Concerning the Kingdoms and Marvels of the East, Book I*. Vol. I. Edited by Henry Yule. London: John Murray, 1903, pp. 260–263. Translation slightly modified by Lawrence Morris.

TIMELINE   2000 1900 1800 1700 1600 1500 1400 1300 1200 1100 1000 900 800 700 600 500 400 300 200 100 1 BCE

What You Need to Know

This is an excerpt from the thirteenth century writings of Venetian traveler Marco Polo on Mongol warriors. (Like many of his contemporaries, Polo refers to the Mongols as Tartars.)

The Mongols is the term used to describe a collection of people originally inhabiting the vast Mongolian Plateau of east-central Asia, who are ethnically related and speak a variety of Mongolic languages. The term, which linguists believe is derived from *mong*, meaning "brave" in Mongolic languages, dates back to the late first millennium CE and was first used by the Chinese to describe certain peoples on their northern frontier.

The Mongolian Plateau is a land of extremes. The Gobi, one of the world's largest deserts, covers its southern part while high mountains dominate its north and west. About 10 percent of it is covered in forest, but most is steppe land, flat grassy plains ideal for raising livestock. The climate is harsh. Winds blowing down from Siberia create icy conditions in winter, with average temperatures of −20 Fahrenheit in January. But it is the rainfall, or frequent lack of it, that has made things especially hard for the region's inhabitants through history, with frequent droughts drying up grasses and threatening herds and the people who depended on them.

Such conditions shaped both the Mongol spirit and way of life. It made them self-reliant and tough in the face of obstacles, human or natural. Living in such a harsh environment, they looked on the more temperate and fertile lands of the civilizations surrounding their harsh desert home as suitable places for conquest.

A Closer Look

The Mongol homeland was a harsh and unforgiving land, never more so than during times of drought. Indeed, it is a great drought that led the Mongols, under their extraordinarily ruthless and brilliant leader Genghis Khan, to expand outward from the Mongolian Plateau to eventually conquer much of the Eurasian landmass, from Korea to Eastern Europe, in the thirteenth and fourteenth centuries, forever changing the course of history.

Genghis's military success was built on two factors. One was the terror he instilled in his enemies. He prided himself on plunder and massacre, so when his envoys approached an enemy people and told them to surrender or face the consequences, they often took the offer. Although ruthless to those who resisted, Genghis was lenient to those who accepted his authority, giving them much local autonomy and, in the process, gaining more recruits for his armies.

The second factor behind his success was his warriors, as this excerpt from Polo's writing attest. They were extraordinarily gifted archers and horsemen, who, as he notes, attacked when the enemy was weakest and then retreated if faced with a greater force. They were also capable of extreme privation, living off of the land for long periods, which enhanced their ability to strike wherever and whenever they pleased.

1 100 200 300 400 500 600 700 800 900 1000 1100 1200 1300 1400 1500 1600 1700 1800 1900 2000 CE

1.10.14 Marco Polo on Chinese Paper Money

China
Thirteenth Century CE

The Emperor's mint then is in this same city of Cambaluc, and the way it is wrought is such that you might say he hath the secret of alchemy in perfection, and you would be right! For he makes his money after this fashion.

He makes them take of the bark of a certain tree, in fact of the mulberry tree, the leaves of which are the food of the silkworms—these trees being so numerous that whole districts are full of them. What they take is a certain fine white skin which lies between the wood of the tree and the thick outer bark, and this they make into something resembling sheets of paper, but black. When these sheets have been prepared they are cut up into pieces of different sizes. The smallest of these sizes is worth a half tornesel; the next, a little larger, one tornesel; one, a little larger still, is worth half a silver groat of Venice; another a whole groat; others yet two groats, five groats, and ten groats.

With these pieces of paper, made as I have described, he causes all payments on his own account to be made; and he makes them to pass current universally over all his kingdoms and provinces and territories, and whithersoever his power and sovereignty extends. And nobody, however important he may think himself, dares to refuse them on pain of death. And indeed everybody takes them readily, for wheresoever a person may go throughout the Great Khan's dominions he shall find these pieces of paper current, and shall be able to transact all sales and purchases of goods by means of them just as well as if they were coins of pure gold. And all the while they are so light that ten bezants' worth does not weigh one golden bezant.

Furthermore all merchants arriving from India or other countries, and bringing with them gold or silver or gems and pearls, are prohibited from selling to any one but the Emperor. He has twelve experts chosen for this business, men of shrewdness and experience in such affairs; these appraise the articles, and the Emperor then pays a liberal price for them in those pieces of paper. The merchants accept his price readily, for in the first place they would not get so good a one from anybody else, and secondly they are paid without any delay. And with this paper-money they can buy what they like anywhere over the Empire, whilst it is also vastly lighter to carry about on their journeys. . . .

When any of those pieces of paper are spoilt—not that they are so very flimsy neither—the owner carries them to the mint, and by paying three per cent on the value, he gets new pieces in exchange. And if any baron, or any one else soever, hath need of gold or silver or gems or pearls, in order to make plate, or girdles, or the like, he goes to the mint and buys as much as he list, paying in this paper-money.

Source: Polo, Marco, and Rustichello of Pisa. *The Travels of Marco Polo: The Complete Yule-Cordier Edition*. 2nd ed. Edited by Henry Yule and Henri Cordier. New York: Scribner, 1903, pp. 423–426. Slightly modified by Lawrence Morris.

TIMELINE   2000 1900 1800 1700 1600 1500 1400 1300 1200 1100 1000 900 800 700 600 500 400 300 200 100 1 BCE

What You Need to Know

The passage here comes from Marco Polo's volume on China and describes paper money.

Money—that is, an exchange medium that facilitates trade—dates back at least 3,000 or 4,000 years to ancient Egypt. For several millennia, money took the form of widely desired commodities. These included cattle in some parts of the world, cowry shells in Asia, and metal rings or bars in the Middle East. The Lydians, a seafaring and trading people from Western Anatolia, were the first to actually manufacture money in the form of coins around 700 BCE. The Greeks and Romans continued this tradition, as did civilizations across Eurasia, which soon expanded on the idea by minting coins of various values.

These coins had intrinsic value. That is, the metal they were made from was worth close to the face value of coin. The next major step in the history of money was the development of a medium, the value of which was representative rather than intrinsic—that is, a form of money not inherently precious but whose value was guaranteed by an issuing government. Such representative money came in two forms: nonprecious coinage and paper money. It was the Chinese, specifically the Tang dynasty, who came up with the idea for the latter sometime in the ninth century.

A Closer Look

Although Europeans had been traveling to China and East Asia since ancient times, contact between the two ends of the Eurasian landmass had declined markedly after the fall of the Western Roman Empire in the fifth century CE. It was revived in the later centuries of the Middle Ages, most notably, by traders from Italy. The most famous of these was Marco Polo, a Venetian merchant born in 1254. His widely read travelogue *Book of the Marvels of the World* was divided into four books dedicated to different regions of the world—the Middle East and Central Asia; China and the Mongols; other parts of East and South Asia, as well as the eastern coast of Africa; and Russia, which also contains accounts of the Mongol Wars.

Paper money was a marvel to Polo and presumably to his readers back in Europe. What amazed him most about it was the fact that something of no intrinsic value, in this case, paper made from the bark of trees, could be accepted as a medium of exchange. He likens the exchange to alchemy, or the medieval, the pseudo-scientific pursuit of a substance that would turn base metals into gold. This acceptance, of course, was based on the prestige and power of the government that created it and backed its value. Polo examines not just how this money is manufactured but how its value is established, noting the sophisticated economic understanding of the Chinese imperial court.

1 100 200 300 400 500 600 700 800 900 1000 1100 1200 1300 1400 1500 1600 1700 1800 1900 2000 CE

1.10.15 The Women of Kublai Khan's Court

China
Thirteenth Century CE

[Kublai] has four wives of the first rank, who are esteemed legitimate, and the eldest born son of any one of these succeeds to the empire, upon the decease of the grand khan. They bear equally the title of empress, and have their separate courts. None of them have fewer than three hundred young female attendants of great beauty, together with a multitude of youths as pages, and other eunuchs, as well as ladies of the bedchamber; so that the number of persons belonging to each of their respective courts amounts to ten thousand. . . . Besides these, he has many concubines provided for his use, from a province of Tartary named Ungut, having a city of the same name, the inhabitants of which are distinguished for beauty and features and fairness of complexion. Thither the grand khan sends his officers every second year, or oftener, as it may happen to be his pleasure, who collect for him, to the number of four or five hundred, or more, of the handsomest of the young women, according to the estimation of beauty communicated to them in their instructions. . . .

Upon the arrival of these commissioners, they give orders for assembling all the young women of the province, and appoint qualified persons to examine them, who, upon careful inspection of each of them separately, that is to say, of the hair, the countenance, the eyebrows, the mouth, the lips, and other features, as well as the symmetry of these with each other, estimate their value at sixteen, seventeen, eighteen, or twenty, or more carats, according to the greater or less degree of beauty. . . .

Upon their arrival in his presence, he causes a new examination to be made by a different set of inspectors, and from amongst them a further selection takes place, when thirty or forty are retained for his own chamber at a higher valuation. These, in the first instance, are committed separately to the care of the wives of certain of the nobles, whose duty it is to observe them attentively during the course of the night, in order to ascertain that they have not any concealed imperfections, that they sleep tranquilly, do not snore, have sweet breath, and are free from unpleasant scent in any part of the body. Having undergone this rigorous scrutiny, they're divided into parties of five, one of which parties attends during three days and three nights, in his majesty's interior apartment, where they are to perform every service that is required of them, and he does with them as he likes. When this term is completed, they are relieved by another party, and in this manner successively, until the whole number have taken their turn. . . .

The remainder of them, whose value had been estimated at an inferior rate, are assigned to the different lords of the household; under whom they are instructed in cookery, in dressmaking, and other suitable works; and upon any person belonging to the court expressing an inclination to take a wife, the grand khan bestows upon him one of these damsels, with a handsome portion. In this manner he provides for them all amongst his nobility. It may be asked whether the people of the province do not feel themselves aggrieved in having their daughters thus forcibly taken from them by the sovereign? . . . [T]hey regard it as a favour and an honour done to them; and those who are the fathers of handsome children feel highly gratified by his condescending to make choice of their daughters.

Source: Polo, Marco. Excerpts from *The Travels of Marco Polo the Venetian, Book II, Ch. IV*. Edited by E. Rhys. Translated by J. Masefield. New York: Dent, 1908, pp. 162–165.

TIMELINE   2000 1900 1800 1700 1600 1500 1400 1300 1200 1100 1000 900 800 700 600 500 400 300 200 100 1 BCE

342

What You Need to Know

This excerpt is by the great Venetian travel chronicler Marco Polo, who visited the court of Kublai Khan in the thirteenth century.

Compared with other civilizations of the time, women in Mongol society had a greater degree of autonomy and even power, especially compared with the women of China, Japan, and other East Asian civilizations. Mongol women, for instance, had the right to own property and to initiate divorce. Part of this higher status was due to their economic role. It was Mongol women who were responsible for maintaining the herds of horses that their warrior men folk rode into battle.

At the same time, the young women of Kublai Khan's court, recruited from the various lands the Mongols conquered, were prized for their beauty, manners, and health. So many were brought to the court that there developed a small bureaucracy of officials, as well as standards, by which to judge them before their final assignment as concubines or servants.

A Closer Look

While traditional Mongol nomadic society offered women a degree of respect and equality, that became less the case after the great Mongol conquests of the thirteenth century. Ruling civilizations who had a more elaborate material culture than their own and whose populations were much greater, the Mongols tended to assimilate their customs and traditions as they settled down to rule over them. Such appears to be the case in this description of the court of Kublai Khan offered by Marco Polo, who visited his court in the late thirteenth century. Grandson and successor to Genghis Khan, Kublai expanded the Mongol Empire into southern China and other regions during his reign from 1260 to 1294.

Polo first describes the legitimate wives of Kublai Khan, who numbered four. He notes how each of them were titled empresses and had their separate courts. From this description, one can understand why the Mongol Empire ultimately succumbed in part to succession crises.

More remarkable is the description of the Khan's vast number of concubines, and the methods used to procure them. They came by the hundreds from across the empire and were largely selected for their physical attractiveness. Those less attractive were relegated to household service. While his European readers might think that this wholesale seizure of beautiful young women might antagonize the Mongol leader's subjects, Polo informs them that the fathers of these women considered it an honor that their daughters were chosen to serve the great Khan.

1 100 200 300   400   500   600   700   800   900   1000 1100 1200 1300   1400   1500   1600   1700 1800 1900 2000 CE

1.10.16 Yoshida Kenko on Sake

Japan
1282–1350 CE

There are many things in this world that I do not understand. For example, you give other people sake to drink, and you think this is enjoyable. I can't understand why. The drinker grimaces, he frowns, he watches for an opportunity to throw away the sake or to escape, but the host traps him, holds him back, and forces him to drink. Next, intelligent men become all at once fools and do stupid things. Healthy people fall ill under our very eyes, and lie down, dead to the world. What an absurd way to celebrate a festival! The next day they have a headache, they can't eat anything, they let out long sighs, they can no longer remember the things of the night and say that they were in another life. They neglect both private and public business, no matter how important, and become ill. To make people go through this is neither hospitable nor decent. How can one who has seen such harsh things not view them with distaste and irritation? If we heard that a similar custom existed in some foreign country, we would undoubtedly find it bizarre and outrageous.

Seeing these things happen shocks the heart. Some thoughtful people, who are important, foolishly hold themselves proudly and start gabbing. They tilt their hat, they unknot their belts, they roll up their sleeves; they have such a stunned look that they become almost unrecognizable. Women push back their hair, shamelessly showing their forehead. They throw back their heads and seize the hand of the man to whom they are offering the drink. Some rude fellow, taking a bit of fish, raises it to someone else's lips and then eats the rest himself—a disgusting sight! Everyone sings at the top of their lungs and dances. An old monk, urged to dance, uncovers a dark black shoulder and performs a strange unwatchable dance. The people who look at this in enjoyment repulse and detest me. Next, the drunkard boasts greatly of his skills and qualities (which the others find hideously tiresome), and he cries out in his drunkenness. Commoners quarrel and argue, generating fear and anxiety. The intoxicated crowd behaves like ruffians; they grab things that you do not want to give them. . . .

In this world, sake brings with it a host of wrongs—the victim loses his money and his health. Although one calls the man of a hundred cures, ten thousand diseases come to him. Although it's said that sake makes you forget sadness, in fact drunk people remember past miseries and bemoan them. With regard to the future life, sake destroys the wisdom of men, it burns like fire the roots of goodness, increases one's faults, encourages one to violate all the commandments and to fall into hell. "He who gives other people drink will be born without hands for five hundred lives." That is what Buddha said about the matter.

Although sake is indeed detestable, there are some occasions when one cannot justly refuse it. Sake increases pleasure if offered on a bright moonlit night, on a snowy morning, or amongst the flowers when you are at peace. If, on a tedious day, a friend suddenly arrives, then it is enjoyable to receive him with a bit of sake.

Source: Yoshida Kenko. Excerpt from *Tsurezuregusa*. In *Anthologie de la literature japonaise des origins au xxe siècle*. Edited by Michel Revon. Paris: Delagrave, 1919, pp. 297–299. Translated from the French by Lawrence Morris.

TIMELINE   2000 1900 1800 1700 1600 1500 1400 1300 1200 1100 1000 900 800 700 600 500 400 300 200 100 1 BCE

What You Need to Know

In the text included here, Yoshida Kenko, a Buddhist monk, discusses sake drinking.

First brewed in Japan, and still the country's national drink, sake is an alcoholic beverage made from fermented rice, which has been stripped of its bran and then polished, and *koji*, a mold native to East Asia. The word *sake* translates as "liquor." Historians are not certain of its origins, although most believe it dates to the Nara period from 710 to 794.

Originally, sake had a rather low alcoholic content but quickly became the most popular of drinks, imbibed at festivals, in taverns, and even during religious rituals. The government maintained a monopoly over sake production during the early Heian period of the eighth and ninth centuries, its production gradually slipped under the control of monasteries, which earned much of their income selling it. By the eighteenth and nineteenth centuries, most of the beverage was produced by landowners who gradually gave up farming and turned to full-time sake manufacturing. Some Japanese sake firms today date back hundreds of years.

A Closer Look

One of the most celebrated of medieval Japanese authors was Yoshida Kenko. Born the son of a government official around 1282, Kenko is best known for his collection of short literary pieces *Tsurezuregusa*, or Essays in Idleness. The work, which consists of a preface and 248 passages of varying length, is an early example of a Japanese style of writing known as *zuihitsu*, which literally means "follow the brush," but is best translated as "stream of consciousness" writing. The essays cover a variety of topics from abstract concepts to the doings of everyday life, from the wonders of the natural world to the concerns of humans. Contemplative in tone, there is also much nostalgia in the book as the author laments the passing of traditional ways even as he explores the idea that often what makes things beautiful is their transience.

As with many of Kenko's other essays, this one looks at the subject from different angles. On the one hand, he condemns the widespread drunkenness he sees around him, which produces bad actions and a loss of reason. But he is not a teetotaler either. He draws a portrait of an ideal form of sake enjoyment that entails the drinking of moderate amounts in a beautiful natural setting or surrounded by good friends. In fact, it is not so much alcohol that Kenko is criticizing but the unfortunate public scenes drunkenness leads to.

1 100 200 300 400 500 600 700 800 900 1000 1100 1200 1300 1400 1500 1600 1700 1800 1900 2000 CE

1.10.17 Liu Chi on Corruption during the Yuan Dynasty

China
Fourteenth Century CE

At Hangchow there lived a costermonger who understood how to keep oranges a whole year without letting them spoil. His fruit was always fresh-looking, firm as jade, and of a beautiful golden hue; but inside—dry as an old cocoon.

One day I asked him, saying, "Are your oranges for altar or sacrificial purposes, or for show at banquets? Or do you make this outside display merely to cheat the foolish as cheat them you most outrageously do." "Sir," replied the orangeman, "I have carried on this trade now for many years. It is my source of livelihood. I sell; the world buys. And I have yet to learn that you are the only honest man about, and that I am the only cheat. Perhaps it never struck you in this light. The baton-bearers of to-day, seated on their tiger skins, pose as the martial guardians of the State; but what are they compared with the captains of old? The broad-brimmed, long-robed Ministers of to-day pose as pillars of the constitution; but have they the wisdom of our ancient counsellors? Evil-doers arise, and none can subdue them. The people are in misery, and none can relieve them. Clerks are corrupt, and none can restrain them. Laws decay, and none can renew them. Our officials eat the bread of the State and know no shame. They sit in lofty halls, ride fine steeds, drink themselves drunk with wine, and batten on the richest fare. Which of them but puts on an awe-inspiring look, a dignified mien?—all gold and gems without, but dry cocoons within. You pay, sir, no heed to these things, while you are very particular about my oranges."

I had no answer to make. Was he really out of conceit with the age, or only quizzing me in defence of his fruit?

Source: Liu Chi. "Outsides." In *A History of Chinese Literature. Book VI: The Mongol Dynasty.* Ch. I. Edited by Herbert Allen Giles. New York: D. Appleton and Co., 1901, pp. 254–255.

TIMELINE   2000 1900 1800 1700 1600 1500 1400 1300 1200 1100 1000 900 800 700 600 500 400 300 200 100 1 BCE

What You Need to Know

This passage from poet Liu Chi's satirical piece "Outsides" describes the corruption in Mongol-controlled China during the Yuan dynasty.

In the thirteenth and fourteenth centuries, the Mongols, a nomadic peoples from north-central Asia, conquered virtually all of Eurasia. Their conquest of Song dynasty China occurred in two stages. Northern China was captured by Genghis Khan in the early thirteenth century, while the Southern Song fell to his grandson and successor Khubilai Khan (Kublai Khan) in 1279.

The Mongols were not just great conquerors but also effective administrators. Marco Polo, the great Venetian travel writer of the late thirteenth century, noted as much in his description of Hangzhou, the commercial capital of the Mongol-ruled China, which was known as the Yuan dynasty. Polo describes regular police-style patrols of the city of nearly a million people, aimed at discouraging both crime and political dissent. While noting their rigorous enforcement of the law, he also notes that the accused had certain rights, such as the right to appear before a magistrate and the right to plead innocence.

A Closer Look

The Yuan dynasty of the Mongols in China instituted a number of reforms to improve policing in urban areas. How effective the Yuan dynasty's law enforcement really was is questioned by the poet Liu Chi in "Outsides." Liu lived during the waning years of the Yuan dynasty, from 1311 to 1375. The dynasty fell eight years before his death, a result of squabbling over dynastic succession, natural disasters, and unjust treatment of the local Han people.

Part of that mistreatment arose from the corruption that permeated Yuan dynasty society, from the court of the emperor down to the petty corruption of street vendors, such as the Hangzhou costermonger, or fruit seller, depicted in the poem of Liu Chi, reprinted here. New taxes to pay for an imperial court filled with highly paid officials were arbitrarily imposed, and the collection turned over to local officials who often used their authority, and the police, to extract even more from poor town dwellers and peasants. Corruption at the top bred a general contempt for Confucian principles of honesty and social harmony, resulting in cheating, fraud, and bribery at all levels of society. There was much resentment and frustration with this state of things, leading to a series of peasant revolts that ultimately brought down the dynasty. What Liu describes here, however, is not as momentous. Instead, it describes the petty corruption of a Hangzhou costermonger, or someone who sells fruit on the street.

1 100 200 300 400 500 600 700 800 900 1000 1100 1200 1300 1400 1500 1600 1700 1800 1900 2000 CE

1.10.18 Medical Treatment as Described in *The Romance of the Three Kingdoms*

China
Fourteenth Century CE

"Dr. Hua," explained the officer, "is a mighty skilful physician, and such a one as is not often to be found. His administration of drugs, and his use of acupuncture and counter-irritants are always followed by the speedy recovery of the patient. If the sick man is suffering from some internal complaint and medicines produce no satisfactory result, then Dr. Hua will administer a dose of hashish, under the influence of which the patient becomes as it were intoxicated with wine. He now takes a sharp knife and opens the abdomen, proceeding to wash the patient's viscera with medicinal liquids, but without causing him the slightest pain. The washing finished, he sews up the wound with medicated thread and puts over it a plaster, and by the end of a month or twenty days the place has healed up. Such is his extra-ordinary skill. One day, for instance, as he was walking along a road, he heard someone groaning deeply, and at once declared that the cause was indigestion. On inquiry, this turned out to be the case; and accordingly, Dr. Hua ordered the sufferer to drink three pints of a decoction of garlic and leeks, which he did, and vomited forth a snake between two and three feet in length, after which he could digest food as before. On another occasion, the Governor of Kuang-ling was very much depressed in his mind, besides being troubled with a flushing of the face and total loss of appetite. He consulted Dr. Hua, and the effect of some medicine administered by him was to cause the invalid to throw up a quantity of red-headed wriggling tadpoles, which the doctor told him had been generated in his system by too great indulgence in fish, and which, although temporarily expelled, would reappear after an interval of three years, when nothing could save him. And sure enough, he died three years afterwards. In a further instance, a man had a tumour growing between his eyebrows, the itching of which was insupportable. When Dr. Hua saw it, he said, 'There is a bird inside,' at which everybody laughed. However, he took a knife and opened the tumour, and out flew a canary, the patient beginning to recover from that hour. . . ."

"The pain in your Highness's head," said Dr. Hua, "arises from wind, and the seat of the disease is the brain, where the wind is collected, unable to get out. Drugs are of no avail in your present condition, for which there is but one remedy. You must first swallow a dose of hashish, and then with a sharp axe I will split open the back of your head and let the wind out. Thus the disease will be exterminated."

Source: Luo Guanzhong. Excerpt from *The Romance of the Three Kingdoms*. In *A History of Chinese Literature. Book VI: The Mongol Dynasty*. Ch. III. Edited by Herbert Allen Giles. New York: D. Appleton and Co., 1901, pp. 278–280.

What You Need to Know

The accompanying excerpt comes from a historical novel titled *The Romance of the Three Kingdoms*, attributed to the writer Luo Guanzhong, who lived from about 1330 to 1400.

The Chinese have a medical tradition that stretches back roughly 5,000 years and is based on ideas that are very different from its Western counterpart. First, traditional Chinese practitioners hold that human physiognomy is composed of two essential principles. These are *yin*, the inner and negative principle, and *yang*, the outer and positive principle. When these are not in balance, illness results. Chinese tradition also says that the principles of yin and yang determine the flow of vital energy that makes life itself possible. That vital energy consists of energetic particles, blood, and other bodily fluids. The energy is part of the yang principle and is warm and dry; it is kept moist and cooled by the liquids of the body, which are part of the yin principle. When these are out of order, the organs will not function properly. While such principles run counter to the understanding of human physiognomy offered by modern medicine, the diagnostic tools of Chinese doctors seem sound even today. There were four of these: observation of symptoms, questioning of the patient, analysis of the sounds and odors of the body, and measurement of the heartbeat and pulse.

A Closer Look

*The Romance of the Three Kingdom*s tells the story of the War of the Three Kingdoms, a civil conflict that occurred near the end of the Han dynasty in the third century CE. The passage printed here relates to the treatment given to a soldier who had been struck on the head by a sword yielded by the spirit of the pear tree he was trying to cut down. So bad is his suffering that his commanding officer recommends he be treated by a highly respected doctor named Hua. The passage then relates other cases handled by the doctor. While the book is about events more than a thousand years before, the medical techniques it describes were contemporary, including references to acupuncture.

Some of the medicine it describes seems remarkably sound, even by modern standards. In the case of the soldier, he is anesthetized with hashish before the surgery. After opening up the patient's abdomen, the doctor applies medicine to the wounded area and then sews up his stomach using sutures that appear to have been treated with an antiseptic. Another patient is given a purgative to remove what seems to be a tapeworm. Yet there are also cases that seem fantastical, such as the bird that flies out of a tumor on a patient's face or the winds released from the brain of an emperor suffering from headaches.

1.10.19 Yuan Dynasty Jingdezhen Blue-and-White Porcelain Ewer

China
ca. 1335 CE

Credit: DeAgostini/Getty Images

TIMELINE   2000 1900 1800 1700 1600 1500 1400 1300 1200 1100 1000 900 800 700 600 500 400 300 200 100 1 BCE

What You Need to Know

The ewer, or pitcher, shown here was manufactured around the year 1335. It is made of white glazed porcelain and decorated with a blue flower motif in its underglaze, derived from the mineral cobalt.

The Mongols were a nomadic warrior people from Central Asia, who in the thirteenth and fourteenth centuries conquered much of the Asian landmass from the Middle East to Korea, including China. Initially raiders and plunderers, they soon settled down and established governments over the people they conquered, even as they assimilated the culture of these civilizations. In China, they established the Yuan dynasty, which lasted from 1271 to 1368.

Although relatively short-lived, the Yuan dynasty was marked by the energy and expansiveness of its Mongol rulers. It sent out great maritime expeditions to explore and conquer and its trading networks spread as far as the Spice Islands of today's Indonesia to Western Europe. Ultimately, the Yuan succumbed to the problems of earlier dynasties—namely, a series of incompetent emperors and internal court intrigue, leading to its overthrow by the Ming dynasty. Among the greatest artistic accomplishments of the Ming were its exquisite ceramics, but that tradition actually began under the Yuan.

A Closer Look

Ceramics are brittle, impermeable, and heat-resistant materials made by firing a nonmetallic mineral, such as clay, at a high temperature. Porcelain is a subset of ceramics, noted for its white, translucent color. So associated is porcelain with China that the English term for dishware made of it is called "china."

There is good reason for this, as historians believe it was the Chinese under the Han dynasty from 226 BCE to 220 CE who first developed it. Since Han times, the best Chinese porcelain came from Jianxi Province in southeast China, and specifically from the so-called city of porcelain, Jingdezhen, still a center of production. Traded across China, Jingdezhen porcelain was manufactured on an industrial, rather than artisanal, scale, especially from the Yuan dynasty on. The ewer shown at right is not particularly elaborate in its design or execution and was probably destined for the household of moderate means, where it would be used to dispense water or wine. Ones like it, but of a higher quality, might have been destined for the foreign trade, as Chinese porcelain in the fourteenth century was sold as far away as the Middle East, India, and even Europe.

1   100   200   300   400   500   600   700   800   900   1000   1100   1200   1300   1400   1500   1600   1700   1800   1900   2000 CE

1.10.20 Scene from *Aya no Tsuzumi*, a Japanese *Noh* Play

Japan
ca. Fourteenth–Fifteenth Centuries

Courtier: I am a courtier at the Palace of Kinomaru in the country of Chikuzen. . . . [S]o it happened that one day the old man who sweeps the garden here caught sight of the Princess. And from that time he has loved her with a love that gives his heart no rest.

Some one told her of this, and she said, "Love's equal realm knows no divisions," and in her pity she said, "By that pond there stands a laurel-tree, and on its branches there hangs a drum. Let him beat the drum, and if the sound is heard in the Palace, he shall see my face again." . . .

Chorus (speaking for the gardener): And hope stretched out from dusk to dusk.
    But now, a watchman of the hours, I beat
    The longed-for stroke.

Gardener: I was old, I shunned the daylight,
    I was gaunt as an aged crane;
    And upon all that misery
    Suddenly a sorrow was heaped,
    The new sorrow of love. . . .

Chorus: She has not come. . . .
    Then weary of himself and calling her to witness of his woe,
    "Why should I endure," he cried,
    "Such life as this?" and in the waters of the pond
    He cast himself and died . . .

Princess (speaking wildly, already possessed by the Gardener's angry ghost, which speaks through her): Listen, people, listen!
    In the noise of the beating waves
    I hear the rolling of a drum.
    Oh, joyful sound, oh joyful!
    The music of a drum.

Courtier: Strange, strange!
    This lady speaks as one
    By phantasy possessed.
    What is amiss, what ails her?

Princess: Truly, by phantasy I am possessed.
    Can a damask drum give sound?
    When I bade him beat what could not ring,
    Then tottered first my wits

Source: Excerpt from *Aya no Tsuzumi*. In *The Noh Plays of Japan*. Edited by Arthur Waley. New York: Knopf, 1922, pp. 134–141.

TIMELINE   2000 1900 1800 1700 1600 1500 1400 1300 1200 1100 1000 900 800 700 600 500 400 300 200 100 1 BCE

What You Need to Know

This selection is from one of the best known dramas of the Ashikaga shogunate, *Aya no Tsuzumi*, or *The Damask Drum* in English.

For much of its medieval history, through the first half of the second millennium CE, Japan was ruled as a shogunate. Under this system, the emperor remained a ceremonial figurehead, a semi-divine incarnation who represented the oneness of the Japanese people. The actual day-to-day administration of the government was in the hands of a regent. To maintain control over the powerful lords of the country, the Shogun required that they live much of the year at the imperial court. Because they had so little to do there, life at court during the Ashikaga shogunate was highly ritualized and shaped by a rigid social hierarchy, where courtiers and officials engaged in endless ceremonies and intrigues of both the sexual, romantic, and political varieties, which was reenacted in drama. Indeed, theater going was a major activity of court nobles who themselves often wrote up plays of their own. When not indulging in theatrical activities, the nobles engaged in conspicuous consumption of luxury, oftentimes competing with one another and, in the process, driving themselves into debt. To meet their financial obligations, some were forced to sell ancestral lands, which further weakened their power vis-à-vis the shogunate.

A Closer Look

The Noh is a form of musical drama dating to roughly the thirteenth century. The name *noh* is derived from a Chinese term for "talent." Traditionally, the actors in *noh* dramas were all male. Masks allowed them to play a host of characters, including female ones. In medieval times, *noh* dramas were played in sets of five, with short and humorous *kyogen* one-act plays (*kyogen* means "crazy talk") interspersed throughout. Performances typically lasted all day.

Noh dramas were a hybrid of popular and aristocratic dramatic forms and reached their apogee during the Ashikaga shogunate. Like the imperial courts, and the courts of local princes, where they were often performed, *noh* dramas were highly formalized, with rules about who characters could be, the type of language that could be used, and the subject matter that might be depicted.

Although the identity of the playwright is not certain, many scholars believe it was penned by Zeami Motokiyo, who lived from 1363 to 1443. The play tells the tale of a gardener and a princess who fall in love but, because of their differences in status, cannot fulfill that love. *Aya no Tsuzumi* thus captures the essence of court life in medieval Japan, with its rigid social hierarchy and obsession with romantic love and sexuality.

Part 11:
Europe in the Middle Ages

Fifth–Fifteenth Centuries CE

1.11.1 Merovingian Grooming Accessories

Gaul (Western Europe)
Fifth–Eighth Century CE

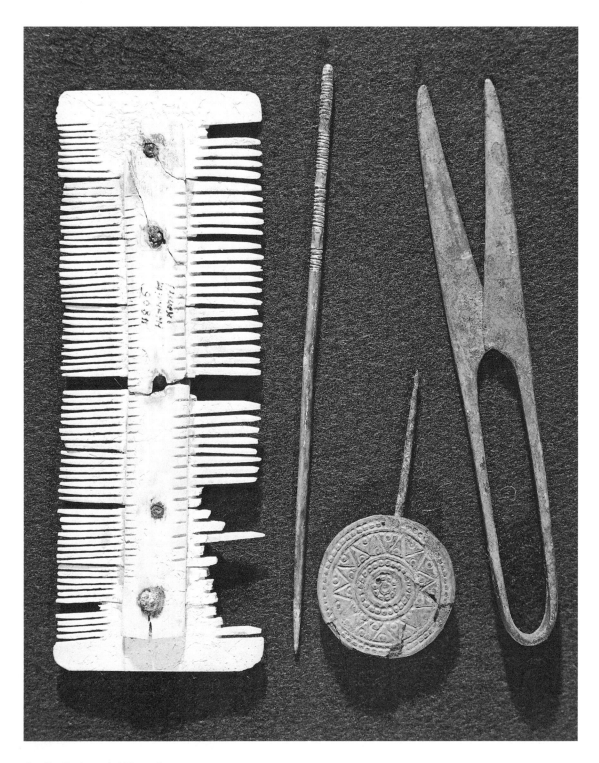

Credit: DeAgostini/Getty Images

What You Need to Know

This set of women's hair grooming accessories from Merovingian France of the fifth to eighth centuries, includes a comb, hair pins, and a clipper.

Personal hygiene and grooming were not common attributes of life in the European Middle Ages. While peasants and common folk might bathe and adorn themselves for special events in their lives or for high holidays, day-to-day personal care was largely the preserve of the noble class. Implements for grooming were rare and expensive and water for bathing had to be laboriously drawn from wells, transported to dwellings, and then slowly heated with firewood that itself had to be gathered.

There were also other cultural factors involved. In a highly religious age that valued the spirit over the body, fashionable grooming and adornment were often frowned upon as examples of sinful pride. Indeed, bathing itself—allowing water to wash over one's naked body—was likened to sexual debauchery in some medieval literature. And even for those who did not see it as sin, there were health concerns, as many felt that bathing was a source of disease.

A Closer Look

Unlike their Roman predecessors, the Merovingian kings who ruled over much of northwestern Europe from the fifth through the eighth centuries favored long-flowing hair and beards for men. Indeed, the shaving of the head and beard was a form of disgrace and punishment among the aristocracy.

As in much of the Middle Ages, women in this period preferred to wear their hair, which was a mark of a woman's fertility and sexuality, long as well, typically down to the waist. The hair was then twisted into braids that could hang down or be tied up in a chignon atop the head, using the hairpins seen in the accompanying image of hair grooming utensils of the Merovingian era. The scissors shown were used not only for cutting tresses at their ends but around the forehead, which was considered among the most attractive features of a woman's face and thus kept clear of hair.

While brushes were unknown in medieval times, combs were widely used and not just for styling but to rid hair of lice, a major problem in an era of long hair, little bathing, and communal sleeping.

1 100 200 300 400 500 600 700 800 900 1000 1100 1200 1300 1400 1500 1600 1700 1800 1900 2000 CE

1.11.2 Salic Law on the Punishment for Stealing Livestock

Northern Europe
ca. 507–511 CE

II. Concerning thefts of pigs

1. If any one steal a suckling pig and it be proved against him, let him be judged guilty of chrane calcium, i.e. 120 denarii, which make 3 solidi.

2. If any one steal a pig that is weaned and it be proved against him, let him be judged guilty of chrane calcium, i.e. 40 denarii, which make 1 solidi. . . .

14. If any one steal 25 pigs and there be no more in the herd, and it be proved against him, let him be judged guilty of sonista, i.e. 2500 denarii, which make 62 solidi.

III. Concerning thefts of cattle

4. If any one steal the unyoked bull which is the leader of the herd, let him be judged guilty of charohitum, i.e., 8,000 denarii, which make 45 solidi.

5. But if that bull be kept for the cows of three villages in common, let him who stole it be judged guilty of chammitum, i.e., three times 45 solidi.

6. If any one steal the king's bull, let him be judged guilty of anteotho, i.e., 3,600 denarii, which make 90 solidi, besides capitale and delitura.

IX. Concerning damage done among crops or in any enclosure

1. If any one find cattle or a horse or any flocks among his crops he ought not to harm them in any way.

2. And if he does so and confess it, let him pay capitale in place of the damage; but he shall keep the injured beast for himself.

3. But if he does not confess, and it be proved against him, let him be judged guilty of 600 denarii, which make 15 solidi, besides capitale and dilatura.

Source: Salic Law. Excerpt in *Germanische Rechtsdenkmäler*. Edited by H. G. Gengler. Erlangen, Germany: F. Enke, 1875, p. 267. In *A Source Book for Medieval Economic History*. Edited by Roy Cave and Herbert Coulson. New York: Biblo and Tannen, 1965, pp. 307–308.

What You Need to Know

The accompanying document comes from the Salic Law of the Franks, a Germanic people who inhabited Central and Western Europe in the early Middle Ages. The excerpts here, from the early sixth century, concern the laws on stealing livestock.

The vast majority of people in the European Middle Ages worked on the land. Most labored either as peasants or serfs, depending on their relationship with the lord of the manor, the obligations in labor and taxes they owed him, and the degree of freedom they enjoyed.

Compared with modern agricultural practices, medieval farming methods were extremely primitive and unproductive. Not only was their no machinery, even hand tools were scarce. Plows were made of wood and so barely broke the surface of the soil. Grain was cut with a sickle and grasses with a scythe. Fertilizing the soil was barely understood and consisted mostly of spreading around animal manure. Farms were also small because there were few effective tools to clear forests and as much as a third of the land that was cleared was left to lie fallow.

A Closer Look

With little in the way of pasturage or cut grains and grasses for animals to feed on, livestock were few and generally of small stature in medieval times. The average full grown bull measured only slightly larger than a calf on a modern farm today, while the typical sheep might produce two ounces of wool per shearing, compared with as much as ten pounds today. Oxen were the most valuable animals because they served as the main beasts of burden, but they required an enormous amount of feed. For this reason, they were not typically owned by an individual but were shared by a community of peasants.

Despite this low productivity, or perhaps because of it, livestock was highly valued, as these excerpts from a Germanic legal code of the seventh century make clear. There were no public prisons in the lands of central Europe inhabited by Germanic-speaking peoples, and thus persons found guilty of stealing livestock were punished with fines. And these could be quite high, especially for cattle, with the theft of a bull resulting in a fine of 8,000 denarii, a form of silver specie. So highly valued were livestock that, even when an animal damaged a neighbor's crop, the victim was proscribed from harming the creature, at the risk of a major fine.

1 100 200 300 400 500 600 700 800 900 1000 1100 1200 1300 1400 1500 1600 1700 1800 1900 2000 CE

Italy
529 CE

Clause 3. About Calling in the Brothers to Take Counsel

Whenever anything of importance is to be done in the monastery, the abbot shall call together the whole congregation, and shall himself explain the matter in question, and, having heard the advice of the brothers, he shall do what he considers most advantageous. . . . But even as it behooves the disciples to obey the master, so it is fitting that he should arrange all matters with care and justice. In all things, indeed, let every one follow the Rule as his guide; and let no one rashly deviate from it. Let no one in the monastery follow the inclination of his own heart. And let no one boldly presume to dispute with his abbot, within or without the monastery. But, if he should so presume, let him be subject to the discipline of the Rule.

Clause 16. How Divine Service Shall Be Held Through the Day

As the prophet says: "Seven times in the day do I praise Thee." Which sacred number of seven will thus be fulfilled by us if, at matins, at the first, third, sixth, ninth hours, at vesper time and at "completorium" we perform the duties of our service; for it is of these hours of the day that he said: "Seven times in the day do I praise Thee." For concerning nocturnal vigils, the same prophet says: "At midnight I arose to confess unto thee." Therefore, at these times, let us give thanks to our Creator concerning the judgments of his righteousness; that is, at matins, etc.

Clause 33. Whether the Monks Should Have Anything of Their Own

More than anything else is this special vice to be cut off root and branch from the monastery, that one should presume to give or receive anything without the order of the abbot, or should have anything of his own. He should have absolutely not anything, neither a book, nor tablets, nor a pen—nothing at all. For indeed it is not allowed to the monks to have their own bodies or wills in their own power. But all things necessary they must expect from the Father of the monastery; . . . All things shall be held in common.

Clause 48. Considering the Daily Manual Labor

Idleness is the enemy of the soul. And therefore, at fixed times, the brothers ought to be occupied in manual labor; and again, at fixed times, in sacred reading. Therefore we believe that both seasons ought to be arranged after this manner, so that, from Easter until the October 1, going out early, from 6 a.m. until 10 a.m. they shall do what labor may be necessary. From 10 a.m. until about noon, they shall be free for reading. After the meal at noon, rising from the table, they shall rest in their beds with all silence, or, perchance, he that wishes to read may read to himself in such a way as not to disturb another. And the second meal shall be moderate and eaten about 2:30 p.m.; and again they shall work at what is to be done until evening prayer.

Source: Benedict of Nursia. Excerpts from *The Rule of St. Benedict*. In *Select Historical Documents of the Middle Ages*. Translated and edited by Ernest F. Henderson. London: George Bell & Sons, 1892, pp. 278, 283, 289, 297. With slight modifications.

TIMELINE   2000 1900 1800 1700 1600 1500 1400 1300 1200 1100 1000 900 800 700 600 500 400 300 200 100 1 BCE

What You Need to Know

Saint Benedict of Nursia, who founded 12 monasteries in Italy in the early sixth century, formalized the rules of monastic life in the Catholic tradition, some of which are excerpted here.

Monasteries were—and are—institutions founded, inhabited, and run by religious observants as a place for contemplating spiritual matters. Although known to many of the world's religions, monasteries in the Western tradition date back to the late Roman Empire, when some Christians fled persecution and established communities in which they could safely practice their faith.

Monasticism, or monastic life, was first practiced in the eastern half of the Roman Empire but, by and shortly after the fall of the Western Roman Empire in the fifth century, they had spread as far as Gaul (France), England, and Ireland. In 540, a Roman senator named Cassiodorus founded a monastery on his estate in Italy, where he set monks to work copying sacred and secular texts, thereby establishing one of the principal occupations of monasteries—education and the pursuit of scholarship. But no one is more central to the tradition of monasticism in western Christendom than Saint Benedict.

A Closer Look

Celebrated as a saint by Catholics and Anglicans, St. Benedict, who lived from around 480 to 543 or 547, wrote down in 529 what has come to be known as *The Rule of St. Benedict*, a brief guideline for the monks of the monastery he had established at Monte Cassino, in central Italy. The excerpts here highlight Benedict's three main principles of monastic life: community, work, and prayer, all to the purpose of understanding, praising, and fulfilling the word of God. Benedict made it clear that monks, while retreating from the bustle and temptation of secular life, were not hermits but rather members of a brotherhood.

The community element is made clear in Clause 3, which states that abbots, or head monks, should consult the community of monks before making any important decision. At the same time, he advises that no single monk should consider his opinions necessarily superior to those of other monks. The communal nature of monastic life is reiterated in Clause 33, which states that all possessions belong not to individuals but to the brotherhood as a whole. Clause 48 urges the monk to labor, not just to sustain the community but for his own salvation as "[i]dleness is the enemy of the soul." Finally, citing Christ's own admonition, Clause 16 calls for frequent, near round-the-clock prayer and masses for the lord.

1 100 200 300 400 500 600 700 800 900 1000 1100 1200 1300 1400 1500 1600 1700 1800 1900 2000 CE

1.11.4 A Vassal's Contract

France
Seventh Century CE

To that magnificent lord _____, I, _____. Since it is well known to all how little I have wherewith to feed and clothe myself, I have therefore petitioned your piety, and your goodwill has decreed to me, that I should hand myself over, or commend myself, to your guardianship, which I have thereupon done; that is to say, in this way, that you should aid and succor me, as well with food as with clothing, according as I shall be able to serve you and deserve it.

And so long as I shall live I ought to provide service and honor to you, compatible with my free condition; and I shall not, during the time of my life, have the right to withdraw from your control or guardianship; but must remain during the days of my life under your power or defense. Wherefore it is proper that if either of us shall wish to withdraw himself from these agreements, he shall pay _____ shillings to the other party, and this agreement shall remain unbroken.

Source: Cheyney, Edward P., trans. *University of Pennsylvania Translations and Reprints*. Vol. IV, no. 3, pp. 3–4. In *A Source Book of Mediaeval History*. Edited by Frederic Austin Ogg. New York: American Book Company, 1908, pp. 205–206.

TIMELINE   2000 1900 1800 1700 1600 1500 1400 1300 1200 1100 1000 900 800 700 600 500 400 300 200 100 1 BCE

What You Need to Know

The accompanying document is a standard vassal's contract from seventh century France, meant to be used by peasants seeking to be vassalage under a lord.

A vassal in medieval Europe could be anyone who stood as the inferior in a binding relationship with another person. The vassal agreed to provide services and loyalty in exchange for some form of payment and protection, the latter necessary in a world where central governments provided little security for the people living under them. A vassal could be a noble, trading loyalty, military services, and goods in exchange for a king's grant of land. Knights were also vassals, who exchanged military duty for a grant of land or goods from a lord. Most typically, however, vassals were peasants who agreed to provide labor and part of their crop and livestock to a lord. In exchange, the lord granted the peasant some land and provided him protection. The vassal was not only expected to serve his lord but to offer his obedience in all matters of daily life, from settling legal disputes to officiating over his marriage.

A Closer Look

In this document, the reader should note that the contract had blanks where the names of the lord and the vassal, along with the price for ending the vassalage, were left to be filled in later. At first glance, the document seems akin to a modern employment contract—labor for pay. But a closer reading reveals major differences. First, the vassal to be, who is clearly indigent, because he does not have the "wherewith to feed and clothe" himself, binds himself over to the lord, making of the latter his guardian. In exchange, the lord will provide him not with monetary pay but with food and clothing.

Equally noteworthy is the fact that the vassal pledges his services to the lord for life. The only way that either party could get out of the contract was by making a payment in money. But, in seventh-century France, a peasant might in fact never possess or even see money in his lifetime, as there was little in the way of a commercial economy at that time. Thus, only a lord might have the means to sever the contract. In effect, this turned the peasant into a slave in all but name. Although that status did not necessarily pass on to the vassal's heirs, as was the case with slavery in subsequent eras, it was most likely that the vassal's children would agree to their own vassalage with the lord upon coming to maturity.

1 100 200 300 400 500 600 700 800 900 1000 1100 1200 1300 1400 1500 1600 1700 1800 1900 2000 CE

1.11.5 Laws Concerning Anglo-Saxon Women

Wessex, England
Ninth Century CE

8. If anyone takes a nun from a nunnery without the permission of the king or bishop, he shall pay 120 shillings, half to the king, and half to the bishop and the lord of the church, under whose charge the nun is.

i. If she lives longer than he who abducted her, she shall inherit nothing of his property.

ii. If she bears a child, it shall inherit no more of the property than its mother.

iii. If her child is slain, the share of the wergeld due to the mother's kindred shall be paid to the king, but the father's kindred shall be paid the share due to them.

9. If anyone slays a woman with child, while the child is in her womb, he shall pay the full wergeld for the woman, and half the wergeld for the child, [which shall be] in accordance with the wergeld of the father's kindred.

i. Until the value amounts to 30 shillings, the fine shall be 60 shillings in every case, when the [said] value amounts to this sum, the fine shall be 120 shillings.

ii. Formerly the fines to be paid by those who stole gold and horses and bees, and many other fines, were greater than the rest. Now all fines, with the exception of that for stealing men, are alike—120 shillings.

10. If anyone lies with the wife of a man whose wergeld is 1200 shillings, he shall pay 120 shillings compensation to the husband; to a husband whose wergeld is 600 shillings, he shall pay 100 shillings compensation; to a commoner he shall pay 40 shillings compensation [for a similar offence].

11. If anyone seizes by the breast a young woman belonging to the commons, he shall pay her 5 shillings compensation.

i. If he throws her down but does not lie with her, he shall pay 10 shillings compensation.

ii. If he lies with her, he shall pay 60 shillings compensation.

iii. If another man has previously lain with her, then the compensation shall be half this amount.

iv. If she is accused of having previously lain with a man, she shall clear herself by an oath of 60 hides, or lose half the compensation due to her.

v. If this outrage is done to a woman of higher birth, the compensation to be paid shall increase according to the wergeld.

18. If anyone lustfully seizes a nun, either by her clothes or by her breast, without her permission, he shall pay as compensation twice the sum we have fixed in the case of a woman belonging to the laity.

TIMELINE   2000 1900 1800 1700 1600 1500 1400 1300 1200 1100 1000 900 800 700 600 500 400 300 200 100 1 BCE

What You Need to Know

This selection of laws regarding women is part of a larger collection of Anglo-Saxon laws codified during the reign of King Alfred the Great, who ruled Wessex, now southwestern England, from 879 to 899 CE.

As in much of medieval Europe, women in Anglo-Saxon England of the late first millennium CE enjoyed few rights and privileges under the law. Indeed, they were often viewed as a form of property or, at least, as objects of other's actions rather than agents in their own right. This was particularly true when it came to sex. What made a woman esteemed or valued most highly was her chastity. It was expected that women remain virgins until marriage and monogamous once in marriage. To do otherwise was to have their value diminished in the eyes of society and the law. Because women were seen as belonging to others, it was to those others, typically a husband or male relative, that compensation was paid when a crime, such as rape or fornication (consensual sex outside of marriage), that destroyed the woman's chastity and hence diminished her value, was committed.

A Closer Look

Under Anglo-Saxon law, all persons and things had an underlying monetary value assigned to them. This was known as the *wergeld* and was derived from the Germanic *were*, for man (as in werewolf), and geld, or fee.

Thus, when something was stolen, damaged, or destroyed, the guilty party was expected to pay compensation for that thing to the property's owner. Similarly, when a person suffered bodily harm, which, as this extract from Alfred the Great's legal code makes evident, could apply to a woman's chastity, compensation was also to be paid. To whom, however, varied depending on the woman's status. Unlike in modern-day America, the law in medieval England did not consider all persons equal before it.

Not surprisingly, an assault against an aristocratic woman required that a greater wergeld be paid than an assault on a commoner. This also applied to nuns as well, but not necessarily because they were holy but because most were of aristocratic birth. Paradoxically, aristocratic women were afforded less liberty, or autonomy as human beings, precisely because they were more valuable. Thus, the laws of Anglo-Saxon England determined that the wergeld for an aristocratic woman be paid to a husband or male relative—or, in the case of a nun, a bishop—while that for a common woman was paid directly to the woman herself.

1   100   200   300   400   500   600   700   800   900   1000   1100   1200   1300   1400   1500   1600   1700   1800   1900   2000 CE

1.11.6 Anglo-Saxon Vendetta and Tort Law

Wessex (England)
Ninth Century CE

42. Also we enjoin, that a man who knows his adversary to be residing at home, shall not have recourse to violence before demanding justice of him.

i. If he has power enough to surround his adversary and besiege him in his house, he shall keep him therein seven days, but he shall not fight against him if he will consent to remain inside. And if, after seven days, he will submit and hand over his weapons, he shall keep him unscathed for thirty days, and send formal notice of his position to his kinsmen and friends.

ii. If, however, he flees to a church, the privileges of the church shall be respected, as we have declared above.

iii. If, however, he has not power enough to besiege him in his house, he shall ride to the *ealdorman* and ask him for help. If he will not help him, he shall ride to the king before having recourse to violence.

iv. And further, if anyone chances on his enemy, not having known him to be at home, and if he will give up his weapons, he shall be detained for thirty days, and his friends shall be informed [of his position]. If he is not willing to give up his weapons, then violence may be used against him, he shall pay any sum which he incurs, whether wergeld or compensation for wounds, as well as a fine, and his kinsman shall forfeit his claim to protection as a result of his action.

v. We further declare that a man may fight on behalf of his lord, if his lord is attacked, without becoming liable to vendetta. Under similar conditions a lord may fight on behalf of his man.

vi. In the same way a man may fight on behalf of one who is related to him by blood, if he is attacked unjustly, except it be against his lord. This we do not permit.

vii. A man may fight, without becoming liable to vendetta, if he finds another man with his wedded wife, within closed doors or under the same blanket; or if he finds another man with his legitimate daughter or sister; or with his mother, if she has been given in lawful wedlock to his father.

44. 30 shillings shall be given as compensation for a wound on the head, if both bones are pierced.

i. If the outer bone only is pierced, 15 shillings shall be given as compensation.

45. If a wound an inch long is inflicted under the hair, one shilling shall be given as compensation.

i. If a wound an inch long is inflicted in front of the hair, 2 shillings shall be paid as compensation.

46. If either ear is struck off, 30 shillings shall be given as compensation.

i. If the hearing is stopped, so that he cannot hear, 60 shillings shall be given as compensation.

47. If anyone knocks out a man's eye, he shall give him 66 shillings.

Source: Excerpts from the laws of King Alfred. In *The Laws of the Earliest English Kings*. Edited and translated by F. L Attenborough. Cambridge: Cambridge University Press, 1922, pp. 83–91.

TIMELINE   2000 1900 1800 1700 1600 1500 1400 1300 1200 1100 1000 900 800 700 600 500 400 300 200 100 1 BCE

What You Need to Know

This excerpt from the law code issued by King Alfred the Great, who ruled the Kingdom of Wessex (in what is now southwestern England) from 871 to 899, lays out the fines to be imposed for various crimes that would today fall under the general category of assault and battery.

England, in the Anglo-Saxon era, roughly from the fall of the Western Roman Empire in the fifth century through the Norman Conquest of 1066, did not have public prisons and thus a legal system that punished people by placing them under lock and key. There was also no distinction between criminal and civil offenses, at least as far as punishment was concerned. All criminals were treated under what passed for tort law, forced to pay a fine for an offense rather served a prison sentence.

Anglo-Saxon England also did not have a strong central authority to which those fines would be paid. Instead, a criminal offender would provide compensation directly to the victim or, in the case of death, to the victim's family. In addition, it was usually the victim's family, rather than the government, who enforced the ruling.

A Closer Look

The list here is lengthy and detailed: 15 shillings for piercing "an outer bone," 30 shillings for a head wound, 66 shillings for knocking out a person's eye, and so on. These fines were based on the Anglo-Saxon concept of *wergeld*, or man-fee, the idea that all persons and things had an underlying monetary worth, the basis for the modern concept of tort law.

King Alfred's legal code also describes the means for ensuring that such fines be paid, which were largely based on vengeance. Because there were no police and no real courts to enforce payment, it was up to the victim or his family to exact it. The only exception to this rule was if the victim or his family had little resources to accomplish that or faced a much stronger adversary. Then the local authorities might step in to enforce the ruling.

Although the methods of exacting payment might strike the reader today as crude and primitive—besieging the perpetrator's house, for instance—it did represent a step forward toward modern forms of justice in that it systemized fines and required victims to follow certain procedures rather than immediately exact vengeance. The only exception to the latter was in crimes of passion—such as a husband finding his wife in bed with another man—where the law allowed the victim, that is, the cuckolded husband, to exact immediate vengeance.

1 100 200 300 400 500 600 700 800 900 1000 1100 1200 1300 1400 1500 1600 1700 1800 1900 2000 CE

1.11.7 A Monastic Fish Farm

Duchy of Saxony (Germany)
832 CE

In the name of our Lord and Saviour, Jesus Christ. Louis, by the grace of God, Emperor Augustus. If, of our charity, we have provided churches in places dedicated to divine worship, and in the same place have made refuges for the servants of God, we not only thereby adhere to the honorable custom of royal munificence, but we hope to receive the reward of eternal life through this distribution of temporal gifts.

Wherefore be it known to all, both present and future, that, by these presents, we have granted for the love of God and for the salvation of our soul, to the monastery which is called New Corvey, which we built in Saxony in honor of Saint Stephen, the first martyr, and at the head of which is our faithful cousin Warin, its first abbot, a certain fishery in the River Weser. This fishery is in the village called Wimode, adjoining the villa of Liusci, the earldom of Count Abbo. And because it is constructed in the likeness of stakes which the inhabitants of the district call *Hocas*, it is known by the natives under the local name of *Hocwar*. It is at present within our right, and the same Count Abbo formerly held it as a benefice from us. But seeing that the same fishery without serfs, who were thought of in this provision, could not be very useful to the brethren, we have granted thirty-two serfs to be wholly and entirely in possession of that monastery. And we have also granted to the monastery whatever Abbo had in benefice pertaining to that same fishery for as long as the monks living there continue to pray for divine clemency for us. And in order that this charter may be held in high regard, and accepted by our faithful people in future, we have ordered it to be sealed with our seal below, and we have signed it with our hand.

Source: N. Schaten, *Annales Paderbornenses*. Reprinted in Roy C. Cave & Herbert H. Coulson, *A Source Book for Medieval Economic History*. New York: The Bruce Publishing Co., 1936; reprint ed., New York: Biblo & Tannen, 1965, pp. 60-61. Translation adjusted by Lawrence Morris.

What You Need to Know

In this document, the Frankish king Louis the Pious donates a fish farm to the monastery at New Corvey, in what today is Germany.

In 529, a Italian religious man named Benedict of Nursia wrote what came to be called *The Rule of Saint Benedict*, a kind of handbook for monks and monasteries. Along with communal life and frequent prayer, Benedict emphasized work. While the admonition was meant to reinforce faith—"idleness is the enemy of the soul," he wrote—it also had practical implications.

In the wake of the slow collapse of the Western Roman Empire in the fourth and fifth centuries, urban life in Europe virtually disappeared, as the city was superseded by the self-sustaining rural manor headed by local strong men. Although organized for different purposes and ruled along different lines, monasteries were akin to manors. They were economically self-sufficient, providing everything the monks and the communities of laypersons who supported the monks would need. Indeed, many were extremely successful, expanding agricultural production through innovation, as well as engaging in manufacturing and even finance. The profits they generated were then used to pay for the services the monasteries offered, such as copying manuscripts, educating the young, comforting the sick, and providing alms for the poor. However, those profits could also enrich the abbots who ran the institutions.

A Closer Look

Aside from their self-sufficiency and the enterprise and ingenuity of the monks, monasteries of the European Middle Ages had another important advantage—faith. This was not only a means of motivating monks to serve God but was also a bargaining chip to be used in the relationship monasteries had with secular authorities. Simply put, monarchs and lords believed they could win God's favor, and a path to eternal salvation, by donating to the monasteries.

This document from Louis the Pious, who served as king of the Franks, a people inhabiting much of what today is northern France and western Germany, illustrates how this process worked. In it, the king in 732 grants the monks of the Abbey at New Corvey a local fishing spot, as well as 32 serfs legally bound to the land. The serfs would do the actual work while the monastery would reap the profits. In exchange, the writ declares, "We [the royal 'we'] hope to receive the reward of eternal life through this distribution of temporal gifts."

In fact, there was more to this quid pro quo than meets the eye. At the time of the bequest, New Corvey's abbot, or head monk, was none other than the king's cousin. Thus, by donating the pond, the king was enriching his own family and securing an important economic alliance, thereby revealing how intricately connected secular and sacred authority were in the Middle Ages.

1 100 200 300 400 500 600 700 800 900 1000 1100 1200 1300 1400 1500 1600 1700 1800 1900 2000 CE

1.11.8 *Song of Roland* on Frankish Military Culture and Chivalry

The Pyrenees
Eleventh Century CE

"Comrade Roland, sound the oliphant [horn], I pray;
If Charles [Charlemagne] hear, the host he'll turn again;
Will succour us our King and baronage."
Answers Roland: "Never, by God, I say,
For my misdeed shall kinsmen hear the blame,
Nor France the Douce fall into evil fame!
Rather stout blows with Durendal [his sword] I'll lay,
With my good sword that by my side doth sway;
Till bloodied over you shall behold the blade.
Felon pagans are gathered to their shame;
I pledge you now, to death they're doomed today." . . .

Says Oliver: "The wastes I saw, and all the farthest plains.
A muster great they've made, this people strange;
We have of men a very little tale."
Answers Roland: "My anger is inflamed. . . .
Never by me shall Frankish valour fail!
Rather I'll die than shame shall me attain.
Therefore strike on, the Emperor's love to gain." . . .

Pride hath Roland, wisdom Olivier hath;
And both of them shew marvellous courage;
Once they are horsed, once they have donned their arms,
Rather they'ld die than from the battle pass.
Good are the counts, and lofty their language. . . .

Then Roland feels that death to him draws near,
For all his brain is issued from his ears;
He prays to God that He will call the peers,
Bids Gabriel, the angel to himself appear. . . .
There he falls down, and lies upon the green;
He swoons again, for death is very near. . . .

On the green grass count Roland swoons thereby.
A Sarrazin him all the time espies, . . .
He's seized Roland, and the arms, that were at his side,
"Charles' nephew," he says, "here conquered lies.
To Arabia I'll bear this sword as prize."

Source: Moncrieff, Charles Scott. *The Song of Roland, Done into English in the Original Measure*. London: Chapman and Hall, 1919, pp. 35–37, 74. Modified slightly.

TIMELINE   2000 1900 1800 1700 1600 1500 1400 1300 1200 1100 1000 900 800 700 600 500 400 300 200 100 1 BCE

What You Need to Know

First sung and later written down in French, *chansons des gestes*, or "songs of heroic deeds," were poems that told of the exploits of military leaders and their knights. The most famous of these was the *Song of Roland*, first transcribed in the eleventh century. Inspiration for this epic poem came from the Battle of Roncesvalles, in what is now the Basque Country of northern Spain, in 778. The battle was part of the great medieval emperor Charlemagne's efforts to extend his realm into the Iberian Peninsula. In fact, the loss to Basque warriors represented Charlemagne's only defeat and the emperor forbade anyone to speak of it. Nevertheless, poets of the era sung the exploits of a Frankish warrior named Roland who lives and fights by the chivalric code before dying on the battlefield at Roncesvalles. In the telling of Roland's exploits, the Basques become Saracens, that is, Muslim infidels, and the warrior dies a martyr's death in defense of the Christian God.

A Closer Look

The poem has all of the elements of the chivalric code, as Roland and his fellow captain Oliver lead a small group of knights against a vast Muslim army, prepared to test their strength and courage in a one-sided struggle to defend their emperor and their Christian faith. Notably, the Song of Roland was not written down until late in the eleventh century, just in time to inspire nobles and knights as they set forth on the First Crusade to wrest control of the Holy Land from its Muslim guardians.

The audience for these chansons were the nobles, who patronized the poets who created them. Nobles in the early Middle Ages were largely warriors, who either fought for themselves or pledged their military services to a king, who then granted them control of an estate and the peasants and serfs who worked it.

Even more so than today, military service in the Middle Ages had an ethos of its own, marked not just by bravery and honor but also a faith in God and undying loyalty to the king or, in the case of a knight, to a lord. It also included rules and rituals to make sure that the violence so common to military life in the era did not get out of hand. Among other things, this ethos, as laid down in the unwritten chivalric code, pledged the warrior to the protection of women, children, the elderly, and any other person incapable of defending themselves under arms.

1 100 200 300 400 500 600 700 800 900 1000 1100 1200 1300 1400 1500 1600 1700 1800 1900 2000 CE

1.11.9 Viking Rune Stone

Oland Island, Sweden
Eleventh Century CE

Credit: DeAgostini/Getty Images

What You Need to Know

Rune stones were large tablets containing runic writings, based on the non-Latin alphabets used by Germanic peoples since ancient times, and primitive imagery. An example from eleventh-century Oland Island, now part of Sweden, is shown here.

In the late eighth century, there arose in Europe a new and frightening force. They were known as the Northmen, Normans, or Vikings, the latter from the Old Norse word for "creek" because they often laid in wait there to attack passing ships. They came from Scandinavia and their fierce martial culture, combined with advanced shipbuilding technology and superb seamanship, made them the terror of the continent for 200 years. "Save us, O God, from the violence of the Northmen," was a prayer heard from the North Sea to the Mediterranean.

They enslaved thousands and lived by plunder, attacking along seashores and in river valleys, wherever their boats took them, from the British Isles to southern Italy to deep into what is now Russia. Gradually, however, they began to settle in the lands they conquered, become Christianized, intermarry with the local population, and establish dynasties such as the Norman kingdoms of England, France, and Sicily. By the eleventh century, the Viking threat was over, although their influence over Europe's political and economic development was lasting.

A Closer Look

Typically, rune stones consisted of an upright tablet made of local stone, sometimes cut and sometimes in its natural state, in which artisans etched words and then colored them with various form of mineral- and plant-based paints. Most rune stones were situated at places where people gathered—river fords, bridges, crossroads, and outdoor assembly spots.

The first rune stones date from fourth-century Scandinavia and were erected to commemorate great men, battles, or other historical events. They also identified who had made them. Villages and tribes fashioned most of them in the early periods, but by the ninth and tenth century, many were erected by kings to herald their achievements and mark their domains. Increasingly as these kings adopted Christianity and tried to convert their peoples to the faith, the stones included religious messages and symbols, as does the one pictured here, from Oland Island, Sweden. Indeed, it was in the eleventh century, when this rune stone was erected, that the people of Oland Island, which is situated in the Baltic Sea, just off the southeastern coast of Sweden, became Christianized.

1 100 200 300 400 500 600 700 800 900 1000 1100 1200 1300 1400 1500 1600 1700 1800 1900 2000 CE

1.11.10 Land Grant to a Jewish Community in Medieval Germany

Speyer, Germany
1090 CE

In the name of the Holy and Indivisible Trinity, I, Rudiger, surnamed Huozmann, Bishop of Speyer, when I made the villa of Speyer into a town, thought I would increase the honor I was bestowing on the place if I brought in the Jews. Therefore I placed them outside the town and some way off from the houses of the rest of the citizens, and, lest they should be too easily disturbed by the insolence of the citizens, I surrounded them with a wall. Now the place of their habitation which I acquired justly (for in the first place I obtained the hill partly with money and partly by exchange, while I received the valley by way of gift from some heirs) that place, I say, I transferred to them on condition that they pay annually three and a half pounds of the money of Speyer for the use of the brethren.

I have granted also to them within the district where they dwell, and from that district outside the town as far as the harbor, and within the harbor itself, full power to change gold and silver, and to buy and sell what they please. And I have also given them license to do this throughout the state. Besides this, I have given them land of the church for a cemetery with rights of inheritance. This also I have added that if any Jew should at any time stay with them, he shall pay no thelony.

Then also just as the judge of the city hears cases between citizens, so the chief rabbi shall hear cases which arise between the Jews or against them. But if by chance he is unable to decide any of them, they shall go to the bishop or his chamberlain. They shall maintain watches, guards, and fortifications about their district, the guards in common with our vassals. They may lawfully employ nurses and servants from among our people. Slaughtered meat which they may not eat according to their law, they may lawfully sell to Christians, and Christians may lawfully buy it. Finally, to round out these concessions, I have granted that they may enjoy the same privileges as the Jews in any other city of Germany.

Lest any of my successors diminish this gift and concession, or constrain them to pay greater taxes, alleging that they have usurped these privileges, and have no episcopal warrant for them, I have left this charter as a suitable testimony of the said grant. And that this may never be forgotten, I have signed it, and confirmed it with my seal as may be seen below. Given on Sept. 15th, 1084, etc.

Source: Altmann, Wilhelm, and Ernst Bernheim, eds. *Ausgewählte Urkunden zur Erläuterung der Verfassungsgeschichte Deutschlands im Mittelalter.* Berlin: Weidmannsche Buchhandlung, 1904.

TIMELINE   2000 1900 1800 1700 1600 1500 1400 1300 1200 1100 1000 900 800 700 600 500 400 300 200 100 1 BCE

What You Need to Know

In this text, Bishop Rudiger Huozmann states the rights and restrictions of Jews living in the city of Speyer (in what is now Germany) at the end of the eleventh century.

With a heritage stretching back more than 3,000 years, the Jews are believed to have originated in northern Mesopotamia and then relocated to Palestine sometime in the second millennium BCE. Rebellious under imperial rule, their capital city of Jerusalem was sacked and their main temple destroyed by the Romans in 70 CE. Thousands of Jews were killed in that war and subsequent conflicts with the Romans. Meanwhile, Jewish communities had emerged around the empire, forming the Jewish diaspora community.

By the early Middle Ages, there were Jewish communities scattered across Europe, tolerated to a degree but never fully accepted, as Jews were commonly held by ordinary Christians and church officials to have been the slayers of Christ. Forbidden from owning lands in most jurisdictions, they congregated in towns and cities, where they became traders and moneylenders, professions that exposed them to charges of economic exploitation of Christians. The rise of a commercial economy in Europe in the twelfth century, which often left nobles and others in debt to Jews, is believed to have been the source of rising anti-Semitism, an attitude further fueled by widespread rumors of "blood rites," apocryphal stories about Jewish religious ceremonies that required the use of Christian blood.

A Closer Look

The ambivalence felt by European Christians toward Jews before the twelfth century is evident in this document issued by Bishop Rudiger Huozmann in 1090. Like other city officials across Europe, the Bishop of Speyer mistrusted Jews for their unwillingness to accept Christianity which, at a time when religious faith and secular authority overlapped, meant that they were potential enemies of the state. At the same time, he valued the Jews for their business and financial skills and capital. Speyer wanted to improve his city's economy, and he knew he needed the Jews for that to happen.

Thus, on the one hand, he grants them broad rights to engage in trade and finance, including currency exchange, in a special district in town and around the harbor. He also granted them an exemption from a tax on trade and allowed Jews to have special rabbinical courts of their own. Notably, these courts would not only hear cases between Jews but even cases brought by Christians against Jews. He even granted them a special district where they could live. But it was to be outside the city, separate from the Christian community within the walls of Speyer.

1   100 200 300   400   500   600   700   800   900   1000 1100 1200 1300   1400   1500   1600   1700   1800   1900   2000 CE

1.11.11 The Fall of Jerusalem during the Crusades

Jerusalem
1099 CE

Later, all of our people went to the Sepulchre of our Lord rejoicing and weeping for joy, and they rendered up the offering that they owed. In the morning, some of our men cautiously ascended to the roof of the Temple and attacked the Saracens [Muslims] both men and women, beheading them with naked swords; the remainder sought death by jumping down into the temple. When Tancred heard of this, he was filled with anger.

The Duke and the Counts of Normandy and Flanders placed Gaston of Beert in charge of the workmen who constructed machines. They built mantlets and towers with which to attack the wall . . . .

There were twelve or thirteen hundred knights in our army, as I reckon it, not more. I say this that you may realize that nothing, whether great or small, which is undertaken in the name of the Lord can fail, as the following pages show.

Our men began to undermine the towers and walls. From every side stones were hurled from the *tormenti* and the *petrahae*, and so many arrows that they fell like hail. The servants of God bore this patiently, sustained by the premises of their faith, whether they should be killed or should presently prevail over their enemies. The battle showed no indication of victory, but when the machines were drawn nearer to the walls, they hurled not only stones and arrows, but also burning wood and straw. The wood was dipped in pitch, wax, and sulphur; then straw and tow were fastened on by an iron band, and, when lighted, these firebrands were shot from the machines. They were bound together by an iron band, I say, so that wherever they fell, the whole mass held together and continued to burn. . . .

When the morning came, our men eagerly rushed to the walls and dragged the machines forward, but the Saracens had constructed so many machines that for each one of ours they now had nine or ten. . . .

By noon our men were greatly discouraged. They were weary and at the end of their resources. There were still many of the enemy opposing each one of our men; the walls were very high and strong, and the great resources and skill that the enemy exhibited in repairing their defences seemed too great for us to overcome. But, while we hesitated, irresolute, and the enemy exulted in our discomfiture, the healing mercy of God inspired us and turned our sorrow into joy, for the Lord did not forsake us. While a council was being held to decide whether or not our machines should be withdrawn, for some were burned and the rest badly shaken to pieces, a knight on the Mount of Olives began to wave his shield to those who were with the Count and others, signalling them to advance. Who this knight was we have been unable to find out. At this signal our men began to take heart, and some began to batter down the wall, while others began to ascend by means of scaling ladders and ropes. . . .

Now that the city was taken, it was well worth all our previous labors and hardships to see the devotion of the pilgrims at the Holy Sepulchre. How they rejoiced and exulted and sang a new song to the Lord! For their hearts offered prayers of praise to God, victorious and triumphant, which cannot be told in words.

Source: d'Aguiliers, Raymond. Excerpts from *Historia Francorum qui Ceperint Iherusalem*. In *The First Crusade: The Accounts of Eyewitnesses and Participants*. Edited by August C. Krey. Princeton, NJ: Princeton University Press, 1921, pp. 257–262.

TIMELINE   2000 1900 1800 1700 1600 1500 1400 1300 1200 1100 1000 900 800 700 600 500 400 300 200 100 1 BCE

What You Need to Know

Despite the general illiteracy and lack of academic learning among the knights who fought in the First Crusade, a number of them wrote down accounts of their adventures. This excerpt comes from Raymond d'Aguiliers, a clerk from the monastery of Vézelay, Burgundy, in modern-day France, and tells of the capture of Jerusalem.

Inspired by Pope Urban II, the Crusades of the eleventh and twelfth centuries were a series of holy wars launched by Christian Europe to seize the Holy Land of the Bible away from its Islamic inhabitants. The most successful of the Crusades was the First, which led to the capture of Jerusalem, the holiest city for Christians, and the establishment of the Kingdom of Jerusalem, in what is now Israel and Jordan, from 1099 to 1291.

Most of those who fought in the Crusades were knights, armed retainers of European lords and monarchs. In a famous 1095 speech at Clermont, France, Pope Urban urged them to put aside their petty squabbles and fight for God. He even offered them the indulgence, or remission of temporal penalties for sin, if they joined the Crusade. Many of the knights who went forth were inspired by faith, but others merely sought adventure or earthly fortune in the form of fiefs, or land grants from lords or monarchs, in the Middle East. Whatever the motive, the knights, who felt they were fighting for God, showed little mercy to the Islamic defenders and inhabitants of the Holy Land.

A Closer Look

D'Aguiliers ascribes the victory at Jerusalem to two critical factors. One was technology. He tells of invading crusaders constructing complicated siege machines, towers supporting bridges that could be used to scale the high walls of Arab castles. To drive back defenders, the crusaders used flaming arrows. The second factor was faith. The attackers firmly believed that God was on their side, a certainty that fortified them with courage and confidence. At one point in his account, a mysterious knight appears on the Mount of Olives, adjacent to the walls of Jerusalem, urging the attackers forward to victory.

D'Aguiliers's account also belies the modern mythology surrounding medieval combat: that it was a genteel and highly ritualized affair. In fact, the capture of Jerusalem was brutal and chaotic, involving torture and dismemberment. And despite their supposed chivalric code, the crusading knights did not spare women from their wrath.

1 100 200 300 400 500 600 700 800 900 1000 1100 1200 1300 1400 1500 1600 1700 1800 1900 2000 CE

1.11.12 Bankruptcy in Medieval England

England
Twelfth Century CE

Master: ... The chattels which are lawfully sold, then, of debtors who do not of their own will pay what is demanded of them are those goods which are movable and which move themselves: such are gold, silver, and vessels composed of the same; also precious stones, and changes of vestments and the like; also both kinds of horses, the ordinary ones, namely, and the untamed ones; herds also of oxen and flocks of sheep, and other things of this kind. The nature of fruits also and of some victuals is movable, so that, namely, they may be freely sold, deducting only the necessary expenses of the debtor for his victuals—so that, namely, he may provide for his needs, not his extravagance, and likewise may satisfy nature, not gluttony. Nor are these necessaries furnished to the debtor alone, but to his wife and children and to the household, which he was seen to have had while he was living at his own expense. ...

And mark that if that debtor who is not solvent have once obtained the belt of knighthood, though the other things are sold, nevertheless a horse, not any one but the one he uses, shall be reserved for him; lest he who, by rank, has become a knight, may be compelled to go on foot. But if he be a knight who "Delights in the glory of arms, finds pleasure in using his weapons" and who, his merits demanding, ought to be reckoned among the brave, all the armature of his body, together with the horses necessary to carry it, shall be left entirely free by the sellers; so that, when it is necessary, equipped with arms and horses, he can be called to the service of king and kingdom. ...

The sheriff, moreover, shall take care to warn his seller that, with regard to the things to be sold, they observe this order: the movable goods of anyone shall first be sold, but they shall spare, as much as possible, the plough oxen, by which agriculture is wont to be carried on; lest, that failing him, the debtor be still further reduced to want in the future. But if even thus, indeed, the sum required is not raised, the plough oxen are not to be spared. When, therefore, all the saleable things that belong especially to him have been sold, if the amount is still not made up, they shall approach the estates of his bondsmen and lawfully sell their chattels, observing at the same time the aforesaid order and rule; for these are known to belong to the lord, as has been said above. ...

Likewise the sheriff is to be warned that he diligently and carefully investigate, as well as he can, if there is anyone in his county in debt to that debtor for the payment of money lent to him or deposited with him. But if it be found that there is, the sum which is required from his creditor, the man bound to the king, shall be exacted from that debtor, and he shall be prevented by authority of the public law from being answerable for it to that creditor.

Source: Attributed to Richard, son of Bishop Nigel of Ely. "Dialogue Concerning the Exchequer." In *Select Historical Documents of the Middle Ages*. Translated and edited by Ernest F. Henderson. London: George Bell & Sons, 1905, pp. 117–119.

TIMELINE   2000 1900 1800 1700 1600 1500 1400 1300 1200 1100 1000 900 800 700 600 500 400 300 200 100 1 BCE

What You Need to Know

This excerpt is from a dialogue between a master and a student on the bankruptcy laws of England's Exchequer, which served as a central bank and an accounting office in medieval times. The document is attributed to Richard FitzNeal, who served as both Bishop of London and Lord High Treasurer to King Henry II.

One of the critical ingredients in the expansion of the European economy from the eleventh century onward was the increased availability of credit. Landholders, of course, had the collateral to borrow and frequently did so. Sometimes this was done for solid economic reasons, such as to expand commercial agricultural output, and sometimes to sustain an aristocratic lifestyle beyond the financial means of the borrower. With that credit, of course, came debt and the potential for bankruptcy, which in turn required laws for the settlement of outstanding debts, protections for creditors, and the means to liquidate the assets of insolvent borrowers.

Given the rigid social hierarchies of the Middles Ages, and the fact that medieval law did not treat all members of society equally, it is not surprising to find that laws concerning bankruptcy gave special dispensations to those of high rank. Further complicating such laws was the fact that persons had nonfinancial legal and customary obligations to others, including the labor and military duties of a vassal to the lord or king.

A Closer Look

As the master explains, the debtor who, in this case, is clearly a man of high rank with many assets had numerous protections under the law. Similar to bankruptcy laws today, those of twelfth-century England allowed the debtor liquidating his assets to retain those possessions necessary to maintain life and his economic livelihood. Specifically, the debtor could keep his house and his lands. Moreover, the debtor was allowed to hold onto food supplies of his household, which included not just relatives but servants and other dependents.

Privileges of rank were also protected, as evidenced by the protections offered the knight. Because horses were not just a symbol of knighthood but a means to serve his lord, taking away such an animal meant in effect the demotion of the knight to the ranks of common men, a setback, in medieval Europe, perhaps more catastrophic than losing one's home.

Still, as the dialogue makes clear, creditors had protections, too, including the right to seize the assets of those legally bound to the debtor, such as the peasants who lived on the lord's land and owed him allegiance.

1.11.13 Pledging Allegiance to the Count of Flanders

County of Flanders (Belgium)
1127 CE

Through the whole remaining part of the day those who had been previously enfeoffed by the most pious count Charles, did homage to the count, taking up now again their fiefs and offices and whatever they had before rightfully and legitimately obtained. On Thursday, the seventh of April, homages were again made to the count, being completed in the following order of faith and security:

First they did their homage thus. The count asked if he was willing to become completely his man, and the other replied, "I am willing," and with clasped hands, surrounded by the hands of the count, they were bound together by a kiss. Secondly, he who had done homage gave his fealty to the representative of the count in these words, "I promise on my faith that I will in future be faithful to Count William, and will observe my homage to him completely, against all persons, in good faith and without deceit." Thirdly, he took his oath to this upon the relics of the saints. Afterwards, with a little rod which the count held in his hand, he gave investitures to all who by this agreement had given their security and homage and accompanying oath.

Source: de Bruges, Galbert. Excerpt from "De multro, traditione, et occisione gloriosi Karoli comitis Flandirarum." Translated by Edward P. Cheyney in *University of Pennsylvania Translations and Reprints*. Vol. 4, no. 3, p. 18. In *A Source Book of Mediaeval History*. Edited by Frederic Austin Ogg. New York: American Book Company, 1908, pp. 218–219.

TIMELINE   2000 1900 1800 1700 1600 1500 1400 1300 1200 1100 1000 900 800 700 600 500 400 300 200 100 1 BCE

What You Need to Know

The passage here describes an 1127 ceremony, in which a number of vassals pledge their loyalty and service to William, Count of Flanders (in what is now Belgium), in exchange for property and rights.

Feudalism was the political order common across Europe from roughly the end of the chaotic "Dark Ages" in the ninth century through the rise of secular nation-states in the thirteenth and fourteenth centuries. Under this system, political power was not centralized in a king but widely dispersed among local lords, who treated it as their own personal possession.

At the top of the feudal order were counts, who were both royal officials and possessors of great estates of their own. Beneath them were armed retainers, known as knights, who were expected to pledge their loyalty to the counts, just as the counts were expected to pledge their loyalty to the king. Many counts granted estates to their knights to maintain the their loyalty and to help them maintain their own households. At the bottom of the social hierarchy were the peasants, who were tied to the manor, or estate, by oath and circumstance; in exchange for the lord's protection, they granted him labor and a portion of their crops.

A Closer Look

A fief, or "feoff" in Middle English, was a piece of property or a special right granted by a lord or a king to a vassal. As such it was at the heart of the feudal system. Fiefs should not be understood as private property in the modern sense because the granter of the fief held final say over it and could take it away should the vassal fail to live up to his obligations as sworn to in oaths.

As in modern courts, the oath was a legally binding statement, witnessed by man and God. In important oath-taking ceremonies, participants swore their allegiance to the lord or king in the presence of saint's bones and relics. Thus, to disobey an oath meant not only breaking a kind of legal contract but violating God's will, as the taker of the oath swore by the Almighty to uphold it. In an age of great faith, this was a frightening prospect, for it potentially condemned the oath breaker to eternal damnation.

As this excerpt demonstrates, oath taking was a highly ritualized activity. This ceremony consisted of several steps, including kneeling before the lord, paying him homage, and swearing loyalty upon saint's relics. By the time the ceremony was over, lord and vassal had established an intimate economic and political relationship, sealed by the divine.

1   100   200   300   400   500   600   700   800   900   1000   1100   1200   1300   1400   1500   1600   1700   1800   1900   2000 CE

1.11.14 *The Rights of Individuals* on Anglo-Saxon Social Classes

England
Twelfth Century CE

2. Geneat-right. Geneat-right is various according to the rule of the estate; in some places he must pay land-rent, and a swine yearly for grass-rent, and ride and carry with his beasts, and haul loads, work and provide food for his lord, reap and mow, cut deer-hedges, bring travelers to the township, pay church-scot, and alms-money, keep watch and guard the horses, and go on errands far and near, wherever he is ordered.

3. Cotter's right. The cotter's right is according to the custom of the estate; in some places he must work each Monday in the year for his lord, or two days in each week at harvest-tide. He has not to pay land-rent. He is wont to have five acres; more, if it is the custom of the estate. And if he have less, it is too little; for his service must be frequent.

4. Gebur-right. The gebur's duties are various, in some places heavy, in others light. On some estates the rule is that each week in the year he shall do two days of week-work, whatever is enjoined on him; and three days from Candlemass to Easter; if he lends his horse, he shall do no work while his horse is away. At Michaelmas he must pay ten pence for gafol [tribute]; and at Martinmass twenty-four sesters [a liquid measure roughly equal to a quart] of malt and two hens; at Easter a lamb or two pence.

Source: *The Rights of Individuals*. Excerpt in *Select Charters and Other Illustrations of English Constitutional History from the Earliest Times to the Reign of Edward the First*. 9th ed. Edited by William Stubbs. Revised by H. W. C. Davis. Oxford: Clarendon Press, 1913, pp. 89–90. Slight modifications by Lawrence Morris.

TIMELINE   2000 1900 1800 1700 1600 1500 1400 1300 1200 1100 1000 900 800 700 600 500 400 300 200 100 1 BCE

What You Need to Know

The Rights of Individuals, or *Rectitudines Singularum Personarum*, is an early twelfth-century Latin translation of a collection of Anglo-Saxon laws, many of the original texts now lost to history, from around the year 1000.

Social class was integral to life in the European Middle Ages. But it was defined very differently than it is today in several ways. First, it was not necessarily based on money or lifestyle alone. Medieval peoples did not refer to themselves as rich or middle class or poor. Second, it was not a loose social concept as it is now; in modern democracies, all people are equal under the law and so class has no real meaning under the law. Class, in medieval Europe was just the opposite—a specific legal definition with clearly laid out rights and obligations attached to it. Moreover, there was little social mobility; the class one was born into was the class one remained in all one's life and the class one's children were born into. Most people worked on the land, specifically on manors controlled by lords; some were serfs, bound to the lord's manor legally, while others were peasants who had obligations to the lord in the form of labor or monetary rent. This began to change in the late Middle Ages, as towns, industry, and trade grew, providing opportunities for serfs to obtain their freedom or for peasants to leave the land.

A Closer Look

The laws described in *The Rights of Individuals* were devoted to rural life, and defined oaths, fines, marital practices, and other legal and social matters. The excerpt here covers the duties and obligations for three classes of peasants. Ranging from highest to lowest these were the *geneat*, loosely defined as a tenant who works for a noble landholder or lord; a cotter, also known as a *costetla*, literally someone who labors for the lord in exchange for a cottage in which to live; and a *gebur*, defined as either a farmer or keeper of animals.

The relative status of each class, according to the laws laid out in *The Rights of Individuals*, was defined by how much service they owed to the lord. At the bottom, geburs were required to work at least two days a week through the year and three days between Michalmas in early February and Easter in March or April, roughly coinciding with planting time; cotters were obligated to a single day of labor per week and two at harvest time; and geneats had no specific labor obligations, but were required to pay money rent for their land. Unmentioned in this excerpt but equally important in defining each class was the land the lord was required to let them use, with geneats getting the most and geburs the least.

1 100 200 300 400 500 600 700 800 900 1000 1100 1200 1300 1400 1500 1600 1700 1800 1900 2000 CE

1.11.15 Charter for a Butchers' Guild

Paris, France
1182 CE

In the name of the Holy and Indivisible Trinity, Amen. Philip, by the grace of God, King of the Franks. Be it known to all present and future generations that the butchers of Paris came to our presence asking that we could grant and permit them to hold in peace their ancient customs, just as our father and grandfather, Louis of good memory, and other predecessors of ours—the Kings of France—had granted them. On the advice of those who attended us we heard their petition, but, since those customs granted by our father were not in a written charter, we have ordered them to be put into writing, and to be confirmed with our seal.

These are the customs:

1. The butchers of Paris can buy living and dead cattle, and whatever pertains to their trade, freely without tax and without giving any pedagium [a traveler's toll] within the area of Paris, from wherever they come, or wherever they are taken, if by chance it should happen that they are being taken anywhere. Fish of the sea, and fish from fresh water, they may likewise buy and sell.
2. No one can be a Paris butcher, nor shall other butchers have their rights, namely, food and drink, unless they wish to concede them of their own will.
3. On the Octave of Christmas, every butcher will give us annually twelve denarii [units of money]; on the Octaves of Easter and of St. Denis, thirteen denarii to him who holds it in fief from us.
4. Every butcher shall owe a noble [a unit of money] for stallage to our reeve for every Sunday on which he cuts pork or beef, and every butcher owes every year to us, at the vintage, one hautban [a measuring unit] of wine.

And in order that all these things may remain secure forever, we have strengthened this charter by the addition of our seal and signature.

Done at Paris in the year of the Incarnation of the Lord, 1182, in the fourth year of our reign. Witnesses, etc.

Source: Fagniez, Gustave. *Documents Relatifs à l'Histoire de l'Industrie et du Commerce en France*. Vol. 1. Paris: Picard, 1898, p. 91; Keutgen, F. *Urkunden zur Städtischen Verfassungsgeschichte*. Berlin: Felber, 1901, p. 360. Adjusted by the Lawrence Morris.

What You Need to Know

This excerpt is from the 1182 charter for the Paris butchers' guild.

The vast majority of people in medieval Europe were peasants or serfs, living on a local lord's lands, providing goods to that lord in exchange for protection and other services. The tiny minority who lived in cities—many of them artisans and craftsmen—were freer than their rural counterparts but also lacked the protection provided by the lord. One of the ways urban dwellers provided for themselves was through guilds.

A kind of mutual protection society, guilds thrived as towns and the manufacturing and trade that took place within them revived in the late Middle Ages, after centuries of dormancy. The city of Cologne, in modern-day Germany, for example, had no less than 42 craft guilds in the fifteenth century. But guilds, which tried to regulate who could engage in various crafts and the prices they could charge, began to come under stress as early as the fourteenth century as urban economies and population expanded beyond the ability of guild members to control.

A Closer Look

Guilds, which existed for almost every type of craft in medieval European cities, were set up for two basic reasons. One was insurance. These organizations, as this excerpt from the Paris butchers' guild reveals, required members to pay various fees and dues, sometimes in money and sometimes in goods. The fees were then used to take care of members should they become injured or sick or to pay their funeral expenses and to take care of their widows and orphans should they die.

The second reason behind guilds was to regulate trade, largely to ensure that members could charge a decent price for their products. This was done in several ways. First, guilds set high standards for their members. Not only did this ensure that the products they sold were of high quality, so as to command a premium on the market, but also to keep out the less skilled, thereby restricting supply. Indeed, the members of the Paris butchers' guild enjoyed a near monopoly over the city's trade in meat and fish. To become a butcher in the guild, members were forced to undergo long apprenticeships, which also restricted the number of masters who owned butcher shops and stalls.

But as Paris's population grew in the late Middle Ages, more and more youth were drawn to apprenticeships in butchery and other trades. Gradually, it became impossible for many of them to become master butchers, as the guild set a limit on how many masters could practice their trade. This produced much dissatisfaction and led to many apprentices setting up butcher stalls without guild approval, thereby undermining the latter's authority.

1.11.16 Description of Students at the University of Paris

Paris, France
Thirteenth Century

Almost all the students at Paris, foreigners and natives, did absolutely nothing except learn or hear something new. Some studied merely to acquire knowledge, which is curiosity; others to acquire fame, which is vanity; others still for the sake of gain, which is cupidity and the vice of simony. Very few studied for their own edification, or that of others. They wrangled and disputed not merely about the various sects or about some discussions; but the differences between the countries also caused dissensions, hatreds and virulent animosities among them and they impudently uttered all kinds of affronts and insults against one another.

They affirmed that the English were drunkards and had tails; the sons of France proud, effeminate and carefully adorned like women. They said that the Germans were furious and obscene at their feasts; the Normans, vain and boastful; the Poitevins, traitors and always adventurers. The Burgundians they considered vulgar and stupid. The Bretons were reputed to be fickle and changeable, and were often reproached for the death of Arthur. The Lombards were called avaricious, vicious and cowardly; the Romans, seditious, turbulent and slanderous; the Sicilians, tyrannical and cruel; the inhabitants of Brabant, men of blood, incendiaries, brigands and ravishers; the Flemish, fickle, prodigal, gluttonous, yielding as butter, and slothful. After such insults from words they often came to blows.

I will not speak of those logicians before whose eyes flitted constantly "the lice of Egypt," that is to say, all the sophistical subtleties, so that no one could comprehend their eloquent discourses in which, as says Isaiah, "there is no wisdom." As to the doctors of theology, "seated, in Moses' seat," they were swollen with learning, but their charity was not edifying. Teaching and not practicing, they have "become as sounding brass or a tinkling cymbal," or like a canal of stone, always dry, which ought to carry water to "the bed of spices." They not only hated one another, but by their flatteries they enticed away the students of others; each one seeking his own glory, but caring not a whit about the welfare of souls.

Having listened intently to these words of the Apostle, "If a man desire the office of a bishop, he desireth a good work," they kept multiplying the prebends, and seeking after the offices; and yet they sought the work decidedly less than the preeminence, and they desired above all to have "the uppermost rooms at feasts and the chief seats in the synagogue, and greetings in the market." Although the Apostle James said, "My brethren, be not many masters," they on the contrary were in such haste to become masters that most of them were not able to have any students except by entreaties and payments. Now it is safer to listen than to teach, and a humble listener is better than an ignorant and presumptuous doctor. In short, the Lord had reserved for Himself among them all only a few honorable and timorous men who had not stood "in the way of sinners," nor had sat down with the others in the envenomed seat.

Source: de Vitry, Jacques. *Historia Occidentalis.* Excerpt from Book II, Ch. VII. In *Translations and Reprints from the Original Sources of European History.* Vol. II, Ch. III. Translated and edited by Dana Carleton Munro. Philadelphia: University of Pennsylvania Press, 1907, pp. 19–21.

What You Need to Know

This passage is from a description of students at the University of Paris, by Jacques de Vitry, a thirteenth-century French intellectual and church official.

The late Middle Ages saw a surge in the need for educated persons, particularly for the expanding bureaucracies of the Catholic Church, then undergoing administrative reform, and the governments of the secular states emerging across the European continent. To meet this need, universities, derived from Latin word *universitas*, meaning corporation or guild, were established, beginning in the late eleventh and early twelfth centuries.

Various universities were famed and, hence, drew students for their specialized focuses: the University of Paris was known for religious studies that of Bologna for the law and Salerno's for medicine. Still, most universities offered a broad education and were divided into faculties, or departments, specializing in the sciences, law, the arts, and theology. The standard method of teaching was the lecture, which in its original Latin sense meant a "reading." Professors would read from a holy or secular text and then explain its meaning in what was known as a gloss, as his students took copious notes. Examinations were given orally and conducted every few years, rather than at the end of each course of study.

A Closer Look

Before the establishment of universities, academic education took two forms—either a one-on-one tutorial by a priest or in classes conducted in monasteries. But as the need for educated bureaucrats expanded, monks pulled back, unwilling to upset their quiet seclusion with the noise and chaos of youthful lay students. Into the breach stepped urban church schools and schools established by municipalities.

Cities were ideal locales for the new universities because they were places where people from different lands came together and exchanged not only goods but ideas that might not always meet the approval of the church. Thus, universities reflected both the cosmopolitanism and increasing secularism of the cities where they were established. And as this excerpt makes clear, these attributes could be both good and bad.

In his description de Vitry, bemoans the students' focus on careerism and intellectual sophistry, as opposed to saving their own and others' souls. Surrounded by peoples from different lands, the writer also indulges in the national stereotypes that a cosmopolitan place, such as a university, made evident. The dyspeptic de Vitry spared no one—Englishmen were drunkards, Germans prone to anger, and even his fellow Frenchmen "proud" and "effeminate."

1.11.17 Knight Chess Piece from Florence

Florence, Italy
Thirteenth Century

Credit: DeAgostini/Getty Images

What You Need to Know

The ivory knight's piece shown here was part of a Florentine chess set from the thirteenth century.

Ivory, a white bonelike material that comes from the tusks and teeth of various mammals, was highly prized in medieval Europe—and not just for its beauty and the ease with which it could be carved. It was also extremely rare. The elephant tusks from which much of it derived, whether in eastern Africa or southern Asia, were transported to Black Sea and eastern Mediterranean ports by Arab merchants. They were then sold to Christian traders who brought them to Europe. High transport costs and the many middlemen in the trade meant that ivory was expensive and thus reserved for the most important of objects.

For much of the Middle Ages, this meant ecclesiastical objects, including reliquaries, to hold the bone and artifacts of saints, ornamental plaques for church furniture, and covers for holy texts. But the revival of trade in the latter part of the age saw an increase in the supply of ivory, allowing for its use in secular objects, such as chess sets, for royalty, nobility, and the wealthier merchant class.

A Closer Look

Chess is one of the oldest games known to humankind. Originating in India around the sixth century CE, it soon spread to Persia and via the Arab world to Europe around the tenth century. It grew in popularity and, by the twelfth and thirteenth centuries, was being played across the continent, this despite various church prohibitions and sanctions against it. In general church officials frowned on games, seeing them as a means for gambling and a distraction from holy matters. Chess was particularly suspect since it came, as far as contemporary Europeans understood, from the rival Islamic world.

Despite such reservations, Europeans made important innovations to the game, most notably by styling the various pieces into stock characters. Naturally, these depicted familiar characters and, in the case or rooks, objects of medieval life—kings and queens, bishops, knights, and pawns, the latter derived from peon, or foot soldier in medieval Latin.

Chess, in the Middle Ages, was a pastime of the nobility, as this knight's piece from thirteenth century Florence, made from rare and expensive ivory indicates, and was highly valued by those who considered themselves cultured because it was a game of skill rather than chance. Indeed, practitioners of the game defended themselves against the condemnation of church officials by citing this fact.

1   100   200   300   400   500   600   700   800   900   1000   1100   1200   1300   1400   1500   1600   1700   1800   1900   2000 CE

1.11.18 Thirteen-Century Charters for English Cities

England
1200–1215 CE

Confirmation for the Citizens of York, 1200 CE

John, by the grace of God, etc. Know that we have granted to our citizens from York all the freedoms and laws and customs, including their merchant guild and their trade guilds in England and Normandy, and the landing tax along the sea coast, just as they held them, freely and well, in the time of King Henry, our great grandfather. And we desire and resolutely instruct that they hold and possess the aforementioned freedoms and customs along with all the freedoms pertaining to the aforementioned merchant guild and trade guilds, freely, peacefully, and without annoyance. . . . Moreover, know that we have granted and have confirmed with the present charter to all our citizens of York the quittance of all landing tax, wreck fees, bridge tolls, road tolls, trespass, and all customs. . . . Wherefore we desire and resolutely instruct that they should be left in peace, and we prohibit anyone to harass them upon pain of a ten pound penalty, as the charter of King Richard, our brother, clearly indicates.

Charter to Cambridge, 1207 CE

John, King of England by the grace of God, etc. Know that we have granted and confirmed with this charter to our burghers from Cambridge, the town of Cambridge along with all things pertaining to it, to have and to hold in perpetuity, from us and our heirs and their heirs, provided that they pay annually to our Exchequer the traditional payment, namely 40 white pounds plus twenty pounds profit. . . . Wherefore, we desire and firmly instruct that the aforementioned burghers and their heirs have and hold the aforementioned town with all things pertaining to it, freely and peacefully, etc., along with all freedoms and free customs. We have granted to them also that they should create for themselves a reeve, whomever they want whenever they want.

Charter to London, 1215 CE

John, King of England by the grace of God, etc. Know that we have granted, and have confirmed with this charter, to our barons of the city of London that they should elect a mayor for themselves every year, who shall be loyal to us, wise, and suitable for city management, and that, once he has been elected, he shall be presented to us, or to our justiciar if we are absent, and should swear loyalty to us; and that, if they wish, they can remove him at the end of the year and put another in his place, or they can keep him, provided that he be shown to us, or to our justiciar if we are absent. We have also granted to these barons, and we have confirmed it with this charter, that they should possess, freely, peacefully, fully, and without annoyance, all the liberties which they have hitherto enjoyed, both in the city of London and outside of it, both on land and on sea, and everywhere.

Source: Stubbs, William, ed. *Select Charters and Other Illustrations of English Constitutional History from the Earliest Times to the Reign of Edward the First*. 9th ed. Revised by H. W. C. Davis. Oxford: Clarendon Press, 1913, pp. 311–312. Translated and adapted by Lawrence Morris.

TIMELINE   2000 1900 1800 1700 1600 1500 1400 1300 1200 1100 1000 900 800 700 600 500 400 300 200 100 1 BCE

What You Need to Know

These excerpts are from a series of charters granted to the citizens of York, Cambridge, and London between 1200 and 1215 by King John, who ruled over England and a number of regions, such as Normandy and Aquitaine, in what is now western and northern France.

Throughout the Middle Ages, the vast majority of Europeans lived in rural areas, usually on manors controlled by noble men for whom commoners worked and to whom they were tied by numerous legal, political, and economic obligations. Even the few towns of the early Middle Ages were controlled by local lords.

But as commerce, industry, and trade began to expand from the eleventh century onward, towns and cities grew in size and importance. The local burghers, or merchants, chafed under noble rule and demanded certain freedoms and rights to conduct business and go about their lives as they pleased. Reinforcing these demands was money. The merchants had it, and kings, eager to assert their authority over local lords and expand their realms against other monarchs, needed it to finance their growing armies. To enhance the economic potential of towns and cities, kings began to grant their inhabitants certain political and economic concessions, formalized in charters.

A Closer Look

The charters offered certain rights and privileges, both economic and political, to the merchants and artisans of these cities. This excerpt from the charter for York highlights two privileges critical to business. First, the merchants and artisans, as well as their guilds or associations, were exempted from paying certain customs and duties. Second, they were offered security for their trade through the king's promise to "prohibit anyone to harass them upon pain of a . . . penalty."

The charters for Cambridge and London illustrate the political concessions the crown was willing to grant the citizens of these municipalities. In the former, the king grants the burghers the right to appoint their own reeve, or city manager, in exchange for an annual tax to the exchequer, or royal treasury. The charter for London offers the merchants the right to elect their own mayor, although on the condition that he swear loyalty to the crown. John wanted to make sure that self-government would not get out of control and that he would hold ultimate power. This, perhaps, is not a surprising request given that in that same year, 1215, John was forced to concede certain governing powers to the landed barons of his realm under the Magna Carta, a document that limited royal prerogatives.

1.11.19 Acknowledgment of King's Authority over Vassal's Marriage

Melun, France
1221 CE

I, Matilda, countess of Nevers make known to all who shall see this present letter, that I have sworn upon the sacred gospels to my dearest lord, Philip, by the grace of God, the illustrious king of France, that I will do to him good and faithful service against all living men and women, and that I will not marry except by his will and grace. For keeping these agreements firmly I have given pledges to the same lord king from my men whom I had with me, on their oaths, in this wise, that if I should fail to keep the said agreements with the lord king, (though this shall not be), these are held to come to the lord king with all their lands and fiefs which are held from me, and shall take their oaths to him against me until it shall have been made good to him to his satisfaction. And whenever the lord king shall ask me I will cause him to have similar oaths from my men who were not present with me before the lord king, that is to say from all whom I may have, in good faith, and without evil intention, and similarly the fealty of my town. And in order that this may remain firm and stable, I have written the present letters supported by my seal. Given at Melun, in the year of the Lord 1221, in the month of February.

Source: Thatcher, Oliver J., ed. *The Library of Original Sources*. Vol. IV. New York: University Research Extension, 1907, p. 307.

TIMELINE   2000 1900 1800 1700 1600 1500 1400 1300 1200 1100 1000 900 800 700 600 500 400 300 200 100 1 BCE

What You Need to Know

This document, from 1221, is a pledge made by a French countess to King Philip II Augustus of France. In it, she declares that she will not marry without the king's approval.

Marriage in the European Middle Ages was rarely about love, and even more rarely was it the sole decision of the betrothed. Instead, marriage, particularly among the aristocracy, was a calculated arrangement, usually made by the families, for the purposes of forming a political or economic alliance between them.

Such arrangements were a reflection of society itself. The Middle Ages knew little of the individualism we prize today. People of that time did not view themselves as autonomous actors, free to shape their own destiny. Instead, in the feudal order that dominated the epoch, they were defined by their relationships to others and their predetermined place in society. Middle Age European society was thus highly hierarchical, with peasants at the bottom and an aristocracy on top, each owing allegiance to those above and duties to protect those below. Above all was the king, to whom all owed obeisance and who controlled the destiny of his subjects.

A Closer Look

As the countess of Nevers, a region in central France, Matilda was a vassal of King Philip II Augustus of France, who reigned from 1180 to 1223. A vassal in medieval Europe was typically a member of the landed aristocracy, whose position stemmed from his or her relationship with the king.

This relationship between lord and king was defined by mutual obligation, as this 1221 document in which Matilda agrees that Philip will have final say over her marriage decision indicates. She vows that she will obey his wishes in this matter, as part of her promise to be a "good and faithful" servant. For male vassals, service to the king typically meant military or political service. For female vassals, this typically meant marrying into a family the king approved of to further his interests and having children, who would also become faithful vassals.

Matilda also notes that, failing this, she shall surrender her lands to the king and that all those landholders who received land from her shall no longer owe her allegiance but shall have their allegiance transferred directly to the king. This represented the other half of the mutual obligation between king and vassal. In exchange for the vassal's allegiance, he or she was granted a fiefdom, or landed estate—and in a time of serfdom, the people who worked those lands—by the king. Thus, the vassal never actually owned the land outright but was merely given the right to rule over and exploit it at the king's pleasure.

1 100 200 300 400 500 600 700 800 900 1000 1100 1200 1300 1400 1500 1600 1700 1800 1900 2000 CE

Scandinavia
ca. 1241 CE

Halfdan's Marriage to Hjort's Daughter

Now King Halfdan was in Hedemark at the Yule entertainments when he heard this news; and one morning early, when the king was dressed, he called to him Harek Gand, and told him to go over to Hadeland, and bring him Ragnhild, Sigurd Hjort's daughter. Harek got ready with a hundred men, and made his journey so that they came over the lake to Hake's house in the grey of the morning, and beset all the doors and stairs of the places where the house-servants slept. Then they broke into the sleeping-room where Hake slept, took Ragnhild, with her brother Guthorm, and all the goods that were there, and set fire to the house-servants' place, and burnt all the people in it. Then they covered over a magnificent wagon, placed Ragnhild and Guthorm in it, and drove down upon the ice. Hake got up and went after them a while; but when he came to the ice on the lake, he turned his sword-hilt to the ground and let himself fall upon the point, so that the sword went through him. He was buried under a mound on the banks of the lake. When King Halfdan, who was very quick of sight, saw the party returning over the frozen lake, and with a covered wagon, he knew that their errand was accomplished according to his desire. Thereupon he ordered the tables to be set out, and sent people all round in the neighborhood to invite plenty of guests; and the same day there was a good feast which was also Halfdan's marriage-feast with Ragnhild, who became a great queen. Ragnhild's mother was Thorny, a daughter of Klakharald king in Jutland, and a sister of Thrye Dannebod who was married to the Danish king, Gorm the Old, who then ruled over the Danish dominions.

Halfdan's Dream

King Halfdan never had dreams, which appeared to him an extraordinary circumstance; and he told it to a man called Thorleif Spake (the Wise), and asked him what his advice was about it. Thorleif said that what he himself did, when he wanted to have any revelation by dream, was to take his sleep in a swine-sty, and then it never failed that he had dreams. The king did so, and the following dream was revealed to him. He thought he had the most beautiful hair, which was all in ringlets; some so long as to fall upon the ground, some reaching to the middle of his legs, some to his knees, some to his loins or the middle of his sides, some to his neck, and some were only as knots springing from his head. These ringlets were of various colors; but one ringlet surpassed all the others in beauty, luster, and size. This dream he told to Thorleif, who interpreted it thus: There should be a great posterity from him, and his descendants should rule over countries with great, but not all with equally great, honor; but one of his race should be more celebrated than all the others. It was the opinion of people that this ringlet betokened King Olaf the Saint.

Source: Sturluson, Snorri. *The Heimskringla or Sagas of the Norse Kings*. Translated by Samuel Laing. 2nd ed. Vol. I. New York: Scribner and Welford, 1889, pp. 336–339.

What You Need to Know

The Viking poem, the *Heimskringla*, or "house of kringlia," excerpted here, tells the history of the kings of Norway. The author—or rather, the chronicler—was Snorri Sturluson, a parliamentarian and historian from Iceland, which had been discovered and settled by Vikings from Norway in the ninth century.

To Europeans of the Middles Ages, the Vikings, who raided the continent for plunder and slaves in the eighth and ninth centuries, were a devilish scourge. Indeed, Vikings came from Scandinavia, then beyond the pale of Christendom and what passed for civilization in medieval Europe. The violence they inflicted on others was also an endemic part of their own culture, marked as it was by frequent feuds and internal power struggles.

But Viking culture was also rich and complex. They were master craftsmen, as evidenced in their weaponry and most notably in their ships, whose speed, maneuverability, and endurance excelled anything in the rest of Europe at the time. They were also intrepid explorers, eventually reaching all the way to North America 500 years before Columbus. And they were great poets, singing and eventually writing down epic poems, or sagas, of warriors and kings, feuds and alliances, battles and expeditions.

A Closer Look

The poems of the Vikings were originally told orally and were meant to serve as tales heralding kings, warriors, and sometimes entire families. Only centuries later, after the Vikings had settled down in some of the lands they conquered in continental Europe, did the poems get collected and written down into the sagas we know today.

In one part of the *Heimskringla* saga, Sturluson relates the story of Halfdan the Black, a late ninth-century king, who founded the dynasty that would rule Norway. Although Sturluson does not shy away from depicting the violence of Halfdan's rise to the throne, he does not consider him a brute but a man who uses his military might to uphold justice and Viking law. One of the excerpts here captures the seemingly mindless violence of Viking life but also the importance of politics, as mediated by marriage. Indeed, Halfdan's marriage to Ragnhild is meant to cement an alliance between Norway and Denmark.

The second excerpt relates to the importance of dreams and the supernatural to Viking life. Here, Halfdan's first dream is interpreted to mean that his descendants will rule over many lands but not always honorably. Still, one will lead to the rule of King Olaf the Saint, who would do much to convert his people to Christianity during his reign from 995 to 1030.

1 100 200 300 400 500 600 700 800 900 1000 1100 1200 1300 1400 1500 1600 1700 1800 1900 2000 CE

1.11.21 Running a Manorial Estate in England

England
1280 CE

Survey your lands and tenements by true and sworn men. First survey your courts, gardens, dove-houses, cartilages, what they are worth yearly beyond the valuation; and then how many acres are in the demesne, and how much is in each *cultura*, and what they should be worth yearly; and how many acres of pasture, and what they are worth yearly; and all other several pastures, and what they are worth yearly; and wood, what you can sell without loss and destruction, and what it is worth yearly beyond the return; and free tenants, how much each holds and by what service; and customary tenants, how much each holds and by what services, and let customs be put in money. And of all other definite things, put what they are worth yearly. And by the surveyors inquire with how much of each sort of corn you can sow an acre of land, and how much cattle you can have on each manor. By the extent you should be able to know how much your lands are worth yearly, by which you can order your living, as I have said before. . . .

If your lands are divided in three, one part for winter seed, the other part for spring seed, and the third part fallow, then is a ploughland nine score acres. And if your lands are divided in two, as in many places, the one half sown with winter seed and spring seed, the other half fallow, then shall a ploughland be eight score acres. Go to the extent and see how many acres you have in the demesne, and there you should be confirmed. Some men will tell you that a plough cannot work eight score or nine score acres yearly, but I will show you that it can. . . . You know well that a furlong ought to be forty perches long and four wide, and the king's perch is sixteen feet and a half; then an acre is sixty-six feet in width. Now in ploughing go thirty-six times round to make the ridge narrower, and when the acre is ploughed, then you have made seventy-two furlongs, which are six leagues, for be it known that twelve furlongs are a league. And the horse or ox must be very poor that cannot from the morning go easily in pace three leagues in length from his starting-place and return by three o'clock.

And I will show you by another reason that it can do as much. You know that there are in the year fifty-two weeks. Now take away eight weeks for holy days and other hindrances, then there are forty-four working weeks left. And in all that time the plough shall only have to plough for fallow or for spring or winter sowing three roods and a half daily, and for second fallowing an acre. . . .

At the beginning of the fallowing and second fallowing and of sowing, let the bailiff, and the messer, or the provost, be all the time with the ploughmen, to see that they do their work well and thoroughly, and at the end of the day see how much they have done, and for so much shall they answer each day after unless they can show a sure hindrance. And because customary servants neglect their work it is necessary to guard against their fraud; further, it is necessary that they are overseen often; and besides the bailiff must oversee all, that they all work well, and if they do not well, let them be reproved.

Source: Walter of Henley. Excerpts from *Husbandry*. Translated by Elizabeth Lamond. London: Longmans, 1890, pp. 7–9, 11, 19, 23–27, 69, 79–81. Modified slightly by Lawrence Morris.

TIMELINE   2000 1900 1800 1700 1600 1500 1400 1300 1200 1100 1000 900 800 700 600 500 400 300 200 100 1 BCE

What You Need to Know

In *Treatise on Husbundry*, excerpted here, a thirteenth-century English manager explains how to run a large manor.

Rural manors, huge estates controlled by wealthy nobles, were where the vast majority of Europeans lived in the Middle Ages. They were also the sites where most economic activity occurred. In the early Middle Ages, the manors were largely isolated from one another, from the few towns and cities that survived the fall of the Western Roman Empire in the fifth century, and from the larger world. As such, they needed to be almost entirely self-sufficient.

That economic self-sufficiency, although still important, gave way to a more commercial outlook in the late Middle Ages after the eleventh century, as towns and cities grew and long-distance trade expanded. Manorial operations and finances grew increasingly complex as the estates began to manufacture goods and raise crops and livestock for sale and profit. This required the nobles who owned the estates and, more critically, those who ran the day-to-day operations for them to become both efficient managers and profit-oriented businessmen.

A Closer Look

Around the year 1280, a manager, or bailiff as they were known, a man named Walter of Henley (Henley was a market town on the Thames River in southern England), wrote down his thoughts on estate management in *Le Dite de Hosbondrie*, or Treatise on Husbundry. The title in old French reflects the linguistic divide in medieval English life between the upper classes, often of Norman dissent, and the Middle English–speaking Anglo-Saxon peasantry. As the excerpt here illustrates, the manor Walter managed was a complex agricultural and industrial enterprise that included cropland, pastures for livestock, forests for timber, "dove-houses," beehives, "cartilages" (butcheries) and numerous other sources of income.

The sheer number of enterprises required huge work forces, which at this time would have been composed of both free peasants and serfs bound to the land. Thus, Walter spends much time discussing how labor was to be managed and rewarded. As the paid manager of the estate, he wanted to get as much work and profit out of his laborers as possible. This, he said, required much diligence. As he noted, workers were prone to laziness and pilfering. Still, they also had certain rights. Since the time of King Alfred the Great hundreds of years earlier, all workers were granted several holiday periods per year totaling some eight weeks off, an extended kind of vacation that employees today might regard with envy.

1.11.22 Illustration from the Luttrell Psalter of English Servants

England
ca. 1330 CE

celum + terram
Celum celi domino: terram autem
dedit filiis hominum

Credit: The British Library/StockphotoPro

What You Need to Know

This illumination from the Luttrell Psalter, an English liturgical book from around 1330, shows servants working in the kitchen of an English manor.

The medieval European household typically consisted of much more than a nuclear family, often including various generations and sometimes quite distant relations. For wealthy and aristocratic families, households also contained a legion of live-in servants. Nobles were not expected to labor manually or serve others. Moreover, an extensive service staff was necessary given the large households and the near total absence of laborsaving household conveniences.

As with medieval society at large, servants in the household of a large rural manor were divided into a rigid social hierarchy. Each of the general areas of servant labor—personal service, food preparation, cleaning, security, and overall administration—had stewards at the top, with what might be called middle management below them and the basic laborers at the bottom. Whole families of servants would live either in the manorial house or in small dwellings near it, depending on the service they were expected to render, and all ages, from young children to elderly adults, were put to work.

A Closer Look

More servants in a medieval manorial estate were engaged in food preparation and service than any other task inside the manor house itself. There were, of course, no appliances, refrigeration, other than cold cellars, or sources of heat other than open flames. This meant that all food had to be prepared by hand; all foodstuffs had to be laboriously preserved by salting, drying, and other means; and cooking meant constant monitoring of heat and adjustments to the fuel source, usually wood. Drawing and carrying water was a major task for the lowliest of kitchen servants, although this eased somewhat by the late Middles Ages, when this illumination from the Luttrell Psalter was made. By that time, many manor houses had water piped directly into the kitchen, although it still needed to be heated over an open fire.

Virtually all of the food consumed on the manor was grown there. Situated around the manor house would be herb gardens, pens for various animals, and even fishponds. Generally two full meals a day would be served, one in the late morning to early afternoon and the other around nightfall. For reasons of fire safety, kitchens were maintained some distance from the great hall of the manor where meals were served. Given the large size of medieval households, this meant a large retinue of servants was required, as this image illustrates, to carry the food from the kitchen to the great hall.

1   100   200   300   400   500   600   700   800   900   1000   1100   1200   1300   1400   1500   1600   1700   1800   1900   2000 CE

1.11.23 Account of the Black Death at Avignon

Avignon, France
1348 CE

The disease is threefold in its infection; that is to say, firstly, men suffer in their lungs and breathing, and whoever have these corrupted, or even slightly attacked, cannot by any means escape nor live beyond two days. Examinations have been made by doctors in many cities of Italy, and also in Avignon, by order of the Pope [Clement VI], in order to discover the origin of this disease. Many dead bodies have been thus opened and dissected, and it is found that all who have died thus suddenly have had their lungs infected and have spat blood. The contagious nature of the disease is indeed the most terrible of all the terrors (of the time), for when anyone who is infected by it dies, all who see him in his sickness, or visit him, or do any business with him, or even carry him to the grave, quickly follow him thither, and there is no known means of protection.

There is another form of the sickness, however, at present running its course concurrently with the first; that is, certain aposthumes [swellings] appear under both arms, and by these also people quickly die. A third form of the disease—like the two former, running its course at this same time with them—is that from which people of both sexes suffer from aposthumes in the groin. This, likewise, is quickly fatal. The sickness has already grown to such proportions that, from fear of contagion, no doctor will visit a sick man, even if the invalid would gladly give him everything he possessed; neither does a father visit his son, nor a mother her daughter, nor a brother his brother, nor a son his father, nor a friend his friend, nor an acquaintance his acquaintance, nor, in fact, does anyone go to another, no matter how closely he may be allied to him by blood, unless he is prepared to die with him or quickly to follow after him. Still, a large number of persons have died merely through their affection for others; for they might have escaped had they not, moved by piety and Christian charity, visited the sick at the time.

To put the matter shortly, one-half, or more than a half, of the people at Avignon are already dead. Within the walls of the city there are now more than 7,000 houses shut up; in these no one is living, and all who have inhabited them are departed; the suburbs hardly contain any people at all. . . .

The like account I can give of all the cities and towns of Provence. Already the sickness has crossed the Rhone, and ravaged many cities and villages as far as Toulouse, and it ever increases in violence as it proceeds. On account of this great mortality there is such a fear of death that people do not dare even to speak with anyone whose relative has died, because it is frequently remarked that in a family where one dies nearly all the relations follow him, and this is commonly believed among the people. Neither are the sick now served by their kindred, except as dogs would be; food is put near the bed for them to eat and drink, and then those still in health fly and leave the house.

Source: Gasquet, Francis Aiden. *The Black Death of 1348 and 1349*. London: George Bell and Sons, 1908, pp. 44–46

TIMELINE   2000 1900 1800 1700 1600 1500 1400 1300 1200 1100 1000 900 800 700 600 500 400 300 200 100 1 BCE

What You Need to Know

This letter was written by a fourteenth-century church official from Avignon, France, to his friends about the plague.

Although the increase in long-distance trade in the late Middle Ages brought renewed prosperity to Europe, it also created a grave new problem—the spread of infectious disease. The worst such outbreak was the bubonic plague, also known as the Black Death, because the gangrene it caused in its victims discolored their skin.

Historians are not sure where and when the plague originated, although most think it was somewhere in Asia in the early fourteenth century. Overland caravans and ships brought the disease to Europe, where it proved devastating to a population with little or no immunity. In a series of outbreaks in the mid- and late fourteenth century, it wiped out as much as a third of Europe. Horrible as it was, the plague did have an upside. Population loss made laborers more valuable and land more available, permitting many peasants to break free of their lords and demand more return for their labor, laying the foundation for the development of modern capitalist Europe.

A Closer Look

As this excerpt makes clear, contemporaries understood that the Black Death came in various forms: one that manifested itself in swelling in the arm pits and groin; the other through bleeding in the lungs.

But, of course, medieval Europeans did not understand what caused the disease. (In the late nineteenth century, scientists identified the source as the bacillus *Pasteurella pestis*.) That was one of the reasons the disease invoked such fear. We know now the plague was brought to Europe by rats in the holds of ships or, more precisely, by fleas in the rats' fur. This was the source of the bubonic form, which caused extreme swelling in the glands. But once in Europe, a pneumonic form took hold, which was passed directly from person to person. That was another source of the panic, as the letter makes clear. People shunned anyone who showed signs of the disease; doctors would not treat the sick, and even family members avoided one another.

The disease also struck panic because of its awful symptoms; victims typically died in terrible agony. But it was the sheer deadliness of the illness that truly horrified people. Entire families were wiped out; villages and towns emptied in a matter of weeks. Forensic pathologists today estimate that the plague killed between one-third and three-quarters of those who came down with it. It is no wonder, then, that in an age of deep faith and great scientific ignorance, most saw the disease as from the devil or a vengeful God punishing humanity for its sins.

1 100 200 300 400 500 600 700 800 900 1000 1100 1200 1300 1400 1500 1600 1700 1800 1900 2000 CE

1.11.24 The Statute of Laborers from Fourteenth-Century England

England
1351 CE

Whereas late against the malice of servants, which were idle, and not willing to serve after the pestilence, without taking excessive wages, it was ordained by our lord the king, and by the assent of the prelates, nobles, and other of his council, that such manner of servants, as well men as women, should be bound to serve, receiving salary and wages, in the same places where they were serving in the twentieth year of the reign of the king that now is, or five or six years before; and that the same servants refusing to serve in such manner should be punished by imprisonment of their bodies, as in the said statute is more plainly contained. Whereupon commissions were made to diverse people in every county to inquire and punish all them which offend against the same statue; and now forasmuch as it is given the king to understand in this present parliament, by the petition of the commonalty, that the said servants having no regard to the said ordinance, but to their ease and singular covetousness, do withdraw themselves to serve great men and others, unless they have livery and wages to the double or treble of that they were wont to take in the said twentieth year, and before, to the great damage of the great men, and impoverishing of all the said commonalty, whereof the said commonalty asks for remedy. Wherefore in the said parliament, by the assent of the said prelates, earls, barons, and other great men, and of the same commonalty there assembled, to refrain the malice of the said servants, be ordained and established the things underwritten:

First, that carters, ploughmen, drivers of the plough, shepherds, swineherds, dairy maids, and all other servants, shall take the same liveries and wages as were given in the said twentieth year, or four years before; so that in the country where wheat was usually given, they shall take for the bushel ten pence, or wheat at the will of the giver, till it be otherwise ordained. And that they be allowed to serve by a whole year, or by other usual terms, and not by the day; and that none pay in the time of plowing or hay-making but a penny the day; and a mower of meadows for the acre shall get five pence, or by the day five pence; and reapers of corn in the first week of August two pence, and the second three pence, and so till the end of August, and less in the country where less was wont to be given, without meat or drink, or other courtesy to be demanded, given, or taken; and that such workmen bring openly in their hands to the merchant-towns their instruments, and there they shall be hired in a common place and not privy.

Source: White, Albert Beebe, and Wallace Notestein, eds. *Source Problems in English History*. New York: Harper, 1915, pp. 147–148. Slightly modified by Lawrence Morris.

What You Need to Know

Demands for more autonomy and higher wages by peasants and urban laborers sparked concern among the nobility and monarchy that they were losing control of the populace. They also disliked the idea that more of the nation's wealth was accruing to commoners and less to themselves. In response, King Edward III and Parliament, which was then largely controlled by the landed aristocracy, issued the Statute of Laborers in 1351, excerpted here.

Between 1347 and 1351, England, like much of Europe, was struck by the bubonic plague. Also known as the Black Death, the plague is estimated to have killed off at least one third of England's inhabitants, perhaps more. Aside from the sheer human tragedy of the event, the plague had enormous economic repercussions. Initially, these were quite dire. In the absence of laborers and the desolation of towns and cities, agricultural and industrial production plummeted, triggering shortages and rapid wage and price inflation.

Historians in recent decades, however, have pointed out that the longer-term economic consequences of the plague may, in fact, have been positive. England may have been overpopulated before 1347, with the land unable to support so many people, given the primitive agricultural practices of the day. The plague not only brought things back into balance but offered negotiating leverage to those laborers who survived, allowing them to demand higher wages and greater freedom from feudal obligations. Then, with more money in their pockets, they spent more, spurring economic growth.

A Closer Look

While ostensibly written to curb the inflation rampant in the wake of the Black Death, a move that would serve commoners as well as the aristocracy, the Statute of Laborers is clearly written in the interests of the upper classes. First, it attempts to reign in the high prices and "excessive wages" demanded by peasants and laborers, as this caused "great damage of the great men." The statute also attempted to reinforce old medieval obligations that peasants remain on the manors in which they currently labored, rather than seek out better terms with other lords, hence the restriction that workers "serve by a whole year, or by other usual terms, and not by the day." In short, the lords were attempting to create a kind of cartel over the hiring of labor.

Ultimately, the Statute of Laborers was largely a failure. For one thing, it was almost impossible to enforce. More important, it ran counter to basic economics of the marketplace, revealing the economic ignorance of government officials of the day. Simply put, because goods were in short supply, prices were inevitably going to rise. In addition, a limited labor supply meant peasants and workers could command more wages from their lord or employers or find a new employer willing to pay higher wages.

1   100   200   300   400   500   600   700   800   900   1000   1100   1200   1300   1400   1500   1600   1700   1800   1900   2000 CE

1.11.25 University of Heidelberg's Charter of Privileges

Heidelberg, Germany
1386 CE

Lest in the new community of the city of Heidelberg, their misdeeds being unpunished, there be an incentive to the scholars of doing wrong, we ordain, with provident counsel, by these presents, that the bishop of Worms, as judge ordinary of the clerks of our institution, shall have and possess, now and hereafter while our institution shall last, prisons, and an office in our town of Heidelberg for the detention of criminal clerks. These things we have seen fit to grant to him and his successors, adding these conditions: that he shall permit no clerk to be arrested unless for a misdemeanor; that he shall restore any one detained for such fault, or for any light offense, to his master, or to the rector if the latter asks for him, a promise having been given that the culprit will appear in court and that the rector or master will answer for him if the injured parties should go to law about the matter. . . . And we desire that he will detain honestly and without serious injury a criminal clerk thus arrested for a crime where the suspicion is grave and strong, until the truth can be found out concerning the deed of which he is suspected. And he shall not for any cause, moreover, take away any clerk from our aforesaid town, or permit him to be taken away, unless the proper observances have been followed, and he has been condemned by judicial sentence to perpetual imprisonment for a crime.

We command our advocate and bailiff and their servants in our aforesaid town, under pain of losing their offices and our favor, not to lay a detaining hand on any master or scholar of our said institution, nor to arrest him or allow him to be arrested, unless the deed be such that that master or scholar ought rightly to be detained. He shall be restored to his rector or master if he is held for a slight cause, provided he will swear and promise to appear in court concerning the matter; and we decree that a slight fault is one for which a layman, if he had committed it, ought to have been condemned to a light pecuniary fine. Likewise, if the master or scholar detained be found gravely or strongly suspected of the crime, we command that he be handed over by our officials to the bishop or to his representative in our said town, to be kept in custody.

By the tenor of these presents we grant to each and all the masters and scholars that, when they come to the said institution, while they remain there, and also when they return from it to their homes, they may freely carry with them both coming and going, throughout all the lands subject to us, all things which they need while pursuing their studies, and all the goods necessary for their support, without any duty, levy, imposts, tolls, excises, or other exactions whatever. And we wish them and each one of them, to be free from the aforesaid imposts when purchasing corn, wines, meat, fish, clothes and all things necessary for their living and for their rank. . . .

Lest the masters and scholars of our institution of Heidelberg may be oppressed by the citizens, moved by avarice, through extortionate prices of lodgings, we have seen fit to decree that thenceforth each year, after Christmas, one expert from the university on the part of the scholars, and one prudent, pious, and circumspect citizen on the part of the citizens, shall be authorized to determine the price of the students' lodgings.

Source: Ogg, Frederic Austin, ed. *A Source Book of Mediaeval History*. New York: American Book Company, 1908, pp. 348–350. In *Select Historical Documents of the Middle Ages*. Edited and translated by Ernest F. Henderson. London: George Bell & Sons, 1896, pp. 263–265. With slight modifications.

TIMELINE   2000 1900 1800 1700 1600 1500 1400 1300 1200 1100 1000 900 800 700 600 500 400 300 200 100 1 BCE

What You Need to Know

This selection from the Charter of Privileges by Rupert I, Count Palatine of the Rhine, issued in 1386 to the University of Heidelberg (in what is now Germany), addresses the appropriate treatment of students at the university.

The new universities that emerged across Europe in the late Middle Ages reflected a changing social, economic, and political landscape. Rising secular states and an expanding Catholic Church created the need for educated persons to fill the bureaucracies that increasingly ran these entities. Along with theology, they provided students with a broad-based secular learning essential to understanding an increasingly complicated world.

In particular, the new bureaucracies created opportunities for privileged sons of the aristocracy. (Daughters were not admitted to medieval universities and women were not allowed to fill political positions in the church or in secular government.) Before this period, the younger sons, lacking the landed inheritance provided to the first born, had few options beyond priesthood, the monastery, or serving as itinerant knights for hire.

But bringing together large numbers of aristocratic students to cities full of lower-class persons—both laborers and merchants, the latter deemed of the lower classes as well, despite the wealth some of them may have possessed—brought the potential for social clashes. In short, the medieval university established the pattern of "town versus gown" tensions that exist in many college towns to this day.

A Closer Look

Medieval society was one marked by a strict and formal hierarchy. Not only were aristocrats deemed socially superior to commoners, they also enjoyed legal privileges at a time when the concept of equality before the law was virtually unknown. Such was the case for the largely aristocratic students attending universities, as attested to by this excerpt from the Charter of Privileges issued to the University of Heidelberg in 1386.

First among these privileges for the students was that they were not subject to local secular authorities but to university officials and the bishop, thus benefitting from a legal system set aside for themselves. They were also not obligated to pay fines immediately and did not have to sit in jail while awaiting trial. They also enjoyed economic favors as well. Authorities enforced rent control laws on landlords to prevent the "extortionate prices of lodging" inevitable when large numbers of students poured into town. And they were free of local taxes, meaning that although often having access to greater familial wealth than their nonstudent neighbors, they paid the fewest taxes.

1 100 200 300 400 500 600 700 800 900 1000 1100 1200 1300 1400 1500 1600 1700 1800 1900 2000 CE

England
Early Fifteenth Century

Thou, Sir, whatever you be, great or little, that would teach a man to be a good hunter, first he must be a child past seven or eight years of age or little older, and if any man would say that I take a child in too tender age for to put him to work, I answer that all nature shortens and descends. For every man knoweth well that a child of seven years of age is more capable in these times of such things that he liketh to learn than was a child of twelve years of age (in times that I have seen). And therefore I put him so young thereto, for a craft requires all a man's life ere he be perfect thereof. And also men say that which a man learns in youth he will hold best in his age. And furthermore from this child many things are required, first that he love his master, and that his heart and his business be with the hounds, and he must take him, and beat him when he will not do what his master commands him, until the time that the child dreads to fail. And first I shall take and teach him for to take in writing all the names of the hounds of the hues of the hounds, until the time that the child knoweth them both by the hue and by the name. After I will teach him to make clean every day in the morning the hounds' kennel of all foul things. After I will learn him to put before them twice a day fresh water and clean, from a well, in a vessel there where the hound drinks, or fair running water, in the morning and the evening. After I will teach him that once in the day he empty the kennel and make all clean, and renew their straw, and put again fresh new straw a great deal and right thick.

Source: Edward, Second Duke of York. *The Master of Game*. Edited by W. A. Bailie-Grohman and F. Bailie-Grohman. New York: Duffield & Company, 1909, pp. 123–124.

TIMELINE   2000 1900 1800 1700 1600 1500 1400 1300 1200 1100 1000 900 800 700 600 500 400 300 200 100 1 BCE

What You Need to Know

This passage from the early fifteenth-century treatise, *The Master of Game: What Manner and Condition a Good Hunter Should Have*, by Edward, the Second Duke of York and cousin of King Henry V of England, describes how to be a good hunter.

Hunting in medieval Europe, particularly of big game such as hart deer or boar, was the exclusive preserve of the nobility, who had the skills, the weapons, the horses, and the hunting dogs, to pursue it. Moreover, the nobility excluded the peasantry from the private forest preserves where most of the big game lived.

But for the aristocracy, hunting was about more than putting meat on the table. It was also a means for developing the social and leadership skills a nobleman needed. It helped establish camaraderie between noble families, fostered an ability to direct men in a common pursuit, and taught critical martial skills, such as horsemanship and weapons handling. It was for all of these reasons that fathers within the nobility made a point of teaching their sons early the many skills required for a successful hunt.

A Closer Look

As this excerpt from *The Master of Game*, from early fifteenth-century England, indicates, an important part of a boy servant's duties was minding the hounds used for hunting.

Childhood in the Middle Ages was very different from what it is today, particularly after children had reached the age when they could be effectively tutored in the skills and learning they would need in adulthood. For children of the aristocracy, life was mostly play until about age seven. At that point, male offspring who were not destined for a life in the church were typically placed in the households of a father's friends or relatives. There, they became both a servant and a pupil. The boy was put to work either at table or as a personal valet to the lord. He was also given formal tutoring in letters and other academic topics, as well as the martial skills critical to a nobleman's life. The latter was nurtured through the hunt, as made clear in the accompanying excerpt.

On the hunt, as in the manor house, the child was both servant and pupil. As the writer makes clear, the child was not only to learn the qualities of the hounds so critical to medieval hunting but was expected to take care of them, including cleaning up their excrement. More important, the child was expected to both love and obey his master, with stern physical punishment forthcoming should he not practice the latter. This taught him not only to respect his elders but to understand the rigid hierarchy that applied to all social relationships in medieval Europe.

1 100 200 300 400 500 600 700 800 900 1000 1100 1200 1300 1400 1500 1600 1700 1800 1900 2000 CE

1.11.27 Wax Seal with Hanseatic Cog

France
Fifteenth Century

What You Need to Know

This French red wax seal dates to the fifteenth century and features a cog, or type of trading ship. Seals were used by monarchs, church officials, city governments, and merchants in the Middle Ages to verify both the originator of a document and the fact that the document had not been tampered with in transit to the receiver. This particular seal was used by members of the Hanseatic League, a trading alliance in northern Europe.

With the resurgence of the European economy in the late Middle Ages came a revival of long-distance trade and the port cities that were supported by it. This revival was a continent-wide phenomenon, but it was especially marked in northern Europe, which had been on the periphery of European civilization in ancient times.

Critical to this expansion in trade was the Hanseatic League. Founded in the Baltic Sea port of Lübeck, in what is now Germany, in 1159, the Hanseatic League soon consisted of hundreds of Hansa ports—the word *Hansa* comes from the medieval German term for a military garrison—around the North and Baltic Seas. Later, it would expand to include seaports as far away as France, Italy, Spain, and Portugal, as well as inland trading cities.

Membership in the Hanseatic League offered mutual security, exclusive trading rights, and in some cases, a monopoly for a member city over a particular trading good.

A Closer Look

Seals were used by monarchs, church officials, city governments, and merchants in the Middle Ages to verify both the originator of a document and the fact that the document had not been tampered with in transit to the receiver.

This particular impression is for a French trading town in the Hanseatic League and includes writing that identifies the source of the document surrounding an image of a cog, a single-masted, square-rigged ship widely used for coastal trade by Hanseatic merchants from around the twelfth century onward.

Cogs transported a host of goods in and around Northern and Western Europe. The primary trade route, however, was along an axis stretching from Russia via the Baltic and North Seas to Germany, Britain, and northern France. Traded goods included cloth, furs, dried fish, wine, salt, metals, the timber the cogs were made from, and the wax used in this seal.

The documents sealed by this wax included accounting registers, a critical business instrument pioneered by the League. By listing their debts and deals in these registers, merchants received a league guarantee that the transactions in the document would be honored, a key development in the spread of credit and commerce across Europe.

1 100 200 300 400 500 600 700 800 900 1000 1100 1200 1300 1400 1500 1600 1700 1800 1900 2000 CE

1.11.28 Helmet and Bevor

Innsbruck, Austria
1460 CE

Credit: DeAgostini/Getty Images

What You Need to Know

These pieces armor, a helmet and bevor, were manufactured by the firms of Vetterlein and Treytz, of Innsbruck, Austria, in the fifteenth century.

Warfare was endemic to Europe in the Middle Ages and Renaissance, with any number of causes. In the early part of the era, much of the fighting occurred between local lords and kings, as the former fought to protect their autonomy against the encroaching authority of the latter. In the later Middle Ages, as proto-nation states emerged, the struggles became larger in scope.

There were basically three types of war in the era: civilization-based, foreign, and civil. The first involved grand struggles, such as that between Christian and Islamic Spain from the eighth to fifteenth centuries or the Crusades from the eleventh through the thirteenth centuries. The second pitted monarchs against each other, each trying to expand their realms or assert their control over other kingdoms, such as the Hundred Years War between England and France in the fourteenth and fifteenth centuries. And there were civil wars, where various alliances of noble families fought to control the throne, as in the late fifteenth-century War of the Roses in England.

A Closer Look

A defensive weapon, armor, or the covering of warriors and sometimes war animals, in a protective shield, usually of metal, was widely employed in Europe from ancient times through the advent of guns and gunpowder, which rendered armor ineffective, in the sixteenth century. But before that, there was a kind of arms race between armor and offensive weapons, such as daggers, swords, lances, longbows, and crossbows. As the latter became more effective, armor evolved.

It began as chain mail, a type of armor consisting of intermeshed iron rings that could repel arrows and spears. By the thirteenth century, improvements in offensive weapons had rendered mail less effective. Armorers began to develop plate armor in response. At first, such plates were attached to the chain mail to protect particularly vulnerable parts of the body, such as the chest and groin. By the fifteenth century, when this helmet and bevor were made, armor had reached its zenith, put together into suits that covered the entire body. (In this image, the helmet covered the skull, while the bevor, a separate piece, protected the lower face and neck.) The material in the armor also changed in the fifteenth century from untreated iron to stronger carburized, or case-hardened, steel, which by infusing iron with carbon offered more protection with less weight, an important consideration given that a full suit could weight upward of 100 pounds.

1 100 200 300 400 500 600 700 800 900 1000 1100 1200 1300 1400 1500 1600 1700 1800 1900 2000 CE

Italy
1447–1478 CE

Credit: DeAgostini/Getty Images

What You Need to Know

Depicted on this tarot card from the workshop of Bonifacio Bembo, an Italian painter and miniaturist of the mid-fifteenth century, is the Knight of Wands.

As with so many other innovations that became central to European life in the late Middle Ages and early modern era, playing cards were originally invented in China and came to the West via the Islamic world in the fourteenth century. Although today tarot cards are largely used for divination, they were originally developed for recreational purposes. Invented by an unknown person in early fifteenth-century Italy, the 22 tarot cards were added to the standard four-suit playing deck, which then consisted of 56 cards. These cards trumped or triumphed over all regular cards and so were known as *carta da trionfi*, or *tarocco*, in Italian, from which the English word tarot is derived.

But while largely used for recreational purposes, the tarot served a higher purpose as well. People of the Middle Ages imbued them, as with all other cultural artifacts, with a higher religious meaning. The cards of the tarot with their allegorical drawings were meant to illustrate how the divine informed ordinary life and activities. It was not until the sixteenth century, however, that there emerges evidence of the tarot being used to predict the future or discern other unknowable things.

A Closer Look

Like the other figures depicted on tarot cards, the knight had an allegorical meaning. To understand that meaning, one has to understand what knights had come to represent. While in the early Middle Ages they had been tied to a specific lord and manor, by the fifteenth century they had become itinerant warriors, recruited by kings to fight wars across Europe and beyond, as in the case of the earlier Crusades in the Middle East. They survived not only by their martial skills but also by their wits. Thus, the knight signified intelligence, innovation, progress, knowledge, and energy.

There were allegorical meanings to everything on the tarot card. The horse stood for speed and natural instinct, and the wand was a symbol not of magic as it is today, but authority, much like a scepter, and male virility and strength, as a kind of phallic symbol. Together, all of these elements conveyed a message to the person wielding the card in a game: think about what you are going to do next but do not let too much second-guessing impede your actions. Later, when tarot cards were used for divining one's fortune, the Knight of Wands conveyed a similar idea—if one took action in one's life, good things would result.

1 100 200 300 400 500 600 700 800 900 1000 1100 1200 1300 1400 1500 1600 1700 1800 1900 2000 CE

1.11.30 Marriage of Margery Paston

England
1469 CE

On Friday the bishop he sent for her [Margery] by Ashfield and other[s] that are right sorry of her demeaning. And the bishop said to her plainly, and put her in remembrance how she was born, what kin and friends that she had, and should have more if she were ruled and guided after them; and if she did not, what rebuke, and shame, and loss should be to her, if she were not guided by them, and cause of forsaking of her for any good, or help, or comfort that she should have of them; and said that he had heard say that she loved such one [Calle] that her friends were not pleased with that she should have, and therefore he had her be right well advised how she did, and said that he would understand the words that she had said to him, whether it made matrimony or not. And she rehearsed what she had said [in promising marriage to Calle], and said if those words made it not sure, she said boldly that she would make it surer ere than she went thence, for she said she thought in her conscience she was bound, whatsoever the words were. These lewd words grieve me and her grandam as much as all the remnant. And then the bishop and the chancellor both said that there was neither I nor no friend of her would receive her. . . .

I was with my mother at her place when she [Margery] was examined, and when I heard say what her demeaning was, I charged my servants that she should not be received in my house. I had given her warning, she might have been aware afore, if she had been gracious; and I sent to one or two more that they should not receive her if she came. She was brought again to my place for to have been received, and Sir James [Gloys] told them that brought her that I had charged them all and she should not be received; and so [the bishop has sent her to] Roger Best's. . . . I am sorry that [Best and his wife] are cumbered with her, but yet am I better paid that she is there for the while than she had been in other place, because of the sadness [i.e., seriousness] and good disposition of himself and his wife, for she shall not be suffered there to play the brethel [i.e., whore]. I pray you and require you that you take it not pensily [i.e., heavily] for I wot [i.e., know] well it goes right near your heart, and so does it to mine and to other[s]. But remember you, and so do I, that we have lost of her but a brethel, and set it the less to heart, for, an' she had been good, wheresoever she had been, it should not have been as it is, for, an' he [Calle] were dead at this hour, she would never be at mine heart as she was. . . . For wot it well, she shall full sore repent her lewdness hereafter, and I pray God she might so.

Source: Warrington, John, ed. *The Paston Letters*. London: J. M. Dent and Sons, 1924. Revised edition, 1956.

What You Need to Know

This is an excerpt from a letter written by wife Margaret Paston in 1469 to her son Sir John Paston on the marriage of their daughter.

England was a land divided in the fifteenth century, torn by political strife. The source of the problem was a weak monarchy, which could not enforce the peace against rival factions of the aristocracy. As the population in the countryside, still decimated by the plague that had struck in the middle years of the previous century, continued to decline, local landlords found their revenues shrinking. Lands lay fallow for lack of labor power as unrest and crime grew.

Still, old values persisted, particularly those concerning gender roles. For girls, childhood was largely a preparation for married life, where they learned the skills and values—primarily obedience—expected of a good wife. Courtship was largely arranged through the parents and, at least for those with property, with an eye toward what would improve the family's economic and political standing. Families were hierarchically structured, with property and decision making largely invested in the male head of the household. Women and children were expected to be submissive in almost all things though wives often had control over the practical matters of the household as well as child-rearing, especially for girls and very young boys.

A Closer Look

Marriage and family were the central institutions of life in England in the fifteenth century. This was as true for the peasantry as it was for the gentry, although the former left few records for us to understand what marriage meant to them. But we do have documents left to us by the middle and upper classes. And the letters exchanged between John and Margaret Paston, an upper-middle-class couple from Norfolk, and their children are among the most detailed and evocative of these. In 1439, their parents arranged for them to get married.

Once married, John was usually in London on business and legal matters while Margaret managed their properties. Her duties included running a large household, arbitrating among the tenant farmers who worked the family's lands, and running the estate. The couple had eight children who survived to adulthood. Among these was a daughter named Margery.

In 1469, at the height of the War of the Roses, Margery secretly married the family's bailiff, a man named Richard Calle. In this context, a bailiff meant someone who aided large property owners in the management of their estates. As such, he was considered of a lower class than great landlords, such as the Pastons. Marrying beneath one's social class was shunned in the highly stratified English society of the fifteenth century. And, indeed, in this letter from Margaret to her eldest son John, she explains why she had to disown his younger sister.